Faith and Race in American Political Life

Race, Ethnicity, and Politics

Luis Ricardo Fraga and Paula D. McClain, Editors

Faith and Race in American Political Life

Edited by Robin Dale Jacobson
and Nancy D. Wadsworth

University of Virginia Press   *Charlottesville and London*

University of Virginia Press

© 2012 by the Rector and Visitors of the University of Virginia

All rights reserved

Printed in the United States of America on acid-free paper

First published 2012

9 8 7 6 5 4 3 2 1

LIBRARY OF CONGRESS CATALOGING-IN-PUBLICATION DATA

Faith and race in American political life / edited by Robin Dale Jacobson and
Nancy D. Wadsworth.

   p.   cm. — (Race, ethnicity, and politics)

  Includes bibliographical references and index.

  ISBN 978-0-8139-3195-1 (cloth : alk. paper) — ISBN 978-0-8139-3205-7 (ebk.)

  1. United States—Race relations—Political aspects. 2. Race—Political aspects—United States.
3. Religion and politics—United States. 4. Minorities—United States—Politics and government.
I. Jacobson, Robin Dale. II. Wadsworth, Nancy D., 1968–

  E184.A1F314 2012

  305.800973—dc23
                                                 2011019288

Contents

Introduction: Intersecting Race and Religion   1

Foundations

Religion, Race, and the American Constitutional Order   33
  Eric Michael Mazur

Quakerism and Racialism in Early Twentieth-Century U.S. Politics   56
  Carlos Figueroa

Race, National Identity, and the Changing Circumstances of Jewish
Immigrants in the United States   80
  Susan M. Gordon

What Would Robert E. Lee Do? Race, Religion, and the Debate over the
Confederate Battle Flag in the American South   103
  Gerald R. Webster and Jonathan I. Leib

Acting Out

The Black and White of Moral Values: How Attending to Race Challenges
the Mythology of the Relationship between Religiosity and Political
Attitudes and Behavior   127
  Robert P. Jones and Robert D. Francis

Latino Religion and Its Political Consequences: Exploring National and
Local Trends   149
  Jessica Hamar Martínez, Edwin I. Hernández, and Milagros Peña

The Stranger among Us: The Christian Right and Immigration   170
  Robin Dale Jacobson

Possibilties and Limits

Political Advocacy through Religious Organization? The Evolving Role
of the Nation of Islam   189
  Catherine Paden

A Demanding Conversation: The Black Manifesto in the Mennonite
Church, 1969–1974   207
  Tobin Miller Shearer

Religion and Race: South Asians in the Post-9/11 United States   231
  Sangay Mishra

Ambivalent Miracles: The Possibilities and Limits of Evangelical Racial
Reconciliation Politics   249
  Nancy D. Wadsworth

Racial Justice in the Protestant Mainline: Liberalism and Its Limits   275
  Antony W. Alumkal

Notes on Contributors   299

Index   303

Faith and Race in American Political Life

Introduction

Intersecting Race and Religion

In March 2008, presidential candidate Barack Obama's campaign is nearly upset by the release of footage of his former preacher, Jeremiah Wright, employing black theology to critique aspects of U.S. history and policy. This ignites a political firestorm, culminating in Obama's denouncement of Wright's "extremism" and an unprecedented speech directly focusing on the issue of race in America (Kantor 2008).[1]

As late as August 2010, after President Obama has been in office for more than a year and a half, the number of Americans believing he is a Muslim continues to rise, with almost one in five saying he is a Muslim. The proportion of individuals believing he is a Christian as he professes drops to its lowest two-year point of 34 percent ("Growing Numbers of Americans" 2010).

In 2010, a spate of controversies emerges regarding the role of the Muslim faith in America, fueled by a planned Islamic center in downtown New York near the site of the former World Trade Center. President Obama is criticized for not speaking as boldly and as quickly in defense of Muslim Americans as President Bush did—but also criticized when he does defend Muslim Americans (Gustin 2010). Obama is critiqued for not being as strong a defender of racial minority interests as he is of religious minorities (McAllister 2010).

The early experiences in office of the first African American president pulled back the curtains on a complex drama about faith and race in American political life that has not been well understood. Separately, each incident demonstrates a different way in which the forces of race and religion in the United States intersect. Collectively, they illuminate that neither race nor religion in this moment can be responsibly understood without a thorough grasp of how the two categories function in concert.

That Barack Obama could be simultaneously accused of being Muslim and insufficiently protective of Muslim Americans, of being too black and not black enough, of belonging to a church that is "too political" in its faith and of not being Christian, could only happen in the United States. Why would being a Muslim American citizen be a liability, in the land of *E Pluribus Unum* and constitutionally enshrined separation of church and state? Why has Obama's blackness become equated, for many Americans, with religious otherness, and vice versa? How could President Bush be praised for defending Muslim Americans after the events of September 11, 2001, while two-thirds of Americans worry about President Obama doing the same thing?[2]

The controversy over Reverend Wright's speech provides a sense of just how differently groups of Americans think about the relationship between race and religion. (Race and religion are understood here both as historical influences and as deeply held identities.) One way of putting it is that the racial segregation of most Americans at eleven o'clock Sunday morning results in radically divergent ways of interpreting race and political events. For many African Americans (and other groups of color), religious faith has long been an important resource for enduring and overcoming American racism and a lens through which to critique it. From that perspective, Wright's views, while perhaps extreme, could be understood to fit into a larger context of surviving white supremacy. For many whites, however, the idea of using theology to critique racism or to build racial solidarity is foreign—even though their own religions have facilitated exactly those functions. But in a nation deeply informed by racial and religious hierarchies, both whiteness and Christianity have drawn their political power partly from their invisibility to those who most benefit from the privileges accorded to them. Thus, many whites do not recognize the combined influences of race and religion in their own histories.

The two related controversies the president faced in connection to Islam illuminate additional aspects of the interplay between race and religion in the United States. First, that Obama *in particular* was (and still is) accused of being Muslim derives from the reality that many religious minorities have, from America's beginnings, been marked as "other" along racial as well as religious lines. Islam is one of the most glaring examples today, but it follows on the heels of numerous predecessors. The rolls of racially othered religious minorities include Native Americans, Hindus, and Buddhists—and also, for a time, groups that eventually became "white," such as Irish Catholics and Jews. This racialization of religion developed because the dominant religion—first Protestant Christianity, later broadened to include any religion in the Judeo-Christian tradition—was, from the start, partnered with the dominant racial category, whiteness.

And there is more to it. In ways the essays in this book illuminate, the meaning and the political effects of racial categories have often been channeled through religion. Because this racial-religious framework is so deeply embedded in American political development, Obama's racial otherness even today gets him "religionized," so to speak, as a (suspicious) Muslim. In this way, we can understand the president's possible actions toward Muslim Americans as reflecting religious diversity issues circumscribed by a long racial legacy that is always in play with religion. This brings us to a third insight drawn from the examples above: a fear of growing minority power often occurs at the intersection of racial and religious minorities; the threat to the dominant white Christian majority is often perceived as an unknown amalgam of anti-Christian, brown-skinned forces.

These examples, and others provided in the twelve essays collected here, illustrate that to understand American religious politics, we need to understand the role of race therein. Likewise, to fully grasp American racial controversies, past and present, we need to know something about American religious history. Race and religion are always important to the political discourse, not just in moments when a black man is president or when the headlines focus on how to incorporate religious minorities into the polity. Race and religion may also be central to the campaigning of a mainstream white candidate. However, in moments when the actors or the issues diverge from our historical experiences with expected or familiar racial and religious categories, the importance of the intersection is illuminated.[3] In those moments when race and religion are thrust into the national conversation in unexpected ways, the artificial normalizations of white and Christian identity suddenly become visible.

Faith and Race in American Political Life provides a framework and lessons for understanding the many ways in which race and religion are historically intertwined and still actively having an impact on U.S. politics. These essays explore political figures and diverse religious and racial groups, organizations, and citizens to demonstrate how Americans often engage race and religion simultaneously. To understand the political behavior of any of these actors or the outcome of particular forces requires a nuanced exploration of the intersection of religion and race that is sensitive to the social, historical, and political contexts that give the categories meaning and shape how they change over time.

In the remainder of this introduction, we show what can be gained by considering race and religion *together*. We often use the term *co-constituted* to capture this phenomenon, and here we have recourse to the useful methodology of intersectionality. When we say that religion and race are co-constituted we mean that the categories are defined, in part, by each other, both in their meanings and in their political effects. The study of identities not in isolation but in constitution provides an important place to situate the exploration of race and religion. We argue that an exploration of race and religion as fundamentally related factors is essential not just to understand particular events, groups, or individuals in American political life but also to help us theorize conceptions of national identity. The inclusion of religion in intersectional scholarship, as well as race in work on religion, and vice versa, opens avenues for answering key questions in multiple areas of inquiry.

Starting with a brief, critical review of American political history, we show how race and religion have been in conversation with each other from the outset, that neither has meaning absent the other, and that the politics around race and the politics around religion have always been heavily informed by each other.[4] The historical story also shows how the intersection of religion and race has resulted in both oppression *and* liberation, depending on context. There is no single normative assessment to take from the history we tell. We neither bemoan nor celebrate this intersection. But we do argue that what it reveals is important for understanding American political history.

Next we turn to scholars already working to understand intersectional identities, often with emancipatory or social justice goals. We ask why religion may have been ignored in the scholarship thus far, and what the inclusion of the religion-race intersection might contribute to such work. Finally, we preview the essays and provide a synoptic view of what we learn collectively from the contributions. Through what specific mechanisms do race and religion intersect? We trace out a number of key pathways of intersection, a number of ways in which the two categories define each other, and a number of ways in which the intersection limits or opens up political possibilities.

Racialized Religion and Religious Race

As Alexis de Tocqueville (1839), W. E. B. Du Bois (2003), and many others have observed, religion stands as the cultural backbone of the United States in a way that is unique among modern nation-states. The long-term influence of early religious immigrants on American political culture is undeniable, but the nation's founding by religious outcasts such as the Puritans is only part of it. Before Western rational, secular knowledge became the primary interpretive framework for social organization, most American colonists drew from religion to make meaning of the world (Fredrickson 2002; Waldman 2008). Deists notwithstanding, many colonists refused a church establishment government not because they reviled religion but because they revered it. With the development of the Constitution and the Bill of Rights, the nation became simultaneously one of the world's most radical Enlightenment projects, through its legally codified separation of church and state, and easily one of the most religious countries in the world (Kramnick and Moore 1997).

With religious pursuits free to proliferate into myriad competing denominations, sects, and churches in the most open marketplace of faith on the planet, religion became an engine of civic life and the dominant ideological and civic influence for many Americans (Bellah 1975; Marsden 1990; Putnam 1993; Moore 1994). Religion (most of it Christian through the nineteenth century) organized volunteer societies, social movements, and broad cultural practices. It fueled civic republicanism and even justified laissez-faire liberalism (Smith 1993). Indeed, religion was part and parcel of political party institutions until the mid-twentieth century (Orren and Skowronek 2004). It should be no surprise, then, that in a religious nation, religion has often been the primary lens through which Americans understood race and the power hierarchies organized around it.

Even as early American colonists codified technical or prima facie religious freedom, Christianity underwrote the young nation's ideological framework—with devastating results for peoples considered nonwhite or non-Christian. Dominant American Christianity has historically been racialized, which is to say it has built on and in turn constructed white privilege—not just in the sociological sense of who worships with whom but theologically, culturally, and politically. This happened alongside the critical countervailing force of African American Christianity, itself a major tradition in American religion and religious politics (Gravely 1997). As whiteness scholarship has amply demonstrated, the power of whiteness derives in part from its ability to exist unnamed or unmarked, while nonwhites are named as different, marked as other and therefore inferior, often through the vehicle of religious ideology (McIntosh 1989; Roediger 1991; Steyn 2001; Bush 2004; Lipsitz 2006). White Christianity in the United States and other imperialist frontier outposts has positioned itself and its whiteness as the universal norm, thereby rendering the racial and religious baggage behind it invisible (though hardly invisible to people of color).

Indeed, it was rebellious Protestant offshoots of white Christianity that made a claim to religious freedom in the New World. Religion justified the creation and expansion of the new nation, and this had everything to do with race (Pearce 1967). Almost all the early Anglo-Saxon colonists rationalized the deeds of their "civilizing" project, especially as it concerned indigenous people, through religion. "Civilized" *meant* Christian for the colonizers. "Christian" was defined very specifically (and conveniently) and was realized in specific forms of agricultural cultivation, Lockean definitions of property, and worshipping a certain kind of monotheistic god.[5] It also meant spreading the religion and imposing it, forcibly if necessary, on "barbarians," "heathens," and "pagans"—that is, Indians and African Muslims. For many, it meant expanding westward. While fear of racial others encroaching was central to this drive to expand (Hietala 1985), manifest destiny also had no coherence without a religion that claimed its believers were conscripted by God to conquer a land and build a political community (Horsman 1981).

Freedom of religion was a founding precept, but the interpretation of the extent and limits of that freedom was circumscribed by religious inclinations of the dominant racial group, and through the racial markers they constructed and policed to their own advantage. Most of the original colonies had legally codified religious tests for citizenship. The eventual abandonment of those tests did not necessarily help religious minorities in the United States, who had to fight tooth and nail for their freedom. Nor did a nominal commitment to religious freedom curtail forced enrollment of Indians in federally funded missionary societies (Tinker 1993). Even in winning measures of freedom, religious minorities often had to sacrifice unique aspects of their faith. This applied particularly to Native Americans, who, by virtue of having spiritual forms linked to land, have never enjoyed true, state-protected religious freedom (Mazur 1999). In effect, freedom of religion in the United States was a white, and often Christian, privilege; for a long time it did not apply to Indians, slaves, and certain unpopular immigrant groups.

Religion was used both as the basis for enforcing a racial hierarchy and to craft critiques of the political implications of that racial hierarchy. Some used white Christianity to justify the taking of people from Africa for chattel slavery under the proposition that they were either godless heathens or hopeless pagans, while other Christians disagreed and even fought slavery, some in radical terms (Olson 2007). As Morone (2003) and others have chronicled, racist Christians used notions of polygenesis (the theory that God chose one race over other inferior races he created), Ham's curse, and other narratives to justify the forced employment of black slaves in a "mud sill class" at the socioeconomic bottom (Goldenberg 2005).[6] Christians fighting slavery also utilized religion at the center of their argumentation. Yet few ceased to believe white Christians were chosen by God to bring a better religion and way of life to people of color they largely still regarded as inferior.

Battles over immigration and membership at this time were inextricably linked to the religious and racial debates over slavery. The conflation of religion, race, and nation is revealed in the anxieties over Chinese immigration and inclusion that occurred in parallel with the slavery system. Debates over "coolie" labor revealed that some employed religion as a tool to hone the perceived threat of a racialized other. Arguments against Chinese labor were constructed in the context of a white Christian national identity struggling with slavery and its legacy. Those against slavery argued against coolie labor because it violated free (white) labor. This was true not just because conditions for Chinese laborers were so poor as to be equated with slavery but also because of the perpetual foreignness, for white Americans, of the Chinese. Different religious practices were central to the perpetual foreignness that would prevent the Chinese contract laborer from being anything other than essentially a slave. Others, defenders of slavery, relied on religious arguments to argue that coolie labor was *worse* than slavery. Here the reasoning was that the divinely ordered differences between the races were being subverted through the use of Chinese labor and without the protections of slavery: "To alleviate the fancied sufferings of the accursed posterity of Ham, you sacrifice, by a cruel death, two-thirds of the children of the blessed Shem, and demand the applause of Christians, the blessing of Heaven!" (quoted in Jung 2005, 691).

After the Civil War, the Chinese question continued during debates over the Reconstruction Amendments and their enforcement. The possibility of including the Chinese as citizens and potential voters was read as a danger because of the perpetual foreignness of the Chinese constructed at the intersection of race and religion. During debates over the Fifteenth Amendment and the possible inclusion of the Chinese, Representative William Higby of California stated, "The Chinese are nothing but a Pagan race" (quoted in Torok 1996, 80). The threat of Chinese suffrage as a result of enforcement of the Fifteenth Amendment alarmed Oregon senator Henry W. Corbett: "The Chinese . . . a pagan nation," if allowed to vote, would establish "pagan institutions in our midst which would eventually supersede . . . Christian influences" (quoted in Torok 1996, 83).[7] The construction of the Chinese as a racial-religious other during the debates over the Reconstruction Amendments anticipated the racialized religious other at the center of the debate over Chinese exclusion and interpretations of the Fourteenth Amendment that would come later. A congressman from California in 1882 spoke to the lasting connections among slavery, religion, and the dispute over Chinese labor when he spoke of the "Chinese coolly [sic] contract system" and polygamy as being the "twin relic[s] of the barbarism of slavery." In his words, the United States was "the home of the down-trodden and the oppressed . . . [but] not the home for millions of cooly slaves and serfs who come here under a contract for a term of years to labor, and who neither enjoy nor practice any of our religious characteristics" (Representative Horace F. Page, quoted in Jung 2005, 667).

Multiple uses of religion in racial definition and struggles took new shape as nineteenth-century battles carried into the twentieth. Questions about national identity and immigration continued and the centrality of race and religion persisted, in legislative battles, the courtroom, and the popular imagination. At the turn of the twentieth century, the term "Hindu" was used to refer to a racial group, Asian Indian immigrants, that did not necessarily match people's actual religious practices (Takaki 1989, 295; Haney López 1996, 87–88).

In the South, two culturally distinct civil religions competed for consensus over racial equality (Manis 1987). Most (though not all) white Christian denominations wielded the Bible to defend Jim Crow and perpetuate status quo inequalities, while the black church—the only institution blacks had unrestricted access to and full ownership of—and its Jewish and Christian mainline white allies[8] became a powerful ideological and institutional force for organizing the civil rights movement, especially the Southern Christian Leadership Conference (Morris 1986; Harris 1999; Williams 2003; Lippy 2007; Noll 2008).[9]

Race did not disappear from the post–civil rights era political landscape but was transformed. What we might call religious-racial politics shifted in response to the new political terrain. By the 1980s white evangelicals, many of them based in the South, had built a political backlash weapon that embraced Reagan-era neoconservatism in matters of economics, race, welfare, and foreign policies while focusing its efforts on other matters of morality (Liebman and Wuthnow 1983; Diamond 1989, 1995; Hunter 1991). Meanwhile, many black and Latino church organizations worked on an entirely different menu of concerns: urban community and development, affordable housing, poverty, fatherlessness, and immigration rights (Perkins 1995). By the 1990s Christians of color, including theologically conservative evangelicals, were challenging their white counterparts to deal with embedded racism and apply their theology to a broader spectrum of issues than "family values" policy (Wadsworth 2008). Whites and people of color embraced faith-based initiatives from different directions. Meanwhile, people of color who ascribed to other minority religions—Muslims, Hindus, Buddhists—struggled to make a place for themselves in white- and Christian-dominated America (Eck 2002).

Despite a history of liberatory religious racial traditions, racial segregation in religious communities persists. This is not simply a matter of free people preferring to worship with their own kind, with the side effect that people become concentrated into distinct demographic subsets of each particular denomination (Emerson and Smith 2000). While religious segregation began as a component of racial hierarchy, distinctive racial and ethnic religious cultures grew into a source of community, power, and survival for many religious communities of color. Thus, it is not only intentional exclusion by whites but also the fact that many Americans of color sought and seek membership in monoracial faith communities that helps explain how 90 percent or more of American church communities remain composed almost entirely of one racial group (Emerson and Kim 2003; Chaves, Anderson, and Byassee 2007). Churches are still counted as the most racially segregated arena of American life (Yancey 2003).

As this historical sketch suggests, religion in the United States has never been raceless. Nor can we ever fully disarticulate race in this country from the religious history that has helped invent and promote racial stratification. Christianity was employed to construct—but also to challenge—patterns of segregated and unequal religious community.[10] With this as background, the essays in this volume explore phenomena revealing how some religious Americans perpetuated racist systems, others challenged racism, and some struggled—and continue to struggle—to figure out how to navigate race and racism.

Approaches to Race and Religion

The abiding connection between race and religion has yet to be fully recognized. The literatures on race in American politics and on religion in American politics have tended to exist on separate islands. However, developing work that looks at the intersection of identities provides an important model for exploring how race and religion have worked together to craft American political life.

Explorations of race in the United States would benefit from a thorough examination of how religion has been fundamentally linked to American racial history and thus to the social movements, political structures, and individual and collective identities that flow out of that history—not only for people of color but also for whites.[11] Unfortunately, religion tends to be siphoned out of the picture in studies of racial and ethnic politics. This leads to the curious phenomenon of race being treated as a political topic, while religion often gets relegated to the realm of "culture"—that is, outside politics—except when considering the actors and movements identified as conspicuously political, such as the Religious Right or the Southern Christian Leadership Conference's involvement in civil rights political movements. This leads to the false impression that religious content—by which we mean systems and beliefs, not just material resources such as churches—does not inform the political lenses or strategies of Americans of color.

Additionally, race tends to be separated from studies of religion and politics, resulting in the perception that race has little to do with the religious activism of whites.[12] Indeed, until recently, the exciting religion in politics subfield of political science only rarely engaged race in its analysis, and then primarily to capture groups marked as minorities. The unintended impact of studying race and religion as separate political topics may be that the influence of whiteness in religious politics gets naturalized (through its relative invisibility). Fortunately, new scholarship is beginning to demonstrate that neither race nor religion is free of the influence of the other in the United States (Harris 1999; Badger and Ownby 2002; Williams 2003; Wilson 2008). We see this volume as a contribution to that emerging field.

The body of research now circulating under the banner of intersectional scholarship is perhaps the most promising and relevant arena for our purposes. The last two decades have seen an exciting expansion of the application of intersectionality across the social sciences, from legal studies to anthropology to economics. Intersectional scholars, led by black feminist thinkers, have richly theorized the interplay between and co-constitution of social categories that foundationally inform the organization of power, privilege, agency, and resistance in the United States. This work began at the intersection of race and gender to capture the complex positioning of black women, which could not be understood along a single axis (hooks 1989; Caldwell 1991, 365; Collins 1991; Crenshaw 1991).

Intersectional scholarship challenges mainstream empiricists who try to capture political behavior by simply "adding" topics such as race and gender to their analyses of political phenomena. By looking at the experience of, for example, black women within the criminal justice system or with employment discrimination law, intersectional scholars find that black women's experiences cannot be explained as a subset of black or women's experiences. Nor can we add up those two categories, race plus gender, and understand the unique experience of black women—or even expand it to other actors and their treatment of subordinated groups. Instead, intersectionality scholars emphasize "inter-category diversity—that is, the tremendous variation within categories such as 'Blackness' or 'womanhood'" through research that explores the relationship within and across categories of experience (Hancock 2007b, 66).

While intersectional analysis has been developing rapidly, it is still being refined to answer broader theoretical questions and extend its usefulness beyond case studies of particular groups.[13] Applying intersectional frames not just to study individual and group experiences but also to analyze the ways in which categories such as race, gender, sexuality, and class intersect and help constitute and inform institutional and cultural power structures is a work in progress. A challenge for the "second wave" of intersectional scholars is to move beyond the analysis of specific intersectional groups (e.g., black women, working-class whites) and into theoretical explorations of how intersectionality works more broadly.[14]

Such scholarship has so far not included religion but certainly lends itself to it.[15] Insofar as religion has, especially in the United States, powerfully influenced gender, sexual, racial, and class normativity, it is essential to consider how religion intersects with other identities to understand American political life. Indeed, in a nation where the vast majority of the population has historically been and still is religious, religion has been a core, if not the primary, feature informing most of these social categories.

Like the second wave of intersectional scholarship, studies of race and religion are now ready to move beyond case studies of particular groups. A few important studies have been done looking at race and religion simultaneously. Most tend to be topic-driven. Such studies might, for instance, examine the political engagement of a racial or religious group in the United States through a survey model. These projects offer snapshots of the political orientations of particular niche groups, such as Latinos or American Muslims (Pew Forum on Religion & Public Life 2007). They might also employ case studies to examine the value of religion to one racial or cultural group's political perspective (e.g., Alumkal 2003; Guest 2003; Jeung 2004; Joshi 2006). Like first-generation intersectional work on other identities, these studies have their uses for understanding certain constituencies.

But we also need to explore the intersectional relationship between and across categories and more fully theorize how religion informs particular racial identities or politics for these actors, and how race enables or forecloses different religious identities or politics. Important questions emerge here: How do people experience the intersection of religious and racial identities? How do they simultaneously (or not) construct and navigate their racial and religious identities? How has history helped constitute these identities? How do different constituencies relate to each other? What do different combinations of race and religion mean for American political culture on the whole? Our approach provides a method for engaging such questions and attempts to bring the study of race and religion into the second, more theoretically invested wave of intersectional work, and in doing so further the development of an intersectional paradigm.

Entering the Intersection

Because religion is so central to U.S. political life and to questions of race, gender, sexuality, and other aspects of American identity, it belongs in intersectional research. But in considering why it has largely been excluded, some distinctions merit discussion. Religion is perceived as being different from categories typically treated in intersectionality research (race, class, gender, sexuality) in at least two key ways. As we work though those differences, we will see why theories of intersectionality should consider religion.

First, for some, in certain contexts, religion can be viewed as a choice and not (at least not permanently) externally inscribed on the individual. Second, religion does not fall neatly on one side or the other of a power dichotomy; certain religious identities do not always lead to marginalization or privilege. Only through sociopolitical and historical context can we understand how religious identities are formed and function. However, this is true for understanding how any identity category functions at any moment. Context determines what ascriptive categories are given cultural meaning and why; how institutions create, privilege, and discipline identities; and how power and disempowerment vary across time and place. Incorporating religion into intersectional analysis forces these insights to the fore for intersectional work, and for explorations of any identity politics.

Scholars of identity politics ask: Are social categories, identities, and their meanings (such as "Asian woman" or "queer man") ascribed to people by outsiders, or are they instead (or also) chosen by those who occupy them? Under what circumstances are they ascribed or chosen, and with what social, political, and institutional results?

Religiosity as a social category should be subjected to the same set of questions because the relationship between choice and religion is equally complicated. Although religious subjective identity may be chosen, it is rarely chosen simply. One may choose, for instance, to identify with a church, to have a relationship with religion. One may also choose to what degree that relationship will be publicly pronounced. Yet people are most often born into a religion they did not initially choose, and because of this, religious identity can sometimes feel, and indeed be, as difficult to escape as ethnicity (as testified by the examples of Orthodox Jews, Mormons, or "good Catholic girls"). Is religion qualitatively different from other categories because displays of religion (at least in some nation-state contexts) are understood as a choice, because one cannot always "see" the belief structure or identity that guides, constricts, stigmatizes, or empowers individuals?

The exclusion of religion from intersectional analysis might rest on the idea that while race and gender are bodily inscribed categories in the United States, religion in this country can be and generally is regarded as privatized and therefore not the same kind of politically constructed identity. If the visible markers of religion are not constant, the importance of religious identities and the patterns of power attached to them are variable and avoidable. In this framing, public pronouncements of religion are understood as a choice, one that individuals can symbolically perform, or not, through their religious behaviors or through the display of cultural signifiers such as bumper stickers, fish symbols, crosses, and stars of David. The question of choice looks different, however, if we consider the cases of Hasidic Jews, religious women who wear head coverings, men with religiously prescribed beards and turbans, Amish individuals traveling any great distance, or simply observant Catholics on Ash Wednesday (Brah and Phoenix 2004; Vakulenko 2007; Rottman and Ferree 2008). In these examples, individuals do not have a choice about whether or not to mark themselves visually, as engaging in the faith requires a public display. In fact, the exceptions are so numerous that religious identification can be regarded as a choice only if we consider a narrow set of religious faiths.

Too, it is important to recognize that although religious identities are not necessarily knowable by others or are not automatically marked in the ways race or gender may be, race and religion, especially for minorities, are often conflated in American society as ascribed identities. The Indian Hindu confused with the Muslim after 9/11 illustrates this issue, as Islam has long been a racialized religion in the American context. Nativism directed against the Irish in the late nineteenth century was manufactured at the intersection of religion (Catholic), class (laboring), and ethnicity (Irish), and all of this was inscribed on the corporeal entity. Also to be noted are the gendered variants, such as the fecund Irish (or Italian) women who would presumably produce children faithful to the pope and as a result further the race suicide of the Anglo-Saxon Protestant race. The Buddhism and Hinduism that Asians brought to the United States were often received as (again, in racialized terms) un-American religions. Visible religious difference has often been interwoven with racialized schemas that are anything but politically neutral. Where a (white) Amish person may be stigmatized on the basis of culture and religion, an African Muslim immigrant cannot necessarily disentangle the religious cultural stigma she experiences from her racial (and gendered) marginalization.

But choice is a relative concept for most categories of identity. Like religion, race has always been constructed by social custom and legal definition and, while rarely a matter of choice, has itself been variable, depending on context. In the

1840s a person could be legally coded black in one state but white in another, depending on how race was defined through bloodline. Variable definitions meant people could sometimes pass for or be persecuted as belonging to another race, depending on location (Harris 1993). The racial formation process, the rewriting of racial meanings and their categories, happens when movements that envision new racial categories and meanings challenge the dominant racial terrain (Winant 2004). Similarly, Americans are born into class, but not only economic institutions determine where they remain; they also make individual and collective choices that may move them across class striations. Disability is likewise not static; physical and health status can change many times in one's life span.

The consideration of religion alongside other forces helps us problematize questions of choice and permanence, of where the physical ends and the cultural begins in the realm of identity. As Judith Butler (1999) and others have argued, while we may not choose our born biology, we certainly may choose to "perform" our gender, our sexuality (a linked subcategory of gender), even our race, ethnicity, or class, in any number of traditional or boundary-crossing ways.[16] Moreover, all individuals bear—and choose—crosscutting identities. The prominence of any of these, their combined meaning, and their relative social power exist only in the context of an individual's overall identity and the social norms, institutions, and other power structures that frame it. Mobilization can and does occur at the intersection of identities. Religion and race, considered intersectionally, are not only central to American identity, and therefore shouldn't be ignored, they also serve to highlight the importance of historical and social context, as well as intersections for *all* core political identities.

A second reason religion may have been undertheorized in intersectionality research is that the latter tends to focus on exploring how categories of disadvantage function, and religion is not easily situated in respect to power.[17] Intersectionality scholarship, with an eye toward liberatory politics, tends to focus on forces of disadvantage.

Religion, then, with the potential to be employed on the side of advantage or disadvantage—or even both, in different political contexts—might prove problematic for such a framework. Religion has been implicated in enforcement of racial hierarchies and has also been critical in the fight against them. People of color have used religion both to hope for a better day in heaven and to fight oppression on earth. Christianity may be a source for dissent for one black woman (say, Sojourner Truth) and an instrument of oppression for another, such as a black gay person with AIDS (Cohen 1999). Moreover, people who experience marginalization along one axis of identity (say, race) may draw on another intersecting aspect of their identity (say, membership in a dominant Christian majority) to leverage privilege or advantage. This privilege can then be politically wielded against another disadvantaged identity group (say, a sexual minority). Religion has been a particularly useful tool, in this respect, for otherwise disadvantaged groups in the United States to access relative power. But one can't immediately or automatically determine what side of power religion will be on, especially when it functions in combination with other intersecting identities.[18]

Additionally, the "power" behind any religion changes over time. Being Catholic rendered a nineteenth-century U.S. citizen vulnerable to exclusion, prejudice (often racialized), and attack in a way that is not true today. Evangelical Christians were dismayed to discover in 1925 that their worldview, once the norm, had been effectively marginalized by the forces of modernism (Harding 1991). Baptists were once besieged religious mavericks; now they represent the largest and most powerful Protestant denomination in the country (Ammerman 1990). This dynamic and shifting relationship between religion and power, in combination with other categories of identity, makes religion a less static force for considering intersectionality than race, class, sexuality, or gender, in which one side of the equation (e.g., "male") has been definitively dominant.

Lisa García Bedolla's work, however, offers a helpful approach to understanding how identity categories that sit in multiple places in power hierarchies can (and should be) incorporated into intersectional work. She argues that intersectional research helps scholars interrogate the "crosscutting political effects of both marginalization and privilege" and analyze how the "relative stigma and power" of identities works for different groups (2007, 235). As with gender and sexual identities, collective identities always contain relational aspects, and the referent (or context) helps determine whether the identity is a source of empowerment or an agent of oppression (241). Moreover, it may not be possible to disentangle a single aspect of one's identity (southern, e.g.) from another (black Pentecostal), given that people have multiple potential crosscutting memberships.

Religion highlights the importance of a multidimensional approach to intersectional work as it does not fall neatly on an axis of disadvantage, as some have treated gender or sexual orientation or race. Power and privilege have in the United States been granted through ideological frames, institutional forms, and political systems (e.g., law) that favor some religious identities and distinctly marginalize or overtly oppress others, *in combination with gender, race or ethnicity.* But again, context always informs power's contours.

Thus, wherever race, gender, class, and sexuality are in U.S. political history, religion further complicates the picture in important ways. Being a white male may garner certain automatic degrees of privilege, but such privileges would have gone only so far for a Jehovah's Witness in the early 1900s who declined to salute the flag because he refused to put allegiance to the founding fathers before his faith. It was one thing to be a white Protestant woman pamphleting against polygamy in the 1860s and another power position altogether to be a Mormon woman fighting to defend it as a matter of religious freedom, despite the shared racial or gender identity (Gordon 2002). What about being a black Seventh-Day Adventist woman in 2008, an Asian Muslim girl in 1920, or a white lesbian growing up in a Pentecostal church in the 1960s? If we consistently siphon religion out of our explorations of intersectional power structure—and too often we do—we miss huge influences on identity, culture, and history.

Including religion is vital to continuing the reconceptualization of power and privilege begun by intersectional scholars. Including context, not only the historical and political moment but also other intersecting social forces, is essential to understanding how power or disadvantage works and is experienced. While "male" has certainly been the gender connected with power, it is in particular contexts and through intersectional identities that we can see moments when particular lived experiences might differ from the theoretical expectations equating maleness with advantage. A young black man's encounter with a white police officer may be freighted with more danger, for example, than a female's encounter with the same officer. For the social justice and policy purposes expressed as the center of this work, religion, with its ambiguous power credentials, is an important addition to the paradigm of intersectionality as its methods and meaning are worked out.

While arguing for its inclusion in intersectional scholarship, it is important to identify religion's singular distinctiveness from some other categories, including race, in the United States. Most important, religion was constitutionally granted a privilege that race-, gender-, sexuality-, and class-based categories never enjoyed: the privilege of being constitutionally codified from the start as deserving equal protection under the law. This de jure equality under the First Amendment was not always de facto; indeed, it was frequently violated, especially for racially marginalized peoples. But explicit formal equality secured something that could be appealed to by persecuted or marginalized religious groups in their search for rights. This is a significant structural power advantage; the explicit promise of free exercise is a huge legal benefit over vague phrases like "all men are created equal," whose interpretation is entirely wedded to existing social hierarchies. That said, which groups enjoyed religious freedom and which didn't depended on racial and ethnic categorizations because religious privilege was also distinctly racialized, in practice, in the United States by virtue of being granted first to whites.

In a nation that allowed for the multiplication of and competition within religious sects, some individuals and communities were able to carve original, even eccentric, nonmainstream religious identities and still be more or less left alone as long as they didn't threaten the state's authority. This was rarely possible with nondominant gender and racial groups. In this way, religion historically has turned out to be much more flexible than race: a site for oppression and simultaneously a site for community building and liberatory politics. People might be stereotyped and persecuted (e.g., the Latter-Day Saints, Jehovah's Witnesses, Hindus) but were generally allotted more freedom by the institutional apparatus of the state to develop this aspect of their identity than, for instance, sexual minorities were. In short, because religion enjoyed formal political equality, there are more cracks in the power structure of the dominant religious order in any given historical period than there are in the dominant racial order.[19] However, the relative power and privilege of religious categories, just as for race, class, sexuality, and gender categories, depend on the cultural and political conditions in which they are embedded.

Finally, religion and race in combination are more than the sum of their parts in the context of American sociohistory and institutions. Put differently, race is not simply an additive factor to religion (and vice versa); the categories of race and religion in American political life are often defined through and against each other to create complexly layered individual and collective identities and institutional realities. Given that most groups of color experienced both racial and religious subordination because of the way the two categories have historically functioned together in the United States, religion cannot be left off the table of intersectional analysis.

Like race, and like gender, religion has founded identities, provided interpretive frames, and channeled a wide variety of social forces throughout the history of American political life. Religion has been a major mode of identification for many Americans, another way in which people position themselves relative to others. Religion is, then, a vehicle for membership, affiliation, and solidarity, but also for exclusion, competition, adversarial status, discrimination, and exploitation. Religion (including the identity of "nonreligious") crosscuts every other identity category. Like and alongside race, religion can be a source of privilege, status, disadvantage, or resistance, depending on where one is positioned in relation to larger power structures and institutions. Institutions can and do reflect or privilege certain religious identities and belief systems above others, with power and advantage aligning accordingly.

Theoretical Gains

There is much to gain when we analyze the functioning of religious frameworks, identities, and movements in deep combination with other organizing social categories, *especially* race. We find that race never existed apart from religious influence in the United States, and that religion was never exempt from the crucible of racial hierarchy. We also discover the myriad ways in which Americans employed their religion to provide counternarratives to American racism, to survive it, and to forge pathways of resistance.

"Foundations"

The first set of essays in this volume, "Foundations," illuminates how race and religion craft the meaning of each other. Through a variety of political institutions and political struggles, we see race and religion together redefining the concept, the content, and the import of the other category. We also see that the definitional process has an impact on the execution of political struggles and the temporary conclusions that are reached. To understand a range of U.S. policy, then, requires understanding the co-constitution of race and religion.

Eric Michael Mazur in "Religion, Race, and the American Constitutional Order" argues that to understand contemporary jurisprudence on a large variety of issues requires understanding how the very meanings of race and religion are defined in concert. He notes that changes in the Supreme Court's approach to race must be viewed against a backdrop of changes in understandings of the relationship of religion to society. Race and religion transition together from a group identity to individual identities as the constitutional order becomes increasingly authoritative. Through this analysis Mazur can explain the outcome of particular Supreme Court cases, such as the recent decision in *Parents* on public school assignments and race.

In the next essay, "Quakerism and Racialism in Early Twentieth-Century U.S. Politics," Carlos Figueroa investigates the co-constitution of race and religion by looking at the intersection of Quakerism and racialism. His exploration of the work of Quaker Albert K. Smiley and Congregationalist Lyman Abbott at the Lake Mohonk Conference illuminates the ideological struggles between and among race, religion, and empire. Both these religious political thinkers—at the center of discussions between imperialists and anti-imperialists—were guided by what Figueroa refers to as a "Christian evolutionary racialist theory." The "intersection of pragmatic Quakerism and evolutionary racialism" informed how the Quaker Lake Mohonk Conference directed U.S. state actors to deal with the conflict between American liberalism and American imperialism in the context of governing (and racializing) U.S. overseas territories at the turn of the twenti-eth century.

Not only do religion and race define each other conceptually, they also define the content of those categories, the racial or religious divisions. Religion is central to the racialization process through which group identities are formed and gain meaning. In "Race, National Identity, and the Changing Circumstances of Jewish Immigrants in the United States," Susan M. Gordon demonstrates how contextual variables affect the ways in which religion defines racial categories. She explores the changing political process of racializing religious identities through a study of the experience of Jews with the U.S. immigration state apparatus. Immigration bureaucracies in the early twentieth century defined race not just by color but also by geography, assimilation, and religion. For Jews after World War II, however, U.S. state institutions went some distance toward disentangling race and religion. Through explorations of movies and academic writings of the time, Gordon shows how racial categories opened up, allowing for change in official naturalization policy. Immigration service documents and census categories help Gordon demonstrate how the state deracialized Jews. The political context following World War II fundamentally changed the intersection of race and religion in crafting political identities for Jews at an institutional level.

The essay by Gerald R. Webster and Jonathan I. Leib, "What Would Robert E. Lee Do?," illuminates the use of religious discourse and resources in racialized politics through an exploration of the centrality of religion to defining white southern identity and the crusade for maintaining its heritage. Both sides in the Confederate flag debate draw on religion to buttress the justness of their views on the use of the flag. Many of the actors in the battle are influential pastors or groups of ministers, and the debates are theological as much as secular. In the clash between the theological racism tradition of pro-flaggers and the racial justice tradition articulated by critics we see the flexibility of Christianity in racial politics as it is "tactically interjected." Religious institutions, ideas, and identities serve as a central and unique resource, then, for those engaged in racial politics.

"Acting Out"

The mutual construction of racial and religious identities takes place not only in American institutions and among political leaders but also on the ground: the intersection of race and religion is a lived experience. The second section of this volume, "Acting Out," sharpens the insights gained into political behavior by recognizing the codefinition of racial and religious categories, in which religion serves as a site or vehicle for mobilization and political action. Race and religion intersect not just in a deep definitional manner but also in crafting strategies and mobilizing resources and individuals.

Robert P. Jones and Robert D. Francis in "The Black and White of Moral Values" use survey and exit poll data to show that the impact of religion on political behavior cannot be understood independent of race; blacks and whites are not affected by religion in the same way. It is only by looking at the intersection of race and religion that we can begin to make sense of contemporary public opinion on issues such as abortion and voting patterns and party support in elections this century.

In the next essay, "Latino Religion and Its Political Consequences," Jessica Hamar Martínez, Edwin I. Hernández, and Milagros Peña look at the differences in civic participation and voting patterns between Catholic and Protestant Latinos. While considerable attention has been paid to the growing Latino portion of the electorate, these scholars argue that unless religion is included alongside the other more commonly studied issues of nativity and ethnicity, Latino political behavior cannot be fully understood. A growing sector of Latino Protestants has higher civic participation rates and is more likely than Latino Catholics to identify with the Republican Party.

In "The Stranger among Us," Robin Dale Jacobson argues that to understand the activity of religious organizations in the political realm requires recognizing the racial terrain on which the group walks. A look at the Christian Coalition's changing stance on immigration over time shows how the religious-racial struggles the evangelical community is involved in at the time affect the political goals of the group across a range of issues. Jacobson also reveals how religion is used discursively to navigate racial politics as the Christian Coalition attempts to posit religion as a key definition of American identity in order to supplant racial divisions.

"Possibilities and Limits"

In the final section of the book, we consider the possibilities and limitations for explicitly locating attempts at racial transformation within religious institutions. Religious resources extended to racial politics produce unique expressions in different communities. In the first essay in this section, "Political Advocacy through Religious Organization? The Evolving Role of the Nation of Islam," Catherine Paden demonstrates the distinctive fashion in which the Nation of Islam can enter into—and sometimes retreat from—American racial politics because of its religious framework. By tracing the shift of the Nation of Islam away from a consciously apolitical body, Paden shows how this religious community offers an alternative framework of racial belonging. This group, she argues, could open up pathways for political mobilization of individuals left out by secular political organizations.

Tobin Miller Shearer's study of the Mennonite response to Black Power demands in "A Demanding Conversation: The Black Manifesto in the Mennonite Church, 1969–1974" shows how religious communities provide a unique space for racial dialogue. The Mennonite imperative for reconciled relationships caused the community to struggle with demands levied against church communities for decades in a way Shearer claims would not have occurred in a secular organization. Through a focused look at this religious community, he observes that "at a time when many white people assumed that the racial revolution died with Martin Luther King, substantive interracial conversation and concrete changes took place under the radar of scholars."

In the next essay, "Religion and Race: South Asian Immigrants in the Post-9/11 United States," Sangay Mishra points out limitations to cross-religious, cross-ethnic organization. He asks why Southeast Asians, while experiencing similar discrimination after September 11, 2001, did not identify common interests and mobilize in a cross-ethnic group. Through in-depth interviews he analyzes the interplay of race, religion, and nation of origin in the racialization of South Asian immigrants in the post-9/11 period and unpacks how this dynamic interaction shaped their differential response to racial targeting and hate crimes.

Nancy D. Wadsworth in "Ambivalent Miracles: The Possibilities and Limits of Evangelical Racial Reconciliation Politics" highlights both possibilities and limitations. She points to racial change that scholars may overlook if they fail to situate it within its religious context, through her exploration of conservative evangelical attempts at racial reconciliation and multiracial church building. She highlights how religious settings, theology, and identity transform racial political engagement, and argues that to understand the implications and outcomes of racial projects we must pay attention to the religious specificity of the participants, resources, and ideas. She notes, however, that pathways to racial change are limited by religious processes and frameworks.

In the final essay, "Racial Justice in the Protestant Mainline: Liberalism and Its Limits," Antony W. Alumkal furthers this insight by demonstrating how religious frameworks and organizational structures can limit the possibilities for racial change and justice. Alumkal concentrates on mainline Protestant denominations. While mainline denominations are able to recognize both structural and individual-level explanations for racial injustice, a strong division between leaders and laity often prevents mainline denominations from achieving some of their goals of diversity. As Alumkal notes, however, religious institutions are not separable from the broader society in which they function; the dominant racial hegemony in society at large limits the ways in which mainline Protestants can achieve reform.

Racial politics cannot be understood apart from their religious dimensions and roots. Religion cannot be understood apart from its growth within a racialized political world. Religion and race do not just come into contact with each other; each actually creates the meaning of the other through intersections in individuals, institutions, and ideologies. A more thoroughgoing exploration of the intersection of race and religion, as begun in this volume, underscores the power of intersectional analysis and points to pathways for development. Such analysis is important because it stresses the contextual nature of power and identity that plagues work that does not consider intersectionality. Looking at one site of intersection, religion and race, furthers these insights. On a theoretical level, this emphasizes the need to recognize the variability of power, the role of agency, and historical context in intersectional scholarship. On an empirical level, the inclusion of religion as a key force in American politics essential to defining hierarchies, political institutions, and behavior is needed to understand much about our political life.

Notes

1. For a transcript of Obama's Philadelphia speech on race on March 18, 2008, see http://www .npr.org/templates/story/story.php?storyId=88478467.

2. By September 2010, 66 percent of Americans objected to building the Muslim community center ("Most Americans Object," September 9, 2010).

3. Talking about "our" experiences can be a dangerous endeavor as experiences are always mediated by our personal identities and positions along a variety of axes, such as gender, class, and, yes, race and religion. However, there might be something useful in talking about our collective national experiences with officeholders, frames, and political contests. In this sense, we have a collective experience to pull from. For example, we have never had a black president, and America has been characterized as a Christian nation by our dominant institutions and narratives. These narratives inform our experiences, although in a multitude of ways.

4. Our overview is not by any stretch of the imagination meant to be a comprehensive history but one that brings forth examples demonstrating the importance and broad trajectory of the co-constitution of racial and religious politics.

5. It is not insignificant in this respect that Locke himself was a Puritan and anchored elements of his social contract theory in Protestant frameworks of land cultivation and divine guidance.

6. The curse of Ham, also known as the curse of Canaan, comes from a passage in Genesis (9:20–27) according to which Canaan, one of the sons of Noah, and his descendants were cursed by God as a result of Canaan having seen his father drunk and naked. Many white Americans, par-

ticularly in the eighteenth and nineteenth centuries, read the story as justifying the enslavement and persecution of people of black ancestry, seen to have been "marked" with darker skin. See also Daly 2004.

7. The conflation of the Chinese with a pagan race is prevalent throughout congressional debates on Chinese immigration and incorporation. Both Republicans and Democrats concerned with Chinese immigration pitch this as a problem about the racialized religious others. Representative James A. Johnson from California, for example, expressed concerns about Chinese suffrage that might result from some proposed provisions of the 1870 Enforcement Act targeting enforcement of the Fifteenth Amendment: "This bill ought to be entitled an act to foster paganism in the States and Territories of the United States; to foster child murder, to strike down Christianity, and to deprive the people of their liberties. . . . These [Chinese] people might become troublesome citizens; might without an effort overthrow our institutions; and further, they would always be pagans. . . . The Chinese empire . . . possesses, perhaps, four hundred million people. This immense, teeming, swarming, seething hive of degraded humanity turned loose upon our country would drown out and destroy our institutions and our race. . . . They will come, and by millions, if invited. Allow them more liberties than they have in their native land, and give them greater compensation for their labor, that is, let them understand that they may not only own the country, but control it, and it will not be long before a white man in California will be a rare sight. . . . I must say, in my humble opinion, the very highest crime a man can commit is committed where he turns against his country and his race. All agitation in favor of enfranchising the Chinese is a war upon the rights of the States and a war against republican self-government—a war in the interest of paganism and against the ever-living God. . . . Laws for the enfranchisement of the Chinese would be . . . manifestly unjust to the white citizens of the Pacific coast" (quoted in Torok 1996, 88).

8. Denominations are institutionally organized subsets of religious groups that distinguish themselves according to church doctrine, worship styles, or theological interpretation. The term "mainline" has differed across historical periods and tends to be contrasted with the term "evangelical." Historically, the majority of American Protestants have belonged to mainline denominations, though from the mid-twentieth century forward, evangelicals have gained ground. In the South during this period, mainline churches included Episcopalians, Lutherans, Presbyterians, American Baptists, and Methodists. See Moorhead 1999.

9. While many scholars have explored the centrality of the black church to the civil rights movement, Adolph Reed (1986) points out that it also sometimes served as an obstacle. A full discussion of the impact of religion on the civil rights movement exceeds the scope of this introduction, but the essays by Shearer, Webster and Leib, Jones and Francis, and Wadsworth speak to the ongoing influence of civil rights era changes on the social and political orientations of American faith communities.

10. Wadsworth (2008) categorizes religiously influenced racial perspectives into three competing religious racial traditions operative across U.S. history: theological racism, religious racial interchange, and religious racial justice.

11. A few examples of studies of American racial politics that reflect these tendencies include Perry and Parent 1995, Walton 1994, Goldfield 1997, Gilliam 1975, Sears, Sidanius, and Bobo 2000, Carmines and Sniderman 2001, and Persons 2001, but this list could be expanded by hundreds of studies. Until about 2004, studies of racial politics in the United States that did not look at religion were more the norm than the exception.

12. A few examples of work on the Religious Right that largely omits race include Wuthnow

1988, Greenwalt 1988, Soper 1994, Himmelstein 1990, Snowball 1991, Diamond 1989, Diamond 1995 (chaps. 7 and 10), Jelen 1991, and Wills 1990.

13. In sociology, it is argued, "Despite its popularity and persuasiveness as an analytic concept . . . intersectionality remains an elusive accomplishment: Sociology is still finding its intersectional legs when it comes to turning intersectional principles into sociological practice" (Luft 2005, 366).

14. Ange Marie Hancock advocates for intersectionality "*both* as a normative theoretical argument *and* an approach to conducting empirical research that emphasizes the intersection of categories of difference (including but not limited to race, gender, class, and sexual orientation)" (Hancock 2007b, 63–64)

15. A word on the tensions being navigated as intersectional scholarship broadens in scope beyond the categories of race and gender: Clearly, there is a risk that new scholarship will expand the categories of interest beyond recognition and without attending to the race and gender dynamics with which black feminist scholars were initially concerned. We maintain, however, that religion is as relevant, and often as central, to the majority of Americans' racial and even gendered identities (even as a background cultural influence for people who aren't actively religious) that failing to theorize its relevance to intersectional analysis would be a serious mistake. We believe all race scholarship must be responsible and that white scholars, of whom we are two, have to be particularly sensitive to our privilege and place in the academy. We also believe that intersectional scholarship can only benefit from exploring domination and subordination, as well as those intersections that problematize a neat hierarchy. The inclusion of religion, so central to American identity, is important for that project.

16. For this reason, sexual orientation has faced some problems being included in the intersectional triumvirate, as evidenced in sociological textbooks.

17. Intersectional models were developed to understand the "simultaneity of oppression" as it affected particular groups, such as black women (Simien 2007). Such models aimed to produce scholarship that continued the liberation of historically subordinated groups but was more sensitive than earlier scholarship to how systems of power affect particular bodies in particularly complex ways, insofar as different structures of oppression and privilege overlap. This goal continues to be central to intersectional work as scholars refine the methodological and theoretical questions raised by earlier perspectives (e.g., Calavita 2006, 253).

18. This is precisely how racial and religiously diverse constituencies could emerge on both sides of political battles over marriage rights, as they have in the past ten years. Wadsworth (2011) explores how intersectionality theory can be used to interpret the multiracial coalitions on both sides of the Proposition 8 battle in California.

19. This has not been true, however, for the religious traditions most deeply subordinated through whites' association of them with racial otherness (such as Native Americans and Muslims).

References

Alumkal, Antony. 2003. *Asian American Evangelical Churches: Race, Ethnicity, and Assimilation in the Second Generation.* New York: LFB Scholarly Publishing.

Ammerman, Nancy Tatom. 1990. *Baptist Battles: Social Change and Religious Conflict in the Southern Baptist Convention.* New Brunswick, NJ: Rutgers University Press.

Badger, Anthony J., and T. Ownby. 2002. *The Role of Ideas in the Civil Rights South: Essays.* Porter L. Fortune Jr. History Symposium (25th: 1999, University of Mississippi). Jackson: University Press of Mississippi.

Bellah, Robert Neelly. 1975. *The Broken Covenant: American Civil Religion in a Time of Trial.* New York: Seabury Press.

Brah, Avtar, and Ann Phoenix. 2004. "Ain't I a Woman? Revisiting Intersectionality." *Journal of International Women's Studies* 5 (3): 75.

Bush, Melanie E. L. 2004. *Breaking the Code of Good Intentions: Everyday Forms of Whiteness.* Lanham, MD: Rowman & Littlefield.

Butler, Judith. 1999. *Gender Trouble.* New York: Routledge.

Calavita, Kitty. 2006. "Collisions at the Intersection of Gender, Race, and Class: Enforcing the Chinese Exclusion Laws." *Law and Society Review* 40 (2): 249–81.

Caldwell, Paulette M. 1991. "A Hair Piece: Perspectives on the Intersection of Race and Gender." *Duke Law Journal* 2: 365–96.

Carmines, Edward G., and Paul M. Sniderman. 2001. "The Future of Racial Politics: Beyond Fatalism." In *The State of Democracy in America*, ed. William Crotty. Washington, DC: Georgetown University Press.

Chaves, Mark, Shawna Anderson, and Jason Byassee. 2007. "American Congregations at the Beginning of the 21st Century (Report)." National Congregations Study. http://www.soc.duke.edu/natcong/.

Cohen, Cathy. 1999. *The Boundaries of Blackness: AIDS and the Breakdown of Black Politics.* Chicago: University of Chicago Press.

Collins, Patricia Hill. 1991. *Black Feminist Thought: Knowledge, Consciousness, and the Politics of Empowerment.* New York: Routledge.

Crenshaw, Kimberle. 1991. "Demarginalizing the Intersections of Race and Sex: A Black Feminist Critique of Antidiscrimination Doctrine, Feminist Theory, and Antiracist Politics." In *Feminist Legal Theory: Readings in Law and Gender*, ed. Katherine Bartlett and Rose Kennedy. Boulder, CO: Westview Press.

Daly, John Patrick. 2004. *When Slavery Was Called Freedom: Evangelicals, Proslavery, and the Causes of the Civil War.* Louisville: University Press of Kentucky.

Diamond, Sara. 1989. *Spiritual Warfare: The Politics of the Christian Right.* Boston: South End Press.

———. 1995. *Roads to Dominion: Right-Wing Movements and Political Power in the United States.* New York: Guilford Press.

Du Bois, W. E. B. 2003. *The Souls of Black Folk.* New York: Modern Library.

Eck, Diana. 2002. *A New Religious America: How a "Christian Country" Has Become the World's Most Religiously Diverse Nation.* New York: HarperOne.

Emerson, M. O., and K. C. Kim. 2003. "Multiracial Congregations: An Analysis of Their Development and a Typology." *Journal for the Scientific Study of Religion* 42 (2): 217–27.

Emerson, Michael O., and Christian Smith. 2000. *Divided by Faith: Evangelical Religion and the Problem of Race in America.* New York: Oxford University Press.

Fredrickson, George M. 2002. *Racism: A Short History.* Princeton, NJ: Princeton University Press.

García Bedolla, Lisa. 2007. "Intersections of Inequality: Understanding Marginalization and Privilege in the Post-civil Rights Era." *Politics & Gender* 3 (2): 232–48.

Gilliam, Reginald Earl, Jr. 1975. *Black Political Development: An Advocacy Analysis.* Port Washington, NY: Kennicat Press.

Goldenberg, David M. 2005. *The Curse of Ham: Race and Slavery in Early Judaism, Christianity, and Islam.* Princeton, NJ: Princeton University Press.

Goldfield, Michael. 1997. *The Color of Politics: Race and the Mainsprings of American Politics.* New York: New Press.

Gordon, Sarah Barringer. 2002. *The Mormon Question: Polygamy and Constitutional Conflict in Nineteenth-Century America.* Chapel Hill: University of North Carolina Press.

Gravely, Will B. 1997. "The Rise of African Churches in America (1786–1822): Re-examining the Content." In *African-American Religion: Interpretive Essays in History and Culture,* ed. Timothy E. Fulop and Albert J. Raboteau, 134–51. New York: Routledge.

Greenwalt, Kent. 1988. *Religious Convictions and Political Choice.* New York: Oxford University Press.

"Growing Number of Americans Say Obama Is a Muslim." 2008. Pew Forum on Religion & Public Life, August 18. http://pewforum.org/Politics-and-Elections/Growing-Number-of-Americans -Say-Obama-is-a-Muslim.aspx.

Guest, Kenneth J. 2003. *God in Chinatown: Religion and Survival in New York's Evolving Immigrant Community.* New York: New York University Press.

Gustin, Delancey. 2010. "Misperceptions and Ineffectiveness: Obama and Islam in America." German Marshall Fund of the United States, September 23. http://blog.gmfus.org/2010/09/23/ misperceptions-and-ineffectiveness-obama-and-islam-in-america/.

Hancock, Ange-Marie. 2007a. "Intersectionality as a Normative and Empirical Paradigm." *Politics & Gender* 3 (2): 248–54.

———. 2007b. "When Multiplication Doesn't Equal Quick Addition: Examining Intersectionality as a Research Paradigm." *Perspectives on Politics* 5 (1): 63–79.

Haney López, Ian F. 1996. *White by Law: The Legal Construction of Race.* New York: New York University Press.

Harding, Susan. 1991. "Representing Fundamentalism: The Problem of the Repugnant Cultural Other." *Social Research* 58 (2): 373–93.

Harris, Cheryl. 1993. "Whiteness as Property." *Harvard Law Review* 106 (8): 1710–69.

Harris, Fredrick C. 1999. *Something Within: Religion in African-American Political Activism.* New York: Oxford University Press.

Hietala, Thomas R. 1985. *Manifest Design: American Exceptionalism and Empire.* Ithaca, NY: Cornell University Press.

Himmelstein, Jerome L. 1990. *To the Right: The Transformation of American Conservatism.* Berkeley and Los Angeles: University of California Press.

hooks, bell. 1989. *Talking Back: Thinking Feminist, Thinking Black.* Boston: South End Press.

Horsman, Reginald. 1981. *Race and Manifest Destiny: The Origins of American Racial Anglo-Saxonism.* Cambridge, MA: Harvard University Press.

Hunter, James Davison. 1991. *Culture Wars: The Struggle to Define America.* New York: Basic Books.

Jelen, Ted. 1991. *The Political Mobilization of Religious Belief.* New York: Praeger.

Jeung, Russell. 2004. *Faithful Generations: Race and New Asian American Churches.* New Brunswick, NJ: Rutgers University Press.

Joshi, K. Y. 2006. *New Roots in America's Sacred Ground: Religion, Race and Ethnicity in Indian America.* New Brunswick, NJ: Rutgers University Press.

Jung, Moon-Ho. 2005. "Outlawing 'Coolies': Race, Nation, and Empire in the Age of Emancipation." *American Quarterly* 57 (3): 677–701.

Kantor, Jodi. 2008. "Obama Denounces Statements of His Pastor as 'Inflammatory.'" *New York Times*, March 15. http://www.nytimes.com/2008/03/15/us/politics/15wright.html.

Kramnick, Isaac, and R. Laurence Moore. 1997. *The Godless Constitution: The Case against Religious Correctness*. New York: W. W. Norton.

Liebman, Robert C., and Robert Wuthnow, eds.1983. *The New Christian Right: Mobilization and Legitimation*. Hawthorne, NY: Aldine.

Lippy, Charles H. "Slave Christianity." 2007. In *Modern Christianity to 1900*, ed. Amanda Porterfield, 291–316. Minneapolis: Fortress Press.

Lipsitz, George. 2006. *The Possessive Investment in Whiteness: How White People Profit from Identity Politics*. Philadelphia: Temple University Press.

Luft, Rachel E. 2005. "Review: *Black Sexual Politics: African Americans, Gender, and the New Racism* by Patricia Hill Collins." *Contemporary Sociology* 34 (4): 366–67.

Manis, Andrew Michael. 1987. *Southern Civil Religions in Conflict: Black and White Baptists and Civil Rights, 1947–1957*. Athens: University of Georgia Press.

Marsden, George. 1990. *Religion and American Culture*. New York: Harcourt.

Mazur, Eric Michael. 1999. *The Americanization of Religious Minorities: Confronting the Constitutional Order*. Baltimore, MD: Johns Hopkins University Press.

McAllister, Lenny. 2010. "Obama's Boldness on Islam vs. His Silence on Race." The Root, August 18. http://www.theroot.com/views/obamas-boldness-islam-vs-his-silence-race.

McIntosh, Peggy. 1989. "White Privilege: Unpacking the Invisible Knapsack." *Peace and Freedom*, July/August, 10–12.

Moore, R. Laurence. 1994. *Selling God: American Religion in the Marketplace of Culture*. New York: Oxford University Press.

Moorhead, James H. 1999. *World without End: Mainstream American Protestant Visions of the Last Things, 1880–1925*. Religion in North America, no. 28. Bloomington: Indiana University Press.

Morone, James A. 2003. *Hellfire Nation: The Politics of Sin in American History*. New Haven, CT: Yale University Press.

Morris, Aldon. 1986. *Origins of the Civil Rights Movement: Black Communities Organizing for Change*. New York: Free Press.

"Most Americans Object to Planned Islamic Center Near Ground Zero, Poll Finds." 2010. *Washington Post*, September 9. http://www.washingtonpost.com/wp-dyn/content/article/2010/09/08/AR2010090806231.html?sid=ST2010090806236.

Noll, Mark. 2008. *God and Race in American Politics: A Short History*. Princeton, NJ: Princeton University Press.

Olson, Joel. 2007. "The Freshness of Fanatacism: The Abolitionist Defense of Zealotry." *Perspectives on Politics* 5 (4): 685–701.

Orren, Karen, and Stephen Skowronek. 2004. *The Search for American Political Development*. New York: Cambridge University Press.

Pearce, Roy Harvey. 1967. *Savagism and Civilization: A Study of the Indian and the American Mind*. Baltimore, MD: Johns Hopkins University Press.

Perkins, John. 1995. *Restoring At-Risk Communities: Doing It Together and Doing It Right*. Grand Rapids, MI: Baker Books.

Perry, Huey L., and Wayne Parent, eds. 1995. *Blacks and the American Political System*. Gainesville: University Press of Florida.

Persons, George A., ed. 2001. *The Politics of the Black "Nation": A Twenty-Five-Year Retrospective.* National Political Science Review, vol. 8. New York: Transaction.

Pew Forum on Religion & Public Life (with Pew Hispanic Center). 2007. "Report: Changing Faiths: Latinos and the Transformation of American Religion." http://pewhispanic.org/reports/report.php?ReportID=75.

Putnam, R. 1993. "The Prosperous Community: Social Capital and Public Life." *American Prospect* 13 (1): 35–42.

Reed, Adolph L. 1986. *The Jesse Jackson Phenomenon: The Crisis of Purpose in Afro-American Politics.* New Haven, CT: Yale University Press.

Roediger, David R. 1991. *The Wages of Whiteness: Race and the Making of the American Working Class.* London: Verso.

Rottman, Susan B., and Myra Marx Ferree. 2008. "Citizenship and Intersectionality: German Feminist Debates about Headscarf and Antidiscrimination Laws." *Social Politics* 15 (4): 481–513.

Sears, David O., James Sidanius, and Lawrence Bobo, eds. 2000. *Racialized Politics: The Debate About Racism in America.* Chicago: University of Chicago Press.

Simien, Evelyn. 2007. "Doing Intersectionality Research: From Conceptual Issues to Practical Examples." *Politics & Gender* 3 (2): 264–71.

Smith, Rogers M. 1993. "Beyond Tocqueville, Myrdal, and Hartz: The Multiple Traditions in America." *American Political Science Review* 87 (3): 549.

Snowball, David. 1991. *Continuity and Change in the Rhetoric of the Moral Majority.* New York: Praeger.

Soper, Christopher. 1994. *Evangelical Christianity in the United States and Great Britain: Religious Beliefs, Political Choices.* New York: New York University Press.

Steyn, Melissa E. 2001. *Whiteness Just Isn't What It Used to Be: White Identity in a Changing South Africa.* Albany: State University of New York Press.

Takaki, Ronald. 1989. *Stranger from a Different Shore: A History of Asian Americans.* Boston: Little, Brown.

Tinker, George E. 1993. *Missionary Conquest: The Gospel and Native American Cultural Genocide.* Minneapolis: Fortress Press.

Tocqueville, Alexis de. 1839. *Democracy in America.* New York: G. Adlard.

Torok, John Hayakawa. 1996. "Reconstruction and Racial Nativism: Chinese Immigrants and Debates on the Thirteenth, Fourteenth, and Fifteenth Amendments and Civil Rights Laws." *Asian Law Journal* 3 (55).

Vakulenko, Anastasia. 2007. "'Islamic Headscarves' and the European Convention on Human Rights: An Intersectional Perspective." *Social and Legal Studies* 16 (2): 183–99.

Wadsworth, Nancy D. 2008. "Reconciling Fractures: The Intersection of Race and Religion in United States Political Development." In *Race and American Political Development*, ed. Julie Novkov, Joseph Lowndes, and Dorian T. Warren, 312–36. New York: Routledge.

———. 2011. "Intersectionality in California's Same-Sex Battles: A Complex Proposition." *Political Research Quarterly* 64(1): 200–216.

Waldman, Steven. 2008. *Founding Faith: Providence, Politics, and the Birth of Religious Freedom.* New York: Random House.

Walton, Hanes, Jr. 1994. *Black Politics and Black Political Behavior: A Linkage Analysis.* Westport, CT: Praeger.

Williams, Johnny E. 2003. *African American Religion and the Civil Rights Movement in Arkansas.* Jackson: University Press of Mississippi.

Wills, Garry. 1990. *Under God: Religion and American Politics.* New York: Simon & Schuster.

Wilson, Catherine. 2008. *The Politics of Latino Faith: Religion, Identity, and Urban Community.* New York: New York University Press.

Winant, Howard. 2004. *The New Politics of Race: Globalism, Difference, Justice.* Minneapolis: University of Minnesota Press.

Wuthnow, Robert. 1988. *The Restructuring of American Religion.* Princeton, NJ: Princeton University Press.

Yancey, George A. 2003. *One Body, One Spirit: Principles of Successful Multiracial Churches.* Downers Grove, IL: InterVarsity Press.

Foundations

Religion, Race, and the
American Constitutional Order

Eric Michael Mazur

> We hold these truths to be self-evident, that all men are created equal, that they are
> endowed by their Creator with certain unalienable Rights . . .
> —The Declaration of Independence

There is little controversy among scholars of American religion that the role of religion in American society has changed dramatically since the Civil War, even if the nature of that change is subject to debate. The fact of change, however, has only more recently been theorized in the context of the relationship of religion to America's public institutions. But by the beginning of the twentieth century, as conservative Protestantism was losing its monopoly on the production and maintenance of the symbols and rhetoric of public authority, the federal religio-political complex, or what I have called elsewhere the American constitutional order—that is, the rites, rules, myths, and rituals of authority and transcendence posited in the federal government—began to eclipse it (Handy 1984; Mazur 1999). As a result, the central tenets of the religio-political order had to be re-conceptualized.

One of the by-products of this transformation has been a parallel one in conceptions of race. As Protestantism was replaced by a state-centered ideology as the public source of symbolic meaning construction and maintenance, the state benefited from a radical individualism that effectively eliminated competition and left it virtually unchecked as a source of authority in American culture. Group-based constructions of identity, including race no less than religion, gave way to this radical individualism, the logical conclusion of a Protestant dominant culture but also a necessity of the state's authority in the American constitutional order. Writes historian of American religion Mark Noll (2008, 2), "rather than any specific configuration of race and religion, it has been the general inter-weaving of race and religion, along with a discernibly religious mode of public argument, that have pervaded the nation's political history." As the "discernibly religious mode of public argument" has itself been transformed, so too has the way religion and race have been understood and themselves been communicated.

The proper analysis of this transformation, therefore, should take into account religion *and* race, examining their shared relationship to the constitutional order rather than as separate factors of change in American public culture. Notes Evelyn Simien (2007, 266) about studies of race and gender, these factors "cannot be reduced to individual attributes to be measured and assessed for their separate contributions in explaining political outcomes," and indeed, people are not, in her terms, "*either* black/white *or* male/female" (emphasis in the original). Rather, people are a blend of many characteristics, and these categories are so intimately integrated that no one can be fully appreciated without taking into account the others (Hancock 2007a, 2007b). In this essay I explore the relationship between religion and race in the American constitutional order by using some of the tools of "intersectionality," an approach that, as Simien (2007, 69) has written, "expects that such identity categories as race, class, and gender"—and, in our case, religion—"fuse to create distinct opportunities," providing us with "an avenue for investigating complex inequalities in the United States." By examining the Supreme Court's evolution as an institution of national ideology, its changing understanding of religion, and changes in the way it understood—or at least articulated an understanding about—race, we should be better able to understand how coincidental these trajectories have been. Following these changes through some of the Court's rulings on public education—particularly where they involve race or religion, or both—will provide us with a window onto one of the most powerful instruments of government indoctrination since the second half of the nineteenth century. The rise of public education as a foundational institution in American society coincides not only with the expansion of religious diversity but also with America's confrontation with questions of race, and the ascension of the American constitutional order. In the public arena, the intersection of religion and race has been one of the defining debates of the American constitutional order. In its decisions related to public education, we may better come to understand how the Supreme Court has negotiated that intersection.

American Religion as an Engine of Supreme Court Dynamism?

Political scientists and historians have long posited stages of institutional development with regard to the federal government. Robert McCloskey's (1960) analysis outlined three stages: the first (roughly from the nation's founding to the Civil War) was characterized by a preoccupation with federalism; the second stage (roughly from *Dred Scott v. Sanford* [60 U.S. 393 (1857)] through *Lochner v. New York* [198 U.S. 45 (1905)] to the presidency of Franklin D. Roosevelt) was preoccupied with individual economic rights; and the third stage (roughly from *Gitlow v. New York* [268 U.S. 652 (1925)] through the civil rights era) was preoccupied with civil rights and individual liberties. Karen Orren and Stephen Skowronek (2004, 143–55) apply categories from American political development to church-state relations, outlining three distinct orders: the religion order, the free exercise order, and (between the two) the order of political parties. However, these orders seem static—"an arrangement of coexisting or 'multiple' orders"— rather than dynamic stages of development that take into account institutional or cultural change. Mark Noll (2008, 64) examines changes in the foundational support for the U.S. government—particularly related to religion and race—but does not relate these changes to the public institutions (like the Court) integral in the connections between the three factors.[1] My own work has sought to track this relationship, using Supreme Court litigation involving Native Americans, Mormons, and Jehovah's Witnesses as case studies (Mazur 1996, 1997, 1999, 2001, 2002b). This order was founded in a relatively homogeneous religious environment in which it was impossible to conceive of government, citizenship, and ethics apart from religion—specifically, Protestantism. Eventually, however, the order evolved separately from the Protestant dominant culture, with interests separate from (and at times opposite to) that culture.

Expressed particularly in the writings of Justice Joseph Story (on the Court from 1811 until his death in 1845), phase one expressed conceptions of federalism from an entirely Protestant point of view, that is, through the doctrine of faith versus works (Hammond, Machacek, and Mazur 2004, 58–60; "Freedom, Religious," forthcoming). Any citizen, regardless of his beliefs or the limits placed on him by any state constitution, could (in theory) participate in the federal government as long as he behaved properly: like a good Christian. Article 16 of the Virginia Declaration of Rights (ratified on June 12, 1776), for example, provided for the free exercise of religious beliefs, but also noted that it was "the mutual duty of all to practice Christian forbearance, love, and charity towards each other." Religious beliefs were protected by the federal Constitution; actions were regulated by the state. As Thomas Jefferson wrote in the Virginia Statute for Religious Freedom (ratified January 16, 1786): "Almighty God hath created the mind free"; but "it is time enough for the rightful purposes of civil government, for its officers to interfere when principles break out into overt acts against peace and good order." "Peace and good order" were determined in the political arena, and therefore reflected a distinctly Protestant sensibility. This American worldview placed significant control of people's actions in the hands of the state government, with the federal government and the authority of the American constitutional order serving as the guarantor of its citizens' various beliefs. Justice Story and others created a jurisprudence of religious liberty that protected every citizen's right to believe what he wanted, while preserving for the state the authority to moderate behavior. This left social order and police powers, as well as limits on political participation, to the states, but made the federal government the supreme guarantor of individual citizens' rights of conscience (Wilson 1990). It was the federal government (Article VI of the U.S. Constitution), and not the states, that prohibited religious tests for participation; a good number of the colonies-turned-states maintained political limitations on members of various religious communities for decades after the ratification of the Constitution.[2] The model Supreme Court decision reflective of this demeanor was authored by Justice Story in *Vidal v. Girard's Executors* (43 U.S. [2 Howard] 127 [1844]), a Pennsylvania probate case involving a will stipulating that part of a bequest be used to teach religion but prohibiting the use of clergy. Challenging this provision as anti-Christian, the descendants sought to invalidate the will. Justice Story, writing for the Court, noted that whereas "Christianity is part of the common law" of Pennsylvania, one need not be a member of the clergy to teach religion. The very Protestant tenet of the "priesthood of all believers" triumphed, and the challenge to the will failed (Hammond, Machacek, and Mazur 2004, 45–83).

In the second half of the nineteenth century, the Court transitioned from Protestant nationalism to (less specifically Protestant) Republican Protestantism. By this time, the conservative Protestant dominant culture's monopoly in American society was loosening, and an increasing level of diversity was having a noticeable impact on American public culture (Handy 1984, 1991). A marked increase in the public participation of Catholics and, to a lesser extent, Jews, and new forms of Protestantism, including Mormons, Seventh-Day Adventists, Jehovah's Witnesses, Christian Scientists, and Spiritualists, as well as fundamentalist, modernist, Pentecostal, and evangelical Protestant camps, threatened the façade of a public cultural monopoly once enjoyed by the largely Congregationalist (Northern) and Episcopalian (Southern) Protestant dominant culture (Hatch 1989). Coupled with a diminished post–Civil War need for the federal government to placate state concerns over issues like religion, this meant that a close connection between citizenship and Protestantism could no longer be assumed. The Union victory in the Civil War meant that the federal government no longer needed the states to affirm its authority, liberating it from nongovernmental systems, institutions, or ideologies—including the Protestant Christianity that had been established de facto if not de jure by the states—for its continued well-being. If relied on at all, the order was more likely to use the symbols and rhetoric of Protestant Christianity (in a more generally applicable form) to justify its actions after the fact (Handy 1991).

Not coincidentally, this second phase saw an increase in Supreme Court activity involving religion and religious institutions, representing an initial distancing of the government from its specifically Protestant foundation.[3] Although there were a number of pragmatic decisions involving religious individuals and institutions in conflicts over taxes, property ownership, and the like,[4] most often during this phase the Court adjudicated matters involving challenges to the government's corporate (i.e., collective yet hierarchical) authority to decide religion-related matters, and regularly affirmed the federal government's supremacy within the collective.[5] A good example of this developing theological self-confidence can be found in *United States v. Macintosh* (283 U.S. 605 [1931]), a case involving a Canadian Baptist whose application for American citizenship was rejected because he had refused—on religious grounds—to promise to take up arms in defense of the nation if ever called upon to do so. Wrote Justice George Sutherland:

> We are a Christian people, according to one another the equal right of religious freedom, and acknowledging with reverence the duty of obedience to the will of God. But, also, we are a nation with the duty to survive; a nation whose Constitution contemplates war as well as peace; whose government must go forward upon the assumption, and safely can proceed upon no other, that *unqualified allegiance to the nation and submission and obedience to the laws of the land, as well those made for war as those made for peace, are not inconsistent with the will of God.* (1931, 625; internal references deleted; emphasis added)

For Justice Southerland and a majority of the Court, the will of the nation and the will of God were in complete agreement, religious sensibilities (including mainstream Protestant sensibilities like those of the Canadian Baptist) to the contrary notwithstanding.

By the beginning of World War II, conditions that had been present since the beginning of the century began to have a profound impact on how the Court understood religion. In large part because of the expansion of free speech protections, those who argued that their right to religious free exercise was related to an individual liberty right stood a much better chance of getting a sympathetic hearing before the Supreme Court. Jehovah's Witnesses, for example, who had argued unsuccessfully before the Court when they relied entirely on religious liberty grounds, were significantly more successful when they integrated (or relied entirely on) free speech justifications (Mazur 1999, 28–61; Hammond, Machacek, and Mazur 2004, 69–83). Increasingly through the 1940s, and particularly by the 1960s, this would lead to an expansion in the protection of individual religious liberty, which grew in conjunction with expansions in the protection of other individual rights and liberties. Decisions of this later period represent a nearly complete break from Protestant sensibilities, affirming religious behavior as equally compelling as religious belief (*Sherbert v. Verner*, 374 U.S. 398 [1963]), and protecting nontheism (*Torcaso v. Watkins*, 367 U.S. 488 [1961]) and sincerely held nonspecific belief systems that were parallel to traditional religious beliefs (*United States v. Seeger*, 380 U.S. 163 [1965]). The fracturing of American Protestantism and the relative explosion of religious diversity more completely liberated the constitutional order from the need to protect increasingly heterogeneous Protestant sensibilities. Indeed, by becoming the undisputed arbiter of religious disputes via the First Amendment, the federal government—as definer and guarantor of religious liberty within the constitutional order—achieved authority over the divine.

The transformation of the Court's relationship to religion (from "Protestant nationalist" to "Republican Protestant" to "constitutional order") reflected the state's growing ideological independence; as it became more self-confident, it exercised its own theology of justification. Although remnants of the Protestant dominant culture could still be found in the underpinnings of the order, increasingly from the latter part of the nineteenth century and most forcefully by World War II the constitutional order had its own transcendent referent—itself. By the end of World War II, Protestant Christianity was still a significant part of American culture, but not the only part, and the independent authority of the American constitutional order—resting on an ideology of radical individualism—enabled the federal government to better incorporate those beyond the Euro-American Protestant dominant culture—such as African Americans—who were either moving to the United States in greater numbers or had been here and were just coming into their own politically.

American Protestantism as the Engine of Racial Dynamism?

In American history there has always been a close relationship between conceptions of religion (particularly Protestantism) and constructions of race. As Craig Prentiss (2003, 2) puts it, "any account of the social construction of race and ethnicity [would] be incomplete if it fail[ed] to consider the influence of religious traditions and narratives," and as Matthew Jacobson (1998, 4) puts it more directly, "Caucasians are made and not born." When the American constitutional order was synchronized most directly with Protestantism, particularly (but not exclusively) in the Protestant nationalist phase before the Civil War, argues sociologist Daniel Lee (2004, 85), "Many White Americans turned to religion as a source of racial and national unity." Well before, but also after, the Civil War, they used religion to construct the very notion of "whiteness." Racial distinctions were based on Old Testament interpretations, either drawn from the curse of Ham narrative (Genesis 9:22) or offered as an explanation for the two creation narratives in the first chapters of Genesis (see Winchell 1880). Lee (2004, 107) concludes:

> At the end of the Civil War, White Americans found it necessary to distinguish themselves from non-White Americans. Initially, they took it for granted that non-Whites were also non-Christians. . . . Thus, White people could safely divide America into two distinct populations: Christians and non-Christians.

Part of this had to do with the habit of understanding race as equivalent to "stock," or roughly what today might be considered "ethnicity." During the debates over the passage of the Civil Rights Act of 1866, members of Congress referred to Chinese, German, "Gypsie," Jewish, "Latin," Mexican, "Mongolian," Scandinavian, and Spanish—in addition to Anglo-Saxon—"races."[6] In this there is a hint that "race" was representative of religious difference; all of the mentioned "races" were predominantly non-Protestant, with the exception of the Scandinavian and German "races," who would have been primarily Lutheran (and, by implication, were either far enough from mainstream American Protestantism or—more significantly—close enough to Roman Catholicism to be considered "other"). This racialization of religion is also apparent in a landmark 1878 religious liberty decision affirming congressional authority to prohibit the Mormon ritual of plural marriage, in which the Court noted that "Polygamy has always been odious among the northern and western nations of Europe"—that is, white Protestants—"and, until the establishment of the Mormon Church, was almost exclusively a feature of the life of Asiatic and of African people"—that is, the nonwhite, non-Protestants (*Reynolds v. U.S.*, 98 U.S. 145 [1878], 164). Forty-five years later, in *United States v. Bhagat Singh Thind* (261 U.S. 204 [1923]), the Court denied American citizenship to a resident noncitizen because of an exclusion of "non-Whites" that Congress had written into immigration law (Snow 2004). Common for the period but also reflective of the interchangeability of religion and race, the aggrieved party's religious identity (Sikh, but mistakenly identified throughout the decision as "high-caste Hindu") is used interchangeably with his national, ethnic, and ultimately his racial identity. One contemporary scholar justified the practice, noting that "each race, beside its special moral qualities, seems also to have special religious qualities, which cause it to tend toward some one kind of religion more than to another kind. These religions are the flower of the race" (Clarke 1875, 16–17; see also Snow 2004, 269).

As late as 1987, the Court affirmed the close connection between religion and race. Ruling in two separate decisions that the concept of race was not limited to the traditional binary categories of black and white, it maintained a definition of "non-White" that included not only peoples of African descent but any peoples who might not have been considered "white" when the early statutes were first debated. In the first of the two decisions (*Saint Francis College v. Al-Khazraji*, 41 U.S. 604 [1987]), this meant people of a geographically based identity (an Arab man suing an employer for alleged racial discrimination); in the second (*Shaare Tefila Congregation v. Cobb*, 481 U.S. 615 [1987]), it meant people of a religion-based identity (a Jewish congregation prosecuting vandals for violating their civil rights).[7] Noted the Court (1987, 610–11) in the former decision:

> The understanding of "race" in the 19th century, however, was different. Plainly, all those who might be deemed Caucasian today were not thought to be of the same race at the time [42 U.S. §]1981 became law . . . It was not until the 20th century that dictionaries began referring to the Caucasian, Mongolian, and Negro races, or to race as involving divisions of mankind based upon different physical characteristics.[8]

The conflation of race (and ethnicity) and religion explains how American pluralism begins with the gradual integration of European "nonwhites"—Roman Catholics and Jews—who, though "racially" and ethnically marginal, could still "pass" in "white" (i.e., Protestant) society. From the anti-Catholic outbreaks of the nineteenth and early twentieth century to Senator John F. Kennedy's victory in 1960, American Roman Catholics moved from margin to mainstream (Mazur 2008).[9] American Jews experienced a similar transition into American public culture, over roughly the same time span (Brodkin 1999). Starting slowly, but culminating just after World War II, the eventual public integration of Roman Catholics and Jews laid the foundation for the later gradual integration into that same society of non-European nonwhites—African Americans ("Americanization" 2008; "Pluralism" 2008), who, by the end of World War II, were slowly beginning to gain wider admission into American public culture. President Harry Truman's Executive Order 9981 to integrate the military—issued on July 26, 1948, but not operationalized until the Korean conflict—was one early step toward the integration of the African American community into the constitutional order.

One religio-racial community that did not seem to benefit from this evolution was the Native American population, but this may have had as much to do with timing as anything else (Mazur 1999, 94–121). Considered unreligious, nonreligious, or inappropriately religious by early Spanish, French, and British settlers, Native American religious and political rights would not improve significantly until the end of the twentieth century. The relatively young American constitutional order worked to integrate willing Native Americans in its midst—and segregate the unwilling. The U.S. Constitution treated as citizens Native Americans living individualized, integrated lives among the former colonists, but treated as nonpersons those living on the "reservation"—identifying them as "Indians not taxed" in Article I §2, and "domestic dependent nations"—foreigners within—by the Supreme Court in *Cherokee Nation v. Georgia* (30 U.S. 1 [1831]). The Civil War, the passage of the Civil Rights Act of 1866, and the passage of the post–Civil War Amendments (13, 14, 15) to the Constitution did nothing to change the collective status of Native Americans. By 1871, with responsibility for official interaction transferring from the Senate to the House of Representatives, Native Americans went from being a foreign threat to being a domestic issue.[10] The General Allotment Act of 1887, also known as the Dawes Act, sought to transfer collective ("tribal") ownership of land to individual Native American landowners, but instead resulted in the wholesale gutting of Native American treaty lands, and finally ended with passage of the Indian Reorganization Act (Wheeler-Howard Act) of 1934. In 1919, U.S. citizenship was finally extended to Native American veterans living on reservations who had served in World War I, and in 1924 the Indian Citizenship Act extended citizenship to all Native Americans born in the United States. Finally, in 1968, the Indian Civil Rights Act extended to Native Americans living on the reservation *most* of the protections of the Bill of Rights—excluding (among other things) some elements of the Fifteenth Amendment, in recognition of the religio-racial aspect of tribal membership (Mazur 1999, 174n16).

It is because of this history of interaction between Native Americans and the

U.S. American constitutional order that religious relations developed the way they did. From the first colonial encounter, Native Americans were seen as a religious threat in need of conversion. From Pope Paul III's 1537 papal encyclical *Sublimus Dei*, identifying Native Americans as human (and therefore worthy of evangelizing), to the "Peace Policy" of President Ulysses S. Grant (which provided federal funds to religious organizations for pacifying Native Americans on the frontier), Native American religions were subject to the overwhelming power of colonial authorities (Beaver 1962; Handy 1984, 1991). The devastation of the Ghost Dance movement in the late 1870s and the prohibition of the Sun Dance in the 1920s only increased the religious marginalization of Native Americans (Wenger 2009). Not until the 1980s would Native Americans bring a religious liberty case to the Supreme Court, and in all the years since, they have never won there (*Bowen v. Roy, 476 U.S. 693* [1986]; *Lyng v. Northwest Indian Cemetery Protective Association, 485 U.S. 439* [1988]; *Employment Division, Department of Human Resources of the State of Oregon v. Smith, 485 U.S. 60* [1988]; *Employment Division, Department of Human Resources of Oregon v. Smith, 494 U.S. 872* [1990]). Precisely because of the transformation of the American constitutional order at the end of the first half of the twentieth century, Native Americans eventually ceased being a missionary field held captive by the federal government to serve vaguely Protestant designs. Later negotiations with Native American communities—understood more meaningfully as diverse across the religio-cultural spectrum—could thus be engaged to the satisfaction of the order, whether or not those ideals met the expectations of Protestant dominant culture; and while no one should argue that relations between Native Americans and the American constitutional order have become completely normalized, the religious imperative driving Euro-American interaction with Native Americans has significantly diminished as far as the federal government is concerned. Federal legislation such as the American Indian Religious Freedom Act (1978), the Native American Graves Protection and Repatriation Act (1990), and even the Religious Land Use and Institutionalized Persons Act (2000) has sought to provide some relief to Native Americans practicing traditional religions.

The interchangeability of the categories of religion and race has been a two-edged sword; equating them permitted religious exclusions based on the prejudices of race, but required an expansion of racial rights when religio-political ideologies shifted. Fifteen years before the Court's decision in *Bhagat Singh Thind*, Justice John Marshall Harlan made this point explicit. In *Berea College v. Commonwealth of Kentucky* (211 U.S. 45 [1908]), a case involving the school's religiously motivated violation of Kentucky's racial segregation statute, Justice Harlan connected the protection of religious freedom with the rights of peoples of all races to participate in U.S. society. We hear in Justice Harlan's dissent a blending of concerns about religion and race, highlighting how, in an American constitutional order increasingly independent of its roots in Protestant dominant culture, a new theology of how citizenship and participation could cross religio-racial lines.

Noting the commercial right to teach "especially, where the services are rendered for compensation," Justice Harland—who had been the lone dissenting vote in *Plessy v. Ferguson* (163 U.S. 537 [1896])—also identifies "the capacity to impart instruction to others," which is "given by the Almighty for beneficent purposes" which cannot be restricted by the government "unless such instruction is, in its nature, harmful to the public morals or imperils the public safety." He questions "what would stop Kentucky from separating children of different races in a church's Sabbath school" or "at a communion table in the same Christian church." "In the eye of the law," he argues,

> [t]he right to enjoy one's religious belief, unmolested by any human power, is no more sacred nor more fully or distinctly recognized than is the right to impart and receive instruction not harmful to the public. The denial of either right would be an infringement of the liberty inherent in the freedom secured by the fundamental law. Again, if the views of the highest court of Kentucky be sound, that commonwealth may, without infringing the Constitution of the United States, forbid the association in the same private school of pupils of the Anglo-Saxon and Latin races respectively, or pupils of the Christian and Jewish faiths, respectively. Have we become so inoculated with prejudice of race that an American government, professedly based on the principles of freedom, and charged with the protection of all citizens alike, can make distinctions between such citizens in the matter of their voluntary meeting for innocent purposes, simply because of their respective races? (*Berea College v. Commonwealth of Kentucky*, 1908, 67–69 [references omitted])

But of course, Justice Harlan's dissent had no immediately visible impact. At that time, the American constitutional order was unprepared to appreciate fully the concept of individual rights. The Court would remain in a more "corporate" phase until it reinterpreted the Fourteenth Amendment, expanding individual rights beyond the arena of economic interests and into the areas of free speech, freedom of religion, and, ultimately, civil rights (Hammond, Machacek, and Mazur 2004, 69–83). If race and religion were as closely connected as we have asserted, such interpretations would only be possible during the third religio-political phase of the American order's maturation, when transcendent reference was located in the state itself, and not during the first or second phase, when it depended—to varying degrees—on conservative Protestant Christianity as its source for definition.

American Public Education as an Engine of Religious and Racial Dynamism?

Developed within the religious world but transformed into a mechanism of state ideological inculcation, public education is a good place to measure the evolution of the state and the changing role of religion and race in U.S. society. In the earliest (Protestant nationalist) period, the education of America's youth was often located (physically and symbolically) in the Protestant church, and was understood entirely as the way in which good Christians became good citizens, and vice versa.[11] Throughout the first half of the nineteenth century conformity to this model was enforced, and state courts adjudicated cases involving students (or their parents), who were punished for objecting to the overtly Protestant nature of public education, most often over the reading of the King James (i.e., the Protestant) version of the Bible in school (Michaelsen 1970, esp. chaps. 3 and 4; Way 1987).

However, concomitant with the American constitutional order's decreasing dependence on the Protestant dominant culture in the second half of the nineteenth century, the ideology of public education expanded beyond those (primarily Protestant) institutions supported by religious communities. Public intellectuals such as John Dewey promoted a theory of education that, although intended as a rebuttal to institutional religion, presented parallel truths supportive of many of the ideals that would be sympathetic to the American constitutional order: good citizenship, respect for authority, dedication to community, and the like (Michaelsen 1970, 135–59). Noted Dewey (1972, 87, emphasis added):

> Ours is the responsibility of conserving, transmitting, rectifying and expanding the heritage of values we have received that those who come after us may receive it more solid and secure, more widely accessible and more generously shared than we have received it. Here are all the elements for a *religious faith that shall not be confined to sect, class, or race.* Such a faith has always been implicitly the common faith of mankind.

Consistent with this, since the beginning of the twentieth century the Supreme Court has dismantled the competition—that is, the Protestant monopoly—over public education. In 1925, the Supreme Court struck down an Oregon law that, by prohibiting private (both religious and secular) education, had granted a de facto monopoly to the Protestant dominant culture in public education at that time (*Pierce v. Society of Sisters*, 268 U.S. 510 [1925]). In 1947, seeing no violation of the separation of church and state, the Court approved public reimbursements to parents of children in private (secular and—de facto—primarily Catholic, but not for-profit) schools who had to take public transportation to get to and from school, Justice Jackson's vaguely anti-Catholic dissent notwithstanding (*Everson v. Board of Education*, 330 U.S. 1 [1947]). The next year, in a decision prohibiting formal religious instruction in public schools, Justice Frankfurter noted that

> The public school is at once the symbol of our democracy and the most pervasive means for promoting our common destiny. In no activity of the State is it more vital to keep out divisive forces than in its schools, to avoid confusing, not to say fusing, what the Constitution sought to keep strictly apart. (*McCollum v. Board of Education*, 333 U.S. 203 [1948], 231)

Starting in 1962, the Court more profoundly disestablished religious (primarily Protestant) authority in education—particularly where the state asserted its own authority—by prohibiting school-sponsored prayer (*Engel v. Vitale*, 370 U.S. 421 [1962]), in-class organized Bible reading (*Abington School District v. Schempp*, 374 U.S. 203 [1963]), and state prohibitions of the teaching of evolution (*Epperson v. Arkansas*, 393 U.S. 97 [1968]). In 1972, the Court ruled that Amish parents could withdraw their children from public school—even though they were still young enough to be required by law to attend—in compliance with community religious sensibilities (*Wisconsin v. Yoder*, 406 U.S. 205 [1972]).[12] By 1980, it would prohibit the public posting of copies of the Ten Commandments (*Stone v. Graham*, 449 U.S. 39 [1980]). Three years later, in what can be seen as a vindication for Justice Harlan's dissent in the *Berea College* decision, the Supreme Court ruled that religious liberty was not necessarily a right superior to individual civil rights. The case pitted two conservative Christian schools—both of which used racially restrictive admissions policies—against the Internal Revenue Service in a fight over tax-exempt status and the enforcement of civil rights statutes (*Bob Jones University v. United States*, 461 U.S. 574 [1983]).[13] Seeming to affirm the independence of the American constitutional order from a Protestant ideological monopoly, the Supreme Court ruled against the schools, noting that while they had the religious right to maintain segregationist policies, they did not have a right to the tax exemptions given by the federal government to "charitable" institutions if they did so. Ultimately, school-sponsored prayers at graduate ceremonies, and even before high school football games, would be ruled unconstitutional (*Lee v.*

Weisman, 505 U.S. 577 [1992]; *Santa Fe Independent School District v. Doe*, 530 U.S. 290 [2000]). And in 1994 the Supreme Court denied a religious community's desire to create an autonomous school district so that local Orthodox Jewish parents of children with special needs could still avail themselves of state services without violating the community's sensibilities related to improper interactions across religious and gender boundaries—that is, they wanted to maintain a form of religious segregation, and the Court said no (*Board of Education of Kiryas Joel v. Grumet*, 512 U.S. 687 [1994]).

The Court's trajectory with respect to the issue of race in public education was roughly parallel to that of religion, if delayed only slightly. Noted historian Mark Noll (2008, 176):

> [T]he Civil War solved the religion and slavery problem, but it did not solve the religion and race problem. Neither did Reconstruction nor the national or regional arrangements that followed Reconstruction. To the extent that the race and religion problem has ever been solved in American life, it began to be addressed only after World War II when an aggressive expression of African-American religion was met by a federal government willing to exert broad national authority on behalf of civil rights.

If our analysis is correct, then the timetable is hardly coincidental. Definitions of religion and race—particularly designations of marginalization used by the Protestant majority—were tied to the relationship between the government and the dominant Protestant culture. As that relationship changed, so too did the definitions of key categories such as race. Once the U.S. constitutional order shed its reliance on a Protestant dominant culture's monopoly in the construction and maintenance of the meaning of public signs and symbols, it could assert a definition of religion and race more suited to its own political needs. Particularly in the area of race—and especially in the area of race and public education—the order increasingly asserted its state-centered ideology on "states rights," (primarily Protestant) Southern states, ultimately disengaging the remnants of a relationship between race and religion.

Within two years of declaring in a 1952 decision involving religion and public education that "We are a religious people, whose institutions presuppose a Supreme Being" (*Zorach v. Clauson*, 343 U.S. 306 [1952], 313), the Court, in its decision in *Brown v. Board of Education* (347 U.S. 483 [1954]), overturned its decision in *Plessy v. Ferguson* (1896), which had affirmed the authority of the Civil Rights Act of 1866 to expand rights for nonwhites without dismantling the system of racial distinction that maintained political marginality—the doctrine of separate

but equal. In so doing, the Court also disengaged some of the official links between Protestantism, public education, and the government's definition of race.
Nonetheless, the Court's decision still relied on corporate categories of race,
strongly suggesting that all African American schools (and by implication, their
schoolteachers) were inherently inferior, and that the only way to "save" African
American children was to integrate them into white schools. Wrote Chief Justice
Earl Warren for a unanimous Court:

> Education is perhaps the most important function of state and local governments.
> Compulsory school attendance laws and the great expenditures for education both
> demonstrate our recognition of the importance of education to our democratic
> society. It is required in the performance of our most basic public responsibilities,
> even service in the armed forces. It is the very foundation of good citizenship. Today
> it is a principal instrument in awakening the child to cultural values, in preparing
> him for later professional training, and in helping him to adjust normally to his en-
> vironment. In these days, it is doubtful that any child may reasonably be expected
> to succeed in life if he is denied the opportunity of an education. (*Brown v. Board of
> Education*, 1954, 493)

In 1978, in a fragmented decision that had greater cultural and political impact than legal authority, a plurality of the Court ruled in *University of California
Regents v. Bakke* (438 U.S. 265 [1978]) that public institutions could not discriminate in a reverse manner—that is, could not overcompensate African Americans
as an undifferentiated social unit at the expense of individual Euro-Americans—
in their admissions process. And in 2002, in a decision hailed by many leaders
in the African American community, the Court ruled that public funds could be
used for "vouchers" to defray the cost of private primary and secondary school
tuition—including religious school tuition—without offending the Constitution's no establishment clause (*Zelman v. Simmons-Harris*, 536 U.S. 639 [2002]).
In fact, the government program would provide the funding to help citizens
avoid sending their children to a public school in their area that was perceived
as "failing" to provide a proper education. In a 2007 statement as direct as it is
reflective of the growing individualism in social categories, Chief Justice Roberts
concluded the Court's opinion in *Parents Involved in Community Schools v. Seattle
School District #1* (No. 05-908 [2007]) by noting that "the way to stop discrimination on the basis of race is to stop discriminating on the basis of race" (quoted
in Greenhouse 2007). Indeed, the central conflict between the Court's majority
and the minority in *Parents Involved* seems to be one over corporate and individual notions of identity.

Radical Individualism and the State

Thus, over the course of the twentieth century, public education went from being controlled by a vaguely Protestant ideology to being an instrument of the state, whose participants went from being the ideal product of a Euro-American Protestant world to being individual citizens (or citizens-to-be) in the American constitutional order, embodying the rise of the American constitutional order and its ideology of state-centered authority.[14] In the act of defining race separately from the historic religio-racial standards of whiteness employed by the Protestant dominant culture, the state was asserting its authority to do so. The power to do so rested entirely on the state's emergence from public Protestantism's cultural dominance and into a position of ideological independence. The political value of being Protestant has diminished as far as the American constitutional order was concerned—not that it didn't matter, but it had no extra cachet as long as the operation and ideology of the State was protected (Mazur 1999, 122–43).

Ironically, this trajectory is based on an element central to the Protestantism that was the original heart of the order (what we initially identified as "Protestant nationalism"), and is that ideology's logical extension. Notes American religion scholar Tracy Fessenden (2008, 139), "The ultimate issue of Protestantism is freedom of conscience, a freedom that leads inevitably to the democratic liberty thought to be the mark of secularism. This is a standard secularization narrative, one in which secularism is dependent on Protestantism and associated with freedom." When mixed with the individualism of democratic order, the Protestant tenets of the individual's relationship with the divine and the priesthood of all believers leads to the complete liberation of the individual, even from Protestantism.

This certainly serves the American constitutional order, which itself has become liberated from the cultural monopoly of public Protestantism. The order can best survive if it is populated by individuals seeking their individual pursuits, rather than if it is dominated by one (or even several) "blocs" monopolizing the instruments of authority. James Madison, in one of his contributions to the Federalist papers (1937, 339–40), noted the value of such a view, particularly in minimizing the risks of the tyranny of the majority. As he put it:

> Whilst all authority in [the society] will be derived from and dependent on the society, the society itself will be broken into so many parts, interests and classes of citizens, the rights of individuals, or of the minority, will be in little danger from interested combinations of the majority. In a free government the security for civil

rights must be the same as that for religious rights. It consists in the one case in the multiplicity of interests, and in the other in the multiplicity of sects. The degree of security in both cases will depend on the number of interests and sects, and this may be presumed to depend on the extent of country and number of people comprehended under the same government.

The more competing "interests" there are, the more fluid the majority, and the greater the possibility everyone will get what he or she wants, sooner or later. That is an asset for participants; the liability is that, in such an environment, the American constitutional order as sole arbiter can govern virtually unchallenged ideologically.

And nothing could better ensure the dominance of the state, standing now as the lone institution of national, public authority of the construction and maintenance of symbols of meaning for its constituents. With the disestablishment of Protestantism—and for many, with all of religion representing a matter of personal choice—and the debate on constructions of race turning more toward individualist rather than group definitions, the state is without peer. Research from contemporary sociologists of religion suggests that this situation was inevitable. Starting with the cultural shifts of the 1960s—which were themselves a reaction to the establishmentarian 1940s and 1950s—American religion has become increasingly focused on the concerns of the individual, at the expense of corporate meaning construction and maintenance (Wuthnow 1998). In part because of the transformations of the baby boom generation, and in part because of the loss of moral and cultural authority of American public institutions in the post–civil rights, post-Vietnam, post-Watergate era, American religious institutions have not only lost their relative monopoly over the construction and maintenance of meaning but have in many ways become just another category of human activity competing for members (Hammond 1992; Roof 1993). Gone is the mediating buffer between the citizen and the government that was at the core of Alexis de Toqueville's nineteenth-century commentary on American society. Rather, and in more Protestant terms, the citizen is now capable of having a much more personal relationship with the divine—only in the current situation, the divine is not the God of Christianity or even Judaism but the god of the American constitutional order.

If there is no competition for the construction and maintenance of meaning, it is no longer necessary to control the method by which citizens become good citizens. From the founding of the nation until the early decades of the twentieth century, being a good citizen meant being a good (white) Christian, and vice versa. For the bulk of the twentieth century, being a good citizen depended on participating in the rites and rituals of the public school (see *Minersville School District v. Gobitis*, 310 U.S. 586 [1940]). By disengaging good citizenship from public education (as in the Amish decision, or in *Zelman*), the Court is affirming the success of the state in its ascent as the dominant (and virtually unchallenged) political authority; by 1972, the American constitutional order was not as ideologically threatened by the challenges of the Amish as it had been in the 1930s by Jehovah's Witnesses who refused to acknowledge the authority of the order by refusing to salute the American flag,[15] or in the 1950s by segregationists who (at least in part) grounded their position in the political ideology of antifederalist states' rights. Today, home-schooling is an acceptable form of education and a method used most by members of the conservative Christian community who feel they have lost their control over the government; since aspects of home-schooling must be certified by some governmental office, it would appear that they are right.

Race, moving as it is toward greater dependence on individual definition, is not only following in the footsteps of religion but is in fact the beneficiary of the same forces that had acted on religious institutions.[16] The modern state, having disestablished religion and freed itself from its Protestant foundations, has as a result not only secured its own authority, it has as a by-product also loosed other social institutions (such as race) from their group definition. Depending as it does on the radical independence of its citizenry to be freed from permanent group affiliations, the state can constantly triangulate the wishes and needs of its constituents while incorporating as many divergent positions as possible. This makes for a healthy democracy, to be sure, but it may also create a new transcendent entity with unchecked authority, never a welcome beast in the garden.

Coda

During the recent 2008 presidential campaign, both race and religion were part of the debate. Senator Obama was accused of being a "secret" Muslim (i.e., a non-Christian), a charge that connected in the minds of some with fears that he was also a "secret" Arab (i.e., a nonwhite)—despite the African birth of his father. Others (National Public Radio 2008) described Obama as a "postracial" candidate—neutralizing concerns of some that he was neither Euro-American nor African American (or, in reality, both) but some additional racial *and* religious "other." Several years earlier, the Census Bureau had expanded racial self-identification options, permitting respondents to identify themselves as being of more than one race ("Census Panel Suggests a Mixed-Race Solution" 1997). While no one could argue that race is no longer a factor in American public life, it seems to be a characteristic that is less authoritative in public discourse, even if it remains central to individual identity. This almost completely mirrors the situation with religion, a category that is not (but for a very few) ascribed. But the election of a man born of an African father would have been impossible before the Civil War and inconceivable before the civil rights era. President Obama's election is as much of a social transformation as the election of the first non-Protestant, Senator John F. Kennedy, in 1960. No other Catholic has since been elected president, but for most Americans, the issue is no longer one of great significance.[17] So too might be the transformation of the Obama election. If so, the American constitutional order will have nearly fulfilled its promise articulated in the first thirteen words of the Declaration of Independence quoted at the beginning of this essay. In many ways, it will also have more nearly fulfilled its ascent to the highest reaches of authority suggested by the latter eleven, and assumed the role of the Creator, who endows rights.

Notes

Versions of this essay were presented at the American Academy of Religion Annual Meeting (2004), Lebanon Valley College (2005), the American Political Science Association annual meeting (2007), and the Western Political Science Association annual meeting (2009). Special thanks to Bette Novit Evans, Bruce Grelle, William S. Mandel, Esq., James A. Morone, Anna Sampaio, and the editors of this volume for their help clarifying my argument, and Heather C. Haskin (Bucknell 2008) for her research assistance.

1. Noll (2008) identifies five stages of development: 1790–1860, in which religion and business predominated but the central government was "latent"; 1860–1876, in which the government was dominant and business influence was significant, but religion was latent; 1876–1932, in which business dominated, the government was "indecisive," and religion was "latent"; 1932–1954/5, in which the market and business predominated but religion was "latent"; and 1954–present, in which all three factors have been competing for dominance.

2. These limitations were common in state constitutions, although most were dismantled by the end of the nineteenth century (see Hammond 1998). They were not declared unconstitutional, however, until the Supreme Court decision in *Torcaso v. Watkins* (37 U.S. 488 [1961]).

3. From 1815 until the end of the Civil War in 1865, the Supreme Court issued decisions in at least fifteen cases related to religion, religious organizations, and religious liberty. From 1866 until FDR's election in 1932, the Court issued decisions related to religion in at least forty-five cases (see Mazur 2000a).

4. Some of the "economic" religion cases had to do with conducting business on the Sabbath (*Hennington v. Georgia*, 163 U.S. 299 [1896]) and church property taxes (*Ponce v. Roman Catholic Apostolic Church*, 210 U.S. 296 [1908]).

5. For example, from 1878 into the 1890s, the Supreme Court issued decisions in at least seventeen cases involving the Church of Jesus Christ of Latter-Day Saints and its adherents, in each strengthening the federal government's territorial authority. Ultimately, the Church was forced to abandon a central religious tenet (plural marriage) and cede political authority over territory in

order to secure a place in the nation (statehood). The Church could remain in Utah, but it could no longer assert ultimate temporal control over the territory controlled by the federal government (see Mazur 1999, 62–93).

6. *Congressional Globe* (1866) shows the following terms: "Latin" (Representative Kasson, 238); "Spanish" (Senator Davis, 251); "Gypsie," "Mongolian," and "Scandinavian" (Senator Cowan, 498–99); "Chinese" (Senator Davis, 523); "Anglo-Saxon," "Jewish," and "Mexican" (Representative Dawson, 542); and "German" (Senator Shellabarger, 1294). The first section of the Civil Rights Act of 1866 (14 Stat. 27 [1866]) reads (in part): "all persons born in the United States and not subject to any foreign power, excluding Indians not taxed, are hereby declared to be citizens of the United States; and such citizens, of every race and color, without regard to any previous condition of slavery or involuntary servitude, except as a punishment for crime whereof the party shall have been duly convicted, shall have the same right, in every State and Territory in the United States, to make and enforce contracts, to sue, be parties, and give evidence, to inherit, purchase, lease, sell, hold, and convey real and personal property, and to full and equal benefit of all laws and proceedings for the security of person and property, as is enjoyed by white citizens, and shall be subject to like punishment, pains, and penalties, and to none other, any law, statute, ordinance, regulation, or custom, to the contrary notwithstanding."

7. It is worth noting that in both cases the parties identified as "non-White" were seeking protection *as* racial minorities, and were not fighting a designation as "non-White" that might exclude them from a "white" majority.

8. 42 U.S. §1981 is the statutory embodiment of the Civil Rights Act of 1866 and the Voting Rights Act of 1870.

9. Historian of American religion Sydney Ahlstrom (1972) identified the period after Kennedy's election as the "post-Protestant" era.

10. The change occurred by legislative sleight-of-hand, when the Senate's authority to ratify treaties with Native Americans was usurped by a rider to a House of Representatives appropriation bill (see Mazur 1999, 104).

11. For example, the Northwest Ordinance reads (in part): "Religion, morality, and knowledge, being necessary to good government and the happiness of mankind, schools and the means of education shall forever be encouraged" (Congress of the Confederation, July 13, 1787, An Ordinance for the Government of the Territory of the United States, Northwest of the River Ohio, Article III).

12. Since the American Revolution, the Amish had categorically been exempted from military service, along with other "peace" churches such as the Mennonites and the Brethren. By the time the Court delivered its decision in *Yoder*, the practices related to conscientious exemption had undergone the same transformation outlined in this essay (see Flowers 2003).

13. One institution, Goldsboro Christian Schools, had a racially discriminatory admission policy. The other, Bob Jones University, admitted African American students but prohibited interracial dating and did not admit those who advocated interracial relationships. Both based these policies on their understanding of Christian scripture.

14. A portion of the material in this section is taken from two earlier collaborative works: Mazur and Ingersoll 1994 and Mazur and Mandel 1998. Thanks to the two co-authors for helping flesh out these ideas.

15. See *Minersville School District v. Gobitis* (1940). *West Virginia Board of Education v. Barnette* (319 U.S. 624 [1943]) was the first Supreme Court victory for Jehovah's Witnesses involving children in the public schools.

16. This is not to suggest that race has disappeared as a social category. As a genetic researcher put it, "You can tell people that race isn't real and doesn't matter, but they can't catch a cab. So unless we take that into account it makes us sound crazy" (Weiss 2005).

17. There was some debate during Senator John Kerry's 2004 presidential campaign, but mostly from fellow Catholics who felt his positions contradicted those of the Church. Little notice was taken of the fact that Senator Biden became the nation's first Catholic vice president.

References

Ahlstrom, Sydney E. 1972. *Religious History of the American People.* New Haven, CT: Yale University Press.

"Americanization." 2008. In *Encyclopedia of Race, Ethnicity, and Society,* ed. Richard Schaeffer, 1:62–64. Thousand Oaks, CA: Sage.

Beaver, R. Pierce. 1962. "The Churches and President Grant's Peace Policy." *Journal of Church and State* 4 (2): 174–90.

Brodkin, Karen. 1999. *How Jews Became White Folks and What That Says About Race in America.* New Brunswick, NJ: Rutgers University Press.

"Census Panel Suggests a Mixed-Race Solution." 1997. *Salt Lake Tribune,* August 25, A3.

Clarke, James Freeman. 1875. *Ten Great Religions: An Essay in Comparative Theology.* Boston: James R. Osgood.

Congressional Globe. 1866. 39th Congr., 1st Sess.

Dewey, John. 1972. *A Common Faith.* New Haven, CT: Yale University Press. First published 1934.

Fessenden, Tracy. 2008. "Disappearances: Race, Religion, and the Progress Narrative of U.S. Feminism." In *Secularisms,* ed. Janet R. Jakobsen and Ann Pellegrini, 139–61. Durham, NC: Duke University Press.

Flowers, Ronald B. 2003. *To Defend the Constitution: Religion, Conscientious Objection, Naturalization, and the Supreme Court.* Lanham, MD: Scarecrow Press.

"Freedom, Religious." 2010. *Encyclopedia of Religion in America,* ed. Charles Lippy and Peter Williams. Thousand Oaks, CA: Sage.

Greenhouse, Linda. 2007. "Justices, Voting 5-4, Limit the Use of Race in Integration Plans." *New York Times,* June 29, 1.

Hammond, Phillip E. 1992. *Religion and Personal Autonomy: The Third Disestablishment in America.* Columbia: University of South Carolina Press.

———. 1998. *With Liberty for All: Freedom of Religion in the United States.* Louisville, KY: Westminster John Knox Press.

Hammond, Phillip E., David W. Machacek, and Eric Michael Mazur. 2004. *Religion on Trial: How Supreme Court Trends Threaten the Freedom of Conscience in America.* Walnut Creek, CA: AltaMira Press.

Hancock, Ange-Marie. 2007a. "Intersectionality as a Normative and Empirical Paradigm." *Politics & Gender* 3 (2): 248–54.

———. 2007b. "When Multiplication Doesn't Equal Quick Addition: Examining Intersectionality as a Research Paradigm." *Perspectives on Politics* 5 (1): 63–79.

Handy, Robert. 1984. *A Christian America: Protestant Hopes and Historical Realities,* 2nd ed. New York: Oxford University Press.

———. 1991. *Undermined Establishment: Church-State Relations in America 1880–1920.* Princeton, NJ: Princeton University Press.

Hatch, Nathan O. 1989. *The Democratization of American Christianity.* New Haven, CT: Yale University Press.

Jacobson, Matthew Frye. 1998. *Whiteness of a Different Color: European Immigrants and the Alchemy of Race.* Cambridge, MA: Harvard University Press.

Lee, Daniel B. 2004. "A Great Racial Commission: Religion and the Construction of White America." In *Race, Nation, and Religion in the Americas,* ed. Henry Goldschmidt and Elizabeth McAlister, 85–110. New York: Oxford University Press.

Madison, James. 1937. *Federalist 51.* In Alexander Hamilton, John Jay, and James Madison, *The Federalist.* New York: Random House. First published 1788.

Mazur, Eric Michael. 1996. "Constitutional Authority and Prospects for Social Justice for High-Tension Religious Communities." *Social Justice Research* 9 (3): 259–80.

———. 1997. "The Supreme Law of the Land: Sources of Conflict between Native Americans and the Constitutional Order." In *American Indian Studies: An Interdisciplinary Approach to Contemporary Issues,* ed. Dane Morrison, 233–59. Baltimore, MD: Peter Lang.

———. 1999. *The Americanization of Religious Minorities: Confronting the Constitutional Order.* Baltimore, MD: Johns Hopkins University Press.

———. 2001. "Religious Minorities and the Pressures of Americanization." *Insights on Law and Society* 1 (2): 8–10.

———. 2002a. "Examining the Canon in Church-State Studies." Paper presented at the annual meeting of the American Academy of Religion, Toronto, November 23–26.

———. 2002b. "Minority Religions and Limitations on Religious Freedom." *Social Education* 66 (3): 149–59.

———. 2008. "Going My Way? Crosby and Catholicism on the Road to America." In *Going My Way: Bing Crosby and American Culture,* ed. Ruth Prigozy and Walter Raubicheck, 17–33. Rochester, NY: University of Rochester Press.

Mazur, Eric Michael, and Julie Ingersoll. 1994. "Corpus Christi: The Holy War over the Body in Public Space." Paper presented at the annual meeting of the American Academy of Religion, Chicago, November 19–22.

Mazur, Eric Michael, and William S. Mandel. 1998. "The Ramifications of a Conflict between Free Exercise and Affirmative Action." Paper presented at the annual meeting of the American Academy of Religion, Orlando, FL, November 21–24.

McCloskey, Robert G. 1960. *The American Supreme Court.* Chicago: University of Chicago Press.

Michaelsen, Robert S. 1970. *Piety in the Public School: Trends and Issues in the Relationship between Religion and the Public School in the United States.* New York: Macmillan.

National Public Radio. 2008. *All Things Considered.* January 28. www.npr.org/templates/story/story .php?storyId=18489466.

Noll, Mark A. 2008. *God and Race in American Politics: A Short History.* Princeton, NJ: Princeton University Press.

Orren, Karen, and Stephen Skowronek. 2004. *The Search for American Political Development.* New York: Cambridge University Press.

"Pluralism." 2008. In *Encyclopedia of Race, Ethnicity, and Society,* ed. Richard Schaeffer, 2:1051–53. Thousand Oaks, CA: Sage.

Prentiss, Craig R., ed. 2003. *Religion and the Creation of Race and Ethnicity: An Introduction.* New York: New York University Press.

Roof, Wade Clark. 1993. *A Generation of Seekers: The Spiritual Journeys of the Baby Boom Generation.* New York: HarperCollins.

Simien, Evelyn M. 2007. "Doing Intersectionality Research: From Conceptual Issues to Practical Examples." *Politics & Gender* 3 (2): 264–71.

Snow, Jennifer. 2004. "The Civilization of White Men: The Race of the Hindu in *United States v. Bhagat Singh Thind.*" In *Race, Nation, and Religion in the Americas,* ed. Henry Goldschmidt and Elizabeth McAlister, 259–80. New York: Oxford University Press.

Way, H. Frank. 1987. "Death of the Christian Nation: The Judiciary and Church-State Relations." *Journal of Church and State* 29 (3): 509–29.

Weiss, Rick. 2005. "A Tiny Mutation: Scientists Have Found a DNA Change That Accounts for White Skin." *Washington Post,* National Weekly Edition, December 26, 31.

Wenger, Tisa. 2009. *We Have a Religion: The 1920s Pueblo Indian Dance Controversy and American Religious Freedom.* Chapel Hill: University of North Carolina Press.

Wilson, John F. 1990. "Religion, Government, and Power in the New American Nation." In *Religion and American Politics: From the Colonial Period to the 1980s,* ed. Mark A. Noll, 77–91. New York: Oxford University Press.

Winchell, Alexander. 1880. *Preadamites: Or, a Demonstration of the Existence of Men before Adam,* 2nd ed. London: Trübner & Co.

Wuthnow, Robert. 1998. *After Heaven: Spirituality in America Since the 1950s.* Berkeley: University of California Press.

Quakerism and Racialism
in Early Twentieth-Century U.S. Politics

Carlos Figueroa

[Our] discussions [at the Lake Mohonk Conference] are of a purely non-partisan and non-political nature, our aim being simply to present the present-day conditions and needs of the Philippines [and Puerto Rico] for the information of the general public in this country.

> —Hicksite Quaker-pacifist Albert K. Smiley to Rev. J. H. Sutherland,
> 28th U.S. Infantry, August 17, 1906

By the addresses, papers and discussions of this Conference we have been impressed afresh with a sense of the worth of other races than our own, and with a conviction that all those who would be of real service to the people of different races and religions with whom the events of the last decade have brought us into close political relations should study sympathetically the national life, the history, the ideals and the racial characteristics of those whom they would help.

> —Lake Mohonk Conference *Annual Report*, 1912

The signing of the Treaty of Paris in 1898 by the United States marked two important political developments: the acquisition of new overseas territories in Puerto Rico and the Philippines, and the inheritance of political authority over the nonwhite races inhabiting those territories (Thompson 1989).[1] Modern U.S. imperialism had begun with the assertion of national sovereignty over nonwhite races. The Treaty of Paris brought both a new challenge to race relations and Christian evolutionary thought to U.S. progressive and imperialist politics. Moreover, the U.S. state gained the political authority to construct political identities and civic communities rooted in a white, Anglo-Saxon, Christian national character. Following the political organization of each territory by 1901, it became clear that this Christian-dominated U.S. national character had created a new race problem in trying to govern insular territories.[2] Political scientist Rogers M. Smith (2003, 9) observes that social and political leaders "who have deployed racialist theories for purposes of political people-building"—such as those involved in U.S. insular territorial politics—"have always portrayed their preferred races as morally meritorious, as playing primary roles in advancing the purposes of God, nature, reason, history, and often the interests of all humanity." As a case in point, in 1904 the Lake Mohonk Conference of Friends of the Indian and Other Dependent Peoples (LMC), by combining racial and religious Christian elements in a co-constituted manner,[3] stepped into the imperialist and anti-imperialist national debates to provide a seemingly neutral forum in which to address the racial and political dimensions surrounding the acquisition of overseas territories and the inheritance of nonwhite peoples.[4]

This essay begins with a brief historical description of Quakerism and racialism in the United States.[5] I then discuss the ideas and thought of Hicksite Quaker Albert K. Smiley, founder of the LMC, in the context of his attempts to shape national political discourses on U.S. insular territories and nonwhite inhabitants. The broader influence of liberal Congregationalist Lyman Abbott, who through his racial and political idealism structured many of LMC institutional activities, was particularly evident.[6] I argue that Quakerism was inextricably linked to and at times mediated U.S. racialized political discourses vis-à-vis the administration of nonwhite peoples in Puerto Rico and the Philippines, as reflected in the work of the LMC. An intersectional approach to understanding the influence of Quakerism and to understanding racialism on a broader stage is particularly useful in grasping nuances of the debates over the politics of U.S. insular territorial affairs.

Quakerism and Politics over the Racial Other

Quakerism, or the teachings of the Religious Society of Friends, as a radical ideological element of Christianity and a religious theological movement, has often entered the public political sphere to confront controversial issues (Davis 1966, 1975; Bowden 1972; Noll 2002; Hamm 2003).[7] George Fox, who founded Quakerism in mid-seventeenth-century Britain, often advocated "industry, frugality, and self-help" for all Quakers. Quaker historian James Walvin (1997, 9) describes Fox as aiming "not to create a sect but to persuade his fellow men and women to worship honestly, not through the intermediary of the priesthood or any religious organization but from within themselves, directly to the Almighty." Fox's ideas amounted to a Quaker affinity to which he "encouraged [Friends] to be hard-working, financially prudent and honest in all their business dealings" (11). Moreover, by practicing their faith in meeting houses, at home, "and in the workplace, Quakers sought to train themselves, their children, and each other in those personal and social qualities , which were at once a reflection of their living faith and a code of everyday conduct" (208). Finally, Fox taught that holding on to beliefs, values, and methods as a Friend "involved subjecting oneself to possible scrutiny of one's personal and professional lift; those whose [behavior] left something to be desired were visited (questioned, helped—or excluded)" (208). These were key attributes guiding LMC interventionist politics.

From 1827 to 1955, U.S. Quakerism was split into several theological and ideological divisions (Ingle 1986; Hamm 2003; Dandelion 2007). Figure 1 shows some of the early Quakerism splits (or schisms) up to the modern period and the suggested theological influences on the LMC. Much of the division had to do with different understandings of the Inner Light notion in Quakerism. (Other areas of conflict were evangelical doctrines, the authority of the elders, the discipline, and antislavery tactics.) Also, from the mid-nineteenth century through most of the first half of the twentieth century, theologically conservative Quakers—traditional Orthodox or Quietist, Gurneyites, Wilburites, and Crewdsonites—assumed an evangelical Christian identity, making up the anti-Hicksite coalition, in which historical Quaker pacifism was abandoned (Dandelion 2007, 93). However, theologically liberal Quakers, or Hicksite Quakers, held on to the traditional silent worship while welcoming both atheists and non-Christians into their fold. Hicksite Quakers were rationalists and progressive in terms of engaging public activities and advocating liberal tenets in social, economic, and political life: egalitarianism, humanitarianism, individualism, and broader tolerance (Forbush 1956; Ingle 1986; Barbour and Frost 1988, 219–29; Dandelion 2007, 83–84). These divisions seemed to prevent politically and socially active Quakers from making any significant advances in the early antislavery movement of the 1830s through 1850s in U.S. political development (Wilson 1975, 5).

Despite this internal schism, Quakers in religious and secular institutions have often concerned themselves with the social and economic well-being and political conditions of those deemed "inferior," "different," "weak," "uncivilized," or broadly categorized as "other."[8] Although humanitarianism and egalitarianism remained constant values throughout the history of Quakerism, some contradictions still existed: many Friends established liberal colonies while owning slaves; others led antislavery campaigns, advocated for women suffrage, held campaigns for the abolition of capital punishment, engaged in electoral politics, and supported the black civil rights movements (Drake 1950; Davis 1966, 291–332, 1975, 213–54; Tully 1977; Frost 1980; Soderlund 1985; Butler 1990). U.S. Quakers in

Figure 1   The evolution of U.S. Quakerism, 1820s–1920s, and its influences on the Lake Mohonk Conference

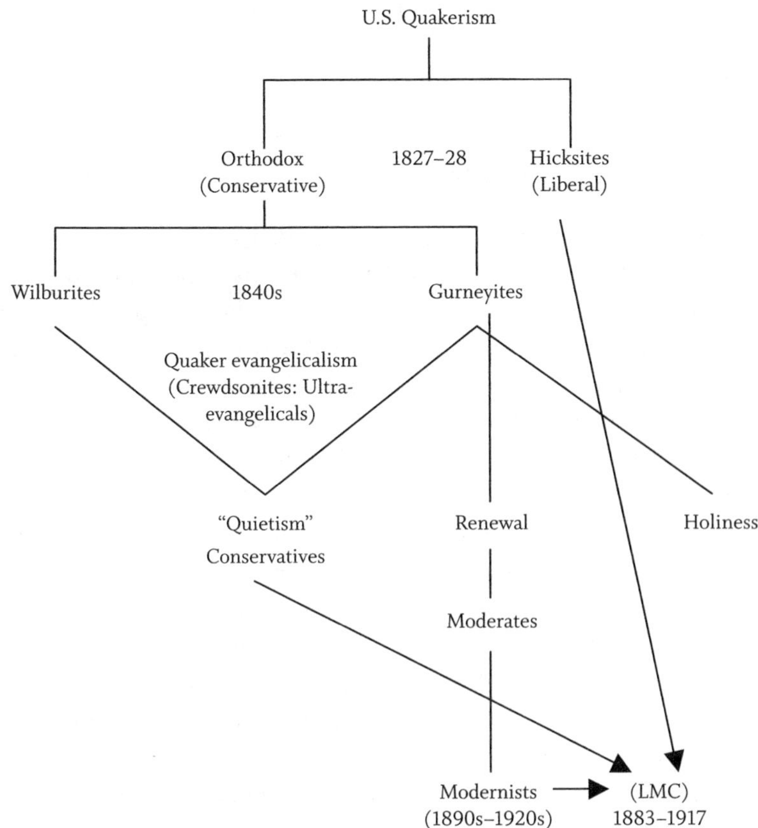

the late seventeenth century "oscillated between active participation in government, as in William Penn's 'Holy Experiment' in Pennsylvania, and quietist withdrawal from the compromises and corruptions of political life" (Wilson 1975, 3). Also, a more active Quakerism in political life was seen in the context of critiquing nation-state–organized violence as a means to achieve political ends (Byrd 1960, 140).[9] More recently, religion historian Diarmaid MacCulloch (2010, 869) found that Quakers in the seventeenth and eighteenth centuries used African slaves to sustain their own Quaker peace haven. In the modern Quakerism period, from the late nineteenth century through the early twentieth century, Friends protested against various wars, and many were active in U.S. Indian affairs (Prucha 1973, 1977, 1979, 1981; Maddox 2005).[10] Within this historical context, liberal Quakers remained tolerant of differences in political, cultural, and ideological perspectives, as well as different socioeconomic positions. Throughout Quakerism's theological and historical evolution, various testimonies consistently guided Friends' engagement in public affairs, peace, equality, and social justice. Thus, the national issues Quakers confronted from the seventeenth to the twentieth century were vast, disparate, and contradictory, but always regarded through the Inner Light.

Spirituality and the Quaker Inner Light

The concept of the Inner Light continues to guide Quaker thought and action. Quaker historian David Hinshaw (1951, 11) comments, "The core of the Quaker belief was the Inner-Light—that intuition of the presence of God which enabled the individual to learn how to discover and realize what is evil for him by avoiding it to bring himself in harmony with the universal spirit." The Inner Light fueled the direct engagement of Quakers in the personal, organizational, social, and political world (Jones 1916, 1965; Byrd 1960). The term (and concept) has been used interchangeably with "Inward Light," "Spirit of God," and "Light Within," among others, to refer to the same experience: "that of God in everyone" (Cooper 2001, 16). The Inner Light concept did not discriminate on the basis of race, religion, gender, or class; it embraced a stronger sense of pluralism than the individualism notions found in classical or modern understandings of liberalism in American political life. The concept of the Inner light made Quakerism "a spiritual religion, a way of life in which people learned to cooperate with God" (Barbour and Frost 1988, 227). Quakerism was known for its form of Christian quietism, characterized by an intentional noninvolvement in domestic and international public affairs, until the late nineteenth century. "The years from 1850 until the outbreak of World War I may be characterized briefly as years during which Friends' interest and involvement in the international scene became more inclusive" (Byrd 1960, 134). The LMC thus surfaced within a dynamic ideological and theological evolution in a broader U.S. Quakerism context that was underwritten by the traditional Inner Light concept.

The Lake Mohonk Conference: Pragmatic Quakerism, Race, and Politics

Hicksite Quaker Albert K. Smiley was the central figure who created the LMC as a national institutional force for dealing with U.S. Indian affairs in 1883 and later officially in 1904 U.S. insular territorial affairs. The idea of a nongovernmental forum with religious underpinnings came to Smiley while he was serving on the Board of Indian Commissioners.[11] In 1879, President Rutherford B. Hayes appointed Smiley to this board to investigate the activities of various "corrupt" bureaucrats engaged in administering Indian affairs (Burgess 1993, 25).[12] Smiley recalls his experience on the board and his frustrations with the manner in which U.S. Indian affairs were conducted:

> At the first meeting I attended . . . I was . . . impressed by the short time given to discussion. . . . I proposed that we should have more time, but all said "You cannot do it. Business men cannot be held in Washington more than one day." Not long after, a large number of us who were interested in the Indians happened to have a meeting in Dakota, where we discussed the Sioux Indian question for three days. "Now," I said, "we are going to have this same thing at Lake Mohonk," and I invited a number of men of experience in Indian affairs to meet here in discussion.[13]

Thus, the LMC was born out of necessity following the political and institutional inefficiency (and apathy) accompanying discussions of the "Indian problem" at the national level.

Smiley's Pragmatic Quakerism and Religious Liberalism

Smiley employed what I call a pragmatic Quakerism to dealing with nonwhite races. This form of Quakerism places an emphasis on open dialogue and practical lived experience guided by traditional Quaker testimonies of peace, equality, fairness, social justice, and spiritual transcendence. Smiley's views were still challenged by racialism at the LMC, which focused mainly on the existence of different racial categories (and hierarchies) that presumed an Anglo-Saxon white racial imperative structuring U.S. insular territorial politics. Smiley's pragmatic Quakerism infused personal, social, and political behavior: plainness of habit, speech, and deportment; wisdom based on lived experience; duty to others; and discipline. Moreover, other traditional Quaker values and methods informed his pragmatic Quakerism, including understanding the social and political significance of business meetings and social questions; commitment to education; and worship centered on the Inner Light, on which communion, fellowship, and public discourse all rely. At times Smiley showed this affinity for the Inner Light and liberal conception of God at the LMC as he discussed race relations and insular territorial politics.

Pragmatic Quakerism allowed a broader discourse on race to infiltrate the various moral perspectives and political debates at the October LMC. This is seen in Smiley's 1904 opening address, as he officially announces the inclusion of "Other Dependent Peoples" at the LMC:

> We don't meet here to scold the [U.S.] Government, by any means. Our object is to discuss conditions in a candid way and to see if we cannot do something to better them. I think it is the general feeling that we should give a prominent share of our attention at this Conference to our new dependent races. . . . In these Conferences we invite discussion by people who hold differing views. The only way to get at the truth is for both sides to be heard fairly, only in a temperate and kind spirit. If once in a while a little warlike spirit breaks out, it generally gets calmed down before the Conference closes.[14]

The inclusion of other dependent races allowed Smiley to strengthen his new forum for more directly engaging U.S. race relations, yet still on the premise that those considered other were racially inferior and thus in need of political and racial uplift. Through Smiley's vision and leadership, and despite his constant reminders that "the conference excludes from its discussions the strictly political questions such as imperialism or anti-imperialism,"[15] the LMC became a respected nongovernmental institutional forum guided by pragmatic Quaker concerns for both domestic and international debates over citizenship, race relations, territorial governance, popular sovereignty, and overseas Americanization projects.

Smiley and other progressives were directly engaged in the national debates between imperialists and anti-imperialists over what to do with the newly occupied overseas territories and their nonwhite inhabitants. Yet Smiley was not considered either an imperialist or an anti-imperialist, which says much about his political and social ideological views and what he hoped to accomplish with the LMC. To illustrate, in a letter, he expressed such views:

> The management of the Conference is opposed to any acrimonious anti-imperialistic discussion, and that the Conference has without exception always declared itself strongly in support of the general policy adopted by the [U.S.] Government. I mention this that you may not be under the impression that this Conference tends against rather than in favor of the efforts of yourself and the other gentlemen who have so faithfully served us in the Philippines.[16]

Smiley seems to have focused on the long-term well-being of Filipinos almost altruistically while avoiding political controversy. His pragmatic Quakerism informed the decision to allow discussion only of rational, not rancorous, anti-imperialistic views, but to a limited extent. In more general terms, the LMC made room for altruism on the part of U. S. imperialists.

However, it was evident that the LMC was a battleground for both imperialist and anti-imperialist elements in the U.S. government. In a letter from Paul Charlton of the Bureau of Insular Affairs it was argued,

> With further relation to the anti-imperialist side of our government . . . if either Mr. Fisk Warren, Mr. Erving Winslow, or Mr. Moorfield Storey, all of Boston, are . . . invited to speak, I would regard it as most important that Mr. Snow be given an opportunity to reply from the view-point of our colonial government and administration. . . . [T]he attacks of the three gentlemen I have named . . . have been so continuous and bitter in the press and through pamphlets and magazine articles, that, if they are to be given an opportunity to speak, it would seem fair that an adequate reply should be made.[17]

Smiley, staying within the Quaker tradition of tolerance, found a middle ground: he decided to keep the peace and cautiously arranged the LMC sessions as fairly as possible. In his reply to Charlton, he wrote, "We do not desire . . . to stifle discussion of those who consider our occupation of the Philippines unfortunate, but we do decidedly wish to exclude such bitter attacks as would be sure to be made by any of those gentlemen. Our only hesitation about Mr. Snow arose from your statement that he is more or less a radical imperialist and it might be unwise to give our Boston friends an opportunity to accuse us of inviting one radical wing while excluding the other."[18] Smiley did not consider his colleagues in Boston, Quakers and non-Quakers alike, radicals either way.

Despite his liberal modernist views, Smiley invoked traditional Quakerism in his LMC addresses. For example, quoting Friends founder George Fox in his opening speech at the 1895 LMC, Smiley attempted to raise the national debate on territorial occupation to a moralistic, nonpartisan, deontological standard by focusing on the discrepancy in social and economic conditions of nonwhite races under U.S. sovereignty. Yet he sidestepped challenging directly the imperialistic policies that might have caused those conditions: "Be faithful to God, and mind that which is committed to you, as faithful servants, laboring in love; some threshing; and some ploughing; and some to keep the sheep, he that can receive this let him, and all to watch over one another in the spirit of God."[19] Smiley's use of Fox reveals his tendency to invoke Quaker ideals to indirectly theologically ground his politics and policy preferences. Moreover, Smiley seems to suggest that some divine spirit (Providence) placed the Anglo-Saxon white race at the pinnacle of a "natural" hierarchy of human races and bestowed with the moral and political responsibility of elevating nonwhite people's living conditions. Smiley presumed a U.S. national character defined in both racialist and moral-religious terms. Thus, his concern for the proper treatment of nonwhite races justified his support for an altruistic tutelage policy in accordance with God's will.

However, Smiley was not religious but spiritual in his liberal theology. He was concerned with God as a notion of lived practical experience, defined by good moral deeds (based on Quaker testimonies and the Inner Light), as opposed to a scriptural or doctrinal God. Invoking Fox also shows how Smiley desired to pursue the truth about U.S. relations with dependent peoples. Accordingly, with every opening statement, Smiley instilled his pragmatic Quakerism both directly and indirectly into everything associated with the LMC, including speaker invitations and committee appointments. Throughout the existence of the LMC, it was the Quaker spirit and moral-religious foundations that guided its public interventionism and political discourses on race, far removed from the bureaucratic and corrupt national, mostly secular, government institutional politics Smiley abhorred.

Pragmatic Quakerism at the LMC was also informed by Smiley's ability to connect with non-Quakers. He was held in great esteem and respected for his "moral influence," and that respect allowed him to create the LMC and gain enough recognition to place the latter on par with national institutions (e.g., the Bureau of Insular Affairs). As one Quaker historian noted, the LMC resembled "a hotel, a home and a church . . . in such a way that no one can tell where one ends and the other begins" (Trueblood 1897, 454). Smiley's character and cooperative reputation made others feel at home in his presence, knowing he was a champion of liberal pragmatic politics yet tolerant of those who had different, more conservative views.[20] This made his adoption of an ambitious if seemingly moderate program at the LMC appear more feasible. How did Smiley reconcile such opposing views at the national level? He relied on his pragmatic Quakerism for achieving practical unity.

Practical Unanimity and Unity as Universal Objectives: Legitimizing the LMC

The Quaker notion of unity also underwrote certain norms and testimonies that were incorporated into Smiley's pragmatic Quakerism. "[Smiley] handled his conferences, emphasizing the Quaker tradition of seeking agreement through unity" (Burgess 1972, 70, 1975, 1980). Smiley was a Hicksite Quaker-pacifist, which meant that connected to his various modern liberal beliefs and often conservative moral imperatives was the idea of creating a universal unanimity, with which all LMC participants had to come to terms when engaging national issues and organizational practices. He saw the objective of practical unanimity as one way to legitimize the work of the LMC and elevate the institution's political stature in the private and public spheres. It demonstrated Quaker-style unity in action and a universal consensus on difficult issues. Also, it allowed Smiley, politically oriented Quakers, and other Christians (and non-Christians) to apply traditional Quaker principles to political discourses on citizenship, self-government, and popular sovereignty not often dealt with by Democrats, Republicans, lobbying groups, or state-level organizations engaged in insular territorial affairs. In his book *Silhouettes of My Contemporaries*, Lyman Abbott (1922, 40) confirmed this point in testimony:

> The attendants were not delegates but invited guests of Mr. Smiley. They included men and women of every variety of temperament and opinion. Roman Catholics, Protestants, and Jews, High Churchmen and Friends, Republicans and Democrats, government officials and newspaper critics, Radicals and Conservatives met to engage in a perfectly free Forum, not to win a victory over each other, but to comprehend each other. Factions were difficult and factional victories were impossible. For from the first it was agreed that no opinion should ever be affirmed to be the opinion of the Conference except by unanimity.

These comments originally appeared in Henry Ward Beecher's Christian Union's new department focusing on current events and instrumental national leaders, which was established by Abbott shortly after becoming associate editor (ibid., 5). The purpose of "The Outlook" department "was not merely to report current events, but to interpret them." This department aimed to "forecast [these events' and people's] relation to the future and the probable effect of their lives upon it" (ibid.) and "was definitely intended to be, as far as practicable, prophetic both of peril and of promise" (vi). Thus, Abbott in large measure revealed the religious-racial-political nexus also found with Smiley's LMC: concepts such as unity, tolerance, and universal assent were intertwined with categories such as religion, race, and gender in the political development of various insular territorial policies. Evidently, the LMC served as a moral-religious guide to the often heated political debates in national organizations and government institutions.

The LMC was unique because of its close conceptual relation to Quaker business meetings. These meetings sometimes "draw out the highest and best that is potential to the group" within a democratic society (Jones 1965, 67). "In all . . . Meetings, Friends openly discussed matters and required near unanimity to make a decision, a method they called the sense of the Meeting" (Benjamin 1976, 6). Moreover, "[The] belief in unanimous decisions . . . attested to the democratic spirit of the faith," which at the LMC was understood as "practical unanimity" (9). But although the LMC "format was not totally identical to the makeup of a Quaker meeting [either the monthly, quarterly, or yearly forms] . . . the basic elements were there: unanimous votes were taken more to formalize the agreements than to secure it" (Burgess 1972, 71). Likewise, "The most effective examples of the Quaker concept 'going forward in unity' . . . were seen in the *spirit* of the Conferences" (ibid., emphasis in original). However, in this case, Fox's Quaker spirit was not clearly defined but rather described in a broader sense by Quaker James Rhoads, who spoke at the 1885 LMC. Rhoads observed the "great importance of unanimity on the part of the Conference . . . both as to principle which should guide their action and as to methods, so far as possible."[21] As suggested, Smiley's practical unanimity objective was closely associated with the Quaker notion of one-ness.[22]

Quaker meetings may "be applicable to larger assemblies . . . and . . . have repercussions upon the whole spirit of democratic discussion" (Pollard, Pollard, and Pollard 1949, 22). Smiley, by integrating the Quaker oneness notion (through practical unanimity) in all circumstances, expected "the Conference [to speak] with authority and practically . . . dictate the government's [insular policies]" (Trueblood 1897, 460). His pursuits of "practical unanimity" in all LMC activities also seem to have prevented any substantive or normative challenges to the dominant Anglo-Saxon racial understanding of U.S. national character. Rather, the racial discourse was embedded in the idea of Christian community. Smiley expected various religious, social, and political groups represented at the yearly assembly to cooperate and almost without much contention reach assent unanimously, despite the presence of divergent pro-expansionist and anti-expansionist camps.[23] Both these ideological-political camps used similar racial grounds (both viewing the Anglo-Saxon as the superior race) along with a moral-religious tenor (missionary or redemptive imperative) in which to support their respective arguments for and against U.S. imperialist policies (Merriam 1978, 369–80). Thus, pragmatic Quakerism seemed to afford a voice for both sides of the ideological and political cultural divide on U.S. imperialism while accepting the notion of Anglo-Saxon race superiority. This was made possible because of Smiley's practice of screening LMC membership lists, topics, and speakers, which often prevented any substantive challenges to the dominant Anglo-Saxonism of the period.

Albert Smiley's Quaker Practical Unanimity Not Quite Liberal Democratic

The historical and archival data reveal that Smiley's pursuit of "practical una-nimity" contradicted a basic liberal democratic value, individual liberty. "Among the hallmarks of the meetings [at Lake Mohonk] were "the blending of expert and non-specialized discussion; concerted attempts to influence government policy, and other organizations; and a persistent effort to provide an environ-ment for open discussion under the influence of 'the Mohonk spirit'" (Burgess 1975, viii). However, this "Mohonk spirit" seems compromised if we look into how Smiley and, later, his younger brother Daniel Smiley screened topics and speakers, and approved the language of yearly platforms. On various occasions prominent potential speakers were prohibited or limited from contributing sub-stantially to topic discussions by one conspicuous rule or another, although the topic may have fallen under the speaker's field of expertise. For example, it was clearly stated that a writer had to present, with some limited exceptions, his own speech; that is, he could not assign someone else to read it. Ironically, Smiley's pursuit of his "practical unanimity" objective both enhanced and constrained liberal free speech simultaneously. Undermining the "moral purity and cheerful restfulness of Mohonk" (Trueblood 1897, 454) was the fact that Smiley, the pri-mary decision maker, organized the institution's meetings and committee work around three precepts—civilization, Christianity, and citizenship—but with a strong hand.[24] He carefully selected all his guests, appointed chairs, and formed all LMC committees while remaining vigilant throughout by "always [attend-ing] the morning and evening meetings" (Abbott 1922, 42). With this process, in large part, Smiley hoped to create an institutional environment that would flourish collegially for both domestic and international discourses. The LMC was to deracinate the various social, political, and economic problems facing white society because of the collective nonwhite races it had inherited (and at times constructed).[25]

In sum, Smiley created the LMC as an ideal forum in which to construct a liberal democratic community guided by the Quaker spirit in the hopes of unify-ing the many voices, ideas, and perspectives into a unanimous political force for redirecting U.S. racial politics by transforming public opinion, shaping institu-tional arrangements, and shifting congressional policies in the context of a rising U.S. imperialist state. In a U.S. political development sense, the intersection of racialism and pragmatic Quakerism accorded the LMC an ecumenical space for national conversations on race and politics in the early twentieth century. In this context, Congregationalist Lyman Abbott was able to import into the national discussions over dependent peoples his own radical Christian evolutionary racialist views.

Lyman Abbott: Christianity, Evolutionary Theory, and Race in U.S. political life

Lyman Abbott, although a Congregationalist Christian rather than a Quaker, became a prominent member of the LMC leadership. He was most noted for his longtime work as editor of the *Christian Union,* a religious weekly that he later renamed *Outlook* magazine (Brown 1953).[26] He was instrumental in melding the moral, theological, and liberal elements in American social and political life, but within a Christian evolutionary racialist framework:

> In the spiritual, as in the physical, God is the secret and source of life; phenomena, whether material or spiritual, are the manifestation of his presence; but he manifests himself in growth, not in stereotyped and statutory forms; and this growth is from lower to higher, from simpler to more complex forms, according to well defined and invariable laws, and by a force resident in the growing object itself. That unknown force is God—God in nature, God in the church, God in society, and God in the individual soul. The only cognizable difference between evolution in the physical and evolution in the spiritual realms is that nature cannot shut God out, nor hinder his working, nor disregard the laws of its own life; but man can and does. (Abbott 1922, v)

Abbott's political thought intertwined with his Christian evolutionary racialism, as seen in several *Outlook* commentaries and in his LMC speeches.

Abbott advocated bringing racial groups, or those characterized in racial terms, for example the "dependent peoples" of the Philippines and Puerto Rico, under the tutelage of U.S. Anglo-Saxon white Christian democracy. He gestured, "Our first duty to a dependent people is just government. The second is a universal system of education. The third is moral and religious culture. We must not only see that their rights to person, property, the family and reputation are respected . . . but must see that their passions are trained to come to heel by a vigorous will, and made the servant of a tender conscience."[27] He further suggested religion as a natural means to accomplish these paternalistic political objectives. "Religion is not a doctrine to be taught, but a spirit to be imparted. To impart it the teacher must possess that spirit of faith and hope and love which constitutes the essence of spiritual life."[28] Like Smiley, Abbott wanted to recast public opinion, but in three distinct yet interrelated areas: economics, politics, and religion. These attributes and common desires led to a close relationship with the LMC. Thus, in 1905, Abbott, because of his prior work with the Quakers, including Smiley, was invited to serve as president of the LMC.[29]

Abbott's Christian evolutionary racialism made its way into all his political, social, and moral discourses. As many social gospel leaders, Abbott held strongly to the belief that Christianity could provide answers to social, political, and economic crisis, including U.S. overseas imperialism. Yet he was a stark defender of Anglo-Saxon racial superiority underpinned by a strong Christian evolutionary ethic, which he melded quite well with his work at the LMC. For good reasons, he appreciated the important institutional power the LMC wielded in certain political circles in the imperialist–anti-imperialist national debates, in particular in the constructing of public opinion through national news outlets, the Associated Press and the National Press.[30] Access to national news outlets lifted the LMC to public prominence regarding race relations in both sectarian and secular circles while enhancing its ability to mold public sentiment in U.S. Indian affairs and, later, insular territorial politics. These aspects appealed to Abbott. Overall, he considered the LMC an important political force in national and international politics while holding the Smiley brothers in high esteem.[31]

Nevertheless, Abbott is relatively unknown and has not been discussed by political scientists or historians in terms of shaping U.S. race relations and imperialist politics through his Christian evolutionary racialist ideas in the early twentieth century. So the question becomes: since Abbott held such explicit racialist political views, and Smiley aimed for a nonpartisan, nonpolitical, and cooperative stance at the LMC, why did Smiley and his fellow Quakers invite Abbott to play such a critical, fundamental role?

First, Abbott represented a different, more nuanced perspective on race in the United States understood in evolutionary Christian terms. Second, his Christian evolutionary philosophy was blended with a significant liberal view of U.S. political life and social practices (i.e., racial and other segregationist views). Abbott held various positions at the LMC besides president, serving as chair of the powerful Business Committee. According to Lucy Maddox, Abbott believed the work of progressive reform at the LMC was "undeniably a Christian project" (Maddox 2005, 79). Thus, as a self-proclaimed Christian evolutionary, Abbott held positions comparable to the LMC's on what he considered "backward races" in Puerto Rico and the Philippines (Abbott 1892, v).

In his 1911 book *America in the Making*, in a chapter titled "Dependent Peoples," Abbott described his position on U.S. race relations more explicitly by focusing on three historical outcomes as various "races" confront each other:

> If you will consider the pages of history I think you will see that there have been three dispositions that have taken place when a superior race and an inferior race have come to occupy the same continent. There have been three results. Sometimes the superior race has destroyed or driven out the inferior race, as the Israelites are supposed to have destroyed the Canaanites and the Anglo-Saxon race in this country has driven from his ancient home the aboriginal Indian. Sometimes the superior race has enslaved the inferior and held them in bondage, making them hewers of wood and drawers of water, as we tried to do with the African race on this continent. Sometimes when a superior has come in contact with an inferior race they have intermarried and a new race has come forth, as Norman and Anglo-Saxon intermarried in England. Extermination, enslavement, intermarriage, are the three alternatives of history. (171–72)

Abbott's statement illustrates that the language of race had already moved away from late nineteenth-century Lamarckian notions, which stood on hereditary assumptions (Reed 1997, 116–21; Hattam 2007, 28). His comments also show a sophisticated view of race relations more embedded in a religious evolutionary logic dominated by Christianity (Quakerism, Catholicism, and Protestantism). In an earlier book, Abbott had suggested that Christian evolutionary racialism provided the most salient and congruent ideological framework in which to structure a political power foundation for properly managing nonwhite peoples. He wrote, "Christianity, whether regarded as an institutional, an intellectual, a social, or a moral life, has exemplified the law of [racial] evolution" (Abbott 1892, 4). The underlying premise of his Christian evolutionary racialist formulation, as articulated in 1911, is that "'there is a power not ourselves which makes for righteousness'; that this power works in and through humanity to a predetermined end, a divine ideal; and that social and political evolution can be understood only as we understand in what direction mankind is moving under this divine direction" (Abbott 1911, v). In sum, his views on race relations and imperialism were guided by the same premise underwriting the pragmatic Quaker sources of Smiley's LMC: "Inward Light of God," which held that "the Light [came] from beyond, as if through a key hole" (Dandelion 2007, 132–33).

Yet earlier, in 1892, Abbott had spelled out the premise of his Christian evolutionary racialism that life is experienced in a systematic way "always from the simple to the complex" forms (Abbott 1892, 6). Related to such a normative stance, his writings and speeches were based on the broader notion that progress meant a steady march "from lower to higher forms of life," with the Anglo-Saxon white race leading the way toward the highest form of civilization (7). With this backdrop, Abbott believed strongly in a social philosophy that placed the Anglo-

Saxon white race not only at the root of Christianity but also as the gatekeeper in a racially segregated society. He early recognized U.S. imperialism as political paternalism, but did not question the unconstitutional and illiberal aspects of imposing national sovereignty on nonwhite races without their consent:

> There have recently come under the sovereignty of the United States four insular possessions, Porto Rico, Hawaii, Guam, and the Philippines. The people who occupy these islands are subjects of the United States, and are under its sovereignty, but these islands are not parts of the United States, and these people have at present no political share in the government of the United States. In the making of America we have a distinct duty towards these so-called dependent or subject peoples. (Abbott 1911, 187)

Abbott then laid out, for the new U.S. imperialist state, the moral-religious and political duties owed the "inherited weaker" races. His text is worth partially reproducing since it shows how pragmatic Quakerism (the tolerant spirit guiding gained practical experiences), as seen in his active participation at the LMC, may allow for an extreme racialism:

> Our first duty is to govern these peoples, who have come under our sovereignty, for their benefits. It is for us, in the exercise of our sovereignty, to determine what is for their benefit, and, as I have pointed out [previously], it is therefore our first duty to govern them for the purpose of making them, at the earliest possible opportunity, self-governing.
>
> But making them self-governing does not necessarily mean either that they shall be independent of the United States, or a part of the United States. It is not true that the only alternative for Porto Rico . . . and the Philippines is independence or statehood. A relation of dependence may be maintained through all time which not only is not inconsistent with self-government, but which may be necessary to preserve self-government in the Dependencies.
>
> It is entirely conceivable that all . . . Dependencies might be left free to regulate their own domestic affairs on the principles of self-government . . . might be brought under the protecting arm of the [United States], and leave all questions which might arise between them and foreign countries to be settled by the [United States]; and yet might have no part in electing the President or the Congress of the United States.
>
> I do not seek now to prophesy the future, or to solve the as yet unsolved problem of our permanent relations to these Dependencies. I do not believe in giving the Statehood to any island population authority to share in electing the President

or the Congress of the United States. But I wish to . . . point out the fact that it is a mistake to suppose that we must either do that or cast off the islands altogether, and leave them in an independent Nationality. (Abbott 1911, 188–91)

Abbott's racial thought, as his political-religious writings demonstrate, corresponds well with the LMC tendency of circumventing the liberal principles of self-determination and individual consent, especially when seen in the context of Filipino demands for increased autonomy or self-government and Puerto Rican's own "home rule" desires. For instance, his 1905 LMC opening presidential address outlines his Christian evolutionary racialism:

[Our] problem for our insular peoples is the same. It is curious how, when we are just beginning to comprehend [the Indian problem], that we have been puzzling over for a quarter of a century, God does not take it away from us, but gives us another that is still harder. This is our problem respecting them: it is not to develop Porto Rico . . . or the Philippines; it is to develop Porto Ricans . . . [and] Filipinos. It is not to get labor to make sugar or fell forests or dig canals or furnish coffee or give us a better livelihood at a cheaper price, it is to make men out of those who are yet but stunted or dwarfed or just beginning to be made.[32]

Abbott reveals the form of imperialism the United States was pursuing outside traditional economic development models. He described the old and new "problems" facing the United States as a consequence of the expansionist policies pursued under the guidance of God's spirit. The emphasis on a Christian God as the appropriate avenue into American democracy, without suggesting racial equality as a liberal value, was an exercise in paternal elite moral safeguarding of Anglo-Saxonism while injecting a sense of pragmatic humanitarianism. In his eyes, U.S. imperialism was still understood in manifest destiny terms, and the inheritance of nonwhite races came with territorial expansionist ambitions. Abbott's speech makes it known that the Anglo-Saxon white national character was the norm for bringing these "others" to the equivalence of men and a civilized American Christian citizenry. Thus, his focus moves away from colonialism, nationalism, or economic development arguments and toward the proper way of racial and political uplift, with a Christian white standard presumably upholding the constellation of American political membership and civic life.

Even so, it is not evident whether or not Abbott developed his ideas at the LMC. However, based on his subsequent writings, it is unquestionable that his association with the Quaker-founded institution over many years allowed him to explore and apply his Christian evolutionary racialism to the politics of "other dependent peoples." Here we may consider Abbott's views toward the Puerto Rican: "I do not see how any one can visit, as I have visited, the West India Islands, or can travel, as I have traveled, from one end to the other of Porto Rico, and not feel . . . the evils that come from the intermarriage of the African with the white man" (Abbott 1911, 190). His Christian racialism is clearly aligned with his politics. Abbott's confluence of racial thinking and religious liberalism became an issue in 1912–14, when he guided the LMC into supporting a platform not sought fully by the Puerto Rican delegation.[33]

In a larger sense, as a Christian evolutionary racialist, Abbott thought systematically about what to do with U.S. dependent peoples: "We cannot exterminate them, we cannot enslave them, and we cannot intermarry with them" (Abbott 1911, 191). His thoughts seem to germinate at the LMC over time and later fully take hold in his 1911 book, *America in the Making*. Abbott put it in empirical terms when he asked, "What then?" regarding the place of extracontinental nonwhite peoples within a homogeneous and seemingly fixed U.S. political community and identity defined by an Anglo-Saxon white Christian national character. His suggestion was an early racial segregation theory but with a cooperative liberal democratic thread to go along with a pervasive imperialistic element:

> We must learn to live separate lives in terms of amity and mutual respect. Democracy has learned how men of different nationality and different traditions can live peacefully together; how men of different religious faiths can live peacefully together, the Protestant not assailing the Roman Catholic and the Roman Catholic not assailing the Protestant. It is your problem to teach a self-governing and co-operative commonwealth how two races can live together and preserve their race purity unimpaired; and yet live happily. It is a great problem; but it is something to know what the problem is, what its only solution must accomplish. (Abbott 1911, 192)

No doubt his proposition of separateness, including Christian sectarianism, flew in the face of many proponents of political assimilation policies at the time in U.S. intellectual, social, and political communities.

Conclusion

This discussion has explored the early twentieth-century politics of U.S. insular territorial relations and political thought through an intersectional historical lens. In the early 1900s in U.S. national political life, religious beliefs and racial thinking were bedfellows. Although political historians and some American political development scholars have previously written important accounts of the significance of religion to politics, not many have taken seriously the interactions between Quakerism and racialism as co-constitutive ideological forces for understanding how the political development of the U.S. imperialist state took shape in the early decades of the twentieth century.

Looking at the intersection of religious beliefs and racial thinking through the work of LMC founder Hicksite Quaker Albert K. Smiley and Congregationalist Lyman Abbott also illuminates the ideological struggles between liberal democratic ideals and the race-citizenship nexus in relation to an emerging U.S. imperialism. Smiley sought to create a balanced institution so participants could discuss regional and national issues notwithstanding their religious or political affiliations or personal identifications. The LMC allowed Abbott to develop his own Christian evolutionary racialist views while also shaping U.S. policies toward nonwhite peoples in acquired overseas territories. Both Smiley and Abbott were interested in shaping the mind, body, and soul of those nonwhite races deemed uncivilized, illiterate, often savage, and dependents of the U.S. imperialist state. Some may see both Smiley and Abbott as impediments to liberal democracy. However, each had broader aims to shape Anglo-Saxon white ideas about the other (or about various dependent peoples), Smiley with his nongovernmental forum, short speeches, and letters, Abbott with his *Outlook* magazine, books, and various leadership roles at the LMC. While Abbott, as a liberal Protestant, was a strong believer in religious liberalism, Hicksite liberal Quaker Smiley was interested in how humanity related to and experienced the world through the Inner Light, or "Spirit of God," although he was not intrinsically religious. The Quaker concept of Inner Light guided the LMC's practical unanimity goal, which not only fueled Smiley's pragmatic Quakerism approach to nonwhite races but also seemed to afford the development of Abbott's Christian evolutionary racialist views.

Finally, studying intersectional politics at the LMC discloses two ways in which religious beliefs and racial thought overlapped to shape political visions. First, race and religion at times co-created the meanings of citizenship in terms of "other dependent peoples." Second, religion played a role in designing the institutional space at the LMC, providing a seemingly neutral place for national conversation on race, citizenship, and political development. These profound influences would otherwise remain latent within either a unitary or a multivariate approach to understanding race relations, citizenship, and empire in American politics.

Notes

1. Treaty of Paris, December 10, 1898, U.S.-Spain, 30 Stat. 1754.

2. By political organization, I mean the two legislative measures that created semidemocratic political systems in the Philippines and Puerto Rico, the Philippine Organic Law of 1902 and the Puerto Rican Organic Law of 1901 (Foraker Act). For a distinction between various U.S. constitutional statuses that make up the hierarchical political structure of the U.S. imperialist state today, see Fallon 1991, 23–41.

3. The chapter focuses on how religious beliefs and racial thought together shaped insular territorial political discourses (and policies) over time in various contexts. For more on the co-constituted character of race and religion, see Nancy D. Wadsworth, "Reconciling Fractures: The Intersection of Race and Religion in United States Political Development" (2008).

4. The LMC was neither a lobbying group, nor a political party organization, nor a state government institution, nor a charitable foundation, but rather a nongovernmental institution founded on Quaker values, principles, and methods, along with liberal democratic ideals. The annual LMC hosted around three hundred participants, including imperialists such as Senator Henry Cabot Lodge, President Theodore Roosevelt, and Vice President Sherman, and anti-imperialists from Andrew Carnegie to Secretary of State William Jennings Bryan. Other intellectuals and political figures were active members: Lyman Abbott, Elmer Ellsworth Huntington, David Barrows, G. Stanley Hall, and George Blakeslee. It gained recognition for its nonbinding resolutions setting certain important moral and political imperatives, with its platforms exerting a significant influence on U.S. political development, institutional arrangements, and public opinion. The institution changed its name twice: from Lake Mohonk Conference of Friends of the Indian to Lake Mohonk Conference of Friends of the Indian and Other Dependent Peoples in 1904, and then later to Lake Mohonk Conference on the Indian and Other Dependent Peoples in 1914. These two changes reflected shifts in U.S. insular territorial politics as well as in the views of the more progressive Quakers who engaged in national political and racial discourses. In the second name of the LMC, "Other Dependent Peoples," a new category of difference appears (Hancock 2007a, 2007b; Simien 2007), racialized Puerto Ricans and Filipinos. For the first historical account of the LMC focused mostly if not exclusively on U.S.-Indian relations, see Larry E. Burgess, "The Lake Mohonk Conference on Friends of the Indian" (1972).

5. Racialism can be thought of as a process of maintaining racial differences through category formation based on one dominant group of people serving as the standard norm for citizenship, self-government, and civic community (e.g., the Anglo-Saxon white race in the United States).

6. The LMC often provided guidelines that Congress later followed. The Dawes Act was passed in 1887 with the help of the LMC (Burgess 1972, 51).

7. The name Society of Friends did not officially appear until much later in the early nineteenth century. See Lloyd 1950, 145.

8. At times, Quakers upheld similar racial assumptions as non-Quakers, who often maintained as hegemonic an Anglo-Saxon white national character that supposedly stood for the racial, cultural, and civic underpinnings of U.S. citizenship and larger "civilized" society (Pearce 1965).

9. U.S. Quakers became engaged in more international relief activities from the late nineteenth century through the early decades of the twentieth century (Byrd 1960, 143). Also, U.S. Quakers became the first organized religious group to oppose the institution of slavery prior to the Civil War,

and later, during Reconstruction, moved on to dealing with the economic and social conditions of the "American Negro," but within the new institution of segregation (Jones [1921] 2008, 609–17).

10. Many Quakers remain politically active through the American Friends Service Committee, a Quaker organization founded in 1917 by several former LMC members, and since 1943 with the Friends Committee on National Legislation, whose sole purpose was to lobby Congress (as the first registered church lobby) but which also played a role in the establishment of the Peace Corps and the Arms Control and Disarmament Agency (Wilson 1975; Hamm 2006).

11. LMC *Annual Report* 1894, 38.

12. LMC *Annual Report* 1906, 9. Smiley already owned property at Lake Mohonk prior to his appointment to the Board of Indian Commissioners. In 1869 he purchased property (discovered by his twin brother Alfred Smiley while on vacation) at Lake Mohonk, New York (Ulster County), where he dedicated time and money to restoring a mountain house resort surrounded by a beautiful natural environment that reminded him of his own Puritan upbringing (Trueblood 1897; Burgess 1980).

13. LMC *Annual Report* 1906, 9; Smiley to Congressman Theobald Otjen, July 12, 1906.

14. LMC *Annual Report* 1904, 9–10.

15. Smith to Dr. H. W. Langhelm of Jamestown, NY, July 31, 1907.

16. Smiley to Henry C. Ide, U.S.-appointed official in the Philippines, June 8, 1908.

17. Paul Charlton to Smiley, June 13, 1908.

18. Smiley to Paul Charlton, June 16, 1908.

19. LMC *Annual Report* 1895, 10.

20. LMC member and editor of the *Methodist Review* William V. Kelley noted Smiley's hospitality, inspired by the Quaker Inner Light. William V. Kelley to Smiley, October 27, 1902.

21. LMC *Annual Report* 1885, 27.

22. Pennsylvania Quaker William Penn expressed the oneness notion in the seventeenth century. To Penn, oneness meant "unity of many" and not the idea of a Trinity as is well-known in Catholicism (Moretta and Penn 2007). Oneness was often "reflected in the unity and egalitarianism of the various communities" (Armstrong 1993, 320).

23. The *Philadelphia Inquirer* in 1909 noted the diversity of political leaders appointed by Smiley to LMC committees (October 21, 1909, 2).

24. In 1894, Dr. Merrill E. Gates of the Indian Services asserted, "Mr. Smiley has a way of arranging everything here for our pleasure, and his sway is an approach to that dangerously attractive rule of the benevolent autocrat which, for the most part, lulls into placid acquiescence the well-pleased subjects" (LMC *Annual Report* 1894, 7–8).

25. Albert K. Smiley's *Will* (Burgess 1972, 18).

26. Abbott was editor for forty-seven years. *Outlook* magazine was highly respected within the various Christian communities—Protestants, Catholics, and Quakers—throughout the United States. Abbott used it as a medium to communicate his religious and racialist views, but mostly aimed to "[popularize] . . . the advancing thought [and ideas] of his contemporaries" including those associated with the LMC (Brown 1953, 2).

27. LMC *Annual Report*, October 18, 1905, 11–12.

28. LMC *Annual Report* 1905, 12. In this context, Abbott responded to his contemporaries who thought his ideas, rooted in a Christian evolutionary racialist foundation, unrealistic in regard to the "inherited" nonwhite populations more broadly (13–14).

29. Abbott was already aware of the national reputation of the LMC, which included an unsuc-

cessful attempt at resolving the so-called Negro problem during the post-Reconstruction 1890s. His history with the LMC and the Smileys gave him the confidence and a warrant to take on the issues of U.S. overseas territorial administration and citizenship, but from his Christian evolutionary racialist perspective.

30. In fact, throughout most of the life of the LMC, public opinion was understood to serve a significant institutional role in shaping U.S. political discourse and public policies. A classic book by James Bryce, *The American Commonwealth* ([1888] 1914), asserted this point. He claimed that public opinion was in all aspects of American politics and social life essential to all who wanted to influence policy or change perspectives on issues. (xxxi–xxxii, 923).

31. Abbott was fond of the Smileys, and thus without hesitation accepted to preside over the LMC during an important period in U.S. political development, as the Anglo-Saxon white race was challenged by its own progressive commitments to overseas imperialist territorial adventurism.

32. LMC *Annual Report* 1905, 10–11.

33. The delegation led by Martin Travieso (a prominent conservative lawyer in Puerto Rico and friend of A. Smiley) protested the LMC's platform and the call for U.S. citizenship while ignoring the home rule demands, which had been effectively argued since 1904.

References

Abbott, Lyman. 1892. *The Evolution of Christianity.* Boston: Mifflin and Co.

———. 1911. *America in the Making.* New Haven, CT: Yale University Press.

———. 1922. *Silhouettes of My Contemporaries.* Garden City, NY: Doubleday, Page & Co.

Annual Reports of the Lake Mohonk Conferences. 1929. New York: Lake Mohonk Conference, 1883–1917.

Armstrong, Karen. 1993. *A History of God: The 4,000-Year Quest of Judaism, Christianity, and Islam.* New York: Random House.

Barbour, Hugh, and J. William Frost. 1988. *The Quakers.* New York: Greenwood Press.

Benjamin, Philip S. 1976. *The Philadelphia Quakers in the Industrial Age, 1865–1920.* Philadelphia, PA: Temple University Press.

Bowden, James. 1972. *The History of the Society of Friends in America.* New York: Arno Press.

Brown, Ira V. 1953. *Lyman Abbott: Christian Evolutionist. A Study in Religious Liberalism.* Cambridge, MA: Harvard University Press.

Bryce, James. 1914. *The American Commonwealth,* vol. 2, *The Party System, Public Opinion, Illustrations, and Reflections, Social Institutions.* New York: MacMillan.

Burgess, Larry E. 1972. "The Lake Mohonk Conference of Friends of the Indian." PhD diss., Claremont Graduate University.

———. 1975. *The Lake Mohonk Conference of Friends of the Indians.* New York: Clearwater Publishing Co.

———. 1980. *An Outing to Paltz Point, Mohonk: Its People and Spirit—A History of One Hundred Years of Growth and Service.* Redlands, CA: Mohonk Mountain House.

———. 1991. *We'll Discuss It at Mohonk: The Smileys: A Commemorative Edition.* Redlands, CA: Moore Historical Foundation.

Butler, Jon. 1990. *Awash in a Sea of Faith: Christianizing the American People.* Cambridge, MA: Harvard University Press.

Bryd, Robert O. 1960. *Quaker Ways in Foreign Policy.* Toronto: University of Toronto Press.

Cooper, Wilmer A. 2001. *A Living Faith*, 2nd ed. Richmond, IN: Friends United Press.

Dandelion, Pink. 2007. *An Introduction to Quakerism*. Cambridge: Cambridge University Press.

Davis, David Brion. 1966. *The Problem of Slavery in Western Culture*. Ithaca, NY: Cornell University Press.

———. 1975. *The Problem of Slavery in the Age of Revolution, 1770–1823*. Ithaca, NY: Cornell University Press.

Drake, Thomas E. 1950. *Quakers and Slavery in America*. New Haven, CT: Yale University Press

Fallon, Joseph E. 1991. "Federal Policy and U.S. Territories: The Political Restructuring of the United States of America." *Pacific Affairs* 64 (1): 23–41.

Forbush, Bliss. 1956. *Elias Hicks: Quaker Liberal*. New York: Columbia University Press.

Frost, J. William, ed. 1980. *The Quaker Origins of Antislavery*. Norwood, PA: Norwood Editions.

Hamm, Thomas D. 1988. *The Transformation of American Quakerism: Orthodox Friends, 1800–1907*. Bloomington: Indiana University Press.

———. 2003. "New Light on Old Ways: Gurneyites, Wilburites, and the Early Friends." In *George Fox's Legacy: Friends for 350 Years*, ed. Charles L. Cherry, Caroline L. Cherry, and J. William Frost, 53–67. Haverford, PA: Friends Historical Association.

———. 2006. *The Quakers in America*. New York: Columbia University Press.

Hancock, Ange-Marie. 2007a. "Intersectionality as a Normative and Empirical Paradigm." *Politics & Gender* 3 (2): 248–54.

———. 2007b. "When Multiplication Doesn't Equal Quick Addition: Examining Intersectionality as a Research Paradigm." *Perspectives on Politics* 5 (1): 63–79.

Hattam, Victoria. 2007. *In the Shadow of Race: Jews, Latinos, and Immigrant Politics in the United States*. Chicago: University of Chicago Press.

Hinshaw, David. 1951. *Rufus Jones, Master Quaker*. New York: G. P. Putnam and Sons.

Ingle, H. Larry. 1986. *Quakers in Conflict: The Hicksite Reformation*. Knoxville: University of Tennessee Press.

Jones, Rufus M. 1916. *The Inner Life*. New York: Macmillan.

———. 1965. "The Faith and Practice of the Quakers." Philadelphia Yearly Meeting of the Religious Society of Friends.

———. (1921) 2008. *Later Periods of Quakerism, II*. Whitefish, MT: Kessinger Publishing.

Lloyd, A. 1950. *Quaker Social History, 1669–1738*. London: Longmans.

MacCulloch, Diarmaid. 2010. *Christianity: The First Three Thousand Years*. New York: Viking Press.

Maddox, Lucy. 2005. *Citizen Indians: Native American Intellectuals, Race, and Reform*. Ithaca, NY: Cornell University Press.

Merriam, Allen H. 1978. "Racism in the Expansionist Controversy of 1898–1900." *Phylon* 39 (4): 369–80.

Moretta, John. 2007. *William Penn and the Quaker Legacy*. New York: Pearson-Longman.

Noll, Mark A. 2002. *America's God: From Jonathan Edwards to Abraham Lincoln*. Oxford: Oxford University Press.

Pearce, Roy Harvey. 1965. *The Savages of America: A Study of the Indians and the Idea of Civilization*. Baltimore, MD: Johns Hopkins University Press.

Pollard, Francis E., Beatrice E. Pollard, and Robert S. W. Pollard. 1949. *Democracy and the Quaker Method*. London: Bannisdale Press.

Prucha, Francis Paul, ed. 1973. *Americanizing the American Indians: Writings by the Friends of the Indian 1880–1900*. Cambridge, MA: Harvard University Press.

———. 1977. *United States Indian Policy: A Critical Bibliography.* Bloomington: Indiana University Press.

———. 1979. *The Churches and the Indian Schools.* Lincoln: University of Nebraska Press.

———. 1981. *Indian Policy in the United States: Historical Essays.* Lincoln: University of Nebraska Press.

Reed, Adolph, Jr. 1997. *W. E. B. Du Bois and American Political Thought: Fabianism and the Color Line.* Oxford: Oxford University Press.

Simien, Evelyn M. 2007. "Doing Intersectionality Research: From Conceptual Issues to Practical Examples." *Politics & Gender* 3 (2): 264–71.

Smith, Rogers M. 2003. *Stories of Peoplehood: The Politics and Morals of Political Membership.* Cambridge: Cambridge University Press.

Soderlund, Jean R. 1985. *Quakers and Slavery: A Divided Spirit.* Princeton, NJ: Princeton University Press.

Thompson, Winfred Lee. 1989. *The Introduction of American Law in the Philippines and Puerto Rico, 1898–1905.* Fayetteville: University of Arkansas Press.

Trueblood, Benjamin F. 1897. "Mohonk and Its Conferences." *New England Magazine* 16 (22): 447–64.

Tully, Alan. 1977. *William Penn's Legacy: Politics and Social Structure in Provincial Pennsylvania, 1726–1755.* Baltimore, MD: Johns Hopkins University Press.

Wadsworth, Nancy D. 2008. "Reconciling Fractures: The Intersection of Race and Religion in United States Political Development." In *Race and American Political Development,* ed. Julie Novkov, Joseph Lowndes, and Dorian T. Warren. New York: Routledge.

Walvin, James. 1997. *The Quakers: Money & Morals.* London: John Murray.

Wilson, E. Raymond. 1975. *Uphill for Peace: Quaker Impact on Congress.* Richmond, IN: Friends United Press.

Race, National Identity, and the Changing Circumstances of Jewish Immigrants in the United States

Susan M. Gordon

In 1776, the Jewish population of the United States was between 1,000 and 2,500, or less than 0.1 percent of the population. One hundred years later, in 1880, Jews accounted for just 0.5 percent of the population. Over the next forty years, however, approximately two million Jewish immigrants (or about one-third of the entire Eastern European Jewish population) would arrive, part of the massive influx of twenty-five million immigrating into the United States during that period. While the vast majority of Jewish immigrants were of European origin, their experiences as immigrants, as a religious minority, and as an emerging ethnic group were shaped by and intimately tied to changing discourses on religion and race in the United States.

The late nineteenth century and early twentieth century were a period of not only high immigration but also major social change. The discourse on immigration was highly racialized, and U.S. immigration and naturalization policy was largely determined by prevailing racial hierarchies that characterized different national groups according to their "fitness for self-government" and "whiteness." Jewish immigrants were generally categorized as legally white, a label that would in theory have ensured their full legal, political, and social acceptance. However, immigration and naturalization policy was dictated not by a simple black-white dichotomy but by broad interpretations of race, which relied on such qualities as geographic origin, skin color, health status, mental ability, and religion to place national groups within a highly variegated hierarchy of races. Accordingly, immigrant groups were differentially treated along a scale of policy options, ranging from outright exclusion to full acceptance, with a wide variety of possible approaches in between.

The situation of Jewish immigrants was complicated by their status as non-Christians arriving in a society that had long defined itself as a nation of Christian Protestants. Most of the early colonies had religious tests for citizenship, and the colonists subscribed to a highly racialized understanding of Christianity that viewed non-Christians as both uncivilized and un-American. As Eric Mazur notes, race and religion were by and large interchangeable categories in U.S. case law during this period, which made Jews' legal position somewhat more precarious (see Jacobson and Wadsworth's introduction to this volume and Mazur, this volume). These policy and social categorizations created a sense of uncertainty for Jewish immigrants regarding both their legal and their social status in their new country. While this uncertainty created strong incentive for Jewish assimilation, many Jews remained ambivalent about becoming "American" because of the (Protestant) Christian orientation of prevailing ideas of national identity, which seemed to many to conflict with their desire to maintain a unique Jewish communal existence.

Following World War II, changes in racial ideologies and, in particular, ideas about the role of Protestant Christianity in American national identity created conditions for Jews to envision moving beyond this "Jewish or American" dichotomy. These broad changes in ideas about what it meant to be an American were accompanied by structural, administrative, and policy changes that made it easier on a practical level for Jews to join the mainstream of U.S. society. Jewish leaders seized on these opportunities, becoming more assertive in expressing and promoting an American ideal that was compatible with their desire to maintain an independent Jewish communal and religious life. At the same time, many Jews adapted their religious practices and aspects of their communal life to conform to these ideals, a common pattern among religious minorities in the United States.

Early Twentieth-Century Racial Ideologies in Flux

The complexity of early twentieth-century Jewish immigrants' status in U.S. society was rooted in part in dramatic changes in prevailing understandings of race at the end of the nineteenth century. The United States' history of chattel slavery and the country's first naturalization act, in 1790,[1] which excluded all but "free white persons of good moral character" from becoming citizens, had virtually ensured that racial distinctions would be central to definitions of citizenship. The 1857 Supreme Court decision in the Dred Scott case and the 1882 Chinese Exclusion Act, which stopped immigration from China and barred Chinese from naturalization, confirmed the precedent of excluding nonwhites from citizenship.[2] By the turn of the twentieth century, however, new scientific notions of race based on social Darwinism and anthropology, in addition to the presence of a large number of ambiguously raced new immigrants, challenged the prevailing classification systems. As a result, notions of a unified, unvariegated white race that had been the basis of the 1790 naturalization act began to give way to a more diverse spectrum of numerous races within and at the borders of whiteness, which made the categorization of immigrant groups such as Jews more ambiguous.

Specifically, there were three competing racial ideologies at the time that complicated the reception of immigrant groups. The first was a scientific notion of race based on Darwinism, genetics, and eugenics that was adopted by American intellectuals in the late nineteenth and early twentieth centuries. Such biological understandings of race were broadly defined and conceptualized, including, "any geographical, religious, class-based or color-based grouping" (Barkan 1999, 2). In this understanding, which was widely viewed as a true statement of fact, belonging to a racial group was "an indivisible essence that was based on a biology that also determined culture, morality, and intelligence, [and] was a compellingly significant factor in history and society" (Pascoe 1996, 48).

These eugenics-inspired theories dominated immigration discourse by 1910, and political debates often focused on the idea that the nation's blood supply was being diluted. Accordingly, many argued that southern and Eastern European immigrants—which included the majority of Jewish immigrants—were unfit for citizenship because of the antisocial and antidemocratic qualities that were theirs by birth. The result of this focus on the new immigrants as racially inferior was a growing movement to exclude immigrants. Limits on immigration enacted every few years after 1891 related to mental and physical health, and political views were directly tied to ideas of scientific racism, as eugenicists and immigration and naturalization officials ranked different nationalities according to their propensities for crime and physical and mental ailments.

Competing with scientific racism were two other views. Cultural anthropology emphasized the changeability of racial classifications and argued that any racial and social qualities the new immigrants displayed would, as Frank Boas testified before the Dillingham Commission, "not survive under the new social and climatic environment of America" (U.S. Immigration Commission 1911, 44). "Commonsense" ideas of race rejected the complicated and obscure categorizations of both eugenicists and the anthropologists for a more straightforward characterization based on phenotype, or who "looked white." In the naturalization courts, conflicts among these three schemes and confusion about the borders of whiteness resulted in different definitions of who could be a citizen at different times and by different courts. In 1909, Armenians were classified as white, even though their origins were technically in Asia; Syrians were defined as white in 1909, 1910, and 1915, but not in 1913 or 1914; Asian Indians were classified as "white persons" in 1910, 1913, 1919, and 1920, but not in 1909, 1917, or after 1923 (Haney López 1996).

Where did Jewish immigrants stand in this highly fluctuating and ambiguous social and legal classification system? Based on my readings of naturalization decisions, Bureau of Naturalization publications, and contemporary discussions of immigration in the press and in popular culture, three principal criteria emerge that determined "commonsense" understandings of who could become a part of the American collective: geographic origin, whiteness, and assimilation, all of which were colored for Jews by their religious otherness. These criteria, which defined most Jews as legally eligible for citizenship, also operated in ways that ensured Jews' continued uncertainty about their legal status and place in society.

Geography

The language of geographic origin pervaded discussions of who could be an American in the early twentieth century. In a quite straightforward manner, Western Europe was the area of automatic and assumed whiteness (Evans 1919, 52). Geographic origin first became part of naturalization law in 1870, which extended eligibility to blacks by referencing geography in speaking of "aliens of African nativity and persons of African descent," and was further institutionalized by the 1882 Chinese Exclusion Act (Klinkner and Smith 2002) and by the 1923 Thind case and the 1924 National Origins Act, which concluded that natives of countries outside Europe were not white and therefore could not naturalize because they were a part of "the white man's burden" (Haney López 1996; Ngai 1999). One implication of these decisions was that by the early 1920s, the question of eligibility for citizenship for southern and Eastern Europeans, including Jews, was resolved in the affirmative.

For Jews, however, geographic origin continued to be intertwined with religion in notions of assimilability. Writing in a 1919 article in the *North American Review*, Hiram Wesley Evans, imperial wizard and emperor of the Ku Klux Klan, distinguished between the "Western Jew," who he believed showed a tendency to "amalgamate" and would likely cease to be a problem, and Eastern Jews, who are "not true Jews, but only Judaized Mongols—Chazars" and thus would never assimilate (Evans 1919, 60). This view was reflected in the 1924 Immigration Act, the most important government statement on the relationship between race and geography in the first half of the twentieth century. The law created immigration quotas based on the 1890 census that severely constrained the influx of southern and Eastern Europeans in favor of immigrants from northern and Western Europe. The difference between the outright exclusion of Asians as racially unfit and the limited inclusion of southern and Eastern Europeans reflected both the emerging racial dichotomy that mapped whiteness onto European, as well as the continued salience of graduated hierarchical notions of race.

The effect of the National Origins Act was to separate race and geography for Europeans, creating hierarchically ranked national-ethnic identities that were separate from the common racial identity as white that made them eligible for naturalization. However, American Jewish leaders such as the prominent writer Maurice Samuel (1924, 215) saw the 1924 act as discriminating against Jews in particular:

> To-day, with race triumphant over ideal, anti-Semitism uncovers its fangs, and to the heartless refusal of the most elementary human right, the right of asylum, is added cowardly insult. We are not only excluded, but we are told, in the unmistakable language of the immigration laws, that we are an "inferior" people. Without the moral courage to stand up squarely to its evil instincts, the country prepared itself, through its journalists, by a long draught of vilification of the Jew, and, when sufficiently inspired by the popular and "scientific" potions, committed the act.

This view was reinforced by testimony from other antirestrictionists, such as Senator Reed of Missouri, who testified that "[a]ttacks have likewise been made upon the Jewish people who have crowded to our shores. The spirit of intolerance has been especially active as to them" (see also MacDonald 2002).[3] This take on the bill contradicted the efforts by many in Congress to depict the 1924 immigration act as primarily about maintaining the ethnic status quo, and not about discrimination. The House majority report favoring the bill specifically addressed this issue, complaining that "[t]he cry of discrimination is, the committee believes, manufactured and built up by special representatives of racial groups, aided by aliens actually living abroad," and defensively insisting that "[t]he continued charge that the Committee has built up a 'Nordic' race and devoted its hearing to that end is part of a deliberately manufactured assault for as a matter of fact the committee has done nothing of the kind."[4]

Nevertheless, American Jewish leaders and the Jewish press were preoccupied with notions of Darwinian scientific racism such as that expressed by Madison Grant in his extremely popular 1921 novel, *The Passing of the Great Race* (Barrett and Roediger, 1997, 10), and in the *American Hebrew* (e.g., March 21, 1924, 554,

625). Accordingly, Jewish leaders were among the principal opponents of the bills.[5] For example, when Louis Marshall of the American Jewish Committee testified in 1924 before the House Committee on Immigration and Naturalization, he stated that the bill reflected the views of the Ku Klux Klan and was inspired by the racialist theories of Houston Stewart Chamberlain (MacDonald 1998).

This insecurity felt by many Jews was reflected in Jewish leaders' strong reaction to anything that might potentially threaten Jews' legal status, such as the Bureau of Naturalization's practice of refusing citizenship to immigrants from the Ottoman Empire. In 1909 the Jewish Committee of New York City inquired why so many immigrants from the Ottoman Empire were being refused citizenship (to which Bureau of Naturalization deputy director Raymond Crist replied they were barred as Asiatics).[6] The Board of Delegates on Civil Rights of the Union of American Hebrew Congregations went further, complaining to Secretary of Labor Campbell about denials of naturalization for Turks, Syrians, Armenians, Palestinians, and Jews, arguing that this decision "would, if living, exclude David and Isaih [sic] and even Jesus of Nazareth himself."[7]

Despite these and similar complaints by other ethnic organizations, there was no mainstream public outcry against the exclusion from citizenship of other natives of the Ottoman Empire. In contrast, the Bureau of Naturalization announcement in 1909 that Armenians would be barred from citizenship led to an extensive debate in the press and between immigrant organizations and the government. The government's exclusion of Armenians was based on geography, which placed Armenia in Asia. This assumption, however, flew in the face of established opinion that distinguished Armenians from others on the border of Europe and categorized them as white on the basis of their Christianity. A San Francisco Newspaper, *The Call*, explained that Turks and Hindus could rightfully be barred as Mongolian, because that racial category excluded such people of "yellow" origin from citizenship. However, the paper argued that it was a travesty that while "the semi-civilized Mongolian Turk with his 'henna' and his 'harem' . . . [can become citizens] if born on American soil," Armenians, who were "from Europe, white, Christian, and have spent their lives fighting the fanatical Mongolians," had difficulty naturalizing.[8] This popular understanding of Armenians as "from Europe" and white can only be explained by their long-standing Christianity (Armenia formally adopted Christianity in A.D. 301, twelve years earlier than the Emperor Constantine), when geographically the region is farther east and no farther north than Turkey. Indeed, as Jacobson and Wadsworth discuss in the introduction to this volume, "civilized" and "Christian" were overlapping concepts for early Americans.

Thus, while in the case of Armenians, their Christianity served to mitigate bad geography, the opposite dynamic appears to have worked for Jews. Jews were clearly religiously racialized in the early part of the century,[9] but for most Jewish immigrants, geography—Western and Eastern Europe—served as a sufficient mitigating factor to guarantee naturalization rights. However, Jews who had not only the wrong religion but also "bad geography" were apparently a racially unfit branch of the "Hebrew race" and denied naturalization as Asiatics (Angel 1982; Papo 1987).

Whiteness

While dominant notions of racial hierarchy categorized all non-Anglo-Saxons as to one degree or another inferior, the differences in reaction to various immigrant groups (exclusion from citizenship and immigration versus immigration restrictions and assimilation programs) is indicative of the importance of skin color in the display of Americanness. Because a dark complexion, or more specifically "blackness," was already established as a mark of distinction between full citizenship and exclusion, differences in complexion among immigrant groups marked them for inclusion or exclusion and suspicion. Nineteenth-century Irish immigrants, who were considered to belong to the inferior Irish or Celtic race, were greeted with disdain during the nineteenth century (although never subject to immigration and naturalization exclusions or restrictions of any kind). However, not only was the Irish race eventually revised in popular culture to be included in the broad category "white," but Irish skin color itself was revised. Originally they were depicted in the nineteenth century as "black Irish," and drawn in contemporary cartoons as dark and simian, over time, emphasis shifted to the relatively light complexions and hair and eye coloring of many Irish immigrants.

For immigrants from outside or on the borders of Europe, the ability to claim whiteness was a determinant of their admissibility. This was particularly true because of naturalization policy that held that, despite the geographic basis for citizenship status (Europe), someone classified as white could naturalize no matter what country he immigrated from. In this atmosphere, in which ideas of racial hierarchy bombarded immigrants not only from government policy and Bureau of Naturalization citizenship education textbooks but from every corner of society, the message was clear: the farther a group was perceived as departing from the ideal of Nordic or Anglo-Saxon whiteness the greater would be its depiction as racially inferior and the greater would be its members' disadvantages at all levels of society. Thus, the desire to avoid the label "racially inferior," and to distance oneself from those who had already been labeled as the farthest from the white ideal, was strong. In October 1909, for example, the president of the United Syrian Society wrote to Secretary Campbell asking about the status of Syrians, in the aftermath of a widely reported statement by Campbell about the inadmissibility of Asiatics. The letter pointed out that naturalization courts had begun denying applications from Syrians, which they previously had not done. It went on to describe how a group of Syrian laborers in Wisconsin had walked off the job, because they didn't want to be characterized as an inferior race (Mongolian).[10]

For their part, Jewish leaders who adopted the discourse of a Hebrew race in the late nineteenth century and spoke of blood ties and shared ancestry when describing their unique social community began to downplay the idea of a separate race by the early twentieth century and to petition the government to abandon the "Hebrew" racial category. Desiring to identify themselves as "white" while at the same time trying to maintain a distinctive communal and social existence, some Jewish intellectuals promoted the term "ethnicity" to describe the unique middle ground they wished to create for themselves. As Victoria Hattam (2004) has explained, Jewish intellectuals writing between 1914 and 1924 such as Horace Kallen, Edward Sapir, Julius Draschler, and Isaac Berkson published works in which they referred to ethnic groups and ethnicity. Kallen, for example, opposed the dominant 100 percent Americanism as advocated by President Woodrow Wilson and the activist Americanizers. As the quintessential pluralist, he and others like him wrote about the importance of preserving ethnic differences and pluralism as central to maintaining a healthy, dynamic democratic culture. Thus, as part of their efforts to navigate between feelings of group solidarity and a desire for acceptance as part of the (white) mainstream, Jewish intellectuals sought both to conform to and to change prevailing racialized definitions of American.

Assimilation

Perhaps the most important strategy for immigrants working to establish or solidify their whiteness in an atmosphere in which both immigration and naturalization laws and decisions were unpredictable and becoming increasingly restrictionist was to "act American." Assimilation into the cultural mainstream was not just a matter of societal pressure, but government policy. Bureau of Naturalization immigrant education texts were strongly assimilationist, admonishing immigrants that "You can not become thorough Americans if you think of yourselves in groups. America does not consist in groups" (U.S. Department of Labor, Bureau of Naturalization, 1918 [F18EN], 4). The texts place earlier, now assimilated, immigrants as an example before the new immigrants, and hold out the promise of full membership in exchange for full assimilation for the European groups to which they're targeted. For example, a 1926 text spends nearly ten pages reviewing the immigration and assimilation histories of immigrants from Ireland, Germany, and Scandinavia, who found it

> difficult to get used to the ways and customs of our Government, especially in the crowded cities, but as time went by they and their children took on the ways of the Americans they met. Now their descendants are thoroughly American and make up a large part of what we call the American people. (Ibid. 1926 [F26N], 143)

Germans in particular are depicted as the ideal immigrant group because they were "too busy making their farms pay to enter into politics, preferring to accept customs already established" (ibid., 141). This example of political nonparticipation and the display of cultural assimilation are promoted by the government as an ideal for immigrant integration. To encourage and aid in such assimilation, the government texts dispense advice for regulating every aspect of immigrants' behavior, including detailed instructions on proper decorum, dress, home decorating, eating habits, and personal behavior (U.S. Department of Labor, Bureau of Naturalization, 1921 [F21SHGC], 10).

One of the primary means of assimilation that was advocated was assimilation into the Protestant mainstream, and Jews' perceptions that they were the main target of the immigration restrictions of the 1920s largely stemmed from the widespread view that the United States was a Christian country in general and a Protestant one in particular. While religion was never specifically mentioned in immigration or naturalization laws, it was nevertheless important in public conceptions of who was an American. For religious minorities such as Jews, Roman Catholics, Orthodox Christians, and Muslims, religion as much as their geographic origin or race marked them as different from Protestant northern Europeans, made them suspect, and was operative in immigration restrictions and general opinion regarding their potential Americanism, although not in naturalization court decisions or in naturalization law. For example, the 1928 presidential election, which pitted Democratic candidate Al Smith against Herbert Hoover, demonstrated the ongoing anti-Catholic sentiment in the country. During the campaign, rural Protestant preachers throughout the country warned congregants that a vote for Smith was a "vote for the devil."[11]

Accordingly, many Jews felt threatened and insecure in their citizenship status, even though their geographic origin in Europe, which was officially equated with whiteness after 1923, meant they were never excluded from immigration or naturalization. This anxiety was supported by government promotion of Christianity as equivalent to Americanism. For example, the Bureau of Naturalization's citizenship education material of the early 1920s is very explicit about the centrality of Christianity to "Americanism." This material, which included instructional textbooks and programs, was intended as a guide for immigrants in preparing for their naturalization examinations. The examination itself was extremely subjective, with decisions based as much on whether the judge believed the applicant to be a person of "good moral character" or loyal to the country and the "American way of life" as on an applicant's knowledge of U.S. civics. Thus, when textbook narratives centering on the activities of the average American family had entire lessons on going to church (U.S. Department of Justice, Bureau of Naturalization, 1924 [F24E], 115–17), featured "the birthday of Christ" prominently as one of the four major national holidays, included the story of the Wise Men, and contained writing drills on Christmas in the immigrant's home country, Jewish immigrants were likely to feel that their religious difference was a potential barrier to their inclusion (ibid., 185, 193). For Jews, then, who were often both politically active and committed to the goal of maintaining their social and cultural uniqueness, the government's promotion of assimilation as a condition for becoming true Americans was a source of anxiety and conflict—particularly because the American ideal to which they were expected to assimilate to was decidedly Christian (Goldstein 2006).

Geography, whiteness, and assimilation—all were areas that were important to public conceptions of the racialized boundaries of Americanism and were complicated for Jews by their religious otherness. For some immigrants, these factors could help or hurt their chances in naturalization courts. For all newcomers, these factors were an important part of the landscape into which they were expected to assimilate.

For immigrants who were on the border of Europe who were fighting for acceptance to citizenship (i.e., Syrians, Armenians, Turks, and others for which naturalization courts had offered contradictory rulings as to their whiteness), the subjective judgments of naturalization officers, naturalization court judges, and the American public were of considerable importance in determining their citizenship and their social status. Even for immigrants such as Eastern European Jews, whose legal status as white had not been challenged, their eligibility for naturalization on the basis of good moral character and attachment to the Constitution, as well as their social status and the eligibility of their family members to immigrate, were at stake. In these struggles, but particularly in the legal struggles in naturalization courts, all of the variables of racial classification outlined above (science, anthropology, and common knowledge) were tried in an effort not to be excluded from the white race, to retain eligibility to naturalize, and to advance one's position in society.

All three of these racial schemes were based on notions of physicality and behavior: Common knowledge was strongly based on geography, religion, and on whether the person "looked white." Anthropological determinations were dependent on racial classification tables and expert opinions that were based on skull measurements and cultural behavior. Eugenics was a scientific linking of physical traits and moral and political attributes. The similarities between what were otherwise considered conflicting, mutually exclusive ways of seeing the world, and the sense of plasticity infused by the diversity of racial schemes, meant that in the early twentieth century, *looking* and *acting* American were becoming increasingly important for one's citizenship status. When viewed in the light of negative stereotypical depictions of African Americans, the low status of African Americans in all areas of American life, and the constant implied questioning of immigrants' moral, hygienic, and cultural fitness for citizenship, a dynamic was created in which immigrants were required to prove, by displaying proper Americanism, that they were physically and morally entitled to citizenship. Increasingly in naturalization trials, whiteness was not judged based on science or even common knowledge but through the "performance" of an applicant's ability to assimilate by demonstrations of "evidence of whiteness in their character, religious practices and beliefs, class orientation, language, ability to intermarry, and a host of other traits that had nothing to do with intrinsic racial grouping."[12]

This assimilationist impulse applied not only to those whose whiteness was in question but also to the masses of southern and Eastern Europeans who had achieved what James Barrett and David Roediger (1997) have termed "provisional whiteness." For them, what was at stake was not necessarily their right to naturalize but their social and economic status, the eligibility of their family members and compatriots to immigrate, and their ability to become "Americans" in a broad sense. For Jews, discrimination came in the form of quotas that restricted elite university and medical school admissions and limited access to jobs in engineering, insurance, and banking. A 1942 survey of the *New York Times* and the *Herald Tribune* found that 30 percent of job advertisements expressed a preference for Christians (Shapiro 1990, 68–69). However, there were also significant self-imposed differences, in particular a desire to remain a separate community and maintain religious and cultural traditions that conflicted with assimilatory impulses and a Protestant individualist ethic. Nevertheless, both ambition and anxiety about immigration and citizenship status served as strong "push factors" encouraging assimilation. The conflict between these two desires was particularly acute (and persistent) because the model of ideal Americanness to which immigrants were expected to assimilate (white, European, Christian) was so at odds with their communal impulses. As a result, for the first half of the twentieth century the adjectives "Jewish" and "American" did not sit comfortably together. For many Jews, this led to an either/or approach to assimilation—either one maintained a primarily Jewish identity and remained steeped in Jewish communal life, or one turned one's back on Jewish life in favor of assimilation to the American mainstream. Leading Jewish intellectuals such as Walter Lipmann, Jerome N. Frank, Isaac Rosenfeld, Alfred Kazin, and Lionel Trilling, for example, distanced themselves from or disparaged Jewish traditions as they advanced in mainstream American society (ibid., 70–71).

Other Jewish intellectuals sought to form a middle ground, to define Jewish difference in terms of ethnicity and thereby distinguish it from race. Writing in the *Menorah Journal*, the premier journal of Jewish-related intellectual and artistic expression, in 1920, Isaac Berkson offered the "community theory" as "the acceptable mode of adjustment for the Jewish group as an ethnic entity," offering it as a "theory of adjustment applicable to all groups which desire to maintain their identity in the midst of American democratic life (Berkson 1920, 311; Hattam 2004, 50). Specifically, Berkson advocated a "change of emphasis from race to culture," building on earlier efforts by another *Menorah* contributor, the non-Jewish anthropologist Alfred Kroeber, to identify a "typical" Jewish character and temperament as a product of environment, not biological fixity (Kroeber 1917, 293; Hattam 2004, 48). Berkson and Kroeber were both part of an alternative discourse on nationality and race associated with ideas of cultural pluralism first advocated by Horace Kallen in 1906, a discourse that positioned ethnicity as an alternative category available to those who wished to escape the phenotype-based category of race. These progressive, pluralist thinkers, who defined ethnicity "against race" were among the first to offer an alternative narrative of American identity that could more easily accommodate Jewish (and other) difference. They set the stage for Jewish communal leaders after World War II to more strongly assert alternative ways of being American that would allow the American Jewish community to comfortably combine these two identities (Shapiro 1990; Goldstein 2006).

Reconciling Assimilation and Difference

World War II and the early Cold War years were a watershed period for both race and religion in American society, as the desire to differentiate the United States from Nazism and fascism made the deracialization of Jews a necessity for Americans. Social scientists rallied to that agenda in such works as Ruth Benedict's 1943 pamphlet *The Races of Mankind*, the Jewish anthropologist Franz Boas's 1945 essay *Race and Democratic Society*, and Ashley Montagu's 1942 *Race: Man's Most Dangerous Myth* (Jacobson 1998, 100–101). Hollywood's contribution included the films *Crossfire* (1947), *Gentleman's Agreement* (1947), *Open Secret* (1948), and *Prejudice* (1948). In *Gentleman's Agreement*, a 1947 Academy Award winner, a reporter goes undercover as a Jew to write an article on anti-Semitism. The film makes two points: first, that you can't tell who is Jewish (thus dispelling racialized conceptions of Jews based on physicality), and second, that Jews think and act like everyone else, making the point that anti-Semitism (and by extension other kinds of prejudice) is unacceptable because there are no real differences between white Protestants and members of other religions and ethnic groups.[13]

Along with this redefinition of Jewish from race to religion, new sociological understandings of the role of religion in American identity began to emerge as well. Writing in 1944, sociologist Ruby Jo Reeves Kennedy argued that American ethnic groups were fusing along religious lines—Jewish, Catholic, and Protestant—and that American assimilation could be explained as a "triple-melting-pot" (Kennedy 1944, 331–39). A similar point was made by Will Herberg in his 1955 book *Protestant-Catholic-Jew*. According to Herberg, the three main religious communities in the United States had become three separate spaces in which ethnic concerns could be expressed, but in which the same faith in "the American Way of Life" and the same values were forged, so that the three religions were "expressions of an over-all American religion, standing for essentially the same 'moral ideals' and 'spiritual values'" (Herberg 1955, 47–48, 50, 94–96; see also Kazal 1995, 450).[14] The implication of Kennedy's and Herberg's work was that this model of segmented assimilation through religious affiliation outside the Protestant mainstream was an acceptable alternative for Jews and Catholics.

These changes were reflected in popular culture of the time as well. Positive images of diversity begin to appear in cartoons, and children's books depicted friendships across ethnic and religious lines (Aleiss 1995; Gerstle 1996). In 1942, the Office of War Information issued a directive to the movie industry that "'Any form of racial discrimination or religious intolerance, special privileges of any citizen are manifestations of fascism, and should be exposed as such'" (Aleiss 1995, 33).[15] As a result, Native Americans changed in Hollywood movies from barbarous enemies to political allies, and World War II movies depicted an integrated military before it was a reality, with multiethnic and at times multiracial platoons (one Jewish, one Irish Catholic, one African American, and two or three Protestant soldiers) that stressed various groups' contributions to the war effort (Aleiss 1995). Similarly, the story of the U.S.S. *Dorchester*, a navy ship sunk during the war by a German U-Boat, was commemorated in several books, on a U.S. Post Office stamp, and promoted to immigrants by INS officials. According to the widely circulated story, four chaplains aboard the ship—two Protestant, one Catholic, and one Jewish, gave their life jackets to enlisted men and went down with the ship, standing proudly, hand-in-hand, in prayer (F48–68G, 88).

Despite (or perhaps because of) high levels of anti-Semitism in the United States both during and after the war (1947 was the all-time high), Jewish leaders saw the change in attitude as an opportunity to influence the national agenda by redefining what it meant to be an American in ways that would both counter anti-Semitism and alleviate some of the conflicts Jews felt about assimilating into the mainstream. Thus, drawing on the pluralist views that "Jews are safe only in a society accepting of a wide range of attitudes and behaviors, as well as a diversity of religious and ethnic groups" (Silberman 1985, 350), Jewish leaders and intellectuals sought to promote ideas of cultural tolerance partially out of the desire to create space for Jewish communal and religious difference within mainstream America. For example, the president of the Jewish Theological Seminary initiated a Conference on Science, Philosophy and Religion and their Relation to the Democratic Way of Life after the war.[16] The conference, which included seventy-nine thinkers and religious figures, had the goal of working for the "preservation of [American] democracy and intellectual freedom" and promoted the idea of a "Judeo-Christian tradition" of democracy as an alternative to the adoption of the term "Christian" by American fascists and anti-Semites during the 1930s (Regents of the University of Michigan 2004).

These changes in racial categories and in public conceptions of the place of religion in American society allowed for changes in official policy and were reflected in the government's approach to Jewish immigrants' religion as well. The American Jewish Committee had been protesting the classification of Hebrew as a race in naturalization records since at least 1930, arguing that government "inquisition" into the question of an applicant's religion was dangerous. Until the war, the solicitor general of the Department of Labor had repeatedly rejected this claim as groundless. After 1940, naturalization forms were revised so that applicants selected their race from a list of those eligible for citizenship: white, African or African descent, and Filipino. In addition, when Earl G. Harrison became Immigration and Naturalization Service (INS) commissioner in 1942, he appointed Henry Hazard to review the possibility of removing "Hebrew" as a race from immigration forms. Hazard responded with a memo concluding that Jews or Hebrews could not be considered a race and that racial classification and, indeed, the definition of the term "race" for immigration and naturalization purposes was to be determined administratively and not according to law or regulation (Smith 2002). As a result, the INS dispensed with the category for naturalization purposes in 1940 and for immigration purposes in 1942 (Smith 2002).[17] For Jews, then, race and religion became disentangled in the official administration of immigration and naturalization in the postwar years.

The INS naturalization textbooks from that period also show subtle changes in the way the role of religion in American life was described. During the war, the INS had discovered that nearly half a million of the country's long-term immigrants had not become citizens. In response, it launched a naturalization campaign that included an extensive citizenship education program with revised textbooks designed to promote "Americanism" to those immigrants. In the INS texts, "Church" is still featured as an important American institution; as a site, along with the family, of moral inculcation ("Children learn what is right in the home and in the church"; F45HECS, 21), and even as a source of personal hygiene ("We try to keep our food clean. . . . We keep our food at the church"; F45HEC, 34). However, religion has been subtly transformed from a Christianity that organizes Americans' daily lives to an institution that is associated in a more general sense with "the right way to do things instead of the wrong way" (F45HEC, 15).

Because it had become much less acceptable to refer to the United States as a Christian country by the 1940s, the texts reconfigure religion, as well as race, as benign "personality" differences, and democracy is shown as respecting all "personalities," whether "black or white, Protestant, Catholic, Jew or unbeliever" (FA43G2, 7). With this de-Christianization of the United States and deracialization of religion, religion began to be infused with political meaning. Religion is emphasized in the texts as the basis of American ideas of equality[18] and assumes a utilitarian function, akin to that of democracy, of helping Americans "live better" (FA43G2, 5). When organized religion is mentioned at all, it is in the context of Americans' freedom to worship as they please and the absence of a state church (although not separation of religion and state explicitly) (FA43G2, 31–33). By 1948, good Americans were no longer only depicted as Protestant churchgoers: one Citizenship Day ceremony depicts Protestant, Eastern Orthodox, Roman Catholic, Jewish, Muslim, Hindu, and Buddhist religions (although most discussions of religion still acknowledge only Protestant, Catholic, and Jewish, or increasingly, simply the Christian-Jewish dichotomy, reflecting both Jews' and white ethnic Catholics' increasing entrance into the mainstream) (F48C, 48).[19]

In the INS texts' discussions of religious diversity, representations of the United States as a Christian country change into depictions of the United States as a religious country in a general sense in which religious terminology is used to describe democracy and the American state. Now, religion's "golden rule" becomes a servant of democracy, and the new golden rule states that "Hate, prejudice, and bigotry, whether religious or racial, tear down and destroy and can have no place in our democracy" (F48–68G, 48). This promotion of religious-like fidelity to the American state reflects broad changes in the place of religion in American life. As Mazur has explained: "Protestantism came to be replaced by a State-centered ideology as the public source of symbolic meaning construction and maintenance . . . that is, the rites, rules, myths, and rituals of authority and transcendence posited in the federal government—would come to eclipse" Protestantism (see Mazur, this volume).

In the postwar period, religious practice accordingly became more "civic." Churches expanded their activities from prayer and charity to recreation, youth programs, and social events, and religious affiliation developed into a lifestyle choice that reflected "the American way of life." In 1940, 64.5 million Americans—or about 50 percent of the population—were church members, compared to only 20 percent in 1860. By 1960, 114.5 million Americans were church members, or approximately 63 percent of the population" (May 1988, 25–60). Increasingly, attendance at religious services became a social event and a way of displaying ideological conformity and affiliation with the American way of life. The INS citizenship education texts express this sentiment well.

One introductory pamphlet offers this view: "Our neighbors do all they can for us. We like this kind of neighbor. We all like the same things. We go to the same church. We go to the same places for good times" (F45HEC, 83). Another states that religious groups "help us to learn the true values of life—what is right or wrong—and about unselfishness and the best way of living" (FA43SG, 41).

Postwar changes in Jewish communal institutions reflect Jews' adaptation to this new model of American religious-civic life. Nineteenth- and early twentieth-century American Jews had organized themselves either in synagogues devoted exclusively to religious activities or social welfare organizations such as the Hebrew Free Loan Society and the Hebrew Immigrant Aide Society. After World War II, Jews moving to the suburbs on the GI bill joined Conservative synagogues, which functioned in part as community centers and attempted to forge a middle ground between Orthodox separation and a Reform Movement that was seen by many as having gone too far in abandoning Jewish traditions (Golinkin and Panitz 2007).[20] The evolution of the Jewish Community Center, which was formed as the Young Men's Hebrew Association (YMHA) in 1854 to help Jewish immigrants, was renamed the Jewish Welfare Board (JWB) in 1917, and became the suburban JCC with recreational and athletic activities, camps, child care, and social and educational events in the second half of the twentieth century, is a case in point.

These changes in American national identity and racial ideologies during and after World War II did not have immediate implications in terms of lifting immigration quotas that had kept the number of Jewish immigrants low since the 1920s. On the contrary, neither immigration nor refugee quotas were increased during World War II, even after the U.S. government and public became aware of the scope of Hitler's final solution, and very few Jewish refugees were admitted in the aftermath of the war.[21]

Nevertheless, changes in public discourse were significant in resolving the conflicts that had plagued Jewish life in the first part of the century. The deracialization of Jews (and fixing of their identity as "white"), moderation of ideas about the centrality of Christianity in American life, and the transformation of religion in public discourse and INS textbooks from a matter of faith to a type of communal activity that was distinctly American contributed to the process. Now Jews could more easily blend their Jewishness with their Americanness, espousing their loyalty to "American ideals" as Jews and participating in Jewish communal activities in ways that were very similar to the ways their Christian neighbors' participated in church activities. While the desire to preserve a distinct Jewish community had conflicted with assimilatory pressures in the early part of the century, in the postwar period displaying Jewish religious affiliation became one more way of performing as an American. This is not to deny that Jews did not continue to experience conflicts between ethnic or religious particularity and assimilation, but changes in ideas of how one could be an American certainly made the Americanization of postwar immigrants a less conflicted matter.

What are the implications of this story for our understanding of the intersection of race and religion in the United States? First, it reinforces our understandings of the interconnectedness of religious otherness and racial otherness. August Hollingshead, a sociologist whose work inspired Arthur Herberg's *Protestant, Catholic, Jew,* wrote in 1952 that "two social worlds have evolved—a Negro world and a white world. The white world is divided by ethnic origin and religion into Catholic, Protestant, and Jewish contingents" (quoted in Schultz 2006). Herberg later drew on the work of Hollingshead and others to argue that in an "other-directed society" like the United States, where one is judged by how one presents oneself, belonging to a recognized group and having a "brand name" were essential to being American. Writing descriptively, Herberg explained that "By and large, to be an American today means to be either a Protestant, a Catholic, or a Jew . . . Not to be a Catholic, a Protestant, or a Jew today is not to be anything, not to have a name" (Herberg 1955, 40). Herberg and Hollingshead describe a process of Jews "becoming American" by becoming white, or rather by changes in society that allowed Jewish (and Catholic) communal affiliation to "count" as alternative ways to demonstrate belonging to white, mainstream America.

Notably left out of Herberg's and Hollingshead's discussions are members of other religious minorities. Indeed, today (and particularly in post-9/11 America), wearing a turban or a headscarf signifies racial otherness in a way that wearing a yarmulke usually does not.[22] This difference can in part be explained by reflection on the political events and intellectual changes that supported the transformation of Jewish affiliation from racialized otherness to an alternative assimilatory path within the white mainstream. Significantly, international politics, particularly post–World War II efforts to differentiate American identity from Nazism and Communism, were important in changing attitudes and official government policies toward Jewish immigrants and Jewish Americans, and toward the idea of the United States as a Christian country.[23] But equally significant were the efforts of community leaders to exploit these opportunities to promote an alternative, more inclusive narrative and the rise of forms of Jewish religious expression that more closely paralleled those of their Christian neighbors.

Finally, that Jewish immigrants, though they never experienced the harshest forms of exclusion and official racialization, nevertheless felt threatened (and were racialized and ostracized in more subtle ways) should also encourage us to appreciate the ways in which international affairs complicate identity issues for religious and racial minorities in the United States. This is obvious in some cases, such as the impact the post-9/11 war on terrorism has had on Arab and Muslim American citizens. But the 1999 firing of Taiwanese American Wen Ho Lee from the Los Alamos National Laboratory and his subsequent arrest for spying for China[24] and the 2001 Hainan island incident, during which many Chinese Americans feared they would be treated as "foreigners in wartime" (Kim 2001),[25] indicate that racial and religious minorities continue to be vulnerable, and that international affairs continue to have an impact on contemporary ideas of American citizenship and American nationality for racial and religious minorities.

Notes

An earlier version of this essay, "Race, National Identity, and the Changing Circumstances of Jewish Immigrants in the United States," was originally presented at the Hurst Seminar Conference on Jewish Immigration in the 20th Century, Dead Sea, Israel, May 2006.

1. Act of March 26, 1790 (1 Statutes-at-Large 103).

2. Chinese Exclusion Act of May 6, 1882 (22 Statutes-at-Large 58).

3. *Congressional Record*, February 19, 1921, 3463 (statement of Senator Reed).

4. House of Representatives, Report 350, 1924, 16.

5. It should be noted, however, that Jews were not the primary victims of the 1921 and 1924 acts. The acts restricted immigration for all southern and Eastern Europeans and accomplished the absolute racialization of "Asiatics" by equating race with nationality and stopping all immigration from Asia by virtue of limiting immigration to those racially eligible for naturalization (Ngai 1999, 69).

6. National Archives and Records Administration, Washington, DC (hereafter NARA), RG 85, entry 26, box 1573, 19783/27, 10/6/09.

7. NARA, RG 85, entry 26, box 1572, file 19783/43, pt. 1.

8. NARA, RG 85, entry 26, box 1573, 19783/29. Despite Bureau of Naturalization director Campbell's strong opinions on the matter and his attempts to influence naturalization decisions, most naturalization courts granted citizenship to Armenians and, while some Arabs and natives of the Ottoman Empire were denied citizenship, many Middle Eastern and European "Asiatics" from all religions, including Syrians, Lebanese, Turks, Egyptians, Armenians, Moroccans, Afghans, and Iraqis, became citizens (Bureau of Naturalization *Annual Report: 1919*, 75 (GAR19); 1921, 17 (GAR21); 1924, 41 (GAR24); 1928, 28 (GAR28); 1929, 33 (GAR 29).

9. See, for example, the Leo Frank case, in which a northern Jewish factory manager was wrongly tried and lynched for raping and murdering a young girl who worked in the pencil factory he managed. The rhetoric of the trial and newspaper accounts described Frank's supposed lust after white women in classically racist terms. The history is recounted in Dinnerstein 1966.

10. NARA, RG 85, entry 26, box 1573, 19783/31. The majority of Arab immigrants to the United States through the 1920s were Christian, mostly natives of Syria and Lebanon, who were referred to (and often referred to themselves) as Syrian. Unlike Armenians, their Christianity did not mitigate their geographic otherness. See Suleiman 1999.

11. See Higham (1955) 1974, chap. 11, and Allan J. Lichtman's *Prejudice and the Old Politics: The Presidential Election of 1928* (Chapel Hill: University of North Carolina Press, 1979).

12. "Constitutional Limitations on the Naturalization Power" 1971.

13. *Gentleman's Agreement* reflected a new postwar modernist racial ideology that viewed racial differences as merely biological, not representative of any true internal differences, and therefore irrelevant. However, while ostensibly about breaking down racial stereotypes, the notion that the reporter and his Jewish friend Dave are "just like us" because they don't look different implicitly accepts racial discrimination against minorities who do look different. Matthew Jacobson's summary of this point as "Do unto others—who could pass for you—as you would have others do unto you—if you could pass for them" correctly exposes the limits of postwar ideas of "tolerance," despite Hollywood's new official "nondiscrimination" position (Jacobson 1998, 129).

14. In a 1949 speech to the D.C. Federation of Women's Clubs, INS director Watson B. Miller said, "Our American way of life is based upon the recognition of the dignity of man as a creature of God. For one man to discriminate against another because of his religion or his national origin is not only un-American—it is an evil in the sight of God" (F49Sa, 2).

15. Quoted from "Government Information Manual for the Motion Picture Industry," Summer 1942, NARA, Office of War Information, Bureau of Motion Pictures (Hollywood Office), RG208, General Records of the Chief, Suitland, Maryland.

16. The Jewish Theological Seminary is the rabbinical and cantorial school of the Conservative Movement in American Judaism.

17. INS *Annual Report* 1941 (GAR41), 9–41; INS *Annual Report* 1948 (GAR48), table 21.

18. "They [the founding fathers] meant there are certain rights every man, woman, and child own simply because they are God's people" (FA43G2, 15).

19. One 1948 text takes great pains to show that all religions have a version of the golden rule (which is defined politically), and that different religious or national backgrounds don't mean that one can't be a true American. It includes quotations from all sorts of people from all sorts of religions about being American, and reports that in World War II, "Every wound, without regard to race, or creed, or social class, bled red" (F48C, 84–86).

20. The Conservative Movement experienced its greatest period of growth in the two decades after World War II, growing from 190 to 778 member congregations between 1945 and 1964. The 1950 decision by the Conservative Rabbinical Assembly to allow driving to the synagogue on the Sabbath was emblematic of the compromise position between modernity and tradition it took. This contrasted to the Reform Movement, which at the time discouraged outward evidence of Jewish difference such as the use of ritual skullcaps and prayer shawls. The Conservative Movement remained the largest among the three major American Jewish denominations until 2000, when it was overtaken by the Reform Movement and threatened by a revitalized Orthodox Movement. The change can be largely explained by demographics and assimilation: with over 50 percent of American Jews marrying outside their faith, Reform acceptance of children of both Jewish men and women as Jewish (in contrast to Conservative and Orthodox acceptance only of children of Jewish mothers) gave it an advantage.

21. See Richard Breitman and Alan Kraut, *American Refugee Policy and European Jewry* (Bloomington: Indiana University Press, 1998), for a detailed discussion of efforts to pass refugee bills and the opposition in Congress, the State Department, and public opinion to increasing quotas that would have allowed Jewish refugees to escape from Nazi-controlled Europe. See also David Wyman, *Abandonment of the Jews: America and the Holocaust 1941–1945* (New York: Pantheon, 1986), for detailed archival material on the issue.

22. Although more esoteric forms of Jewish religious garb still arouse suspicion. See http://www.msnbc.msn.com/id/34973665/ns/us_news-security/.

23. The idea of international politics having an impact on the fate of racial or religious minorities in the United States is not a new one, nor is this a unique case. For example, the differences between the 1864 Chinese Exclusion Act, which officially excluded Chinese from immigrating or becoming citizens, and the 1906 Gentleman's Agreement, which discouraged but didn't formally prevent Japanese immigration, is in part a reflection of Japan's role as important international power at the turn of the century. (The Chinese Exclusion Act, passed in 1862, banned all persons of Chinese descent from citizenship and excluded most Chinese immigrants. The 1906 Gentleman's Agreement, which was negotiated between the United States and Japan, stipulated that Japan would stop issuing permits allowing its laborers to immigrate to the United States.) The same logic applies to the reversal of discriminatory legislation practices: the 1943 repeal of the Chinese Exclusion Act resulted from a desire to placate a World War II ally; the 1954 *Brown v. the Board of Education* decision was partially motivated by a desire to counter Communist propaganda, which emphasized legalized American racial discrimination (Dudziak 2008).

24. Lee was eventually acquitted on fifty-eight of the fifty-nine counts against him. He was convicted only of mishandling computer files.

25. In April, a U.S. naval aircraft and its crew were detained by the Chinese military following a confrontation with a Chinese plane and an emergency landing. The incident was accompanied by anti-Chinese rhetoric and discussions of potential military conflict with China.

References

Primary Sources

For in-text citations of government documents related to citizenship education, the parenthetical abbreviations noted below have generally been used.

U.S. Department of Labor, Bureau of Naturalization. 1918. *Student Textbook,* by Raymond F. Crist. Compiled from material submitted by the State Public Schools to the Bureau of Naturalization (F18EN).

———. 1919. *Annual Report* (GAR19).

———. 1921. *Annual Report* (GAR21).

———. 1921. Student textbook compiled by Bureau of Naturalization from material submitted by state public schools (F21SHGC).

———. 1924. *Annual Report* (GAR24).

———. 1924. Textbook, Part I, *Our Language.* A "narrative of the activities of an average family" (F24E).

———. 1926. Textbook, Part II, *Our Nation* (F26N).

———. 1928. *Annual Review* (GAR28).

———. 1929. *Annual Review* (GAR29).

U.S. Department of Justice, Immigration and Naturalization Service (INS). 1943. *This Democracy of Ours,* by Thomas H. Briggs (FA43G2).

———. 1943. Textbook, *Our Constitution and Government,* prepared by Catheryn Seckler-Hudson (FA43SG).

———. 1945. Textbook, *Home Study Course in English and Government for Candidates for Naturalization,* Section I, *English and Home and Community Life.* "For the helper" (F45HEC).

———. 1945. Textbook, *Home Study Course in English and Government,* Section I, *English and Home and Community Life.* "For the student" (F45HECS).

———. 1948. *Gateway to Citizenship,* ed. Edwina Austin Avery. Revision of 1943 text (F48C).

———. 1968. *Gateway to Citizenship* (F4868G).

———. Speech by Hon. Watson B. Miller at DC Federation of Women's Clubs, in honor of National Brotherhood Week (F49Sa).

U.S. Immigration Commission. 1911. *Changes in Bodily Form of Descendants of Immigrants (Final Report).* Reports of the Immigration Commission 38. 61st Congr., 2d sess. Senate. Doc. 208. William P. Dillingham, chairman. Prepared by Franz Boas. Washington, DC: Government Printing Office.

Secondary Sources

Aleiss, Angela. 1995. "Prelude to World War II: Racial Unity and the Hollywood Indian." *Journal of American Culture* 18 (Summer): 25–34.

Angel, Marc. D. 1982. *La America: The Sephardic Experience in the United States.* Philadelphia: Jewish Publication Society.

Barkan, Elliott Robert. 1999. "Comment: Searching for Perspectives: Race, Law, and the Immigrant Experience." *Journal of American Ethnic History* 18 (4): 136–49.

Barrett, James R., and David Roediger. 1997. "Inbetween Peoples: Race, Nationality and the 'New Immigrant' Working Class." *Journal of American Ethnic History* 16, no. 3 (Spring): 3–44.

Berkson, Isaac B. 1920. "A Community Theory of American Life." *Menorah Journal* 6 (6): 311–21.

"Constitutional Limitations on the Naturalization Power." 1971. *Yale Law Journal* 80, no. 4 (March): 769–810. http://links.jstor.org/sici?sici=00440094%28197103%2980%3A4%3C769%3ACLOTNP%3E2.0.CO%3B2-X.

Dinnerstein, Leonard. 1966. *The Leo Frank Case.* New York: Columbia University Press.

Dudziak, Mary L. 2004. "Brown as a Cold War Case." *Journal of American History* 91 (1): 24 pars. http://www.historycooperative.org/journals/jah/91.1/dudziak.html.

Evans, Hiram Wesley. 1919. "The Klan's Fight for Americanism." *North American Review* 223 (830).

Gerstle, Gary. 1989. *Working-Class Americanism: Politics of Labor in a Textile City, 1914–1960.* Interdisciplinary Perspectives on Modern History. Cambridge: Cambridge University Press.

———. 1996. "The Working Class Goes to War." In *The War in American Culture: Society and Consciousness during World War II,* ed. Lewis A. Ehrenberg and Susan E. Hirsch. Chicago: University of Chicago Press.

Goldstein, Eric L. 2006. *The Price of Whiteness: Jews, Race, and American Identity.* Princeton, NJ: Princeton University Press

Golinkin, David, and Michael Panitz. 2007. "Conservative Judaism." In *Encyclopedia Judaica,* 2nd ed., ed. Michael Berenbaum and Fred Skolnik, 5:171–77. Detroit: Macmillan Reference USA. http://find.galegroup.com/gvrl/infomark.do?&contentSet=EBKS&type=retrieve&tabID=T001&prodId=GVRL&docId=CX2587504582&source=gale&userGroupName=spertusgvrl&version=1.0.

Haney López, Ian F. 1996. *White by Law: The legal Construction of Race.* New York: New York University Press.

Hattam, Victoria. 2004. "Ethnicity: An American Genealogy." In *Not Just Black and White: Historical and Contemporary Perspectives on Immigration, Race, and Ethnicity in the United States,* ed. Nancy Foner and George M. Fredrickson, 42–60. New York: Russell Sage Foundation.

Herberg, Will. 1955. *Protestant, Catholic, Jew: An Essay in American Religious Sociology.* Garden City, NY: Doubleday.

Higham, John. (1955) 1974. *Strangers in the Land: Patterns of American Nativism, 1860–1925.* New York: Atheneum.

Hill, Howard C. 1919. "The Americanization Movement." *American Journal of Sociology* 24 (6): 609–42.

Jacobson, Matthew Frye. 1998. *Whiteness of a Different Color: European Immigrants and the Alchemy of Race.* Cambridge, MA: Harvard University Press.

Kazal, Russell A. 1995. "Revisiting Assimilation: The Rise, Fall, and Reappraisal of a Concept in American Ethnic History." *American Historical Review* 100 (2): 437–71.

Kennedy, Ruby Jo Reeves. 1944. "Single or Triple Melting-Pot? Intermarriage Trends in New Haven, 1870–1940." *American Journal of Sociology* 49 (January).

Kim, Ryan. 2001. "Many Chinese Americans Say U.S. Appears Arrogant: But They fear Impact of Worsening Relations." *San Francisco Chronicle,* April 5.

Klinkner, Philip A., and Rogers M. Smith. 2002. *The Unsteady March: The Rise and Decline of Racial Equality in America.* Chicago: University of Chicago Press.

Kroeber, Alfred L. 1917. "Are the Jews a Race?" *Menorah Journal* 3 (5): 290–94.

MacDonald, Kevin B. 1998. "Jewish Involvement in Influencing United States Immigration Policy, 1881–1965: A Historical Review." *Population and Environment* 19:295–355.

May, Elaine Tyler. 1988. *Homeward Bound: American Families in the Cold War Era.* New York: Basic Books.

Ngai, Mae M. 1999. "The Architecture of Race in American Immigration Law: A Reexamination of the Immigration Act of 1924." *Journal of American History* 86 (1). http://www.historycoop erative.org/journals/jah/86.1/ngai.html.

Papo, Joseph. 1987. *Sephardim in Twentieth Century America: In Search of Unity.* San Jose, CA: Pele Yoetz Books.

Pascoe, Peggy. 1996. "Miscegenation Law, Court Cases, and Ideologies of 'Race' in Twentieth-Century America." *Journal of American History,* June, 44–69.

Regents of the University of Michigan. 2004. *When Jews Were GIs: World War II and the Remaking of American Jewry.* New York: Fathom Knowledge Network. http://www.fathom.com/course/21701756/session5.html.

Samuel, M. 1924. *You Gentiles.* New York: Harcourt, Brace and Co.

Schultz, Kevin M. 2006. "Protestant-Catholic-Jew, Then and Now." *First Things: A Journal of Religion, Culture, and Public Life.* http://www.firstthings.com/article.php3?id_article=72.

Shapiro, Edward S. 1990. "World War II and American Jewish Identity." *Modern Judaism* 10 (1): 65–84.

Silberman, Charles. 1985. *A Certain People: American Jews and Their Lives Today.* New York: Simon & Schuster.

Suleiman, Michael W. 1999. *The Arab Immigrant Experience.* Philadelphia, PA: Temple University Press.

What Would Robert E. Lee Do?

Race, Religion, and the Debate over the
Confederate Battle Flag in the American South

GERALD R. WEBSTER AND JONATHAN I. LEIB

The two most important events in the history of the American South are the Civil War of the 1860s and the civil rights movement of the 1960s. While race clearly played a dominant role in these two historical upheavals, the region's deeply felt religiosity was also central to both events (Miller, Stout, and Wilson 1998). White Southerners viewed the Civil War in theological terms, as a war against Northern apostasy (Webster 2004). As a result, they understood their cause to be righteous and worth any and all sacrifices. Churches and religious leaders also played a central organizing role in the civil rights movement in the last half of the twentieth century. The extreme levels of segregation in the South's churches led to the development of African American leaders in the community's religious institutions, and these leaders provided critical direction for the movement (Webster 2000). This reality led many black churches to becoming targets of violence by those championing the preservation of Jim Crow and racial segregation across the region (Lincoln and Mamiya 1990).

Today, debates over the symbols associated with both the Civil War and civil rights movement underscore how race and religion continue to intersect in the region's political discourse (Webster and Leib 2008). While these debates have pertained to a broad array of issues, the most dominant controversies have been over the proper interpretation of the meaning of the symbols, the memorialization of important notables, and the recognition of historical events associated with the short-lived Confederate States of America (1861–65) (Leib 2002, 2004; Webster 2004). No debate in the region has been more vitriolic than the long-running controversy over the meaning of the Confederate battle flag (Leib and Webster 2007). Because of its use during both the Civil War and civil rights movement, the flag has become imbued with layered meanings that reflect both racial and generational differences of interpretation. Thus, a recent poll in South Carolina found that more than 70 percent of African Americans viewed the battle flag as a "symbol of racism and hate" (Shenin 2007). Yet the battle flag flies at a Confederate memorial on the grounds of the South Carolina state capitol (Webster and Leib 2001).

Similar polls in other states have found substantial contrasts in interpretations of the flag's meaning, with most native white southerners viewing the battle flag as an honorable symbol of heritage and sacrifice and most African American southerners viewing the flag as emblematic of the region's efforts to maintain slavery in the 1860s and segregation in the 1960s (Leib 1998). Discussions over these mutually exclusive views have resulted in harsh rhetoric, given the racial and religious overtones to the debate. Controversies over such symbols are clearly racialized, pitting white and black southerners against one another in passionate debates. It is equally true that some white southerners have found it helpful if not reflexive to intertwine the region's fundamentalist religiosity with Confederate myth to support their spirited defense of Confederate icons as symbols of white southernness and the righteousness of antebellum culture. Using critical race theory and a discussion of religious traditions in the South, this essay seeks to explain why these debates are so polarized and divisive. Before our discussion of critical race theory and southern religious traditions, however, we provide a short history of the Confederate battle flag.

A Brief History of the Battle Flag

In 1861, the provisional government of the Confederate States of America (CSA) formed a "Committee on Flag and Seal" to propose a national flag for the emerging country. The committee reviewed hundreds of proposals, with many bearing a strong resemblance to the United States national flag, or "Stars and Stripes." A substantial number also included religious symbols such as the Christian cross in their design (Cannon 2002). The eventual selection, referred to as the "Stars and Bars," was similar in design to the U.S. flag. Horizontally, the flag was broken into three stripes—red at bottom and top, and white in the middle. A blue canton on the staff end included a star for each member state of the CSA (Coski 2005).

The similarity of the First Flag of the Confederacy to the U.S. national flag soon created problems on battlefields since the flags could be mistaken for one another at a distance. As a result, in May 1863 a new flag was created by the Confederate Congress and referred to as the "Stainless Banner." This Second Flag of the Confederacy was almost entirely white with the exception of a canton that included the familiar battle flag emblem. While some discussions of the flag suggest its white field was "emblematic of the purity of the Cause which it represented" (Cannon 1988, 19), other contemporaneous comments in the CSA indicate the flag's white field was also interpreted in both a religious and a racial manner. In 1863 the *Savannah Morning News,* for example, argued that the flag's white field indicated that "we are fighting to maintain the Heaven-ordained supremacy of the white man over the inferior colored race" and that the new flag would be "hailed as the WHITE MAN's FLAG" (Bonner 2002, 116; Coski 2005, 17–18). Still other interpretations of the Stainless Banner's symbolism were largely if not entirely religious in theme and orientation. This religious theme was strongly reinforced because one of the flag's first uses shortly after its adoption was to drape the coffin at the funeral of Confederate general Stonewall Jackson (Cannon 1988, 19–20). As stated by Bonner (2002, 116), Jackson was "a leader associated far less with slaveholding than with Presbyterian piety." Additionally, there were popular songs written about the Stainless Banner, including "The Star Spangled Cross and the Pure Field of White," which built on the flag's association with religious purity and Christianity (ibid., 116–17). But it is also quite true that religion and race were commonly mixed during the period (Webster 1997; Sebesta and Hague 2002), and it is likely that both race and religion played a role in the Stainless Banner's design and interpretation owing to the dominance of white in its construction.

Problems quickly became apparent with the use of the Stainless Banner on the battlefield—on windless days the flag could be interpreted as a white flag of surrender. As a result, the "final edition" of the CSA's national flag was adopted in March 1865. Somewhat smaller in dimensions, the Third National Flag of the Confederacy added a red vertical stripe to the fly end of the design of the Stainless Banner to avoid being mistaken for a flag of surrender (Cannon 1988). But it is also the case that the flag continued to reflect the Stainless Banner's emphasis on the religious or racial "purity" of the Confederate cause.

Because of the problems associated with the Confederate national flags, by the end of 1861 the Confederate battle emblem had become increasingly common on Civil War battlefields. In light of its notoriety, it is important to note that the battle flag was never the official flag of the CSA. Referred to as the "Southern Cross" or "Starry Cross," the design of the Confederate battle flag is based on St. Andrew's Cross, St. Andrew being the patron saint of Scotland (Hague 2002). Though sometimes referred to as an "X," the symbol is based on the configuration of the decussate cross on which Saint Andrew was reportedly crucified. This flag's designer, Confederate congressman William Porcher Miles (1872), favored this design of the battle flag because "It avoided the *religious* objections about the cross (from the Jews and many Protestant sects), because it did not stand out *so conspicuously* as if the cross had been placed upright" (Beauregard 1872). Thus, there are implicit if not explicit religious overtones to the design of the Confederate battle flag. It is also clearly the case that the Confederate battle flag has become the most recognizable symbol of the short-lived CSA.

The visibility of the Confederate battle flag has been promoted in various ways since the end of the Civil War. In the latter half of the nineteenth century the battle flag was common at Confederate soldier reunions and other celebrations honoring the memory of the "Lost Cause" (Leib and Webster 2007). After the turn of the twentieth century, the notoriety of the battle flag increased substantially as movie producers released a number of films with Civil War themes, including *The Birth of a Nation* in 1915 and *Gone With the Wind* in 1939 (Chadwick 2001). As a result, the battle flag became increasingly acceptable, and was flown by American regiments from the South in different parts of the world during World War II. Public recognition of the battle flag grew substantially as a result of the Democratic Party's national convention in 1948. As a result of various civil rights proposals, many southern state delegations walked out of the convention hall waving the battle flag (Barnard 1985). Later in the summer of 1948, Strom Thurmond was nominated as the presidential candidate of the Dixiecrat Party in Birmingham, Alabama, with the signature symbol of the convention being the Confederate battle flag. The racist themes composing the agenda of the Dixiecrats and their widespread use of the battle flag led it to become the consensus symbol for those wishing to demonstrate their opposition to civil rights initiatives.

The association between those opposing improved civil rights for African Americans and the flag grew substantially after the Supreme Court's 1954 decision in *Brown v. the Board of Education of Topeka, Kansas* (37 U.S. 483 [1954]) and its finding that "separate but equal" educational facilities for black and white children were unconstitutional. In the wake of the *Brown* decision, groups such as the Ku Klux Klan used the flag as a symbol of their opposition to integration, and it became directly associated with the often violent racism of such hate organizations (Webster and Leib 2008). Some state governments also furthered the perceived relationship between the battle flag and those opposing the civil rights movement. For example, in 1963, rabid segregationist Governor George Wallace raised the battle flag over the Alabama state capitol immediately prior to a visit by Attorney General Robert F. Kennedy to discuss the desegregation of the University of Alabama (Clark 1993). It should be noted that Montgomery served as the first capital of the CSA, and its first president, Jefferson Davis, took the oath of office on the steps of the Alabama state capitol.

Alabama was not the only state during the civil rights era to fly the Confederate battle flag. In Mississippi, the battle emblem was added to the state flag by the state legislature in 1894. In 1956 the Georgia state legislature incorporated the Confederate battle emblem into the design of its state flag, while in 1962 the South Carolina state legislature raised the battle flag over the state capitol dome in Columbia. Over the past fifteen years, heated debates have occurred in all four states concerning whether the state government should sanction the flying of the Confederate battle flag (Leib, Webster, and Webster 2000; Leib and Webster 2002, 2004). In both Alabama and South Carolina, the flag has been removed from the top of the state capitol dome and placed in historical context at Confederate memorials on the grounds of the capital (Webster and Leib 2001, 2002). In 2001, Georgia governor Roy Barnes, backed by African American legislators and the state's business community, led a successful effort to remove the battle emblem from the state flag (Leib 1995; Leib and Webster 2007). In Mississippi, a 2001 referendum to remove the battle emblem from the state flag was defeated by a two-to-one margin (Leib and Webster 2003).

Race and Southern Identity

How do race and religion combine to influence the diametrically opposed views of the Confederate battle flag as a southern symbol? While it might be suggested that the emotional attachment to the South by black and white southerners differs, this supposition is contradicted by polls that find that more than 90 percent of both groups feel pride in their "southern heritage" (Associated Press 1994). Arguably, the ongoing and large in-migration of African Americans from the North and Midwest to the South substantiates this emotional attachment. The parents, grandparents, and great-grandparents of many of these in-migrants left the region in the first half of the twentieth century in search of greater freedoms and opportunities in other parts of the United States (Frey 2004).

Despite similar levels of strong positive attachment to the region, black and white southerners interpret many "southern" symbols in contrasting fashion as a result of their different understandings of the region's history and what they define as "southern" (Cobb 1999). Indeed, black and white southerners arguably constitute two separate "nations" that have long inhabited the same region. Because of slavery in the eighteenth and nineteenth centuries and the Jim Crow system of segregation in the twentieth century, during much of the South's history blacks and whites operated in parallel social, economic, and political environments, with only limited or superficial interaction. Thus, it should not be surprising that black and white southerners would come to define their "southern" cultural identities quite differently (Webster and Leib 2001).

While some have suggested that the South should identify and adopt cultural symbols acceptable to both blacks and whites (e.g., Wilson 1995), it seems certain the Confederate battle flag will never be such a symbol. Edward Ayers (1996, 79) argues that the "Confederate flag is a topic of such debate and divisiveness in the South today because it denies all that black and white Southerners share, because it reduces the South to a one-time and one-sided political identity." To most black southerners that "political identity" is clearly the antebellum South and its slave-cotton-plantation economy. In short, the Confederate battle flag defines "southernness" exclusively as "white Confederate southernness." Thus, it is not surprising that Lee Collins, head of the Georgia Committee to Save the State Flag, argued during the Georgia state flag debates of the early 1990s that the battle flag "symbolizes everything that Southerners fight for, Southern heritage, Southern pride, Southern dignity and self-government. This is a true symbol of the Confederacy. . . . [It] does not represent any form of bigotry" (quoted in Leib 1995, 44). Although Collins assumes he is speaking for southerners generally, he is specifically championing the perspective of many traditional white southerners, which has dominated southern outlooks and political debates for most of the region's history.

Critical Race Theory and Whiteness

The concept of "whiteness" is helpful to explain Collins's apparent lack of understanding of black southern contrasting interpretations of the meaning of the Confederate battle flag (see also Gordon, this volume). Conceptually, white people operate as a cultural group, although few whites see themselves as members of such a coherent subdivision. Rather, white people see themselves as the unraced societal standard by which other racialized groups are evaluated, most often as different and lacking (e.g., Frankenberg 1997; Wray and Newitz 1997; Bonnett 2000). Because white culture is both dominant and centered in the United States—and thereby conflated in public narratives with *Americanness*—people of color find it difficult to fully participate in a more complete and accurate definition of American culture.

While whiteness theory is of relatively recent origins, some of its basic tenets and perspectives have been noted for more than a century. For example, in his classic 1903 book *The Souls of Black Folks*, W. E. B. Du Bois (2003, 5) writes of the "double consciousness" of African Americans and that the "American world" "only lets him see himself through the revelation of the other world," in a clear reference to white America. Thus, "One ever feels his twoness,—an American, a

Negro; two souls, two thoughts, two un-reconciled strivings; two warring ideals in one dark body, whose dogged strength alone keeps it from being torn asunder" (ibid., 5). Du Bois (6) goes on to state that

> The history of the American Negro is the history of this strife,—this longing to attain self-conscious manhood, to merge his double self into a better and truer self. In this merging he wishes neither of the older selves be lost. He would not Africanize America, for America has too much to teach the world and Africa. He would not bleach his Negro soul in a flood of white Americanism, for he knows that Negro blood has a message for the world. He simply wishes to make it possible for a man to be both a Negro and an American.

Similarly, in 1945 Lillian Smith wrote an essay titled "Addressed to White Liberals" in which she contended the so-called "Negro problem" was really a white problem. As she argued,

> We have looked at the "Negro problem" long enough. Now the time has come for us to right-about-face and study the problem of the white man: the deep-rooted needs that have caused him to seek those strange regressive satisfactions that are derived from worshipping his own skin color. The white man himself is one of the world's most urgent problems today; not the Negro, not the other colored races. We whites must learn to confess this. (484)

Clearly, both Du Bois and Smith recognized the centered character of whiteness in the definition of Americanness and the challenges for people of color to be accepted as full participants in American society.

The Confederate battle flag debate reflects the centered character of white southern culture in the region. Confederate battle flag supporters assume that white southern culture *is* the "regional culture" and cannot comprehend why black southerners do not feel a strong emotional attachment to such "southern" symbols (Webster and Leib 2001; Leib and Webster 2002). For example, the following exchange took place during a 1993 panel discussion moderated by Georgia governor Zell Miller over whether to remove the battle emblem from the state's flag. Charles Walker was an African American Georgia state senator and Lee Collins was the earlier quoted head of the Georgia Committee to Save the State Flag. The exchange clearly indicates that Collins defines southern culture as white Confederate culture, and questions the "southernness" of those not in agreement.

CHARLES WALKER: As a black senator who's very proud of the state of Georgia, can you
   tell me why I should salute and honor the . . . flag of Georgia?
LEE COLLINS: I don't expect everybody—
WALKER: I represent 30 percent of this state's population. Why should I—
COLLINS: I don't expect everybody to have the same connection to Southern heritage as
   Southerners do.
(Crowd Noise)
ZELL MILLER: Let's have some order.
COLLINS: I understand that you have a reason, perhaps, for feeling offended by the flag,
   and the black population of the state of Georgia may have their reasons for feeling
   offended by the Confederate battle flag.
   I contend there are more important issues to be worrying about. For example, I
   was contacted by several black legislators who told me they supported keeping the
   current flag, but not for the same reasons that Southerners do. Southerners want to
   salute the flag and honor the flag because of their heritage.
REPORTER: Are you suggesting that black Georgians are not Southerners?
COLLINS: No, not at all. I don't know what his origin is—
WALKER: I am an African American born in Georgia. I am the great-grandson of former
   slaves. Should I not have a flag that you and I can share in the Southern heritage . . .
(Applause)
COLLINS: If I honestly thought it was possible to find a flag that everybody in the state
   of Georgia would be proud of, you might have a valid point. (Associated Press 1993)

Many southern whites see the battle flag as an inclusive southern symbol
rather than an exclusive symbol of white southernness. This myopic view results
directly from the manner in which white privilege works—that is, it inhibits the
recognition and understanding that the flag has a racially exclusive history. While
"whiteness" studies indicate that white people tend to see themselves as unraced
in a racialized world, clearly, some whites are obsessive about their whiteness.
As Colin Flint (2004, 2) notes, the "'whiteness' that is usually invisible in mainstream (white) thought and practice is very much to the forefront of the extreme
right." For neo-Confederate groups such as the League of the South, there is an
obsession with the region as a white Christian nation, and they support secession from the United States to create (or, in their mind, to preserve) the purity
of their "nation" (Potok 2000). Thus, the League of the South website (2005)
states that "the League of the South proudly displays the Confederate flags of our
ancestors solely to symbolize our desire to re-establish the Southern nation as a
free and independent Confederacy of sovereign states and to protect and defend
the traditional culture of the South." Rejecting the claim that the flag is a symbol

of racism and hatred, the League's website also makes clear who belongs to the southern nation: "We of the League of the South steadfastly reject the crass bigotry that drives this ceaseless campaign of cultural genocide against the revered Anglo-Celtic symbols of the South." The League of the South has constructed and mythologized its vision of the South as a culturally cohesive white Christian nation directly descended from immigrants hailing from the Celtic area of the British Isles and especially Scotland. This connection to Scotland is highlighted, if not continually reinforced, by the neo-Confederate movement's reference to the battle flag as the St. Andrew's Cross, given its resemblance to the flag of Scotland. Arguably, a flag associated with Scotland is more saleable and defensible than one symbolic of the Confederacy's efforts in the Civil War. By definition, African American southerners are all but excluded from this conception of the region (Webster 2004; Hague, Giordano, and Sebesta 2005). Given the white supremacist ideology that one can read into the second and third national flags of the Confederacy, it is not surprising that the League of the South has now adopted the third national flag as its own.

Religion, Political Culture, and Southern Identity

Religion has also long been intertwined with white southern views of the Civil War generally, and more recently in the many debates pertaining to the Confederate battle flag. As a result, religion has had a central if not dominant role in shaping the political life and political culture of the American South (Elazar 1994; Webster 1997). Early in the region's history of white settlement, high-intensity evangelical and fundamentalist Protestant denominations, including Baptists, rose to prominence (Webster 2000). Charles Reagan Wilson (2005, 9) points out that "evangelical Protestants have been deeply tied to dominant southern cultural styles and traditions, at the very center of a regional context that defined parameters for private selves and public identities." Thus, while the primary impact of the South's traditionalist political culture is the maintenance of the region's social, political, and economic hierarchies, fundamentalist theology often views revisionist threats to this status quo "as creeping 'liberalism' which taints that which is 'normal', traditional and thus 'Godly'" (Webster 1997, 153). Both the region's conservative religiosity and its political culture are therefore resistant to any change that would alter the traditional order. As a result, many traditional white southerners view their "southern" cultural identity in near-religious terms. As Wilson (2005, 23) suggests, "Southern identity today resides most clearly among white conservatives and African Americans, with religion at the core of that identity." To some white southerners, their southern identity is "a spiritual condition, like being a Catholic or a Jew" (Cobb 1999, 147). In keeping with this assertion, Wilson (2005, 23–24) quotes one southerner, who argues that being a southerner is a "way of life," with religion being "central to that way of life."

Explanations of the South's reasons for entering the Civil War became highly intertwined with the region's religiosity in the nineteenth century. Slavery was frequently viewed in biblical terms, as God's plan to Christianize Africans, and as both natural and civilizing. Some viewed the Bible as having created a social hierarchy including God, men, women, children, and slaves, and variation from this societal order as being paramount to a rejection of God (Webster 1997). The Reverend Richard Furman, for whom South Carolina's Furman University is named, penned a biblical defense of slavery in 1822 titled "Exposition of the Views of the Baptists Relative to the Colored Population of the United States in a Communication to the Governor of South Carolina" (Rosenberg 1989). As the Civil War approached, there were growing differences of opinion about the morality of slavery within some national religious organizations. As a result, the South's two largest denominations, the Baptists and the Methodists, split from their national organizations in the 1840s because of sectional controversies over the issue of slavery (Webster 2000). But for many white southerners at the time, the North was an antibiblical enemy, and secession from the Union and the war itself had religious necessity (Sebesta and Hague 2002). "Ministers and churches . . . insisted that the Confederacy was a crusade against the evil empire of the Yankee. It was a holy war" (Wilson 1995, 19).

Prior to the Civil War, slaves in the South were generally prohibited from forming their own organizations, including religious institutions. As a result, slaves were allowed if not encouraged to attend and worship in white churches, with segregated sections such as balconies set aside for their use. During the chaos of the Civil War, many African Americans left predominantly white churches to form their own congregations (Lincoln and Mamiya 1990). After the war's conclusion many more freedmen were forced out of white churches, and southern religious institutions became highly segregated lest they appear to support "racial equality." As stated by Rosenberg (1989, 39), "This expulsion was very much a part of preparation for the legal segregation that was to come," a reference to the subsequent implementation of the Jim Crow system of racial segregation in the latter decades of the nineteenth century.

The military defeat of the Confederacy created a crisis in the South's religious justifications for secession and the conduct of the bloody conflict itself. Had God abandoned them? Had their efforts to meet biblical demands of conduct been insufficient? Or had they simply been wrong about the righteousness of their cause? Wilson (1995, 20) concludes that "Southerners came to believe that God had not abandoned them but instead chastised them, in preparation for a greater destiny in the future." With such an explanation, the mythology of the Lost Cause of the Confederacy was born and became a "functioning religion" in the white South (Wilson 1980, 1995; Manis 2005). This Lost Cause "civil religion" cultivated a "holy" trinity of saints comprising Confederate president Jefferson Davis and Generals Robert E. Lee and Stonewall Jackson. Of the three, Lee clearly became the "white South's favorite icon" (McPherson 1996, 151). Connelly (1977, 3) notes that after the Civil War, Robert E. Lee became a "God figure for [his native] Virginia, [and] a saint for the white Protestant South" generally.

This Lost Cause "holy trinity" was memorialized on the landscape across the South beginning in the latter decades of the nineteenth century and well into the twentieth century. Included among these memorializations were the statues of Lee, Jackson, and Davis on Monument Avenue in Richmond, Virginia, and carvings of the three on the side of Georgia's Stone Mountain (Essex 2002; Leib 2002). Wilson (1995, 21) suggests that in this Lost Cause civil religion, white "southerners were told that they were different and that difference had religious significance. . . . [They] saw religious significance in the Confederate nationalist experience in particular and in regional culture in general." And as Manis (2005, 166) notes, the "Confederate battle flag, of course, constituted the southern civil religion's most sacred object."

Race, Religion, and Support for the Confederate Battle Flag

An explanation of the passionate defense of the Confederate battle flag by some white southerners as symbolic of the integrity of their culture is aided by an understanding of the conflation of Confederate myth and symbols with the region's fundamentalist religious practices. Neo-Confederate groups have been particularly purposeful in bringing religious arguments and symbolism into the debate over the Confederate battle flag (Webster and Leib 2008). From their vantage point, as well as that of many less nationalistic white southerners, the Civil War was first and foremost a theological conflict to defend the purity of Christianity (Sebesta and Hague 2002). The neo-Confederates' views on race relations, religion, and the Confederate battle flag suggest that Paul Harvey's (2005) concept of "theological racism" still exists within a segment of white southern society. Theological racism refers to "the conscious use of religious doctrine and practice to create and enforce social hierarchies" (Harvey 2005, 2), and seems highly pertinent to the efforts of some neo-Confederate groups. For example, Dr. Michael Hill, neo-Confederate activist and founder of the League of the South, argued that the Confederacy entered the Civil War because "it chose to fight Northern [biblical] apostasy rather than submit to an unbiblical world" and that the "distinguishing characteristic of our Confederate ancestors was, without doubt, their Christian faith" (quoted in Webster 2004, 150). Because the battle flag is the pre-eminent symbol of the Lost Cause civil religion, defenses of the flag take on the character of a religious crusade. Hill (n.d.), for example, has stated that the Confederate battle flag is symbolic of "Christian liberty." Railing against those who wish to remove the battle flag from the region's landscape, neo-Confederate *cause célèbre* and restaurateur Maurice Bessinger (2001, xxi) goes so far as to claim that the battle flag is the "cross of God" and that "God can not be happy about this!" Thus, it is no accident that the cover of Bessinger's 2001 autobiography, *Defending My Heritage,* includes pictures of both the battle flag and the Bible.

Two additional examples of the intertwining of neo-Confederate views on religion and the flag are provided by John Weaver and John Thomas Cripps, both Christian clergymen associated with the neo-Confederate movement. John Weaver, a graduate of Greenville, South Carolina's Bob Jones University, served as chaplain to the Sons of Confederate Veterans from 2000 through 2004. He is the author of the pamphlet *The Truth about the Confederate Flag,* which provides a biblical defense of the flag and argues that it is symbolic of Christian government. Clinging to the commonly invoked but highly problematic contention of the dominance of the Scots and the Scots-Irish in the origins of the white Confederate South and within its culture over time (Hague, Beirich, and Sebesta 2008), Weaver (n.d.) argues,

> The Confederate Battle Flag is based upon the national flag of Scotland. The national flag of Scotland is the cross of St. Andrew and the cross of St. Andrew is a symbol of the Christian faith and heritage of the Celtic race. In fact, another name for the Confederate Battle Flag is the Southern Cross. It was adopted consciously, purposefully, elaborately and premeditatedly in order to display faith in the sovereign God of heaven and earth, faith in the providence of that God, the God of history and the God of salvation.

It should be noted that Weaver is also the author of the apologist pamphlet titled *A Biblical View of Slavery.* The pamphlet was being sold in Maurice Bessinger's South Carolina chain of barbecue restaurants and was a principal factor leading to what is now an eight-year boycott of his chain (Webster and Leib 2008). This view is not uncommon among traditional white southerners. For example, in 1996, Alabama state representative Charles Davidson used biblical passages in a speech in the state house's chambers to justify slavery. Davidson argued that those who disagreed with him "are obviously bitter and hateful against God and his word, because they reject what God says and embrace what mere humans say concerning slavery." Davidson also suggested that the descendants of Africans enslaved who embrace Christianity "are most grateful today" (quoted in Webster 1997, 158).

In the early 2000s, the Reverend John Thomas Cripps was president of the Mississippi chapter of the League of the South. He was also a leading battle flag defender and a key figure in the Mississippi state flag debate of 2001. In 2000, Cripps announced his candidacy for the governorship of Mississippi in the 2003 election, running for the nomination of the Southern Party, a secessionist political party formed by the neo-Confederate League of the South in 1999. The press release announcing his candidacy began by stating that "the campaign of ethnic cleansing against Mississippi and the entire South has increased at a disturbing and rapid pace since the inauguration of Governor Ronnie Musgrove" in January 2000. (Musgrove had proposed removing the battle emblem from the state flag once the state supreme court ruled that Mississippi had no official flag, owing to an oversight during an earlier revision of the state's constitution.) Cripps provided seven pieces of evidence for his claim that there was an ongoing "campaign of ethnic cleansing" in Mississippi, all involving challenges to the battle flag. To these challenges, Cripps (2000) responded,

> True Mississippians say: "Enough is Enough!" It's time to free Mississippi from the clutches of big government, big business, big media, and big religion, all of which are complicit in this campaign of ethnic cleansing and cultural genocide. These forces "alien to our Sovereign State" are strangling the life out of our traditional Christian civilization.

That Cripps intertwines religion with the battle flag should not be too surprising because he is also the pastor of Lumberton, Mississippi's Confederate Presbyterian Church, which Cripps refers to as "a denomination in progress" (quoted in Wagster 2000). The Southern Poverty Law Center (2001) notes that in his sermons, "Cripps preaches the virtues of Southern secession."

The foregoing discussion should not be interpreted to mean that only ideological fringe groups view the battle flag as a religious symbol. The Lost Cause civil religion of the white South has evolved over time. In the 1950s and 1960s, the civil rights movement helped spark a backlash revival of the white Lost Cause civil religion that was strongly segregationist, accepted segregation as part of God's plan, and viewed the division as critical for America to fulfill its religious destiny (Manis 2005). Under such a challenge it is arguably not surprising that white southerners adopted the Confederate battle flag as a holy symbol and used it as their "battle flag" in the massive resistance against the civil rights movement and the forces of integration and inclusion.

Manis (2005) argues that since the 1970s, the white South's civil religious struggle against regional social change and pluralism has grown into a national conflict. Conservatives from other parts of the United States have joined southern whites out of their fear that rapid changes generally in American society in recent decades have led to a lessening of their control over society. Thus, the United States has experienced a series of "culture wars" over issues such as the media, abortion rights, the teaching of evolution in public schools, and gay rights. As Manis (2005, 179) argues, however, "For contemporary Southerners, perhaps the most hotly contested battleground of the culture wars remains how to deal with the region's Confederate past . . . [and] . . . no segment of this larger concern is more controversial than debates about the Confederate flag." Placing the battle over the flag within the context of the culture wars, Manis (2005, 179) suggests that "this issue relates directly to the most wrenching culture war of nineteenth-century America, the Civil War, and touches upon symbolic meanings of both America and the Confederate South. Because it does, the battle elevates the emotional temperature wherever and whenever it is joined."

In this context, many of the region's whites, and not just those who belong to neo-Confederate groups, interpret efforts to remove the Confederate battle emblem as another aspect of their loss of control over the region and the further erosion of a way of life. It is also important to note that more mainstream white religious leaders have also been involved in defending the flag. For example, after South Carolina governor David Beasley's call to remove the Confederate battle flag from atop the state house dome in 1996, Beasley was "immediately accused of 'heresy' and being controlled by the 'scourge of political correctness' as 'propagated by liberal intellectuals and their allies in the media' by a group of 16 conservative Christian pastors" (quoted in Webster and Leib 2001, 278). An "interdenominational coalition of pastors" in South Carolina sharply criticized Beasley, issuing a document titled "A Moral Defense of the Confederate Flag" (Moffitt 1997; Sebesta and Hague 2002). The group argued that the flag "is not a symbol of racism, and that the Civil War had less to do with defending slavery than the desire of Southerners to 'resist the federal government's unconstitutional efforts to subjugate sovereign states'" (Moffitt 1997). The ministers strongly suggested that the conflict was also a religious war, arguing that the Civil War was between Confederate Christianity, namely, "the friends of order and regulated freedom," and Union "atheists, socialists, communists, red republicans, [and] Jacobins" (quoted in Sebesta and Hague 2002, 270). "One of the leaders of the group, Pastor Bobby Eubanks of a Southern Baptist church near Charleston, was highly critical of efforts to remove the flag, claiming it was a 'shallow Promise Keepers'-style theology' of racial reconciliation" (quoted in Moffitt 1997).

In Mississippi as well, religious leaders and religiosity became intertwined with the defense of the flag during the 2001 state flag referendum campaign. Along with the very visible role played by John Thomas Cripps in defending the battle flag, the pastor of the Biloxi Christian Church stated publicly, "I am against changing the flag to appease a group of people based on their ignorance of the Civil War." Notably, he also acknowledged that not removing the emblem could lead to an economic boycott of the state (quoted in Schoenberger 2001). Combining religiosity and whiteness, one long-time resident of Mississippi told the state's largest newspaper during the 2001 campaign to the change the state flag, "I don't think we should change something we hold sacred just to make a point to (Northerners). . . . I don't believe in turning over to what the colored people want. We've got our rights, too" (quoted in Schoenberger 2001).

Religion has been tactically interjected into the Confederate flag debates as well. A prime example comes from Georgia Republican state representative James Mills. In 2001, Mills, an ordained Baptist minister, was a little-known white legislator from rural north Georgia. In the 2001 Georgia house debate over changing the state flag to minimize the battle emblem, Mills introduced an amendment to the bill that would have added the U.S. motto "In God We Trust" to the proposed flag. Given the state's religious orientation, the amendment passed. However, despite proposing and voting for the amendment to add the motto, Mills then turned around and voted against the bill to adopt the new flag (which now included the motto he had proposed). While Mills stated that he was not a passionate battle flag defender, he noted that many of his constituents were, and he had pledged not to vote to change the flag. As to why he therefore proposed the amendment in the first place, he responded, "I thought it [the proposed flag] was going to pass and I tried to make it as good as I could, even though I was opposed to it." To those who thought the flag would be too visually complicated with the additional motto, Mills responded that if the flag is "too busy to include 'In God We Trust', then maybe we need to slow down" (quoted in Pettys 2001). Mills's amendment to add God to the new flag while actually opposing the new flag proved ironic. Democratic House floor leaders pushing for passage of the new flag suggested that the addition of the motto may have secured the additional votes necessary for passage of the new flag in the legislative chamber (Pettys 2001).

Race, Religion, and Opposition to the Confederate Battle Flag

Of course, not only did a white civil religion in the South develop after the Civil War, so also did a black civil religion. As Andrew Manis (2005, 167) suggests, the central focus of postbellum black civil religion was "by forcing America to come to terms with racial difference, by pushing America towards racial equality, African Americans helped fulfill both the nation's and their own destinies." Southern black civil religion became revitalized during the mid-twentieth-century civil rights movement. As Manis (2005, 167) argues, the "Civil Rights Movement can be understood as a revitalization of a black civil religion, which heightened both the providential understanding of American history and the particular role of black America within that history." Central to this civil religion, black southerners viewed the end of segregation as the goal for their hopes for the country and its perceived destiny to provide an example that all peoples can live in harmony.

Given southern black civil religion's goals of ending racial divisions in the South, it is not surprising that black religious groups have pressed for boycotts to try to force the region's state governments to remove the Confederate battle flag from public spaces. From their collective perspective, the battle flag constitutes the ultimate symbol of racism, hatred, and racial division. Among black religious groups taking the lead in these efforts were the national Southern Christian Leadership Conference and various chapters of the SCLC in the region (the SCLC was begun by the Reverend Martin Luther King Jr. as a civil rights organization in the 1950s). In response to an economic boycott of South Carolina called for by the NAACP in 1999, three leading black American churches, the African Methodist Episcopal Church, the African Methodist Episcopal Zion Church, and the Progressive National Baptist Convention, all relocated or canceled events scheduled to be held in the state (National Council of Churches 2000). In response to Governor Beasley's 1997 call to remove the flag from the top of the South Carolina state house, "more than 700 ministers of the Baptist Education and Missionary Convention of South Carolina, the state's largest black Baptist organization, called for the flag's removal" (Moffitt 1997).

Moderate, predominantly white religious groups have also entered the region's flag debates. In the Mississippi controversy, many moderate religious leaders came out in favor of removing the battle emblem from the state flag. In December 2000, religious leaders of the state's Catholic, Episcopal, and United Methodist denominations announced they would work toward the adoption of a new state flag because "whatever symbolic meaning one may choose to attach to the Confederate emblem, it is clear that the continued use of our present flag will not unite us for good but will continue to foster division and cripple our future" (quoted in Sawyer 2000). Their position was endorsed by the Mississippi Religious Leadership Conference, a statewide interdenominational group of religious leaders that was organized in the 1960s to rebuild African American churches burned down during the civil rights movement. The Mississippi Religious Leadership Conference (2000) argued that a new flag would allow Mississippians to "make a strong statement and witness within our state and to the rest of the our nation that Mississippi no longer upholds racism and prejudice as commonly held values, and that racism and hatred will not be honored or embraced." The student government at Baptist-affiliated Mississippi College voted by a two-to-one margin to support the new flag. In reference to the vote, a student leader stated that as "a Christian institution, I think we have a particular responsibility to serve as a source of unity in a state that has been so badly divided" (quoted in Kanengiser 2001).

However, such sentiments were not held by all members of the state's religious communities. For example, conspicuously absent from the initial call by religious leaders were those from Mississippi's Southern Baptist Convention, the largest denomination in the state. Of the thirty-eight members signing the Mississippi Religious Leadership Conference letter, only three were Southern Baptists, compared with two Jews, a far smaller religious group in the state, though this is not to suggest that all Southern Baptists opposed the removal of government sanctions for flying the battle emblem. In 2001, the president of the Southern Baptist Convention, a Georgian, endorsed the minimization of the battle emblem in that state's flag (Barnes 2001). In fact, at least one conservative Christian group did endorse the removal of the battle emblem from the Mississippi state flag. The Reverend Don Wildmon, leader of the 40,000-member American Family Association, headquartered in Tupelo, Mississippi, called for Mississippians to vote for the new flag "in part to silence critics who equate Southern pride with racism" (Associated Press 2001). In calling for the flag change, however, Wildmon noted that "At times we have been left with the impression that anyone who votes against the new flag [removing the battle emblem] is a racist. I don't believe that" (quoted in Associated Press 2001).

Possibly the most surprising religious ally of those seeking to lower the battle flag in South Carolina was Bob Jones III, the president of Bob Jones University. In October 1999, in the wake of the NAACP's announced boycott of the state, Jones called for the flag to be removed from the state house dome in Columbia (Burritt 1999). Jones argued that "The Bible speaks against giving unnecessary offense. If the flag, where it is, is an offense to some, their feelings should be addressed." The neo-Confederate Council of Conservative Citizens immediately criticized

Jones's position, stating that "Bob Jones has made a pact with the devil" (quoted in Davenport 1999).

Conclusion

In this essay we have demonstrated the intertwining roles of religion and race in the vitriolic debates over the meanings and display of the Confederate battle flag in the American South. The intertwining of race and religion in the region is not new, and predates the Civil War, with white southerners using the Bible to justify slavery as part of God's plan to Christianize Africa. The Civil War itself was frequently viewed as a religious crusade against perceived northern biblical apostasy and the "evil Yankee." Because the Confederate battle flag became the central icon of the Confederate South, it became imbued with layered racial and religious meanings that are now all but impossible to separate. To many southern whites it became emblematic of the perceived Christian righteousness of the antebellum South, while to African American southerners it symbolized slavery in the nineteenth century and the racism of the Jim Crow system in the twentieth century. With the segregation of white and black churches, religion further played a central role in the twentieth-century's civil rights movement, with black clergy assuming leadership positions and viewing efforts to end segregation as a Christian duty. The preeminent symbol used to oppose their efforts was the Confederate battle flag. As a result, religion not only privileges white racial projects (Winant 2004) but is intertwined with race on both sides of the debates over the meaning and significance of the region's Confederate legacy. Thus, as Manis (2005) points out, this legacy led to the development of two racialized civil religions, one black and one white.

We conclude with a final thought that illustrates how, given the importance of religion in the South, religious imagery is central to the arguments supporting both sides of the Confederate battle flag debate. Because of the strong Christian religiosity of the South, in the early 2000s a favorite question to ask before making a difficult decision was "What would Jesus do?" Not surprisingly, politicians have invoked Jesus' name during the flag debates. In his 2001 speech imploring the state senate to minimize the battle emblem on the state flag, Georgia governor Roy Barnes told the body he had received a letter from a respected former state senator that, as Barnes (2001) noted, "contained these wise words: 'People of faith must be guided by a moral compass that goes beyond political expedience. The Christian faith may ask "What would Jesus do?" about the state flag. I believe Jesus would change the flag to unite people.'"

However, the impact of the white South's civil religion on the Confederate flag debate may have been best addressed by Georgia state representative Bobby Franklin, the legislature's leading battle flag defender. In 2003, Franklin had a change of heart about his support for the battle emblem remaining on the Georgia state flag and proposed an entirely new flag for adoption. Franklin's new flag did not contain the Confederate battle emblem but instead closely resembled the first national flag of the Confederacy (the Stars and Bars). In 2003, Franklin's proposed flag was adopted by the state legislature and signed into law by the governor, and currently flies as the Georgia state flag. In Franklin's speech initially proposing his new flag to the Georgia state House of Representatives, rather than asking "What would Jesus do?" about the appropriateness of having the Confederate battle emblem as part of the state flag, Franklin instead asked, "What would Robert E. Lee Do?" (quoted in Leib and Webster 2006).

References

Associated Press. 1993. "Why Should I Honor the Flag of Georgia?" *Athens Daily News*, January 29, 1.

———. 1994. "Most Southerners Proud of Heritage." *Tuscaloosa News*, February 8.

———. 2001. "Conservative Leader Backs New Flag." *Biloxi Sun-Herald*, February 4.

Ayers, E. L. 1996. "What We Talk About When We Talk About the South." In *All Over the Map: Rethinking American Regions*, ed. E. L. Ayers, P. N. Limerick, S. Nissenbaum, and P. S. Onuf, 62–82. Baltimore, MD: Johns Hopkins University Press.

Barnard, W. D. 1985. *Dixiecrats and Democrats*. Tuscaloosa: University of Alabama Press.

Barnes, R. 2001. "Gov. Barnes Speech to the Georgia Senate." *Atlanta Business Chronicle*, January 30.

Beauregard, G. T. 1872. "The Green Table." *Southern Magazine* 3 (4): 506–9.

Beirich, H., and B. Moser. 2003. "Outfitting Dixie." *Intelligence Report*, Summer. Montgomery, AL: Southern Poverty Law Center.

Bessinger, M. 2001. *Defending My Heritage: The Maurice Bessinger Story*. West Columbia, SC: Lmbone-Lehone Publishing Co.

Bonner, R. E. 2002. *Colors & Blood: Flag Passions of the Confederate South*. Princeton, NJ: Princeton University Press.

Bonnett, A. 2000. *White Identities: Historical and International Perspectives*. Harlow, UK: Prentice Hall.

Burritt, C. 1999. "Flag Dispute Puts S.C. Governor in Crossfire." Associated Press, October 29.

Cannon, D. D. 1988. *The Flags of the Confederacy: An Illustrated History*. Memphis, TN: St. Luke's Press.

———. 2002. "Failed Contestants for the First Confederate Flag." February–March 1861. http://www.confederateflags.org/national/FOTCbm1a.htm.

Chadwick, B. 2001. *The Reel Civil War: Mythmaking in American Film*. New York: Alfred A. Knopf.

Clark, E. C. 1993. *The Schoolhouse Door: Segregation's Last Stand at the University of Alabama*. New York: Oxford University Press.

Cobb, J. C. 1999. *Redefining Southern Culture*. Athens: University of Georgia Press.

Connelly, T. L. 1977. *The Marble Man: Robert E. Lee and His Image in American Society*. Baton Rouge: Louisiana State University Press.

Coski, J. M. 2005. *The Confederate Battle Flag: America's Most Embattled Emblem.* Cambridge, MA: Belknap Press of Harvard University Press.

Cripps, J. T. 2000. "Mississippi League of the South State Chairman, John Thomas Cripps, Announces Bid for Governor." Press release, May 8. Copy available from authors.

Davenport, J. 1999. "Hodges Meets with Business, Legislative Leaders." Associated Press, October 29.

Du Bois, W. E. B. 2003. *The Souls of Black Folks,* Centennial Edition. New York: Modern Library. First published 1903.

Elazar, D. J. 1994. *The American Mosaic.* Boulder, CO: Westview Press.

Essex, J. 2002. "The Real South Starts Here: Whiteness, the Confederacy and Commodification at Stone Mountain." *Southeastern Geographer* 42:211–27.

Flint, C. 2004. Introduction. In *Spaces of Hate: Geographies of Discrimination and Intolerance in the U.S.A.,* ed. C. Flint, 1–20. New York: Routledge.

Frankenberg, R. 1997. *Displacing Whiteness: Essays in Social and Cultural Criticism.* Durham, NC: Duke University Press.

Frey, W. H. 2004. *The New Great Migration: Black Americans' Return to the South, 1965–2000.* Washington, DC: Brookings Institution, Center on Urban and Metropolitan Policy.

Hague, E. 2002. "Flags as Texts: The League of the South and the Development of a Nationalist Intelligentsia in the United States, 1975–2001." *Hagar: International Social Science Review* 3:299–39.

Hague, E., H. Beirich, and E. Sebesta, eds. 2008. *Neo-Confederacy: A Critical Introduction.* Austin: University of Texas Press.

Hague, E., B. Giordano, and E. H. Sebesta. 2005. "Whiteness, Multiculturalism and Nationalist Appropriation of Celtic Culture: The Case of the League of the South and the Lega Nord." *Cultural Geographies* 12:151–73.

Harvey, P. 2005. *Freedom's Coming: Religious Culture in the Shaping of the South from the Civil War through the Civil Rights Era.* Chapel Hill: University of North Carolina Press.

Hill, J. M. n.d. "The Real Symbolism of the St. Andrew's Cross: Christian Liberty vs. the New World Order." www.ncccusa.org/news/00news18.html.

Kanengiser, A. 2001. "Groups at MC, USM Weigh in for New Flag." *Jackson Clarion-Ledger,* April 14.

League of the South. 2005. "The Confederate Flag: Symbol of Southern Culture, Heritage and Sovereignty—Not Racial Hatred." www.leagueofthesouth.net/static/homepage/intro_articles/csa-flags.html.

Leib, J. I. 1995. "Heritage versus Hate: A Geographical Analysis of Georgia's Confederate Battle Flag Debate." *Southeastern Geographer* 35:37–57.

———. 1998. "Teaching Controversial Topics: Iconography and the Confederate Battle Flag Debate in the South." *Journal of Geography* 97:229–40.

———. 2002. "Separate Times, Shared Space: Arthur Ashe, Monument Avenue and the Politics of Richmond, Virginia's Symbolic Landscape." *Cultural Geographies* 9:286–312.

———. 2004. "Robert E. Lee, 'Race', Representation, and Redevelopment along Richmond, Virginia's Canal Walk." *Southeastern Geographer* 44:236–62.

Leib, J. I., and G. R. Webster. 2002. "The Confederate Flag Debate in the American South: Theoretical and Conceptual Perspectives." In *Beyond the Color Line? Race, Representation, and Community in the New Century,* ed. A. Willingham, 221–42. New York: Brennan Center for Justice at New York University School of Law.

———. 2003. "A New 'Stars and Bars'? The Confederate Battle Emblem and Mississippi's 2001 State Flag Referendum." Paper presented at the Association of American Geographers Conference, New Orleans, March.

———. 2004. "Banner Headlines: The Fight over Confederate Flags in the American South." In *WorldMinds: Geographical Perspectives on 100 Problems*, ed. D. Janelle, B. Warf, and K. Hansen, 61–66. Dordrecht: Klüwer Academic.

———. 2006. "District Composition and State Legislative Votes on the Confederate Battle Emblem." *Journal of Race and Policy* 2:53–75.

———. 2007. "Rebel With(out) a Cause?: The Contested Meanings of the Confederate Battle Flag in the American South." In *Flag, Nation and Symbolism in Europe and America*, ed. T. H. Eriksen and R. Jenkins, 31–52. London: Routledge.

Leib, J. I., G. R. Webster, and R. H. Webster. 2000. "Rebel with a Cause? Iconography and Public Memory in the Southern United States." *Geojournal* 52:303–10.

Lincoln, C. E., and L. H. Mamiya. 1990. *The Black Church in the African American Experience*. Durham, NC: Duke University Press.

Manis, A. M. 2005. "The Civil Religions of the South." In *Religion and Public Life in the South: In the Evangelical Mode*, ed. C. R. Wilson and M. Silk, 165–94. Walnut Creek, CA: AltaMira Press.

McPherson, J. M. 1996. *Drawn with the Sword: Reflections on the American Civil War*. New York: Oxford University Press.

Miles, W. P. 1872. Letter to G. T. Beauregard (August 21, 1861). *Southern Magazine* 3 (4): 508.

Miller, R. M., H. S. Stout, and C. R. Wilson, eds. 1998. *Religion and the American Civil War*. New York: Oxford University Press.

Mississippi Religious Leadership Conference. 2000. "Religious Leaders Commend Winter, Flag Commission." Letter to the editor. *Jackson Clarion-Ledger*, December 27. www.clarionledger.com/news/0012/27/27letters6.html.

Moffitt, D. 1997. "Confederate Flag Flap Divides Pastors." *Christianity Today*, March 3, 63.

National Council of Churches. 2000. "National Council of Churches Executive Board 'Weighs In' on Confederate Flag, Hotel Campaigns." Press release, March 3. www.ncccusa.org/news/00news18.html.

Pettys, D. 2001. "Little-Known Lawmaker Has Big Impact on New Flag." *Macon Telegraph*, January 28.

Potok, M., ed. 2000. "Rebel with a Cause." *Intelligence Report* 99, 6–12. Montgomery, AL: Southern Poverty Law Center.

Rosenberg, E. M. 1989. *The Southern Baptists: A Subculture in Transition*. Knoxville: University of Tennessee Press.

Sawyer, P. 2000. "Churches Favor New Flag." *Jackson Clarion-Ledger*, December 20. www.clarionledger.com/news/0012/20/20flag.html.

Schoenberger, R. 2001. "Is State's Image at Stake?" *Jackson Clarion-Ledger*, February 5.

Sebesta, E., and E. Hague. 2002. "The U.S. Civil War as a Theological Struggle: Confederate Christian Nationalism and the League of the South." *Canadian Review of American Studies* 32:253–83.

Shenin, A. G. 2007. "Blacks Still See Flag as Banner of Racism." *The State* (Columbia, SC), September 14.

Smith, L. 1945. "Addressed to White Liberals." In *A Primer for White Folks*, ed. B. Moon, 484–87. Garden City, NY: Doubleday, Doran and Co.

Southern Poverty Law Center. 2001. "Confederates in the Pulpit." *Intelligence Report*, Spring, 51–55. Montgomery, AL: Southern Poverty Law Center.

Wagster, E. 2000. "The Flag: Sign of Heritage or Hate?" *Jackson Clarion-Ledger*, December 19.

Weaver, J. n.d. "The Truth about the Confederate Battle Flag." http://mauricesbbq.itgo.com/truth .html.

Webster, G. R. 1997. "Religion and Politics in the American South." *Pennsylvania Geographer* 35:151–72.

———. 2000. "Geographical Patterns of Religious Affiliation in Georgia, 1970–1990: Population Change and Growing Urban Diversity." *Southeastern Geographer* 40:25–52.

———. 2004. "If First You Don't Secede, Try, Try Again: Secession, Hate, and the League of the South." In *Spaces of Hate: Geographies of Discrimination and Intolerance in the U.S.A.*, ed. C. Flint, 137–64. New York: Routledge.

Webster, G. R., and J. I. Leib. 2001. "Whose South Is It Anyway? Race and the Confederate Battle Flag in South Carolina." *Political Geography* 20:271–99.

———. 2002. Political Culture, Religion, and the Confederate Battle Flag Debate in Alabama. *Journal of Cultural Geography* 20:1–26.

———. 2008. "The Confederate Battle Flag and the Neo-Confederate Movement in the South." In *Neo-Confederacy: A Critical Introduction*, ed. E. Hague, H. Beirich, and E. Sebesta, 169–201. Austin: University of Texas Press.

Wilson, C. R. 1980. *Baptized in Blood: The Religion of the Lost Cause, 1865–1920*. Athens: University of Georgia Press.

———. 1995. *Judgment and Grace in Dixie: Southern Faiths from Faulkner to Elvis*. Athens: University of Georgia Press.

———. 2005. "Preachin', Prayin', and Singin' on the Public Square." In *Religion and Public Life in the South: In the Evangelical Mode*, ed. C. R. Wilson and M. Silk, 9–26. Walnut Creek, CA: AltaMira Press.

Winant, H. 2004. *The New Politics of Race: Globalism, Difference, Justice*. Minneapolis: University of Minnesota Press.

Wray, M., and A. Newitz. 1997. *White Trash: Race and Class in America*. New York: Routledge.

Acting Out

The Black and White of Moral Values

*How Attending to Race Challenges the Mythology of the
Relationship between Religiosity and Political Attitudes
and Behavior*

Robert P. Jones and Robert D. Francis

The 2004 presidential elections revealed two dramatic findings for scholars of
religion and politics. First, race and frequency of religious attendance were the
two most powerful predictors of vote, stronger than other demographic factors such as gender, education, income, or region (Pew Forum on Religion &
Public Life 2005). This correlation between religious attendance and voting behavior quickly gained traction in the mainstream press and resulted in the much-
publicized "religion gap" or "God gap," the popular term for the newly emerged
conventional wisdom that the more religious the voter, the more likely she would
be to vote Republican. This finding, combined with additional Pew data suggesting a growing public perception that the Democratic Party was unfriendly to
religion, also contributed to the inference that Democrats might have a "God
problem" (Smith and Craighill 2006).

Second, in response to a vague exit poll question, more voters chose "moral
values" than any other factor as the most influential "issue" in their vote. This result led many pundits to conjure up the so-called "values voter," a voter who was
at once religious, conservative on social issues, and Republican. "Values voters"
quickly became the media shorthand for religious, socially conservative Republicans, and in short order the term worked its way into the popular and political
lexicons without qualification.

Unfortunately, the survey findings indirectly responsible for the "God gap,"
"values voters," and the Democrats' "God problem" each lost some important nuance in translation to the media and the general public. Most significant, in these
popular treatments, the powerful influence of race dropped out. Voters of color,
especially black Protestants, confound the conventional wisdom about values
voters. Black Protestants are highly religious and conservative on social issues,

but overwhelmingly vote Democratic. Additionally, they demonstrate markedly different understandings of what constitutes moral values than do whites.

Centered on a comparison of white evangelicals and black Protestants across a number of areas—religious belief and behavior, political opinion and behavior, economic issues, social issues, and political ideology—this essay seeks to paint a much more nuanced picture of the confluence of race, religion, and politics in America.[1] We question several of the underlying assumptions in the cultural dialogue surrounding the God gap, values voters, and the Democratic Party's God problem. In doing so, we challenge the prevailing assumption that increased religiosity has a necessarily conservative effect on political behavior. By comparing white evangelical and black Protestant religious similarities and political differences, we also challenge scholarly models that propose a linear, sequential understanding of the impacts of religion and race on political opinion and behavior. Inspired by Bourdieu's (1990) concepts of habitus and field, and drawing on recent data, we argue that a more nuanced model of competing forces better illuminates the interplay of religion, race, and political behavior.

Previous Literature

There is a burgeoning literature addressing the interplay between religion and politics in America, especially as religion has played an increasingly public role in electoral outcomes. The ascension of the Christian Right in the late 1970s, combined with more recent attention to the pivotal "evangelical vote," has drawn particular scholarly attention to conservative Protestantism. Once a homogeneous and mysterious blur on the American religious horizon, conservative Protestantism now benefits from a much more robust and nuanced social-scientific understanding, beginning with how this group is quantitatively and qualitatively measured (Woodberry and Smith 1998; Steensland et al. 2000).

However, even though scholars of religion and politics have long understood the unique nature of the black church and the black vote (Paris 1985; Lincoln and Mamiya 1990; Payne 1995; Manza and Brooks 1999; Dawson 2003; Ahlstrom 2004; Fowler et al. 2004; Wald and Calhoun-Brown 2006), many analyses of religion and politics still often omit in-depth analysis of the religiosity of African Americans. Reliable measures of the American religious landscape distinguish between black and white Protestant traditions (Roof and McKinney 1987; Woodberry and Smith 1998; Steensland et al. 2000; Wald and Calhoun-Brown 2006), and it is no secret to scholars or the general public that African Americans, many of whom are members of socially conservative black churches, vote overwhelmingly Democratic, an alignment that began around the time of the New Deal and solidified during the civil rights era (Manza and Brooks 1997; Fowler et al. 2004). Nevertheless, as Greeley and Hout (2006) note, the nuances are still too often mentioned as an aside on the way toward other analyses, mostly focused on white voters. Moreover, the focus on white evangelicals is often absent from any discussion about race and religion.

The recent analyses that most closely inform our work are Emerson and Hawkins (2007) and Greeley and Hout (2006). Building on the work of Emerson and Smith (2000) using General Social Survey (GSS) data from 1993 to 2001, Emerson and Hawkins (2007) argue that the theologically rooted cultural toolkits of black Protestants and white evangelicals, nurtured in racial isolation, actually drive these groups to more polarized voting behaviors than those of other white and black Americans. Greeley and Hout (2006), in the context of their larger exploration of conservative Christianity, point to black Protestants as proof positive that conservative religion does not necessarily beget conservative politics. Looking at GSS data from 1992 to 2000, they show that the more conservative white evangelicals are across three common measures of religiosity, the more likely they were to vote Republican. Conversely, the more conservative black Protestants become across these same measures, the more likely they were to vote Democratic. Given this, Greeley and Hout see race as an important factor that "directs" religious impact.

We seek to bring this conversation into the contemporary, post–moral values electoral context. Our own analysis suggests that previous models for understanding the relationships among race, religion, and political behavior are too linear and static. Previous analyses seem to start with the fact of religious belief in a vacuum and understand race as an intermediary factor that acts on that religious belief—whether directing, intensifying, or trumping it—in producing political opinion and behavior. In this conception, religion and race are seen as sequential and unconnected rather than simultaneous and dynamically intertwined. We believe Bourdieu's concepts of habitus and field may provide a superior model that better represents both the external fields of influence (the already existing fields of race, religion, and politics) and the ways in which these simultaneously act to form a system of dispositions (the *habitus*).

White Evangelicals and Black Protestants: Similarities in Religious Belief and Practice

White evangelicals and black Protestants are remarkably similar. As figure 1 demonstrates, across five standard measures of religious belief and practice—salience of religion, biblical literalism, certainty of God's existence, and frequency of prayer and church attendance—white evangelicals and black Protestants are nearly identical with one another and notably different from the general public. No other major religious groups in America register percentages as high across these measures (Jones 2006).[2]

Following John Green's work (2004), we used factor analysis to determine that there was a single composite religiosity factor lying behind these five separate measures of belief and behavior.[3] Once we had this composite measure, we used it to subdivide black Protestants and white evangelicals into traditionalists, centrists, and modernists.[4] Nationally, across all religious traditions, Americans are 22 percent traditionalists, 50 percent centrists, 18 percent modernists, and 10 percent secular/nonreligious (Jones 2006). The religious orientations of white evangelicals and black Protestants are similar to each other and different from the public in two main ways. First, both have a significantly higher proportion of religious traditionalists than the general public. Black Protestants have over two-thirds more traditionalists than the public (37 percent vs. 22 percent, respectively), while white evangelicals have twice as many traditionalists as the public (44 percent vs. 22 percent, respectively). Likewise, both groups have about half as many modernists as the public (white evangelicals 10 percent, black Protestants 10 percent, public 18 percent) (Jones 2006).

White evangelicals and black Protestants also demonstrate a distinctly similar outlook on the role of religion in public life and one that is also markedly different from the public's. Americans as a whole are evenly divided in their concerns over the role of religion in public life, with slightly more Americans saying they are more worried about public officials who are too close to religious leaders than about public officials who do not pay enough attention to religion. Black Protestants and white evangelicals are the only major religious groups that are more worried about public officials not paying enough attention to religion. More than six in ten white evangelicals and black Protestants (65 percent and 61 percent, respectively) are worried that public officials do not pay enough attention to religion (Jones 2006).

White evangelicals and black Protestants also share common geographic locations, both being more heavily concentrated in the South and Midwest. Approximately three-fourths of both evangelicals (73 percent) and black Protestants (76 percent) live in the South or Midwest (Jones 2006). Taken together, these shared beliefs and behaviors make the two groups notably distinct from the rest of the general public and from other religious groups in the United States.

FIGURE 1   Two-group comparisons: shared religious orientations

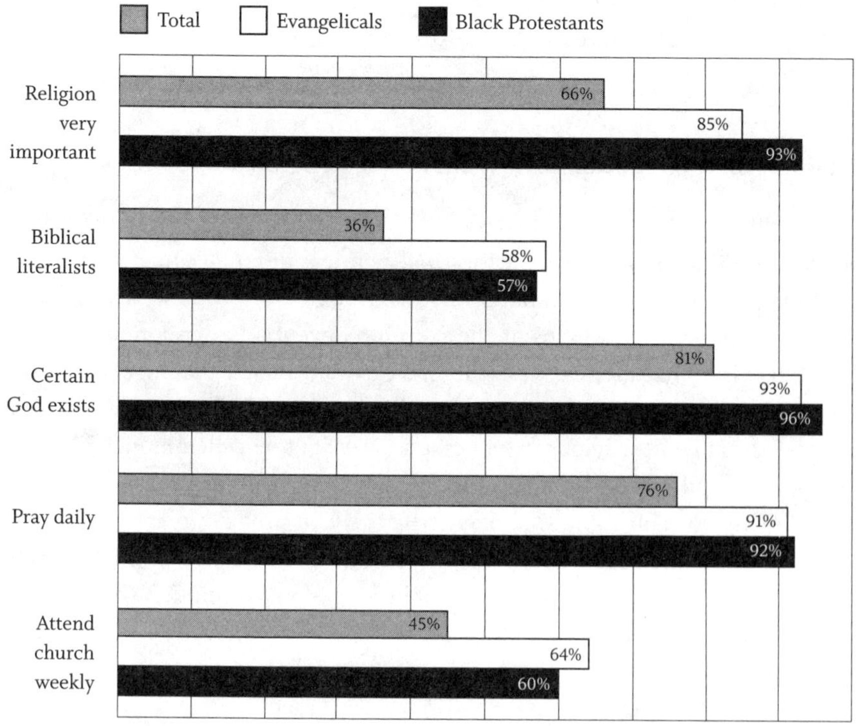

Source: Data weekly.

Voting Differences

Despite these similarities, no two major religious groups display more divergent voting patterns. According to the 2004 National Election Pool (NEP) exit poll, black Protestants voted for Senator John Kerry over President George W. Bush an overwhelming 86 percent to 14 percent, while white evangelicals displayed nearly the same degree of partisanship but in the opposite direction, voting for President George W. Bush over Senator John Kerry by 79 percent to 21 percent.[5] These divergent trends among white evangelicals and black Protestants hold over recent electoral history. Based on analysis of the GSS, Emerson and Hawkins (2007) show that between 1992 and 2000, black conservative Protestant respondents in the sample voted for the Democratic presidential candidate at extremely high rates: Clinton (1992): 100 percent, Clinton (1996): 93 percent, and Gore (2000): 94 percent. Conversely, white conservative Protestants voted for the Republican candidate at relatively high rates: G. H. W. Bush (1992): 60 percent, Dole (1996): 57 percent, and G. W. Bush (2000): 84 percent. Not only did both groups—white and black conservative Protestants—skew to opposite voting behaviors, they were also both more likely to vote for the respective party's candidate than were other voters of their race who were not conservative Protestants.[6]

Challenging Conventional Wisdom about Religion and Politics

The remainder of this essay is devoted to further exploring the implications of these striking religious similarities and political differences between white evangelicals and black Protestants. In this section, we examine how African Americans refute three myths at the core of conventional wisdom about religion and politics in America. First, the God gap myth claims that highly religious Americans are conservative and vote Republican. Second, the values voter myth declares that highly religious voters care more about so-called moral values issues—shorthand for abortion, gay marriage, and stem cell research—than about any other issues. Third, the Democratic Party's God problem myth asserts that Democrats are unfriendly to religion and unable to effectively reach highly religious voters. Underlying all of these conclusions is an assumption that religion has a monolithic, conservative effect on political behavior. As we demonstrate below, all three of these myths are at least incomplete and at worst incorrect, chiefly because they ignore the pervasive power of race.

The God Gap Myth

While we argue that there has been much nuance lost in the uncritical and unqualified adoption of these common assumptions into our faith and politics lexicon, like most myths, these three also contain a kernel of truth. For example, there is indeed a decided Republican advantage among churchgoers who attend weekly or more (Kohut et al. 2000; Layman 2001; Green and Silk 2003; Green 2004; Green et al. 2004; Olson and Green 2006). With data pooled from the American National Election Studies from 1980 through 1994, Layman (1997) found evidence that religiously committed individuals were more likely to vote Republican, although he notably did not separate out African Americans in his analysis. More recently, between 1998 and 2004, Republicans have enjoyed at least a twenty-percentage-point advantage among those attending religious services once a week or more. In the 2004 presidential election, there existed a clear linear relationship between vote and frequency of religious attendance. George W. Bush led John Kerry by twenty-two points among those who attended religious services once a week or more (NEP 2004). Conversely, Kerry performed better among those who attended less frequently or not at all. While these patterns held in the last several election cycles, the 2006 elections saw this Republican advantage cut almost in half, to twelve percentage points, bringing it back to levels comparable to those of the mid-1990s (NEP 2006).

Unfortunately, what most popular commentators and even many journalists failed to notice was that the correlation between attendance and Republican vote held only among white voters. When we break out these God gap findings by race, we see a more nuanced picture of the 2004 election. Figure 2 shows another view of the relationship between religious attendance and voting, showing John Kerry's support by race. Looking at the white vote reveals the much-touted linear relationship between religious attendance and voting from above. However, this linear relationship does not hold for minority groups. Among Latinos, the general trend of more frequent church attendees voting Republican is present, but it is much less pronounced than among white voters, with only Latino "super-attenders" (attending church more than once a week) voting a majority for President Bush. Among African Americans, however, the numbers paint a different picture. African Americans who attend religious service once a week are just as likely to vote Democrat (90 percent) as less frequent attendees, including those who never attend. Even those who attend more than once a week still voted Democrat by 80 percent (NEP 2004).

Thus, the linear relationship between religious attendance and presidential vote at the macrolevel is disproportionately due to strong correlations between these variables among white voters. The effect of race can be seen clearly if one measures the size of the spread between the extremes: the non-attenders and super-attenders in each category. The super-attender/non-attender gap was a full thirty-nine points for whites, but it was only twenty-seven points for Hispanics, and only ten points for African Americans, a mere one-fourth the gap for whites (NEP 2004).[7]

The Values Voter Myth

The second myth proclaims the advent of so-called values voters in the wake of the 2004 presidential election. Even the *New York Times* opined, "a striking portrait of one influential group emerged—that of a traditional, church-going electorate that leans conservative on social issues and strongly backed Mr. Bush in his victory over Senator John Kerry" (Seelye 2004). Several years later one can still find examples of the mainstream press, including the nation's most widely circulated paper, *USA Today* (Page 2008), employing the "values voter" language to refer to social conservatives, reinforcing the assumption that only that voting

FIGURE 2   John Kerry's support by race and religious attendance, 2004

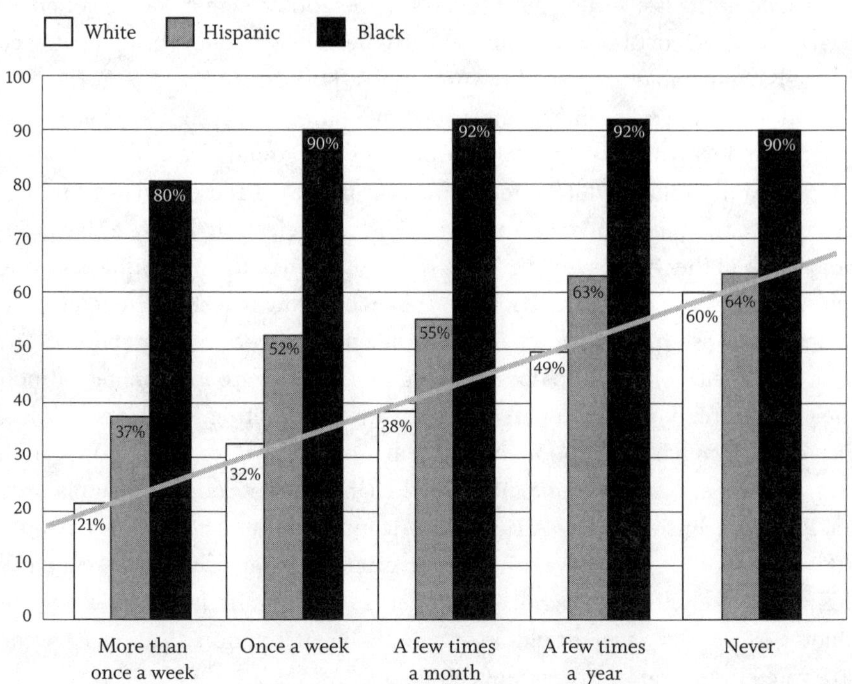

Source: NEP exit poll, November 2004 (NEP 2004). Reproduced with permission.

block prioritizes their values in voting and that abortion, gay marriage, and stem cell research are the true values issues for the highly religious. The Christian Right has been more than happy to strategically capitalize on the currency and traction of this phrase, dubbing their annual Washington, D.C., conference— organized by the Family Research Council—the "Values Voter Summit" and advertising it as "the largest gathering of values voters from across the nation."[8]

Like the God gap myth, the values voter myth contains a kernel of truth. It is strictly true that in the 2004 exit polls, more Americans picked "Moral Values" (22 percent) as the most important issue in their vote than any other issue, outpacing the other choices: "Economy/Jobs" (20 percent), "Terrorism" (19 percent), "Iraq" (15 percent), "Healthcare" (8 percent), "Taxes" (5 percent), and "Education" (4 percent) (NEP 2004). Those who cited moral values as the most important issue influencing their vote backed Bush overwhelmingly (79 percent, with 18 percent for Kerry); those who cited the economy/jobs as the most important issue voted for Kerry by a similar margin (80 percent, with 18 percent for Bush) (Botelho 2004).

Almost immediately, many polling experts and academics objected to the inclusion of the vague category "moral values" alongside specific issues such as economy/jobs and terrorism because the question construct allowed respondents to pick only a single option, implying that other choices were somehow not equally moral concerns. This polling gaffe had the effect of painting the election as a whole in terms that upheld the conventional wisdom that more religious voters are driven by moral values and vote Republican. Unfortunately, while academics and pollsters might know that the question was an exercise in poor polling science, retractions came too late, and it proved difficult to unring that bell in the media and the public consciousness. ABC News polling director Gary Langer, who was a member of the committee that constructed the exit poll, and assistant director Jon Cohen wrote that this question "undermined meaningful analysis of voters' concerns in the 2004 presidential election" and that "the exit poll's 'issues list' distorted our understanding of the 2004 election" (Langer and Cohen 2005). By 2006, even conservative columnist George Will was objecting to the widespread, loose use of the term, asking in a *New York Times* op-ed, "Who isn't a values voter?" (Will 2006).

As with the God gap, these generalizations about the relationship between religiosity and moral values break down when one attends to race. As figure 3 demonstrates, four times as many white evangelicals selected "moral values" as did black Protestants. A remarkable 41 percent of evangelicals selected "moral values" as the most important influence in their vote, while only 13 percent of black Protestants selected this option (NEP 2004). Thus, there is no simple relationship between religion and moral values; while high levels of religiosity were positively correlated with the importance of moral values among whites, high levels of religiosity were positively correlated with the importance of jobs and the economy for African Americans.

Moreover, the assumptions about what people meant by moral values do not hold up to scrutiny. Although the mythology asserted that moral values referred to same-sex marriage, abortion, and stem cell research, the AVS showed that the top things Americans, including white evangelicals, associate with the term moral values are not in fact those narrow, hot-button issues. Rather, four out of ten (39 percent) associate "moral values" with the honesty, integrity, and responsibility of the candidate; 23 percent associate the phrase with eliminating poverty and guaranteeing access to health care, and 21 percent associate it with protecting personal freedoms and individual choices (Jones 2006). Each of these associations far outpaced hot-button issues such as keeping marriage between a man and a woman (9 percent) and restricting access to abortion (3 percent) (Jones 2006). Even among white evangelicals, less than one in five (19 percent)

Figure 3   The black and white of moral values: top three issues in the 2004 presidential vote

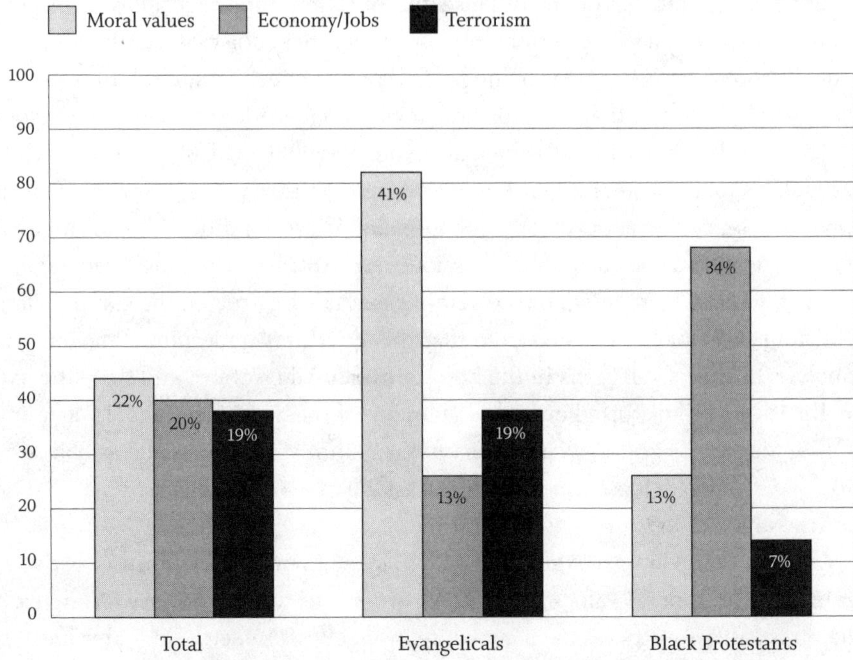

Source: NEP exit poll, November 2004 (NEP 2004). Reproduced with permission.

thought primarily in terms of these controversial issues, and almost equal numbers said that voting their values meant protecting personal freedoms and individual choices (18 percent) (Jones 2006).

The Democrats' God Problem Myth

Finally, there is a public perception that the Democratic Party is less friendly to religion than the Republican Party. In recent years, the Pew Forum on Religion & Public Life began to ask questions about perceptions of the political parties' "friendliness to religion" and found that the Republican Party was perceived to be friendlier to religion than the Democratic Party by at least twenty percentage points (Smith and Craighill 2006). Moreover, the Pew Forum found an eleven-point downward shift in perceptions of the Democratic Party's friendliness to religion between 2002 and 2005. The year 2005 showed the sharpest contrast between the parties, with Republicans being perceived as friendlier to religion by twenty-six percentage points (55 percent to 29 percent, respectively) and less unfriendly by eleven percentage points (9 percent to 20 percent, respectively). In 2006, AVS found that this gap narrowed slightly, so that Republicans held a smaller, twenty-one-point advantage on friendliness (52 percent to 31 percent) and only a three-point advantage on unfriendliness (13 percent to 16 percent) (Jones 2006). Republican Party friendliness to religion remained relatively stable over this period at around 52 percent. It seems the case that—at least as recently as 2006—there was some evidence that Democrats had a God problem (Smith and Craighill 2006).

Like the God gap myth and the values voter myth, however, the Democratic God problem myth also quickly falls away when one attends to race. As table 1 shows, in 2006 white evangelicals demonstrated an exaggerated form of the national pattern. More than twice as many white evangelicals saw the Republican Party as friendly to religion (60 percent) than saw the Democratic Party as friendly to religion (26 percent). Likewise, three times as many white evangelicals saw the Democratic Party as unfriendly to religion (27 percent) than saw the Republican Party as unfriendly to religion (8 percent) (Jones 2006). Among black Protestants, however, the opposite is true. Almost twice as many saw the Democratic Party as friendly to religion (53 percent) than saw the Republican Party as friendly to religion (28 percent). Likewise, almost four times as many black Protestants saw the Republican Party as unfriendly to religion (27 percent) than saw the Democratic Party as unfriendly to religion (7 percent) (Jones 2006).

This section has shown that attending to the influence of race strongly challenges the sweeping conclusions of the God gap, values voter, and Democratic God problem myths. In the next section we step back to think more theoretically about the interplay of religion, race, and voting behavior.

TABLE 1   Friendliness to religion by race and selected religious affiliation

	FRIENDLY		UNFRIENDLY	
	Republican (%)	Democrat (%)	Republican (%)	Democrat (%)
Evangelicals	60	26	8	27
Black protestants	28	53	27	7
Total	52	31	13	16

Source: American Values Survey, 2006 (Jones 2006).

Race and Religion as Competing Forces in Affecting Voting Behavior

A perpetual challenge when explaining behavior is accounting for the simultaneous interplay of multiple variables. Voting behavior is an especially intriguing case because voting in the United States in most cases is essentially a binary choice: Republican or Democrat. Each voter must wrestle all influences and factors toward one either/or decision. In our analysis of race, politics, and voting behavior, we have argued that we think the most appropriate way to understand this complex process is to ask how the fields of race, religion, and politics interact with one another as they "pull" on a social agent when she must make this binary decision in the voting booth.

Some political science literature has assumed race trumps religion. Others talk of race directing religion or of religion shaping and intensifying already established race-based political polarization (Emerson and Smith 2000; Emerson and Hawkins 2007). While helpful, we believe those previous models are too linear and sequential. In their place, we propose an alternative model of race, religion, and politics as competing fields of influence and behavior. We conclude our discussion with a brief voyage into these theoretical waters.

We believe the work of Pierre Bourdieu, particularly his notions of habitus and field, provides a better model to explain the intricate, sometimes counterintuitive patterns we elucidated above. As Bourdieu develops it, *habitus* is a system of dispositions acquired over time and through experience that are simultaneously durable and malleable. While habitus is concerned with social practice from within, a field is the structured social space in which the social agent acts (Bourdieu 1990). As with habitus, fields are also not rigid or timeless but are ever-evolving battlegrounds between continuity and change, the spaces in which social agents adopt stances from among multiple but not infinite options. As Wacquant (2006, 222) helpfully explains, "neither habitus nor field has the capacity unilaterally to determine social action. It takes the *meeting* of disposition and position, the correspondence (or disjuncture) between mental structures and social structures, to generate practice. This means that, to explain any social event or pattern, one must inseparably dissect both the social constitution of the agent and the makeup of the particular social universe within which she operates as well as the particular conditions under which they come to encounter and impinge upon each other."

We suggest that we ought to see race, religion, and politics as competing and interacting fields that exert a kind of gravitational pull on actors who are always already formed by their habitus as they make decisions. Sometimes the sum of these forces pulls an individual agent in the same direction, sometimes the forces compete, and virtually always they shape and alter one another as they interact. As our preceding analysis makes clear, the habitus inhabitated by black Protestants and that inhabited by white evangelicals are structured very differently, even though the religious fields of black Protestants and white evangelicals share many attributes. This divergence is largely because the fields of previous political engagement—largely Democratic for African Americans and Republican for white evangelicals—along with the fields of race, exert different influences on individuals as they are internalized and integrated into a coherent (but never fully consistent) worldview, or at least brought together enough to influence action. The vectors of influence run in every direction with varying strengths: politics to race and religion, religion to politics and race, and race to religion and politics. We see this complex interplay in the political behavior data, and we even hear it explicitly at times from insightful theologians. For example, while white theologians, as the majority group, often eclipse the influence of race in their thinking, black theologians often make these links specific. For example, Cornell West (2003, 109) has noted the importance of this interplay for constructing black theology: "Black historical experience and the biblical texts form a symbiotic relationship, each illuminating the other."

We conclude with one final example that illuminates the distinct individual influence of race and religion on political behavior.[9] We have already noted the high correlations between being white evangelical and voting Republican, on the one hand, and being black Protestant and voting Democrat on the other. To isolate the independent influences of these fields, we developed two different regression models with race and religious affiliation as independent variables and vote as the dependent variable.

A widely cited analysis by the Pew Forum concluded that frequency of religious attendance tied with race as the most powerful single predictor of vote in 2004 (Pew Forum on Religion & Public Life 2005). Although the Pew analysis offers important insights into the powerful influence of religious attendance, the choice of analytical method muted the independent power of race.[10] To provide a more thorough examination, we employed a different analytical tool, multiple logistic regression, to predict rates of Republican voting, utilizing the 2000 and 2004 exit poll data and similar variables as the Pew model: age, religious attendance, income, race, region, gender, education, and union membership (see appendix D).[11]

Using a more nuanced methodology allowed the power of race in the 2004 election to become visible (see table 2). In both 2000 and 2004, race (specifically, being African American) was by far the strongest single predictor of vote:

African Americans were more than twenty times less likely to support the Republican candidate, George W. Bush, than were whites. After race, religious attendance categories were the second and third strongest single predictors of vote: those who attended religious services more than once a week were six times more likely to vote for President George W. Bush, while those who attended weekly were more than three times more likely. While we see that religious attendance is indeed a strong independent predictor of vote, it pales in comparison with the predictive power of being African American.

Translating these findings into the terms of field and habitus can help illuminate these findings. For example, black Protestants approach voting decisions against a backdrop of at least three fields, each of which carries a historical trajectory and institutional structure: the experience of being African American, the context of the black church, and the experience of a political culture that carries a history of being strongly Democratic. According to the regression findings, although race and religion may often lead in the same direction (as they often do in the black church) with regard to voting decisions, when they collide, race carries more than three times the independent power of weekly religious attendance. This finding may help explain why substantial Republican Party outreach to black evangelicals along religious lines leading up to and following the 2004 elections has largely been ineffective (McDaniel and Ellison 2008). It also casts light on why there have been more successes in creating coalitions on certain ballot initiatives, such as same-sex marriage bans, which are separable from partisan voting (Wadsworth 2008).[12] Understanding race, religion, and politics as fields influencing the formation of a distinctive habitus for white evangelicals and black Protestants makes these outcomes more easily understandable. Further study, including some qualitative interview data, could cast some additional light on this phenomenon.

Conclusion

White evangelicals and black Protestants display great similarities across a range of religious measures but manifest virtually opposite partisan voting behavior. This often overlooked phenomenon has important implications for scholarship on race, religion, and politics, as well as for popular understandings of faith in public life. As we have argued, the powerful counterexample of black Protestants refutes the popular if incorrect notion that highly religious voters are necessarily conservative. Our analysis also points to some corrections in scholarly models of the relationship between and among religion, race, and politics. Race and religion should not be seen as static, sequential factors in influencing voting

TABLE 2   Race, then religious attendance, most powerful single predictors in voting

	LIKELIHOOD OF VOTING REPUBLICAN (BUSH)	
Characteristics	*2004*	*2000*
Race: black	−21.3×	−22.7×
Religious attendance: more than once a week	6×	6.8×
Religious attendance: weekly	3.5×	4×
Income: less than $15,000 p.a.	−3.4×	−1.7×
Education: less than high school	3×	1.1×
Gender: male	1.5×	2.3×

Source: National Election Pool (NEP) Exit Poll (NEP 2000, 2004), original multiple logistic regression analysis predicting Republican vote.
Note: Negative factors indicate less likelihood of voting Republican.

behavior. Rather, race, religion, and politics ought to be conceived as dynamic, competing fields of influence that form the environment in which individuals live and that help structure the consciousnesses of individuals. Understanding this complex interplay of these fields is vital for constructing a more accurate understanding of political behavior.

Appendix A: Logistic Regression Analysis

Because religious attendance and race are categorical variables, we can determine the size of the effect by examining the regression coefficients. By simply comparing the size of the regression coefficients on the two relevant categories (black and attending religious services more than once a week) we find that black is much larger, indicating that it is a more powerful explanatory variable. The effect is comparative, indicating a difference between each category and the reference category. For example, the reference category for race is white and the largest effect is seen in the difference between being black and being white, for which the regression coefficient is −3.052 (.14). For religion, as measured by attendance, the largest effect is for those attending more than once a week compared to those who never attend, for which the regression coefficient is 1.791 (.119). These two effects are the largest in the entire model. By examining the relative size of each regression coefficient we conclude that race has more explanatory power than religious attendance in determining vote.

Another way to make this comparison is to examine the odds ratios. The odds ratio approximates the ratio of the corresponding probabilities at the same level of all the other variables. For example, the odds ratio for black is about .047, meaning that blacks are approximately twenty-one times more likely to vote Democrat than whites.[13] For religious attendance the odds ratio is about 6, meaning that individuals attending church frequently are six times more likely to vote Republican than those who never attend. The odds ratio for religious attendance is one-third as large as that for race; however, it still has the second and third largest effect on vote, after race.

Appendix B: Logistic Regression Output (2004)

TABLE 3   Results of multiple logistic regression analysis predicting Republican vote in the 2004 presidential election

	B	S.E.	Wald	d.f.	Sig. (P)	Odds ratio (B)	95.0% C.I. for exp (B) Lower	Upper
Step 1(a)								
Age60			24.748	3	.000			
age60(1)	.139	.100	1.948	1	.163	1.150	.945	1.398
age60(2)	.405	.088	21.074	1	.000	1.500	1.262	1.784
age60(3)	.112	.086	1.703	1	.192	1.119	.945	1.324
Attend			294.060	4	.000			
attend(1)	1.791	.119	226.523	1	.000	5.997	4.749	7.573
attend(2)	1.284	.100	166.246	1	.000	3.611	2.971	4.389
attend(3)	.928	.112	69.076	1	.000	2.530	2.032	3.148
attend(4)	.569	.095	36.182	1	.000	1.767	1.468	2.127
Income6			103.904	5	.000			
income6(1)	−1.236	.142	75.787	1	.000	.291	.220	.384
income6(2)	−.863	.115	56.688	1	.000	.422	.337	.528
income6(3)	−.525	.101	27.086	1	.000	.592	.486	.721
income6(4)	−.278	.095	8.511	1	.004	.757	.628	.913
income6(5)	−.257	.106	5.840	1	.016	.773	.627	.953
Racecode			503.460	3	.000			
racecode(1)	−.879	.258	11.612	1	.001	.415	.251	.688
racecode(2)	−.801	.111	52.276	1	.000	.449	.361	.558
racecode(3)	−3.052	.140	477.824	1	.000	.047	.036	.062
Region			73.700	3	.000			
region(1)	−.328	.092	12.595	1	.000	.720	.601	.863
region(2)	−.122	.090	1.844	1	.174	.885	.743	1.055
region(3)	.395	.090	19.396	1	.000	1.485	1.245	1.770
sex(1)	.442	.061	52.051	1	.000	1.557	1.380	1.755
unionhh(1)	−.676	.073	86.391	1	.000	.509	.441	.587
Educ			115.057	4	.000			
educ(1)	1.107	.175	39.946	1	.000	3.027	2.147	4.267
educ(2)	1.000	.106	88.892	1	.000	2.717	2.207	3.345
educ(3)	.846	.095	79.753	1	.000	2.331	1.936	2.806
educ(4)	.459	.095	23.455	1	.000	1.582	1.314	1.904
Constant	−.933	.145	41.573	1	.000	.393		

Appendix C: Logistic Regression Output (2000)

TABLE 4   Results of multiple logistic regression analysis predicting Republican vote in the 2000 presidential election

	B	S.E.	Wald	d.f.	Sig.	ratio (B)
Step 1(a)						
Age			10.037	3	.018	
age(1)	.296	.104	8.082	1	.004	1.345
age(2)	.241	.090	7.217	1	.007	1.273
age(3)	.164	.092	3.149	1	.076	1.178
Attend			332.602	4	.000	
attend(1)	1.920	.125	234.822	1	.000	6.821
attend(2)	1.380	.103	179.201	1	.000	3.975
attend(3)	.887	.116	58.043	1	.000	2.428
attend(4)	.529	.100	28.048	1	.000	1.697
Income			31.719	5	.000	
income(1)	−.518	.155	11.162	1	.001	.596
income(2)	−.574	.119	23.271	1	.000	.563
income(3)	−.352	.105	11.243	1	.001	.703
income(4)	−.165	.103	2.597	1	.107	.848
income(5)	−.100	.117	.737	1	.391	.905
Educ			50.277	4	.000	
educ(1)	.094	.171	.304	1	.581	1.099
educ(2)	.569	.106	28.746	1	.000	1.767
educ(3)	.610	.096	40.478	1	.000	1.840
educ(4)	.438	.097	20.508	1	.000	1.550
uhouse(1)	−.509	.073	49.084	1	.000	.601
sex(1)	.807	.063	164.263	1	.000	2.241
Region			76.515	3	.000	
region(1)	−.223	.095	5.562	1	.018	.800
region(2)	−.026	.091	.080	1	.778	.975
region(3)	.504	.091	30.745	1	.000	1.656
Racecode			407.407	3	.000	
racecode(1)	−.479	.224	4.557	1	.033	.619
racecode(2)	−.813	.125	42.364	1	.000	.443
racecode(3)	−3.132	.160	382.012	1	.000	.044
Constant	−1.312	.156	70.380	1	.000	.269

Appendix D: Variable Coding

2000	2004
Age (age)	Age (age60)
1. 18–29	1. 18–29
2. 30–44	2. 30–44
3. 45–60	3. 45–60
4. 60+	4. 60+

2000	2004
Education (educ)	Education (educ)
1. No high school	1. No high school
2. High school graduate	2. High school graduate
3. Some college/associate	3. Some college/associate
4. College graduate	4. College graduate
5. Post-graduate	5. Post-graduate

2000	2004
Religious attendance (attend)	Religious attendance (attend)
1. More than once a week	1. More than once a week
2. Once a week	2. Once a week
3. A few times a month	3. A few times a month
4. A few times a year	4. A few times a year
5. Never	5. Never

2000	2004
Region (region)	Region (region)
1. East	1. East
2. Midwest	2. Midwest
3. South	3. South
4. West	4. West

2000	2004
Race (Recoded: racecode)	Race (Recoded: raccode)
1. Asian	1. Asian
2. Hispanic	2. Hispanic
3. Black	3. Black
4. White	4. White

2000	2004
Gender (sex)	Gender (sex)
1. Male	1. Male
2. Female	2. Female

2000	2004
Union (Recoded: uhouse)	Union (unionhh)
1. Union household	1. Union household
2. Non-union household	2. Non-union household

Income	Income (Recoded: income6)
1. Less than $15,000	1. Less than $15,000
2. $15,000–$30,000	2. $15,000–$30,000
3. $30,000–$50,000	3. $30,000–$50,000
4. $50,000–$75,000	4. $50,000–$75,000
5. $75,000–$100,000	5. $75,000–$100,000
6. $100,000+	6. $100,000+

Notes

1. In our analysis, white evangelical refers to those who identify as white, Protestant, and born again, while black Protestant refers to those who identify as black and Protestant.

2. The American Values Survey (AVS) was conducted by Robert P. Jones and Daniel Cox for People for the American Way Foundation, August 9–23, 2006. AVS had 2,502 respondents plus oversampling of African Americans and Hispanics. Including the oversamples, AVS contained 634 white evangelical respondents and 389 black Protestant respondents. For results based on the national sample, the margin of error is ±1.95 percent. The authors thank Daniel Cox for his work on the multiple logistic regression analysis in this essay. For more information about AVS, see http://www.publicreligion.org/research/published/?id=134.

3. White evangelicals and black Protestants were similar to each other on virtually every measure we tested, with one major exception: their approaches to tradition. Having been historically on the weak side of the power dynamics that used religion to support white dominance and discrimination, nearly half of black Protestants (49 percent) said that their church should either adjust beliefs in light of new ideas or adopt modern beliefs and practices, while only 37 percent of white evangelicals agreed (Jones 2006).

4. Traditionalists tend to attend religious services weekly or more, pray daily, believe in a literal interpretation of the Bible, believe without any doubt that God exists, and report that religion is a very important or the most important thing in their lives. Modernists tend to attend religious services once in a while or infrequently, pray occasionally or infrequently, believe that the Bible is inspired but not the literal word of God or that it is an ancient book of myths and legends, believe God exists but have some doubts, and report that religion is fairly important in their lives. Centrists display tendencies that fall in between those of traditionalists and modernists.

5. Notably, the other two major religious groups that favored Senator John Kerry in 2004, Jews and Latino Catholics, were also constituted by ethnic minorities. They voted for him 75 percent to 25 percent and 60 percent to 40 percent over Bush, respectively (NEP 2004).

6. In the GSS sample, white Americans who were not conservative Protestants voted for the Republican candidate at the following rates: G. H. W. Bush (1992): 39 percent; Dole (1996): 33 percent; and G. W. Bush (2000): 57 percent. Black Americans who were not conservative Protestants voted for the Democratic candidate at the following rates: Clinton (1992): 91 percent; Clinton (87 percent); and Gore (85 percent) (Emerson and Hawkins 2007).

7. In addition to the differences in attendance by race, certain religious traditions, such as white evangelical traditions and black Protestant traditions, are much more likely to offer opportunities for and expect attendance at multiple weekly services.

8. See http://www.frcaction.org/index.cfm?c=WASH_BRIEFING.

9. We recognize that the regression model tests only the interplay between race and religion, with political behavior as the dependent variable. It would be illuminating but beyond the scope of this study to run three regression models, taking each variable in turn as the dependent variable.

10. First, Pew chose a particular statistical method that provided more intuitive results, but this method was not ideally suited for this type of analysis. Although the dependent variable (vote) is dichotomous, Pew used ordinary least squares (OLS) regression, a method that is more appropriate to analyzing continuous dependent variables. Second, since Pew was interested only in the relative explanatory power of each variable, the study authors standardized all the regression coefficients in order to compare them. After standardizing the coefficients, they concluded that religious attendance and race were equal (Ð = 28), and thus were equally important predictors of presidential vote. However, regression coefficients don't tell us anything about the *predictive* power of religious attendance and race. Second, because the 2004 exit poll was not yet available at the time of their analysis, Pew compared the Voter News Service (VNS) General Election Exit Poll for 2000 with their own survey, the Weekend Exit Poll for 2004. These polls had three major differences that cause methodological challenges: different data-collecting practices (personal interviews vs. telephone interviews), different sample sizes (13,225 for the VNS 2000 survey and only 2,804 for the Pew survey), and different sampling universes: the VNS exit poll surveyed actual voters, while the Pew survey included self-reporting voters along with those who did not vote and those who may have been ineligible to vote.

11. Our analysis did not include an urban/rural variable primarily because the authors did not believe a priori that it would have any significant effect on vote choice. When a variable for urban and rural was included it had marginal effect on vote choice and did not affect the relative power of other statistically significant variables.

12. Wadsworth found that ballot initiatives affirming traditional marriage received high support from African Americans, often exceeding support from whites (Wadsworth 2008).

13. This number was derived by taking the reciprocal of .047.

References

Ahlstrom, Sydney E. 2004. *A Religious History of the American People: Second Edition*. New Haven, CT: Yale University Press.

Botelho, Greg. 2004. "Exit polls: Electorate Is Sharply Divided." November 3. http://www.cnn .com/2004/ALLPOLITICS/11/02/prez.analysis/index.html.

Bourdieu, Pierre. 1990. *The Logic of Practice*. Stanford, CA: Stanford University Press.

Dawson, Michael C. 2003. *Black Visions: The Roots of Contemporary African American Political Ideologies*. Chicago: University of Chicago Press.

Emerson, Michael O., and Russell Hawkins. 2007. "Viewed in Black and White: Conservative Protestantism, Racial Issues, and Oppositional Politics." In *Religion and American Politics: From the Colonial Period to the Present*, ed. Mark Noll and Luke E. Harlow. Oxford: Oxford University Press.

Emerson, Michael O., and Christian Smith. 2000. *Divided by Faith: Evangelical Religion and the Problem of Race in America*. Oxford: Oxford University Press.

Fowler, Robert Booth, Allen D. Hertzke, Laura R. Olson, and Kevin R. den Dulk. 2004. *Religion and Politics in America: Faith, Culture, and Strategic Choices*. Boulder, CO: Westview Press.

Greeley, Andrew M., and Michael Hout. 2006. *The Truth about Conservative Christians: What They Think and What They Believe.* Chicago: University of Chicago Press.

Green, John C. 2004. "The American Religious Landscape and Politics, 2004." Pew Forum on Religion & Public Life. http://pewforum.org/publications/surveys/green.pdf.

Green, John C., and Mark Silk. 2003. "The New Religion Gap." *Religion in the News* 5:3.

Green, John C., Corwin E. Smidt, James L. Guth, and Lyman A. Kellstedt. 2004. "The American Religious Landscape and the 2004 Presidential Vote." http://www.uakron.edu/bliss/research.php.

Jones, Robert P. 2006. "The American Values Survey (AVS)." Center for American Values in Public Life at People for the American Way Foundation. August 9–21. http://www.publicreligion.org'research/published/?id=134.

Kohut, Andrew, John C. Green, Scott Keeter, and Robert C. Toth. 2000. *The Diminishing Divide: Religion's Changing Role in American Politics.* Washington, DC: Brookings Institution Press.

Langer, Gary, and Jon Cohen. 2005. "Voters and Values in the 2004 Election." *Public Opinion Quarterly* 69:744–59.

Layman, Geoffrey. 1997. "Religion and Political Behavior in the United States: The Impact of Beliefs, Affiliations, and Commitment from 1980 to 1994." *Public Opinion Quarterly* 61:288–316.

———. 2001. *The Great Divide: Religious and Cultural Conflict in American Party Politics.* New York: Columbia University Press.

Lincoln, C. Eric, and Lawrence H. Mamiya. 1990. *The Black Church in the African American Experience.* Durham, NC: Duke University Press.

Manza, Jeff, and Clem Brooks. 1997. "The Religious Factor in U.S. Presidential Elections, 1960–1992." *American Journal of Sociology* 103:38–81.

———. 1999. *Social Cleavages and Political Change: Voter Alignment U.S. Party Coalitions.* Oxford: Oxford University Press.

McDaniel, Eric L., and Christopher G. Ellison. 2008. "God's Party? Race, Religion, and Partisanship over Time." *Political Research Quarterly* 61 (June): 180–91.

National Election Pool. 2004. National Exit Polls. Conducted by Edison Media Research and Mitofsky International.

———. 2006. National Exit Polls. Conducted by Edison Media Research and Mitofsky International.

Olson, Laura R., and John C. Green. 2006. "The Religion Gap." *PS: Political Science and Politics* 39:455–59.

Page, Susan. 2008. "Which Hopeful Is the Face of the New GOP?" *USA Today,* January 24.

Paris, Peter J. 1985. *The Social Teaching of the Black Churches.* Chicago: Fortress Press.

Payne, W., ed. 1995. *Directory of African American Religious Bodies: A Compendium by the Howard University School of Divinity.* Washington, DC: Howard University Press.

Pew Forum on Religion & Public Life. 2005. "Religion in Public Life: A Faith-Based Partisan Divide." Pew Research Center. http://pewforum.org/docs/index.php?DocID=61.

Roof, Wade Clark, and William McKinney. 1987. *American Mainline Religion: Its Changing Shape and Future.* New Brunswick, NJ: Rutgers University Press.

Seelye, Katharine Q. 2004. "Moral Values Cited as a Defining Issue of the Election." *New York Times,* November 4.

Smith, Gregory A., and Peyton M. Craighill. 2006. "Do the Democrats Have a 'God Problem'? How Public Perceptions May Spell Trouble for the Party." Pew Forum on Religion & Public Life. http://pewforum.org/docs/index.php?DocID=148.

Steensland, Brian, Jerry Z. Park, Mark D. Regnerus, Lynn D. Robinson, W. Bradford Wilcox, and Robert D. Woodberry. 2000. "The Measure of American Religion: Toward Improving the State of the Art." *Social Forces* 79:291–318.

Wacquant, Loic. 2006. "Pierre Bourdieu." In *Key Sociological Thinkers*, ed. Rob Stonas. London: Macmillan.

Wadsworth, Nancy. 2008. "Race-ing Faith and Fate: The Jeremiad in Multiracial Traditional Marriage Alliances." *Race/Ethnicity: Multidisciplinary Global Contexts* 1 (2): 313–41.

Wald, Kenneth D., and Allison Calhoun-Brown. 2006. *Religion and Politics in the United States*, 5th ed. Lanham, MD: Rowman & Littlefield.

West, Cornel. 2003. *Prophesy Deliverance! An Afro-American Revolutionary Christianity.* Louisville, KY: Westminster John Knox Press.

Will, George. 2006. "Who Isn't a Values Voter?" *Washington Post*, May 18, A23.

Woodberry, Robert D., and Christian S. Smith. 1998. "Fundamentalism et al: Conservative Protestants in America." *Annual Review of Sociology* 24:25–56.

Latino Religion and Its Political Consequences

Exploring National and Local Trends

Jessica Hamar Martínez, Edwin I. Hernández,
and Milagros Peña

Latinos are the largest and fastest-growing ethnic minority group in the United States, constituting 15.4 percent of the population in 2008 (Pew Hispanic Center 2010). Yet many scholars have noted their lack of political participation compared to other ethnic groups. For example, when it comes to voter registration and turnout, some put Latinos at 10–30 percent lower rates than Anglos (Garcia 1997), and Martínez (2005) finds Latinos are less likely to participate in political protests than non-Latinos. Previous research has found that factors such as immigration status and generation, socioeconomic status, education, local or state anti-immigrant initiatives, and various attitudinal differences contribute to differential political participation among Latinos (Arvizu and Garcia 1996; Garcia 1997; Pantoja, Ramírez, and Segura 2001; Martínez 2005).

In addition to various demographic characteristics that seem to affect political participation, several scholars have noted differences between various Latino subgroups, suggesting the problematic nature of the use of an umbrella term like "Latino" (Calvo and Rosenstone 1989; Diaz 1996; Martínez 2005). For example, when compared with Mexican Americans and Puerto Ricans, Cuban Americans are generally more likely to vote (Calvo and Rosenstone 1989; Diaz 1996) and more likely to identify as Republicans (Garcia 1997), but less likely to participate in political protests (Martínez 2005). Still other studies have suggested that while there are important differences between subgroups of Latinos (based, for example, on national origin or socioeconomic status), Latinos as a group are somewhat cohesive when it comes to political opinion, and the range of opinions on various political issues is smaller within Latinos as a group than between Latinos and other groups, such as Anglos, blacks, or women (Claassen 2004).

While we have some understanding of political behavior, identification, and attitudes among Latinos, we know less about how religion shapes political life for Latinos. According to one study, two-thirds of Latinos see religion as an important influence on their political thinking ("Changing Faiths," Pew Hispanic Center and Pew Forum on Religion & Public Life 2007), suggesting an important relationship between religion and politics for Latinos. Additionally, two-thirds of Latino churchgoers attend heavily Latino congregations, suggesting a strong relationship between ethnic identity and religious worship (ibid.). For Latinos in particular, churches are an important form of voluntary association that serves as a venue for acquiring the civic skills that contribute to political participation (Verba, Schlozman, and Brady 1995; Jones-Correa and Leal 2001). Stepick, Rey, and Mahler (2009) capture the ways in which churches in Miami contribute to enhancing civic engagement that leads to political participation as one of a number of factors in civic engagement. In highlighting the Cuban American experience, they note that "for the first time in American history, a group of first-generation immigrants has assumed control of local political institutions and risen to the top of the local socioeconomic hierarchy" (ibid., 17). All of these examples suggest the importance of exploring the various ways that ethnicity and religion intersect when it comes to shaping political identity and involvement among Latinos.

The relationship among ethnicity, religion, and politics for Latinos is complex. Adding to the complexity is that Latinos are not a homogeneous group when it comes to religion. For example, while a majority of Latinos identify as Catholic (67.6 percent as of 2006), a growing proportion identifies as Protestant (19.6 percent as of 2006) (Pew Hispanic Center and Pew Forum on Religion & Public Life 2007), and religion likely influences different people in different ways when it comes to politics. According to some research, Latino Protestants tend to be more politically active than Latino Catholics (Verba, Schlozman, and Brady 1995). One study cites evangelical Protestant Latinos as being twice as likely as Catholic Latinos to identify as Republican, while Catholic Latinos are more likely to identify as Democrat (Pew Hispanic Center and Pew Forum on Religion & Public Life 2007). Kelly and Kelly (2005) also find that Latino Catholics are more strongly Democratic than Latino Protestants, and that less than 40 percent of mainline Protestant Latinos identify as Democrat, suggesting religion influences Latinos differently than it does non-Latinos.

In addition to religious affiliation, there is reason to believe congregational context also influences the political lives of Latinos. Wald, Owen, and Hill (1988, 531) see churches as "fertile groups for the dissemination of common political outlooks." Jones-Correa and Leal (2001) highlight the importance of the church as a civic association and argue that being active in a church, no matter what religious tradition or denomination, leads to being more active in electoral politics. Still other studies highlight the variable influence of congregational context depending on religious tradition. One study suggests that mainline Protestant Latinos are more likely than Catholics, evangelical Protestants, Pentecostal Protestants, and other Christians to report that their congregation participated in such political activities as helping with voter registration, driving people to the polls, and handing out campaign materials (Espinosa 2006). Another study suggests that in addition to seeing religion as "a moral compass to guide their own political thinking," Latinos "view the pulpit as an appropriate place for the expression of political views" (Pew Hispanic Center and Pew Forum on Religion & Public Life 2007, 57). In other words, many Latinos probably look to their religious leaders for political guidance. While religious beliefs likely guide political thinking, religious communities and leaders possibly influence political views and behaviors as well. Political scientist Catherine E. Wilson (2008) notes that the "definition of religious identity politics suggests that it is both the context and content of religious beliefs, values, and culture that inform social and political action" (63).

The previous examples suggest a few different ways in which religion and politics intersect in the lives of Latinos. In this essay we explore two broad questions about this relationship. First, using data from the Pew Hispanic Center's 2004 National Survey of Latinos, we examine how religious affiliation and participation are related to political identity, political opinion, and political behavior among Latino individuals. Second, using data from the Chicago Latino Congregations Study (Burwell et al. 2009), we examine how religious leaders in Latino congregations encourage political participation among their congregations' members.

Religion and Politics among Latino Individuals: The National Picture

In this section we examine the relationship between religion and politics for Latino individuals.[1] We use the 2004 National Survey of Latinos: Politics and Civic Participation, a survey of Latino adults conducted by the Pew Hispanic Center and the Kaiser Family Foundation.[2] This data source is well suited to answer our questions about Latinos, religion, and politics because surveys were conducted with a large (N = 2,288 after reducing the sample to Catholic and Protestant respondents), nationally representative sample of Latinos in the United States. The survey included several questions about religion and politics. Specifically, we draw on this data source to examine how religious affiliation and religious intensity are related to political party alignment, opinions regarding various political issues, and political involvement.

Following previous studies of Latino politics and religion (Jones-Correa and Leal 2001; Kelly and Kelly 2005), we include both a measure of religious affiliation and a measure of religious intensity. Our categories for religious affiliation are limited to Catholic and Protestant,[3] and religious intensity is operationalized as frequency of church attendance. Respondents who attend religious services at least once a month are considered "religiously active" and those who attend less frequently are considered "religiously inactive." Out of 2,288 Latino/a respondents, 1,489 (65 percent) identified as Catholic and 413 (18 percent) identified as Protestant. Of those identifying as Catholic, 940 (63 percent) considered themselves active Catholics, while 541 (36 percent) considered themselves inactive Catholics. Of those identifying as Protestant, 313 (76 percent) considered themselves active Protestants, while 98 (24 percent) considered themselves inactive Protestants.

In terms of party identification, the 2004 National Survey of Latinos shows that a majority of registered Latino voters (59 percent) identify with the Democratic Party (fig. 1). When we divide Latinos according to their religious affiliation, however, we find that a larger majority of Latino Catholics (64 percent) identify with the Democratic Party than is found among Latino Protestants (52 percent). So too, Latino Protestants are more likely to identify as Republican (38 percent) than are Latino Catholics (28 percent).

Religious intensity also correlates with Latinos' political alignment, but only among Protestants. Specifically, attending church regularly (i.e., once a month or more) substantially decreases the Democratic Party's dominance among Latino Protestants but not among Latino Catholics (see fig. 1). In other words, a smaller percentage of churchgoing Latino Protestants identify with the Democratic Party (42 percent) than do Latino Protestants in general (52 percent), and a larger share of active Latino Protestants identify with the Republican Party (47 percent) than is found in the general Latino Protestant population (38 percent). In contrast, roughly the same percentage of active Latino Catholics identify as Democrats (63 percent) as do Latino Catholics overall (64 percent).

These differences in political party preference between Latino Catholics and Protestants correspond with only slight differences in levels of support for President Bush's handling of the war in Iraq. As figure 2 shows, a somewhat higher percentage of Latino Catholics disapproved of the president's management of the situation (63 percent) than was found among Latino/a Protestants (55 percent). However, religious intensity did increase the level of support for the president

FIGURE 1   Political party alignment, overall and by religious affiliation and intensity

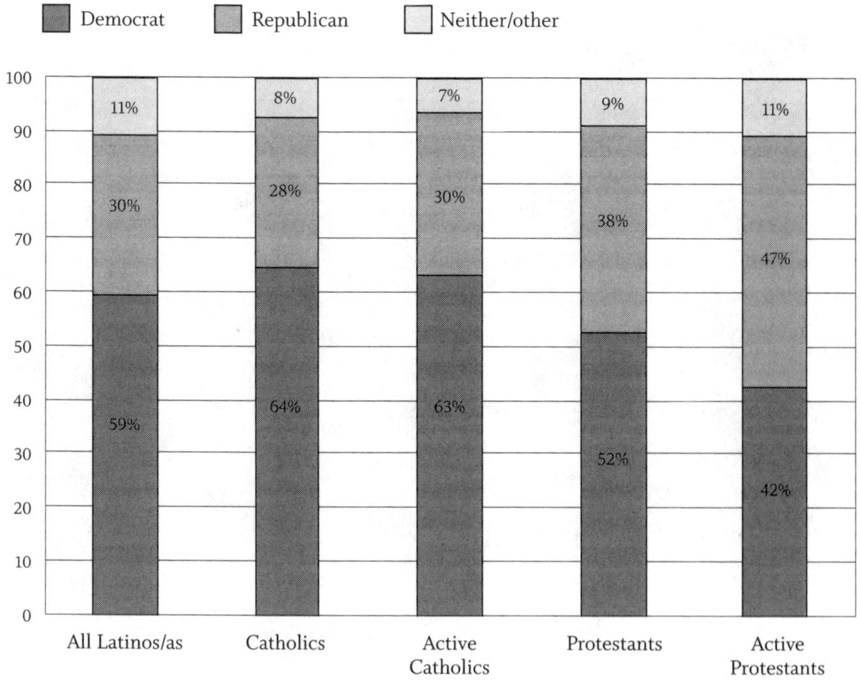

Source: From Hernández et al. (2007). Reproduced with permission.

among Protestants, with 55 percent of the religiously active saying they approved of how he was handling the war—the only group in which a majority expressed such a view.

After the 2004 presidential election, journalistic reports focused on the convoluted results that stemmed from the insertion of "moral values" into the list of issues whose potential influence voters were asked about in exit polls. According to some analyses, 80 percent of the electorate indicated "moral values" as the most important factor influencing their vote for a presidential candidate. However, innovative research by the Pew Research Center found that while "moral values" were an important factor, the "war in Iraq" and "leadership" played more decisive roles in determining voter behavior (Pew Forum on Religion & Public Life 2004).

Interestingly, Latino voters ranked other issues well ahead of both the Iraq War and "moral values." Table 1 compares the issues that Catholic and Protestant Latino voters considered extremely important in the spring prior to the 2004 election. As table 1 shows, though the exact order varies, Latino Protestant and Catholic voters who participated in the 2004 Pew survey identified the same four

Figure 2   View of President Bush's management of the war in Iraq ("Do you approve or disapprove of the way the president is handling the situation in Iraq?")

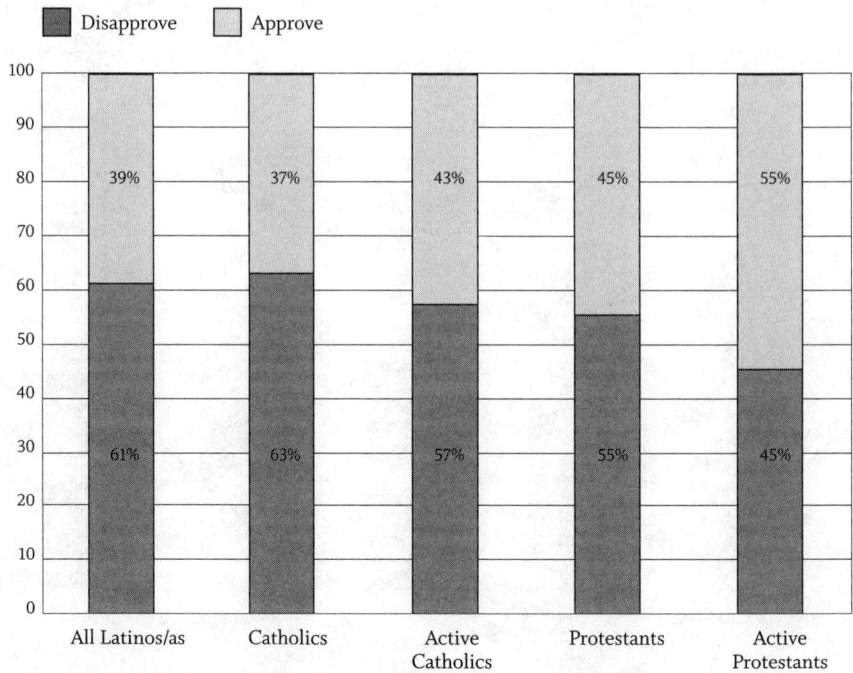

Source: From Hernández et al. (2007). Reproduced with permission.

issues—education, health care and Medicare, the economy and jobs, and the U.S. campaign against terrorism—as their top priorities in the 2004 elections. Latino Catholic and Protestant voters alike ranked "moral values" far beneath most of the other issues polled about (eighth and sixth, respectively), thus indicating that moral values were less critical to their vote than bread-and-butter issues—a finding that holds true even for religiously active individuals. However, more recently, Latino evangelical national organizations have become active in direct political lobbying and organizing efforts around a number of moral value issues, such as antigay legislation, pro-marriage legislation, and immigration reform.[4]

When it comes to political involvement, we can see that general voter registration and voting rates in the 2004 Pew sample were quite high—75 percent of the U.S. citizens indicated they were registered voters, and an overwhelming majority of these registered voters (86 percent) said they had voted in a U.S. election (table 2). These rates are particularly high compared to those reported in previous studies of Latino political involvement. For example, according to the Pew Hispanic Center's recent analysis of the Current Population Survey, ap-

TABLE 1   Comparison of issues that Latino/a Catholics and Protestants identified as being of "extreme importance" in the 2004 elections (among registered voters only)

CATHOLICS			PROTESTANTS		
Issue	*(%)*	*Rank*	*Issue*	*(%)*	*Rank*
Education	52	1	Health care and Medicare	62	1
The economy and jobs	48	2	Education	54	2
Health care and Medicare	47	3	The economy and jobs	54	3
U.S. campaign against terrorism	43	4	U.S. campaign against terrorism	51	4
Crime	40	5	The war in Iraq	45	5
Social Security	39	6	Moral values	45	6
The war in Iraq	38	7	Crime	44	7
Moral values	35	8	Social Security	38	8
Taxes	32	9	Taxes	34	9
The federal budget deficit	29	10	Immigration	30	10
Immigration	27	11	The federal budget deficit	24	11

Source: Findings from the Pew Hispanic Center/Kaiser Family Foundation 2004 National Survey of Latinos: Politics and Civic Engagement. Table from Hernández et al. (2007). Reproduced with permission.

proximately 54 percent of eligible Latino voters were registered to vote in 2006, and 60 percent of registered voters actually voted in that election (Pew Hispanic Center 2007). It is possible that the high rates of voter registration and voting in the 2004 Pew sample are due to either overreporting on the part of participants or, given that the survey was about politics and civic participation, a higher percentage of politically engaged persons agreeing to participate in the survey than is found in the general population.

We also tested to see whether nativity had any impact on registration or voting behavior among Latinos but found no differences between U.S.-born and foreign-born U.S. citizens on either measure. Additionally, we found no differences between Catholic or Protestant voter registration and voting rates among the U.S. citizens in both religious subgroups, as table 2 shows.[5] Further, the registered voters in each denominational cluster reported voting at equally high rates.

Voter registration and voting rates differed between religiously active and inactive Latinos in only a few areas. As table 3 shows, religiously active Catholics register to vote at slightly higher rates than religiously inactive Catholics (81 percent vs. 72 percent). Interestingly, the inverse is true for Latino Protestants, among whom the religiously inactive are more likely to be registered voters (83 percent) than are the religiously active (73 percent). Inactive Protestants also

TABLE 2 Voter registration and voting rates among 2004 National Survey of Latinos, overall and by religious affiliation

	All Latinos/as (%)	Catholics (%)	Protestants (%)
Voter registration rates (%, among U.S. citizens only	75	78	76
Voting rates (% of registered voters who have ever voted in a U.S. election	86	87	92
Percentage who voted in 2002 congressional election	78	79	79
Percentage who voted in 2000 congressional election	82	83	83

Source: Data from Pew Hispanic Center/Kaiser Family Foundation 2004 National Survey of Latinos: Politics and Civic Engagement. Table from Hernández et al. (2007). Reproduced with permission.

TABLE 3 Citizenship and voting rates in 2004 National Survey of Latinos, overall and by religious affiliation and intensity

	Active Catholics (%)	Inactive Catholics (%)	Active Protestants (%)	Inactive Protestants (%)
U.S.-born	36	39	56	56
Foreign-born U.S. citizens	16	14	14	20
Foreign-born non-U.S. citizens	49	47	30	24
Voter registration rates (among U.S. citizens only)	81	72	73	83
Voting rates (% of registered votes who have ever voted in a U.S. election)	89	82	91	94
Percentage who voted in 2002 congressional election	82	71	81	72
Percentage who voted in 2000 congressional election	85	80	84	81

Source: Data from Pew Hispanic Center/Kaiser Family Foundation 2004 National Survey of Latinos: Politics and Civic Engagement. Table from Hernández et al. (2007). Reproduced with permission.

register to vote at higher rates than inactive Catholics (83 percent vs. 72 percent) and report the highest voting rates of any of the subgroups analyzed in table 3 (94 percent); however, the low numbers of inactive Protestants in the sample (N = 98) demand that we interpret these results cautiously.

The high rates of voter registration and voting are not matched by correspondingly high levels of other forms of political engagement. As table 4 shows, only 18 percent of the 2004 Pew survey respondents reported having attended a public meeting or demonstration and only 12 percent had contacted an elected official. While religious affiliation made no apparent difference in these rates, we were not surprised to find that registered voters of either religious identification were more likely to have engaged in these activities.

These low rates correspond to those found in the 2000 Princeton survey (Wuthnow 2000),[6] as table 5 illustrates. This survey found that Latinos are less involved (17 percent) than white non-Hispanics (25 percent) or African Americans (35 percent) in church leadership positions. They are also comparatively less involved in church and other volunteer work. Not surprisingly, and in accordance with other scholars' findings (Segura, Pachon, and Woods 2001), Latinos are also less engaged in political or civic endeavors such as giving money to political candidates and attending political rallies.[7] The widest gap occurs in terms of contact with public officials: only 11 percent of Latinos in the Princeton

TABLE 4   Civic and political involvement in 2004 National Survey of Latinos, overall and by religious affiliation and voter registration status

"In the past year, have you . . . ?"	All Latinos/as (%)	All Protestants (%)	Protestant registered voters (%)	All Catholics (%)	Catholic registered voters (%)
Attended a public meeting or demonstration in the community where you live	18	18	28	17	24
Contacted any elected official	12	14	26	10	19
Attended a political party meeting or function	9	9	14	9	17
Contributed money to a candidate running for public office	8	11	17	7	15
Worked as a volunteer or for pay for a political candidate	4	5	8	4	6

Source: Data from Pew Hispanic Center/Kaiser Family Foundation 2004 National Survey of Latinos: Politics and Civic Engagement. Table from Hernández et al. (2007). Reproduced with permission.

Table 5   Civic and political involvement by race/ethnicity

"During the past twelve months, have you … ?"	Latinos/as (N = 547) (%)	African Americans (N = 509) (%)	White non-Hispanics (N = 3,955) (%)
Contacted an elected official about an issue of concern to you	11	18	29
Given money to a political candidate or party	7	9	14
Attended a political rally or meeting	9	14	11
Worked for a political campaign or voter registration	4	11	5
Attended a class or lecture about social or political issues	15	18	19
Read about social or political issues on the Internet	20	24	31
Done volunteer work at a church or other place of worship	37	56	49
Done volunteer work for an organization other than a church or place of worship	28	39	47
Do you hold any leadership position at your place of worship, such as serving on a committee, serving as an elder or deacon or teaching a class?	17	35	25

Source: Princeton University Religion and Politics survey (Wuthnow 2000). Table from Hernández et al. (2007). Reproduced with permission.

survey indicated they had contacted an elected official, compared with 29 percent of white non-Hispanics.

Overall, and consistent with previous research, Latinos appear to be strongly Democratic. Additionally, Latino Catholics are most likely to identify as Democrats. A higher percentage of Latino Catholics also reported disapproval of President Bush's handling of the war in Iraq. Religious intensity, as measured by church attendance, only seems to matter for Latino Protestants, and tends to have an effect in the conservative direction when it comes to political affiliation. While this means a higher percentage of active Latino Protestants identify as Republicans, it also appears that active Latino Protestants are less likely to register to vote and to vote than inactive Latino Protestants, which perhaps tempers the political effects of this conservative leaning. Also consistent with previous research, we find that Latinos participate in other forms of political engagement at rather low rates (Segura, Pachon, and Woods 2001; Martínez 2005). This seems to be the case regardless of religious affiliation.

Political Encouragement among Latino Religious Leaders: A Congregational Snapshot

While it is clear that religious affiliation affects political views and behaviors for Latinos, it is also likely that the congregational context plays an important role in the relationship (Wald, Owen, and Hill 1988; Kelly and Kelly 2005), especially given the differences based on church attendance shown above. One aspect of the congregational context is the role of the religious leader in encouraging political involvement among congregation members. As Wilson (2008) found in her research of three prominent urban ministries in Chicago, Philadelphia, and New York, Latino religious leaders often find themselves taking "a two-pronged approach: (1) preaching the gospel and (2) taking into account the cultural, structural, and institutional context of the times" (79). To examine this aspect of the congregational context, we draw on data from the Chicago Latino Congregations Study (CLCS) (Burwell et al. 2009). The CLSC, completed in 2007, employed multiple surveys of clergy, lay leaders, and congregants in Latino congregations in the Chicago metropolitan area. (See the appendix for more on methodology.) In particular, we draw on data from a two-part survey of religious leaders in these congregations.

Ideally, we would like to have nationally representative congregational-level data in order to examine religion and politics in the congregational context. However, nationally representative congregational surveys tend to have small numbers of Latino congregations, and limited information about political involvement. While the CLCS focuses on only one metropolitan area, it provides a good opportunity to begin to explore in more detail the ways in which the congregational context affects political identity and behavior among Latino churchgoers.

Out of 82 congregations, 20 (24 percent) were Catholic, 12 (15 percent) were mainline Protestant, 20 (24 percent) were evangelical Protestant, and 30 (37 percent) were Pentecostal Protestant. While there are only a small number of mainline Protestant churches in our sample, there are important differences between mainline Protestant churches and other churches that would be missed if all Protestant churches were condensed into one category. Even with the small number, there are some statistically significant differences between mainline Protestant churches and others, as described below.

To examine the ways that religious leaders may or may not encourage political participation among congregation members, we focus on a few different measures. First, there are direct ways of encouraging political participation, such as asking members of the congregation to engage in particular actions. Second, there are indirect ways, such as inviting a public official to address the congregation, telling the congregation about the importance of political participation in general, and perhaps communicating approval or opposition of the congregation's involvement in certain political activities.

Regarding the more direct approach, survey respondents were asked whether or not they had ever asked members of their congregation to get involved in politics in various ways (table 6), such as signing a petition or calling a public official. More than two-thirds (68 percent) of respondents said they had asked members of their congregation to attend a meeting about a specific social, educational, or political issue. Nearly half of all respondents have asked congregants to sign a petition (48 percent) and to call or write a public official (47 percent). Respondents were much less likely to say they had asked congregants to give money to a political candidate or party (2 percent) or to vote for a particular political candidate (15 percent). It is not surprising that religious leaders would be more likely to be vocal about particular political issues than about particular political candidates or parties, given the requirements for a religious organization to maintain its tax-exempt status.

When comparing congregations across religious traditions, in general, we see higher percentages of Catholic and mainline Protestant religious leaders asking members of their congregations to participate in these particular ways than evangelical and Pentecostal leaders. However, we found two exceptions: asking congregants to vote for a particular political candidate, in which case a higher percentage of Pentecostal leaders answered yes, and asking congregants to give money to a political candidate or party. Only two respondents in total answered yes to the latter question.

While higher percentages of Catholic and mainline leaders tended to answer yes to this group of questions, there are only two differences across religious traditions that are statistically significant. First, leaders in evangelical congregations are less likely than leaders in all other congregations to say they have asked members of their congregation to volunteer time for a voter registration drive or political campaign.[8]

Second, leaders in evangelical congregations are less likely than leaders in Catholic congregations to say they have asked members of their congregation to participate in direct action, such as protests or rallies. Evangelical leaders are also less likely than mainline leaders to say they have asked members this ques-

TABLE 6   Religious leader encouraged political involvement directly

Religious leader asked congegants to:	All (%)	Catholic (%)	Mainline Protestant (%)	Evangelical Protestant (%)	Pentecostal Protestant (%)
Sign a petition	48	60	58	42	40
Call or write a public official	47	50	58	47	40
Attend a meeting about a specific social, educational, or political issue	68	70	83	58	67
Volunteer time for voter registration drive, political campaigns	30	40	58	5	27
Vote for a particular political candidate	15	10	8	11	23
Participate in direct action, such as protests or rallies	41	60	50	21	37
Give money to a political candidate or party	2	0	8	0	3

Source: Data from the Chicago Latino Congregations Study (Burwell et al. 2009).

tion, but this difference is significant only at $P < .100$ and should therefore be interpreted cautiously.

Turning to more indirect ways of encouraging political involvement, approximately 59 percent of all respondents said they had invited a public official or community leader to speak at their congregation. This percentage was fairly consistent across religious traditions. The highest reported percentage came from mainline Protestant leaders (66 percent) and the lowest from Catholic leaders (55 percent), but this difference was not statistically significant.

When asked how often they speak to their congregation about the importance of political participation, more than half (52 percent) of all religious leaders answered either "sometimes" or "very often" (table 7). Comparing across religious traditions, we see that the group with the lowest percentage reporting "very often" is the religious leaders in evangelical Protestant congregations and the highest percentage is found among mainline Protestant religious leaders. When we combine the "very often" and "sometimes" responses, religious leaders in Catholic congregations are more likely than religious leaders in Evangelical congregations and Pentecostal congregations to speak to their congregation about the importance of political participation.[9]

Religious leaders were also asked if they favored or opposed their congregation participating in particular political activities. Table 8 shows the percentage

Table 7   Religious leader speaks to congregation about importance of political participation

Frequency	All (%)	Catholic (%)	Mainline Protestant (%)	Evangelical Protestant (%)	Pentecostal Protestant (%)
Very often	13	16	20	5	15
Sometimes	39	58	40	26	33
Rarely	28	16	20	42	30
Never	20	10	20	26	22

Source: Data from the Chicago Latino Congregations Study (Burwell et al. 2009).

of religious leaders who answered "somewhat favor" or "strongly favor" in regard to three activities. More than four out of five respondents (83 percent) said they favored (somewhat or strongly) their congregation contacting public officials on topics of community concern. Just under half of all respondents (45 percent) were in favor of their congregation engaging in direct action or protests, and less than one-quarter (23 percent) were in favor of their congregation engaging in nonviolent civil disobedience. While the survey questions regarding these matters do not measure whether or not the religious leader expresses his or her favor or opposition toward such actions, it is not unreasonable to expect that the opinions of religious leaders would matter for many churchgoers. As Wald, Owen, and Hill (1988) note, while religious leaders have opportunities to communicate political messages directly to their congregations (as described above), there are also implicit political messages transmitted in congregations. Religious leaders' opinions about various political issues, whether expressed explicitly or not, likely shape the political culture of a congregation and are an important part of the congregational context.

When we compare across religious traditions, two significant differences stand out. First, Catholic leaders are more likely than mainline Protestant leaders to say they are in favor of their congregation contacting public officials, but evangelical and Pentecostal leaders are not significantly more or less likely than any other group. Second, Catholic leaders are more likely than Pentecostal leaders to say they are in favor of their congregation engaging in nonviolent civil disobedience. On all three of these measures, Catholic leaders make up the highest percentage of leaders in favor of their congregations' political activities.

Overall, it seems religious leaders in Catholic churches are most likely to

TABLE 8   Religious leader's support of congregational political activity

Frequency	All (%)	Catholic (%)	Mainline Protestant (%)	Evangelical Protestant (%)	Pentecostal Protestant (%)
Religious leader favors congregation:					
Contacting public officials on topics of community concern	83	95	64	84	82
Engaging in direct action or protests	45	58	50	42	33
Engaging in nonviolent civil disobedience	23	37	30	17	13

Source: Data from the Chicago Latino Congregations Study (Burwell et al. 2009)

encourage people within their congregations to be involved in politics in the various ways explored here. At first glance this may seem contrary to what one would expect, given individual-level results from previous research that suggest Latino Catholics are less likely to be politically involved (Verba, Schlozman, and Brady 1995) or less likely to report that their congregation is politically involved (Espinosa 2006). However, our results in the previous section suggest there are not denominational differences among Latinos when it comes to nonvoting types of political engagement, and Jones-Correa and Leal (2001, 760) argue that their results suggest "Latino Catholics may receive greater encouragement than their Protestant counterparts" when it comes to political engagement. Nonetheless, we can only speculate at this point as to what the effects of encouragement from religious leaders may be on the members of the congregation and their political involvement. Our results suggest that Latinos in Catholic congregations in the Chicago area might be more likely to receive encouragement from their religious leaders to be involved in political activities. The Chicago Latino Congregations Study and other similar research conducted in Chicago and Miami (Kniss and Numrich 2007; Stepick, Rey, and Mahler 2009) suggest the importance of this type of engagement and that religious institutions matter in building broader Latino social and political capacity.

Conclusion

The relationship among ethnicity, religion, and politics among Latinos is complex and multifaceted. Not only do individual experiences and worldviews vary based on factors such as national origin, immigration status, generation, and socioeconomic status, they also vary based on religious factors such as affiliation and participation, thus producing varied political outcomes.

This essay examined how religious factors relate to some political outcomes for Latinos. We approached this relationship from two different directions. First, we looked at how religious affiliation and religious intensity relate to political identity, political opinion, and political behavior among Latinos in the general population. We found that, consistent with previous research, Latinos—and Latino Catholics in particular—tend to identify with the Democratic Party more than with the Republican Party, and that a higher percentage of religiously active Latino Protestants identify with the Republican Party. We also found that while a higher percentage of Latino Catholics disapproved of the way President Bush managed the war in Iraq, there were no significant denominational differences when it came to the political issues considered most important before the 2004 elections: education, health care, the economy, and terrorism. Regarding political behavior, we found that while overall rates of voter registration and voting were rather high, with even higher rates among religiously inactive Latino Protestants, participation in other forms of political activity were rather low for both Latino Catholics and Protestants.

Second, we looked at how religious leaders in a major U.S. city, Chicago, go about encouraging political involvement among individuals in their congregations. In general, we found higher percentages of religious leaders being vocal in their congregations about being involved with certain political issues rather than particular political candidates, campaigns, or parties. Catholic leaders are more likely to report employing various ways to encourage political involvement in their congregations and evangelical leaders are often the least likely. While we cannot speak to the effects of their encouragement at this point, it is likely that religious leaders play an important role in the congregational context that contributes to political involvement among individuals.

Given the dramatic growth of the Latino population, their increased political influence, and the significant role that religion plays in this community, greater attention needs to be given to the intersection of ethnicity, religion, and politics. Particularly promising is exploring how congregational cultures and pastoral cues shape the political values and behaviors of individual congregants. Existing research suggests that one might begin by focusing on better understanding the more complex path that pushes Latinos from the pew to civic engagement and political action.

Our analysis has shown political differences across the Latino Catholic and Protestant divide and that these differences arise from fundamental religious ideology. What factors account for these differences? Among Catholics, the social teachings of the church may have a strong influence on Catholic leaders and parishioners. Social teachings inspire Catholics to be engaged in public policy debates around issues of poverty, labor rights, immigration, abortion, and others (Palacios 2007). They also have a longer tradition of social activism and community organizing than Latino Protestants or evangelicals, though recently Latino evangelicals have organized and begun to flex their political muscle (Lee and Pachon 2007; Wilson 2008).

Another factor is "religious traditionalism," which includes views on the authority of the Christian Bible. Latino Catholics and Protestants have different views on the question of biblical authority. Catholics are less likely to be biblical literalists, while Latino Protestants hold a more literalist interpretation of the Bible, a view that is more closely aligned with Republican values (McDaniel and Ellison 2008). However, religious traditionalism can also galvanize ethnic interests and solidarity. As has been shown (Kelly and Morgan 2008), religious traditionalism can also serve to mobilize political activity, create group consciousness, and challenge policies that threaten minority empowerment. Furthermore, knowing that certain issues can trump Latino partisanship based on national origin (Alvarez and Garcia Bedolla 2003) or religious affiliation (Kelly and Morgan 2008) suggests that Latino political alignment along religious lines is more complex. A case in point is the immigration issue.

Perhaps no other issue has more potential for shattering the Latino Catholic and Protestant political cleavages than the immigration issue. The Latino response to the immigration debate has resulted in a more unified and politically aware community and has created partnerships across the ideological divide, for example between Latino Catholics and Protestants, and between Cubans and Mexicans, that didn't exist before (Suro and Escobar 2006). A sizable number of Protestant and Catholic leaders and parishioners were activated and involved during the 2006 immigration protests, though the Catholic influence was more pronounced (Beyerlein, Sikkink, and Hernández 2007). An important initiative that crosses religious affiliation and barriers is the Campaign for Immigration Reform, organized by one of the largest evangelical Latino organizations in the country, Esperanza.[10] Esperanza has enlisted a sizable number of Catholic, Pentecostal, and mainline Protestant leaders and organizations to unite in an effort to reform immigration laws. Because the immigration issue hits home for so many Latinos across ethnic lines, it has the potential of trumping religious denominations' influence on political affiliation. And if the past results of inter Latino ethnic solidarity in response to the immigration debate of 2006 (Suro and Escobar 2006) is a harbinger of the future, anticipated immigration reform efforts and its opposition, coming primarily from the Republican Party, may further reduce the Catholic, mainline Protestant, and evangelical political divide.

Yet to the degree that Latinos become more pluralistic and the conversion trend from Catholicism to Protestantism continues unabated (Greeley 1997; Hernández 1999; Hernández, Smith, and Burwell 2008), the Latino vote will become less cohesive and increasingly more Republican.

Appendix: The Chicago Latino Congregations Study—Methodology

The Chicago Latino Congregations Study (CLCS) is a multilevel comprehensive study of Latino congregations, clergy, lay leadership, and parishioners.

The researchers initially compiled a comprehensive list of the religious universe of metropolitan Chicago congregations with a significant Latino attendance of 50 percent for Protestant churches and 30 percent or more for Catholic parishes. Churches were then stratified by religious tradition in order to match the Latino population percentage in the categories of Catholic, mainline Protestant, evangelical, and Pentecostal.

The study consisted of several instruments: (1) a shorter leaders' survey that was completed by eighty-four of the churches' leaders; (2) a longer leaders' survey that contained the same questions as the short survey along with others and a self-administered section, which was completed by eighty-two of the churches' leaders; and (3) a survey of adult congregants and (4) a survey of youth congregants that were completed by congregants during or after worship services. In all, 2,368 adults in seventy-four congregations and 607 youth in sixty-three congregations completed the congregant surveys.

Individual-level response rates varied widely by congregation. Based on the field researchers' estimates of attendance at each worship service in which participants were invited to complete the survey, the response rate across all cooperating congregations was about 25 percent. In other words, about 2,368 out of roughly 9,500 attendees completed adult or youth surveys. In general, smaller congregations had better lay response rates than larger congregations, so that in the average participating congregation, approximately 55 percent of worship attendees completed the survey.

To compensate for higher cooperation rates among some religious traditions, a weight was created to ensure that descriptive statistics reflect the population proportions of Catholic, mainline Protestant, evangelical Protestant, and Pentecostal Latino congregations.

For a more detailed description of the methodology for the CLCS, see "The Chicago Latino Congregations Study (CLCS): Methodological Considerations" by Rebecca Burwell, Edwin I. Hernández, Milagros Peña, Jeffrey Smith, and David Sikkink, December 2009, available on the Center for the Study of Latino Religion's website, Institute for Latino Studies, University of Notre Dame, www .nd.edu/~cslr/.

Notes

1. This section is adopted from a previous report from the Institute for Latino Studies at the University of Notre Dame, Indiana: Edwin I. Hernández, Kenneth G. Davis, Milagros Peña, Georgian Schiopu, Jeffrey Smith, and Matthew T. Loveland, *Faith and Values in Action: Religion, Politics, and Social Attitudes Among US Latinos/as*, CSLR publication no. 2007.1, November 2007. All findings reported as significant in this section are statistically significant at $P < .05$ or higher.

2. The Pew Hispanic Center and the Kaiser Family Foundation bear no responsibility for the interpretations offered, or conclusions made based on analysis of the Pew Hispanic Center/Kaiser Family Foundation 2004 National Survey of Latinos: Politics and Civic Engagement Data.

3. Of the participants who answered the religious identification question in the 2004 National Survey of Latinos, 66 percent identified as Catholic, 19 percent identified as Protestant or other Christian, and 15 percent of the sample answered "other" or "none." Only 2 percent of the sample identified as Protestant without also identifying as born again, making it difficult to distinguish among different Protestant subcategories. Therefore, Protestants are grouped together for this portion of the analysis.

4. Examples of Latino evangelical leaders and national organizations involved in political lobbying activities include the Reverend Luis Cortez of Esperanza US and the Reverends Jesse Miranda and Samuel Rodriguez of the National Hispanic Christian Leadership Conference and the Latino Fellowship of InterVarsity Fellowship.

5. Since the survey was conducted before the 2004 presidential election, we do not have voting rates for this. All subsequent discussion of voter registration and voting rate is based only on the U.S. citizens in the 2004 Pew survey. For a more recent analysis of Latino voting behavior, see Pew Hispanic Center 2007 and Pew Hispanic Center 2010.

6. While the results from the Princeton Religion and Politics Survey ($N = 5,317$) enable us to compare Latinos/as, African Americans, and white non-Hispanics, the survey also has limitations because of the small numbers of Latinos/as in the sample (Wuthnow and Evans 2002).

7. It is important to note that there are likely regional differences in faith-based involvement among Latinos (Warren 2003; Silk and Walsh 2008). While we do not control for regional differences in this analysis, Silk and Walsh (2008), for example, have noted an increase in Latino faith-based involvement in places such as Texas and California.

8. All results reported as significant in this section are statistically significant at $P < .050$ or higher unless otherwise noted.

9. The difference between leaders in Catholic congregations and leaders in Pentecostal congregations is significant at $P < .100$, and should be interpreted cautiously.

10. See http://www.esperanza.us/site/c.inKOIPNhEiG/b.5542293/k.4D46/Immigration_Esper anza_For_America.htm.

References

Alvarez, R. Michael, and Lisa Garcia Bedoll. 2003. "The Foundations of Latino Voter Partisanship: Evidence from the 2000 Election." *Journal of Politics* 65 (1): 31–49.

Arvizu, John R., and F. Chris Garcia. 1996. "Latino Voting Participation: Explaining and Differentiating Latino Voting Turnout." *Hispanic Journal of Behavioral Sciences* 18 (2): 104–28.

Beyerlein, Kraig, David Sikkink, and Edwin I. Hernández. 2007. "Latino Religion and Involvement in Immigration Protest." Paper presented at the annual meeting of the Society for the Scientific Study of Religion, Tampa, FL, November 1–3.

Burwell, Rebecca, Edwin I. Hernández, Milagros Peña, Jeffrey Smith, and David Sikkink. 2009. " Chicago Latino Congregations Study (CLCS): Methodological Considerations." Unpublished manuscript, Trinity Christian College.

Calvo, Maria Antonia, and Steven J. Rosenstone. 1989. *Hispanic Political Participation.* Latino Electorates Series. San Antonio, TX: Southwest Voter Research Institute.

Claassen, Ryan L. 2004. "Political Opinion and Distinctiveness: The Case of Hispanic Ethnicity." *Political Research Quarterly* 57 (4): 609–20.

Diaz, William A. 1996. "Latino Participation in America: Associational and Political Roles." *Hispanic Journal of Behavioral Sciences* 18 (2): 154–74.

Espinosa, Gastón. 2006. "U.S. Latino/a Clergy and Churches in Political and Social Action." In *Emerging Voices, Urgent Choices: Essays on Latino/a Religious Leadership,* ed. Edwin I. Hernández, Milgros Peña, Kenneth G. Davis, and Elizabeth Station. Leiden: Brill.

Garcia, F. Chris. 1997. *Pursuing Power: Latinos and the Political System.* Notre Dame, IN: University of Notre Dame Press.

Greeley, Andrew. 1997. "Defection among Hispanics [updated]." *America* 177, 12–13.

Hernández, Edwin I. 1999. "Moving from the Cathedral to Storefront Churches: Understanding Religious Growth and Decline among Latino Protestants." In *Protestantes/Protestants: Hispanic Christianity within Mainline Traditions,* ed. D. Maldonado, 216–35. Nashville, TN: Abingdon.

Hernández, Edwin I., Jeffrey Smith, and Rebecca Burwell. 2008. "A Study of Hispanic Catholics: Why Are They Leaving the Catholic Church? Implications for the New Evangelization." In *The New Evangelization: Overcoming the Obstacles,* ed. Steven Boguslawski and Ralph Martin, 109–41. Mahwah, NJ: Paulist Press.

Jones-Correa, Michael A., and David L. Leal. 2001. "Political Participation: Does Religion Matter?" *Political Research Quarterly* 54 (4): 751–70.

Kelly, Nathan J., and Jana Morgan Kelly. 2005. "Religion and Latino Partisanship in the United States." *Political Research Quarterly* 58 (1): 87–95.

———. 2008. "Religious Traditionalism and Latino Politics in the United States." *American Politics Research* 36 (2): 236–63.

Kniss, Fred, and Paul D. Numrich. 2007. *Sacred Assemblies and Civic Engagement: How Religion Matters for America's Newest Immigrants.* New Brunswick, NJ: Rutgers University Press.

Lee, Jongho, and Harry P. Pachon. 2007. "Leading the Way." *American Politics Research* 35 (2): 252–272.

Martínez, Lisa M. 2005. "Yes We Can: Latino Participation in Unconventional Politics." *Social Forces* 84 (1): 135–55.

McDaniel, Eric L., and Christopher G. Ellison. 2008. "God's Party? Race, Religion, and Partisanship over Time." *Political Research Quarterly* 61 (2): 180–91.

Palacios, Joseph M. 2007. *The Catholic Social Imagination: Activism and the Just Society of Mexico and the United States.* Chicago: University of Chicago Press.

Pantoja, Adrian D., Ricardo Ramírez, and Gary M. Segura. 2001. "Citizens by Choice, Voters by Necessity: Patterns in Political Mobilization by Naturalized Latinos." *Political Research Quarterly* 54 (4): 729–50.

Pew Forum on Religion & Public Life. 2004. "How the Faithful Voted: Political Alignments & the Religious Divide in Election 2004." Event transcript from a forum held in Washington, DC, November 17, 2004. http://pewforum.org/events/index.php?EventID=64.

Pew Hispanic Center. 2007. "The Latino Electorate: An Analysis of the 2006 Election." Pew Hispanic Center, Washington, DC. http://pewhispanic.org/publications/?year=2007.

———. 2010. "Statistical Portrait of Hispanics in the United States, 2008." Pew Hispanic Center, Washington, DC. http://pewhispanic.org/factsheets/factsheet.php?FactsheetID=58.

Pew Hispanic Center and Kaiser Family Foundation. 2004. "2004 National Survey of Latinos: Politics and Civic Engagement." Pew Hispanic Center, Washington, DC. http://pewhispanic.org/datasets/signup.php?DatasetID=3.

Pew Hispanic Center and Pew Forum on Religion & Public Life. 2007. "Changing Faiths: Latinos and the Transformation of American Religion." Pew Hispanic Center, Washington, DC. http://pewhispanic.org/publications/?year=2007.

Segura, Gary M., Harry Pachon, and Nathan D. Woods. 2001. "Hispanics, Social Capital, and Civic Engagement." *National Civic Review* 90 (1): 85–96.

Silk, Mark, and Andrew Walsh. 2008. *One Nation, Divisible: How Regional Religious Differences Shape American Politics.* Matwah, NJ: Rowman & Littlefield.

Stepick, Alex, Terry Rey, and Sarah J. Mahler. 2009. "Religion, Immigration, and Civic Engagement." In *Churches and Charity in the Immigrant City,* ed. Alex Stepic, Terry Rey, and Sarah J. Mahler, 1–38. New Brunswick, NJ: Rutgers University Press.

Suro, Roberto, and Gabriel Escobar. 2006. "2006 National Survey of Latinos: The Immigration Debate." Pew Hispanic Center, Washington, DC. http://pewhispanic.org/reports/report.php?ReportID=68.

Verba, Sidney, Kay Lehman Schlozman, and Henry Brady. 1995. *Voice and Equality: Civic Voluntarism in American Politics.* Cambridge, MA: Harvard University Press.

Wald, Kenneth D., Dennis E. Owen, and Samuel S Hill Jr. 1988. "Churches as Political Communities." *American Political Science Review* 82 (2): 531–48.

Warren, Mark A. 2003. "Faith and Leadership in the Inner City: How Social Capital Contributes to Democratic Renewal." In *Religion as Social Capital: Producing the Common Good,* ed. Corwin E. Smith. Waco, TX: Baylor University Press.

Wilson, Catherine E. 2008. *The Politics of Latino Faith: Religion, Identity, and Urban Community.* New York: New York University Press.

Wuthnow, Robert. 2000. Religion and Politics Survey. Princeton, NJ: Princeton University Survey Research Center.

Wuthnow, Robert, and John H. Evans. 2002. *The Quiet Hand of God: Faith-Based Activism and the Public Role of Mainline Protestantism.* Berkeley: University of California Press.

The Stranger among Us

The Christian Right and Immigration

Robin Dale Jacobson

There is a dearth of work on the Christian Right that deals with race. Some of the important exceptions begin to unpack the dynamics between white and black Christian conservatives. But what happens if we extend the frame beyond black and white? How does the Christian Right approach, and become informed by, the multiracial politics of today? A doorway into answering this question is the issue of U.S. immigration, a racialized topic that at its heart has to do with questions of national identity, culture, and religion.

In this latest, twentieth- to twenty-first-century round of national attention to immigration, Christian Right organizations have taken differing stances on the issue, some arguing for increased restriction, others for increased compassion. Secure Borders and Families First in Immigration are two coalitions that have attracted some stalwarts of the Christian Right, such as the American Family Association, the Reverend Lou Sheldon's Traditional Values Coalition, and Phyllis Schlafly's Eagle Forum, to work for enhanced enforcement and more restrictive policies.[1] While Eagle Forum has long advocated restrictions on immigration, Lou Sheldon's Traditional Values Coalition is newer to the fold. On the other hand, the Southern Baptist Convention (SBC) and the associated Ethics and Religious Liberty Commission headed by Richard Land take a more liberal stance in the debate. In 2006 the SBC adopted resolutions that urge Christians to "follow the biblical principle of caring for the foreigners among us (Deuteronomy 24:17–22) and the command of Christ to be a neighbor to those in need of assistance (Luke 10:30–37), regardless of their racial or ethnic background, country of origin, or legal status," and to "act redemptively and reach out to meet the physical, emotional, and spiritual needs of all immigrants" and help them become a part of American society legally and socially (Southern Baptist Convention 2006). In yet another category are Christian Right organizations that recognize the need to deal with this issue now but have not taken a stand. For example, the Family Research Council, a powerful Christian Right organization, held an immigration conference in April 2006 that brought together thinkers on both sides of the issue. While the council has not formulated an official policy on the issue, a survey of its members suggests that nine out of ten believe illegal immigrants should be deported.

Why, when immigration is on the agenda of the Christian Right, a movement united by an evangelical base that is clearly in support of a restrictionist stance, does the issue divide Christian Right organizations? A look across time sheds some light on this question.

The new Christian Right's relationship with the issue of immigration has changed over time. In the early 1990s there was a growing nativism, which was expressed both at the grassroots level and in many conservative organizations. The Rockford, Cato, and American Enterprise Institutes and the Heritage Foundation took positions on the immigration issue, while many Christian Right groups stayed, for the most part, to the side. This is somewhat surprising, given the growing strength of the Christian Right and the comparative unity on this issue on the right at that time. In the mid-1990s, Christian Right organizations were expanding rapidly and flexing their newfound political muscle. Additionally, the Republican Party was relatively unified on the issue of immigration. Today, however, many Christian Right groups are in decline, and the Republican Party is far from unified. In fact, born-again President George W. Bush was at odds with many restrictionist Republicans. Why, then, would Christian Right organizations, which avoided the immigration issue at a time of strength and consensus, flirt with the topic at a time of weakness and division over the issue?

By answering these empirical puzzles about Christian Right organizational positioning on immigration, we become better able to answer a broader question about the Christian Right and race. An underappreciated part of the Christian Right is the critical role of the racial terrain on which movement actors perform. Immigration is a highly racialized issue in the United States and can provide a window onto the Christian Right's approach to racial politics. Analyzing the varying stances of Christian Right organizations on the issue of immigration, we find that the history of black and white religious politics informs how multiracial politics play out today. Race and religious politics intersect in numerous ways. This essay illuminates how religious political organizations operate and respond to racial politics through their agenda-setting strategies.

Racial identity within religious movements has frequently been treated as a static, independent variable. However, Omi and Winant's (1989) racial formation theory (see also Winant 1994) suggests we should consider it a site of contestation. To so requires placing the Religious Right on a historically specific, racial terrain where religious, racial, and national identities are being fought over and redefined. This allows us to see that Religious Right organizations are both responding to the broader U.S. racial-political terrain and attempting to navigate their position within their own conservative religious political movement. It is at this intersection that we can understand why groups approach the issue of immigration as they do.

To illustrate how these forces help us understand the immigration politics of the Christian Right, I explore the case of a single organization's relationship with immigration through a close reading of the organization's literature. The Christian Coalition is a good case to consider because the organization is central to the early New Christian Right and because it is an example of organizations with a shifting stance on immigration. During the rise of nativism in the early and mid-1990s, the Christian Coalition chose not to get involved in the immigration debate. In response to changes in the organizational and political stature of the group, as well as shifts in the broader racial-political terrain, it began to express a restrictionist stance toward immigration after 2000.

The Christian Coalition is explored not because it is representative of all Religious Right groups, for indeed it is not representative, in part because of its organizational decline since the late 1990s. It is, however, an important case. By looking at how a single religious organization navigates its relationship to immigration in conjunction with changes to its political capabilities, we can begin to tease out the important forces that affect the way race and religion intersect to produce new agendas. This case highlights the importance of the historical narratives of the interaction between race and religion articulated by key actors, as well as the part played by the larger political and racial context and by organizational demands.

Race and the Study of the Christian Right

Scholars exploring the demographics of the Christian Right have found, not surprisingly, that the Christian Right is and most likely will continue to be predominantly white. Knowing that black evangelicals act very differently from white evangelicals on some key political issues, many scholars of the Christian Right have chosen to focus on white actors (Robinson 2006, 592).

A body of work has emerged that attempts to answer why the Christian Right has been predominantly white despite some congruence of political views between white evangelicals and highly religious citizens of color. Noting similar conservative stances on social issues, scholars have considered the prospects for alliances across race and the success of efforts by the Christian Right to bring in African Americans and Latinos (Calhoun-Brown 1998; Greeley and Hout 2006; Green 2006; Robinson 2006). For example, Greeley and Hout, through survey research, conclude that degrees of religiosity (as measured by attendance at church, Bible study, and the like) intensify political views but do not dictate the direction of those views. Rather, race dictates the direction of those views, to the left or right. Religion moves one further toward the ends of the political spectrum; it serves to intensify the political view that is predicted by race (Greeley and Hout 2006, 72). However, other exit poll data may indicate a different relationship between race and religion. An Ohio exit poll taken in 2004 showed that among black Protestants, higher church attendance increased the tendency to vote for Bush for president, indicating that religiosity actually determined which candidate individuals were voting for (Green 2006). Complicating the matter further, support for particular Christian Right candidates and support for Christian Right organizations may not be influenced by the same factors. Robinson (2006) finds that social conservatism does not predict support for Christian Right groups, but religiosity, measured by frequency of religious attendance and intensity of belief, does. However, this does not necessarily translate into different political actions or more votes cast for Republican candidates.

High agreement on social issues between Christian Right organizations and religious citizens of color, such as African American Protestants and Latino Catholics, in conjunction with disparate political behavior suggests that the relationship between religion and political behavior is influenced by race. The impact of the intersection of race and religion on political behavior seems to require a more complicated model than a simple left-right political spectrum. Robinson (2006, 600) suggests distinguishing between economic and social issues, or even between social issues that do not align neatly with religion, such as the death penalty and abortion. Calhoun-Brown (1998) remarks that to understand why black evangelicals are not mobilized by the Christian Right, we must consider symbolic politics. She argues that mobilization or lack thereof can be explained by affective responses rather than by explicit agreement on issues. Although it is clear that religion does not have the same impact on all citizens, it is not clear why this should be the case. Religious affiliation alone does not explain the relationship between individuals and the Christian Right; racial identities are also crucial to consider.

These studies provide snapshots of who makes up the Christian Right. Race, religiosity, and political identity are employed as static, independent variables. These studies raise interesting questions for others to explore about the formation of racial and religious identities, and their contestation.

As scholars in the social sciences and humanities have pointed out, racial and religious identities and their meaning are the result of cultural and political battles. This suggests we need to treat them as dependent variables of political struggles, not only as independent variables explaining coalitions and mobilization. If we are to take the social construction of race seriously, we must not only look at who supports the Christian Right and what issues therein but also examine the role of the Christian Right in creating racial identities and how the political battles over race have an impact on the Christian Right. The relationship between race and religion for the Christian Right is variable and changes over time, across organizations, and in relation to the broader racial-political context.

In the following story on immigration, we see the Christian Coalition attempting to rewrite its racial-political identity as a color-blind, American Christian identity. We see the organization actively involved in the racial formation process as it attempts to forward a new racial project, new definitions of the meaning and import of race, with religion at its core. To push this project, it also must situate itself in the competing "racial institutional orders" (Smith 2005) of the day.

According to Desmond King and Rogers Smith (2005, 75), competing racial institutional orders are coalitions of state and non-state actors, organizations, and institutions that "have adopted (and often adapted) racial concepts, commitments and aims." These racial goals serve both to solidify the coalition and to further the interests of members of the coalition. Change in the racial political landscape, and frequently the political landscape more broadly, can be understood as a result of competition between two competing racial orders, a white supremacist order and an equalitarian, transformative racial order.

Such a racial orders framework helps us understand how the Christian Right can find itself not aligned with its usual political allies on the issue of immigration. What might appear as odd alliances if we privilege economics—for example, an alliance of civil rights organizations and business groups during the immigration reform debates of the 1960s—become more understandable if we foreground race. If we use a framework that looks at the "equalitarian order" and the "antitransformative" or "white supremacist" order, we might find that these strange bedfellows are in fact not strange at all but part of the same racial institutional order.

This suggests that to understand race and the Christian Right requires an investigation into the dynamic intersection of race and religion in constructing the racial-religious projects forwarded by these organizations, as well as how they understand the contemporary racial-political orders.

The Christian Coalition, Race, and Immigration

When the immigration issue hit the conservative political stage in the early 1990s, the Christian Coalition refused to take a stand. It did this in the face of factors that might suggest it should have taken a restrictionist stance. First, the Coalition's elite political allies were engaged in a battle against immigration, and were fairly unified on the issue. Second, the Coalition at this time was attempting to mobilize citizens by broadening the issues the group addressed; at the same time, there was a growing grassroots nativist movement emerging on the political scene. The base was clearly concerned about immigration, and its behavior on the streets, in opinion polls, and at the ballot box demonstrated it was willing to fight for this cause. Despite these factors the Coalition refused to take a stand and did not address immigration as an issue at its conferences, in fund-raising letters, or in its publications.[2]

Many allies of the Christian Coalition supported restrictionist causes in the 1990s. Pat Buchanan, who was writing regularly for the *Christian American*, the Christian Coalition's main publication from 1990 until 1998, in the first two years of its publication, ran a presidential campaign on an America First platform. Phyllis Schlafly, who had a regular column in *Christian American* throughout its life, was and is supportive of restrictive immigration policies as well. The Republican Party was relatively unified on the issue of immigration throughout the 1990s and included fighting illegal immigration in the party's national platform in 1992 and 1996. In 1996, it supported repeal of birthright citizenship and supported Proposition 187, the 1994 California voter initiative designed to deny social services to the undocumented.

The Christian Coalition supported neither Proposition 187 nor a restrictionist stance on immigration, even though it was attempting to reach out to religious citizens on a whole new range of issues and California was a key area for the Coalition's growth. Coalition members were asking the organization to take a stand, and the leadership clearly recognized this. A letter published in the *Christian American* reads, "I can't support any organization that refuses to speak out against the invasion of aliens" (Letters to the Editor 1992, 21). The Coalition continued to refuse to adopt a position after the 1992 election, even though it was consciously trying to enter new and varied issue domains. Ralph Reed, president of the Christian Coalition, set out a five-point organizational strategy in January 1993, one point being to "develop a broad-based issues agenda" to grow and meet people's needs. The Christian Coalition aimed to develop an agenda that matched the most important issues to voters, including crime, schools, and the environment (Reed 1993, 15). The organization did not, however, respond to growing concerns over immigration.

This is also evident when we look at the regional level throughout the early and mid-1990s. California was a hub of the nativist movement and a goal for the Christian Coalition's growth at the time. To better understand the Coalition's silence, it is helpful to consider the subnational racial-religious political setting. Orange County, California, was a hotbed of conservative activism during the McCarthy era. This political movement, combined with the military-industrial complex central to the region's economic well-being, created a unique antisecular conservatism (McGirr 2001, 51). Additionally, while race was important to this movement, it was not the explicitly segregationist form found elsewhere in the country. California has a long history of attempting to craft a raceless (i.e., white) state (Jacobson 2008, xxiii–xxiv). Color-blind conservatism, with its emphasis on individualism and a denial of the importance of race in government and public programs, found a ready home in the conservative movement emanating from Orange County. This background explains why, in the early 1990s, Southern California was central to the Christian Coalition's attempts to expand, and to a flourishing nativist movement.

In 1994, an anti-immigrant grassroots campaign in Southern California culminated in the passage of Proposition 187. The heart of Proposition 187 was also the heart of a central mobilizing drive for the Christian Coalition during the same time period, the first four years of the 1990s. At the first "Road to Victory" conference in 1991, the Christian Coalition reported large growth and mobilization efforts in California. Thirty-two new chapters had been established in six months, and they claimed to run large number of candidates in Southern California. In fact, Southern California was so successful for them that their strategy of targeting low-profile elected offices became known as the San Diego model. At the "Road to Victory" conference, when discussing California, attendees talked about such things as keeping their distaste for Pete Wilson, gubernatorial candidate in California, quiet at county-level meetings but did not mention immigration once, despite a fast-growing nativist movement occurring in the same area at the same time. A 1992 interview with a representative from Southern California published in *Christian American* does not mention the immigration issue either. There is only one article in *Christian American* on the problems of immigrants, and it was published after the vote on Proposition 187. The Coalition made a clear choice not to take a stand on the issue, never offering an editorial or an article by a Coalition leader and publishing only a single article supporting some of the tenets after the election was over.

This same disjuncture between attempts to mobilize in an area where restrictionist causes polled as highly salient and official silence on immigration continued throughout the 1990s. In March and July of 1996, multipage reports on California appeared in *Christian American*. These reports are clear attempts at mobilizing individuals in that state through a discussion of issues not traditionally at the forefront of the Christian Coalition's agenda. While concerns about classroom size and voter fraud are raised, there is not a single mention of immigration, even though it was on the mind of the California electorate and the nation at large.

Why did the Christian Coalition refuse to take a stand on immigration during the 1990s, a time of rapid organizational growth and increasing political power for the group, as well as a time of strong consensus among elite allies and citizen fellow travelers on the issue? Race theory tells us to consider the racial formation process more broadly to better understand a stance on this highly racialized issue. We should consider the racial project—the meaning and import of racial categorizations and interpretations of racial dynamics and politics—being offered by the Christian Coalition. What is the meaning of race embedded in the group's political action? How is the Coalition engaged in the struggle over racial identities and notions of citizenship? By considering the historical political context and the racial stage on which the Christian Coalition is acting, the alternative racial project offered by the Christian Coalition, and the status of the Christian Coalition as an organization, we can see why in the mid-1990s the Coalition did not become involved in the issue of immigration.

The Christian Coalition was responding to what Omi and Winant (1989) call "racial terrain," or what King and Smith call "pre-existing contexts." Each term gets at a similar set of ideas important to understanding the development of the Christian Right in relation to issues of race. The New Christian Right entered the stage in the post–civil rights era. This determined the contours of its arguments. The group's political activity included a racial project that was a response to the existing racial terrain. Two key elements of the racial project advanced by the Christian Coalition in the 1990s were (1) a privileging of religion over racial identities and (2) a redefinition of the political identity of citizens of color. The privileging of religion over race was used to promote a color-blind conservatism and to inject religious identity into the politics of recognition ignited by the civil rights era movements. The Christian Coalition portrays religion, not race, as the contemporary marginalized category.[3] The second agenda item, redefining the political identity of persons of color, was pursued through a campaign that highlighted the existence of socially conservative minorities in an attempt to challenge the depiction of blacks and Latinos as liberals and create a new possible political identity for citizens of color, and new possibilities for political action.

The demands for recognition that emerged out of the civil rights and subsequent identity movements were appropriated by the Christian Coalition (Watson 1997). One of the central issues for the newly formed Coalition was the ability of Christians to participate in the public square. At the beginning of its organizational life, the Coalition utilized a stance as a victim excluded from political dialogue at the center of its mobilization program. This is evident from the fundraising letters that were distributed in the early and mid-1990s. Victimization, or being opposed, is used in all social movements to produce solidarity or a movement identity (ibid., 130). However, the victimization or opposition is turned by the Christian Coalition into demands for recognition. This turn to the politics of recognition must be understood in the context of the identity politics being waged in the post–civil rights era (ibid., 127). Watson does an excellent job of drawing a parallel between the multicultural movement and the Christian Coalition, showing how the Coalition must be understood as responding to the same unstable racial setting as the multicultural movement of the 1990s.

To wage the politics of recognition, the Christian Coalition focused on both pluralism and tolerance in political discussions and a singular Christian American identity. These two potentially conflicting worldviews sat side by side throughout much of the early period of the Christian Coalition in both the organization's publications and its materials soliciting support. Articles in the *Christian American* in the early to mid-1990s focused on defending the United States as a Christian nation. However, this description of the country was in tension with the renewed emphasis on tolerance and acceptance that Ralph Reed brought to the organization. While not emphasized in direct mailings, issues of tolerance and diversity did appear in *Christian American* at the same time.

The tension between these positions was addressed in January 1993. Mississippi governor Kirk Fordice had got into trouble for calling the United States a Christian nation. He was accused of being offensive to Jews. The *Christian American* reported on the story and quoted Fordice, further explaining his statement: "It's the true melting pot of the world. . . . That's the strength of our country, and the strength certainly is not enhanced by denying simple facts that Christianity is the predominant religion" (Zhu 1993). Reed supported Fordice and his explanation: "I think there are two things that have made America great. . . . The first is her essential moral goodness which I think is a derivative of faith. . . . But you also have to acknowledge diversity and pluralism" (quoted in Zhu 1993, 5). Here we see a strong divide between religion and race or ethnicity. As for racial and ethnic diversity, Fordice and Reed suggested American identity is and should remain racially plural, but simultaneously suggested that the country has a strong

Christian heritage that has been, and should continue to be, a source of great strength for America.

In that same issue of *Christian American,* Reed put these ideas into his action plan for the Christian Coalition. Point 3 of his strategy is to "affirm our faith while expressing tolerance of others." The tension between identifying a single unifying national identity and acknowledging diversity is noted: "Our Judeo-Christian heritage and our religio-ethnic pluralism are the twin pillars of American society" (Reed 1993, 14). Effectively, Reed wanted to acknowledge diversity within a single tradition. Pluralism, to the extent that it fell within the Judeo-Christian heritage, was a valuable asset.

The racial project, then, of the Christian Coalition in the 1990s was to privilege religion over the black-white divide and to create a new central, *racialized* religious division.

The meanings of race and its import as offered by the Christian Coalition in the 1990s set up at the outset a racialized religious other, but the others were not blacks or Latinos. In September 1991, the *Christian American* reported that a Muslim prayer opened Congress. This is reported to contrast with America as a Christian nation, a frequent and central claim of the Coalition through its publications from the inception of the organization through today: "On June 25, for the first time in the 200-year history of the United States, the House of Representatives was opened with a Moslem prayer. . . . The prayer, sponsored by Rep. Nick Joe Rahall (D.-W. Va.) who is of Lebanese ancestry, was timed to coincide with the feast of Id al-Adha" ("Moslem Prayer Opens Congress" 1991, 13). Here we see American identity, a "200-year history," being challenged by Islam and a man of Lebanese descent. Catholic and Jewish actors are discursively included in the American Judeo-Christian heritage, as are blacks. However, Muslim actors are effectively framed as other.

The Coalition was offering a new lens with which to view events that privileged a new religious identity that could include blacks, Latinos, and whites over the current understandings of racial politics. In 1996, the Coalition responded to the burning of black churches with money and support. Leaders repeatedly talked about the church burnings as attacks against religion and not as attacks based on race. They cited incidents of attacks on predominantly white Christian establishments to show that this was an attack on religion, not on any racial group: "An analysis of the list of houses of worship targeted by arson and other violence since 1990 reveals that the violence has spread throughout the nation and across racial and denominational lines. . . . In short: the wave of violence has been an attack on places of worship in general even more than an attack on certain ethnic, racial or denominational groups" ("Attacks Span Ethnic, Denominational Spectrum" 1996, 27). This was part of a racial project, a redefinition of racial dynamics and meanings, being offered by the Christian Right that attempted to replace what was understood by others as being about race as being about religion.

The Christian Coalition was also engaged in an active campaign to redefine citizens' racial identities. They wanted to "correct" the biased interpretation of who black religious citizens were. A survey commissioned by the Christian Coalition in 1993 was released under the title "Minority Myths Exploded: Poll Shows Minorities Hold Traditional Values" (Wheeler and English 1993). Part of a campaign to reach out to potential allies of color was to convince them and others that their race did not preclude them from being members of the Christian Right. The Coalition leadership therefore showed high majorities of citizens of color as religious and conservative on key issues. They also distinguished between positions of civil rights leaders and the survey results, suggesting that blacks' and Latinos' political identities had been incorrectly identified with race leaders, such as Jesse Jackson. This was part of the Coalition's strategy of highlighting examples that challenged the dominant image of black citizens as liberal actors (Wheeler 1993; Perkins 1994; Woerner 1994).

The Coalition then took this redefinition of racial religious and political identities to the streets. In the early 1990s the Coalition was experiencing a huge surge in power and influence. To grow further, Reed suggested that minority outreach was an important and natural direction. Based on the 1993 poll, the Coalition began a number of minority outreach campaigns. It targeted black and Latino radio stations and churches and budgeted more than $100,000 for media advertisements in California alone. In 1994, in South Carolina, the Coalition hosted a public forum to mobilize blacks and Hispanics. In 1995, the Coalition gathered one hundred African American leaders in Dallas to talk about a partnership. And in 1996, as mentioned, the Coalition responded to the burning of black churches with money and support. In publicizing their help, the Coalition's leaders depicted their support as an attempt to overcome racial divides. This argument was made simultaneously with the battle to reinterpret the burnings away from a racial frame to a religious one. Here we see two parts of the Coalition's racial project in one moment: the organization tried to reach out through minority-targeted programs even as it downplayed the importance of race and offered a religious identity in its stead.

In 1997 the Coalition introduced the Samaritan Project. This was a set of legislative goals as well as private faith-based programs to address inner-city problems. These projects were highly publicized, promised large amounts of money, and were never fully funded. They were promoted as pieces key to racial reconciliation. Again, through the publicity about the Samaritan Project, the racial project offered by the Coalition becomes visible. It acknowledged a racial past while looking toward a color-blind but religiously coordinated future.

Because of the racial project being offered, the Christian Coalition during this period of rapid growth and increasing influence did not get involved in the immigration issue despite the rising nativism and the near universal conservative anti-immigrant sentiment in the early 1990s. Immigration, a highly racialized issue that targeted Latinos, brought to the fore the tension between minority outreach and color-blind religious identity formation. For this reason, even as other Christian Right groups were expressing restrictive views, the Coalition did not.

The tension between a restrictive stance on immigration and minority outreach is apparent in the November/December 1994 issue of *Christian American*. It is in this issue that the one article on the threatening impacts of immigration published between 1991 and 1997 appeared. This article ran immediately *after* the 1994 election and the passage of Proposition 187. Under a section heading of "multiculturalism," which we know from statements by the Coalition is to be understood as bad and part of a politics of identity that emphasizes race and ethnicity, is the article titled "Welfare Attracts Immigrants: New Immigration Equals Cultural Disintegration" (Feder 1994). The article opens by discussing the economic costs of illegal immigration but concludes with concerns about contemporary immigrants' failure to assimilate, as exemplified by the erection of the statue of an Aztec god in San Jose, California, and Hispanic action against laws requiring that English be spoken in public businesses. While author Don Feder decries new immigrants not learning the language, in the same issue the Christian Coalition advertised free voter education brochures, "Now Available in Spanish."

Much of the restrictionism of the 1990s relied on explicit appeals to racial characterizations of the immigrant. This was at odds with the attempts by the Christian Coalition to craft an inclusive religious political identity. A racial orders approach such as that advanced by King and Smith (2005) helps us understand why the Christian Coalition would avoid the immigration issue. Given the institutional orders of the racial terrain, a call for restriction would have placed the Christian Coalition with the white supremacist racial order. The group wanted to position itself publicly as part of a move toward racial justice, which prevented it from publicly aligning with the nativist movement of the 1990s, firmly a part of the antitransformative racial order of the day. Despite leaders, allies, and a base all supporting a restrictionist stance,[4] the Christian Coalition avoided the issue of immigration and even sometimes supported more liberal immigration policies. We can see the Coalition as responding to the reigning racial orders and offering up an alternative racial project that undergirded its attempt to reach out to minorities. This racial project was at odds with a restrictive immigration stance in the 1990s.

Immigration, Race, and the Coalition Today

In 2006, Christian Coalition leader Roberta Combs allied the Coalition with immigration restrictionists supporting tough enforcement and denouncing any pathway to citizenship. Even in 2003, during the California recall election, there was evidence of the Christian Coalition's supporting a restrictionist stance. The voter guide listed seven issues. Next to partial birth abortion and parental notification for a minor seeking abortion, the Christian Coalition reported the candidates' positions on driver's licenses for the undocumented. Two things changed drastically that allowed the Christian Coalition to approach the immigration issue and adopt a restrictionist posture when it again hit the national scene. The first was the shift in the dominant national racial associations with the immigration issue following the 9/11 attacks. A shift to fearing Muslim and not just Latino immigrants as a key issue can sit easily with the racial-religious project the Christian Coalition was offering in the 1990s. Second, changes in the organizational status of the Christian Coalition from a period of growth to a period of retrenchment meant the organization was not attempting to expand beyond its base of white evangelicals but instead was focusing on shoring up that base. Taken together, these factors explain why the Christian Coalition did not adopt a restrictionist platform in the 1990s, though it does so today.

In the 1990s the Christian Coalition called for a racial melting pot in the name of religious unity. The Coalition attempted to reduce the political importance of race, offering in its stead a religious identity, a Judeo-Christian American identity. Under this project Muslim actors stand out as other. This racial project of cross-racial Judeo-Christian unity was at hand to be capitalized on after the 9/11 terrorist attacks. In 2003, the Christian Coalition held a symposium titled "Muslims and the Judeo-Christian World—Where to From Here?" The conference was billed as one that would educate "Christians of faith and interested Americans about the true nature of Islam" and would discuss "implications for America of the growing Islamic population" (Christian Coalition of America 2003). The speakers listed had previously written and spoken about the dangers of American Muslims and a war between Islam and the West and Christianity, and had made claims about the Koran producing corrupt, violent, and racist societies.[5]

This other permits a post-9/11 stance on immigration as they find an easy way to rewrite the racial battle lines of immigration politics. Immigration restriction after the 2001 attacks on the World Trade Center and the Pentagon begins to have a broader racial appeal. Included in the dangerous other is not just immigrants coming over the southern border to take jobs and services but also Muslim terrorists exploiting the lack of border enforcement. In the April 7, 2006, *Washington Weekly Review,* the on-line publication that replaced *Christian American,* Roberta Combs, the president, writes, "The House and the Senate Conference—assuming the Senate will finally vote for a bill after Democrats have filibustered commonsense amendments such as the one which says people who have broken the law cannot become citizens, etc.—will most likely come up with a bill which looks more like the tough border enforcement (keeping terrorists out of the U.S.A.) that the United States House of Representatives voted for overwhelmingly." In May 2006, the *Washington Weekly Review* reported "most polls" showing that more than 70 percent of people wanting Congress to pass legislation "which emphasizes border enforcement and keeping terrorists out." This was not a reference to any specific poll, just a commentary on public opinion in which the author of the article chose to emphasize terrorism. The racialization of terrorists enabled the Christian Coalition to get tough on immigration while still maintaining an allegiance to part of the racial project, a privileging of religion over a black-white divide, they offered in the 1990s.

The Christian Coalition, however, because of organizational demands, let go of the religious multiracialism of their racial project from the 1990s, the outreach to minorities, and focused on solidifying its base. References to terrorism by the Christian Coalition mirror what happened with other restrictionist forces in the wake of the 9/11 attacks. Terrorism was included side by side with economics and culture as one of the many reasons to support a tough stance on immigration. The Christian Coalition also used arguments about economic issues such as jobs and services in addition to theological arguments about the rule of law and sovereignty. While the Christian Coalition had avoided siding with restrictionist voices in the past, a need to resurrect its base of support led the Coalition to take on this controversial issue and enlist biblical injunctions for others to support tough immigration policies.

The Christian Coalition today is in a critical moment and perhaps on the edge of extinction. While the Christian Right as a movement was seeing success with key leaders at the national level, many Christian Right organizations have suffered. The Christian Coalition has experienced huge membership losses, a serious financial crisis, and organizational secessions, and has been called nearly defunct by friends and foes alike. The changing political environment, in which the organization's goals are now represented at the highest levels and have been mainstreamed into the Republican Party's agenda, has partly caused the decline. The opposition to the Coalition's religious voice is no longer an effective mobilizing tactic. Therefore, to survive as an organization, the Christian Coalition must make efforts to shore up its base, comprising mostly white evangelicals. The group has shifted from a period of growth and mobilizing new members to a period of retrenchment. Outreach to Catholics and religious citizens of color is no longer on its agenda. The immigration issue, one that divides Republicans, can be used as a wedge issue to gain a stronger foothold with those who once were the Coalition's base.

When faced with prospects of its own decline, the Coalition elected Joel C. Hunter as president. Hunter was a much more moderate voice and wanted to expand the Coalition's agenda to include issues such fighting poverty and global warming. Only a little more than a month before he was supposed to take office in January 2007, however, Hunter stepped down, citing resistance in the organization to the expanded agenda. An expansive agenda may not have been the issue as much as the direction of that agenda. Hunter reported, "When we really got down to it, they said: 'This just isn't for us. It won't speak to our base, so we just can't go there'" (Banerjee 2006). Hunter later was one of the individuals who signed on to the Christians for Comprehensive Immigration Reform, a coalition of groups and individuals pushing for more compassionate immigration policies. Barring a political need to return to its base, the Christian Coalition may have been using Leviticus and Matthew to emphasize the care that should be shown toward the stranger among us, rather than biblical passages such as Deuteronomy 27:17, "Cursed is the one who moves his neighbors' landmark." That base is defined not by religion alone but by race and religion operating jointly. Attempting to respond to white evangelicals meant taking a restrictionist stance on immigration.

Through the case of the Christian Coalition, we can see how the unstable racial terrain affects the politics of organizations of the Religious Right and helps determine their agendas. The Christian Right's relationship with immigration is unexplainable if we consider only the religious side of the movement. Race needs to be included, not as a static variable but as a site of contestation. Including the racial formation process is essential to understanding the behavior of the Christian Right, as it includes religion in the struggle over racial meanings. As racial formation theory suggests, understanding the specific logics of the racial project offered by the Christian Coalition is requisite to explaining its behavior. This case suggests we need to ask at all times what role religion plays in the construction of racial projects, and how religion and race work together and in competition to construct central political identities. Following the insights of the racial orders approach advanced by King and Smith, we also need to consider the organizational situation within the political sphere. And to do either we need to understand the Christian Coalition as a religious organization. Through this look at the Christian Right and its relationship to immigration provisions we see how religion is used to redefine racial categories and how religious actors are politically confined by the racial terrain on which they walk; we see the centrality of the intersection of race and religion in political life.

Notes

1. Families First in Immigration called for increased border security and an end to birthright citizenship, or the granting of citizenship to anyone born on U.S. soil. The group argued against the guest worker program being proposed. As part of the compromise, the group promoted legalization for undocumented immigrants already in the United States who were relatives of citizens. Families First in Immigration emerged in January 2007, sending letters to public officials, but the organization has not been heard from since the end of that month.

2. There is one exception, which I discuss below. In 1994, after the election, the Christian Coalition ran an article laying out the problems associated with immigration. However, it did this just once, and at a time that minimized the political impact of the message.

3. Ralph Reed in his writings and speeches suggests that white evangelicals were in fact the marginalized group, in part because of the sin of racism that tarnished white evangelicals' reputation in the public square (see Wadsworth, this volume).

4. Randy Tate began serving as the executive director of the Christian Coalition in 1997. During Tate's one term in Congress he had targeted the undocumented by pushing for enforcement and had worked to make English the official language.

5. The speakers named in the press release included Joseph Farah of WorldNetDaily.com, Daniel Pipes of the Middle East Forum, and Dr. Labib Mikhail. All had written and spoken about the negative impact of Islam on society and its threat to the West.

References

"Attacks Span Ethnic, Denominational Spectrum." 1996. *Christian American* 7 (5): 27.

Banerjee, Neela. 2006. "Pastor Chosen to Lead Christian Coalition Steps Down in Dispute over Agenda." *New York Times*, November 28.

Calhoun-Brown, Allison. 1998. "The Politics of Black Evangelicals: What Hinders Diversity in the Christian Right?" *American Politics Quarterly* 26 (1): 81–109.

Christian Coalition of America. 2003. "Christian Coalition of America to Hold Symposium on Islam." January 14. Christian Coalition of America. Washington, DC: People for the American Way files.

Feder, Don. 1994. "Welfare Attracts Immigrants: New Immigration Equals Cultural Disintegration." *Christian American* 5 (6): 21.

Greeley, Andrew, and Michael Hout. 2006. *The Truth about Conservative Christians: What They Think and What They Believe.* Chicago: University of Chicago Press.

Green, John C. 2006. "Ohio: The Bible and the Buckeye State." In *The Values Campaign? The Christian Right and the 2004 Elections*, ed. John C. Green, Mark J. Rozell, and Clyde Wilcox, 79–97. Washington, DC: Georgetown University Press.

Jacobson, Robin D. 2008. *New Nativism: Proposition 187 and the Debate over Immigration.* Minneapolis: University of Minnesota Press.

King, Desmond, and Rogers Smith. 2005. "Racial Orders in American Political Development." *American Political Science Review* 99:75–92.

Letters to the Editor. 1992. *Christian American*, May/June, 20–21.

McGirr, Lisa. 2001. *Suburban Warriors: The Origins of the New American Right.* Princeton, NJ: Princeton University Press.

"Moslem Prayer Opens Congress." 1991. *Christian American* 2 (5): 13.

Omi, Michael, and Howard Winant. 1989. *Racial Formation in the United States: From the 1960s to the 1980s.* New York: Routledge.

Perkins, Joseph. 1994. "The New Owner on Hauser Street." *Christian American* 5 (July/August): 4.

Reed, Ralph. 1993. "A Strategy for Evangelicals." *Christian American* 4 (1): 14–15.

Robinson, Carin. 2006. "From Every Tribe and Nation? Blacks and the Christian Right." *Social Science Quarterly* 87 (3): 591–601.

Southern Baptist Convention. 2006. "On the Crisis of Illegal Immigration." Southern Baptist Convention Resolutions, June. http://www.sbc.net/resolutions/amResolution.asp?ID=1157 (accessed January 19, 2009).

Watson, Justin. 1997. *The Christian Coalition: Dreams of Restoration, Demands of Recognition.* New York: St. Martin's Press.

Wheeler, John, Jr. 1993. "Innis Raps Reverse Racism: Civil Rights Veteran Says Movement Hijacked." *Christian American* 4 (9): 14–15.

Wheeler, John, Jr., and Paul English. 1993. "Minority Myths Exploded: Poll Shows Minorities Hold Traditional Values." *Christian American* 4 (10): 1, 4.

Winant, Howard. 1994. *Racial Conditions: Politics, Theory, Comparisons.* Minneapolis: University of Minnesota Press.

Woerner, Barbara. 1994. "Conservative African-Americans Speak Out." *Christian American* 5 (3): 7.

Zhu, Connie. 1993. "Fordice Defends Christian Nation." *Christian American* 4 (1): 5.

Possibilities and Limits

Political Advocacy through Religious Organization?

The Evolving Role of the Nation of Islam

CATHERINE PADEN

America is going all over the world selling them on democracy, and the hallmark of democracy is that we have the right to elect and select those who would lead us. But now, we in America, the American electorate, are dropping out of the most important part of being in a democracy—the voting process.

> —Speech delivered by the Reverend Louis Farrakhan at the Get Out the Vote rally,
> Chicago, November 1, 1998

While not an explicitly political organization, the Nation of Islam has been politically relevant since its founding in 1931. The Nation's founding doctrines of racial separatism and economic self-sufficiency for blacks have required that the organization contend with political realities for African Americans. As Jacobson and Wadsworth discuss in the introduction to this volume, the Nation embodies religion as a tool of resistance. Operating at the intersections of race, class, and religion, the Nation is one of few national organizations to specifically target its message and outreach to low-income African Americans. Throughout the organization's history, the Nation's teachings and writings have emphasized the importance of members remaining removed from the American political system. Recently, however, the organization has stepped away from its historically apolitical role, and its leadership has encouraged members to vote and become politically participatory. This essay traces this shift within the organization and considers its implications. Does a shift to mainstream politics detract from the Nation of Islam's role as a more radical organization seeking fundamental changes to the U.S. political system?

The Nation's teachings state that if members participate in any political pursuit, it should be political protest, or other activities that seek to change the U.S.

political system from outside that system. However, in 1984 the Reverend Louis Farrakhan encouraged members of the Nation to vote for the first time in the organization's history. Since 1984, Farrakhan has reemphasized his call to vote, and has publicly touted his own voting history. As the epigraph at the head of this essay suggests, Farrakhan's political rhetoric now includes analysis of the harm brought to a democracy if people do not exercise their right to vote.

This shift was one component of Farrakhan's increasing involvement with the political mainstream, including going to meetings with world leaders and extensive involvement in international affairs. This political engagement does not, however, indicate the Nation's support of the American political system. As Adolph Reed explains, Farrakhan remains critical of politics even as he engages in electoral battles; he presents himself and the Nation as redeemers of a corrupt political system (Reed 1991). Additionally, Farrakhan's calls for participation are consistently tempered by his warnings about the problems inherent in the U.S. political system. In a 1998 speech in Chicago, Farrakhan explained the limits of electoral participation: "I don't have any illusion about telling you to vote. You should vote for those whom you feel will do good for us, but remember, the good that they do is limited by the system they are in" (Farrakhan 1998).

Nonetheless, this shift in the Nation of Islam's activities could potentially change a central purpose of the organization, which has been to resist and critique the political, social, and economic systems of the United States from the outside. Because of its commitment to the poor based on its religious ideology, the Nation is unique in this purpose.[1] In a 1996 interview, Farrakhan explained the importance of hearing the voices of the poor:

> You have between 30 and 40 million Black people, you have a fast growing Hispanic community, you have an Asian and an Arab and an Indian community, and given the dissatisfaction in the country, we need to establish a national agenda that all of these groups can stand on so that in a united way we can leverage our vote to influence the direction of this nation toward the best interest of the poor and the weak rather than a nation held hostage by the rich and the powerful. This is leading . . . to the destruction of this democracy. ("Kennedy and Farrakhan One-On-One" 2007)

Although Farrakhan has recently espoused political activity, the Nation of Islam has not transformed into a political organization. The organization has maintained its founding commitment to religious and political doctrine of separation, as well as controversial positions espoused by its leadership—these positions may preclude traditional political representation while maintaining the Nation's radical voice calling for change within the political system.

In the remainder of this essay, I first introduce the Nation of Islam and the circumstances of its founding. The Nation's organizational evolution illustrates its commitment to its primary constituency—low-income African Americans. Second, I place the Nation within the context of African American political engagement through religious institutions—specifically, the African American church. I argue, as have other scholars, that the Nation's political engagement is very different from that of the church: the organization is reaching out to an undermobilized group through nontraditional political means. The organization's outreach and ideology give it a unique role among religious institutions. Third, I examine the Nation's religious belief system and behavioral requirements, which are intended to appeal to low-income African Americans.

After establishing the organization's commitment to the poor, I assess the Nation's shifting level of engagement with the U.S. political system. Finally, I offer an assessment of the implications of this engagement for the Nation's voice, which has been prominent among interest groups and religious organizations in its critique of the U.S. system and its call for systemic change to address racial hierarchies and economic disadvantage. Although the organization encourages mainstream political participation among its members, its message remains based on a religious doctrine that dictates distrust of the political, economic, and social systems of the United States. The Nation's advocacy on behalf of low-income African Americans brings the political neglect of the poor in American democracy sharply into focus and points to the fallacy of assuming democratic inclusiveness in the U.S. political system.[2]

The Founding of the Nation of Islam

From its inception, the Nation of Islam was founded as an organization based in a critique of the U.S. political, religious, economic, and social systems. According to the Nation's belief, God appeared in the person of W. D. Fard during the summer of 1930 in Detroit, Michigan. Fard introduced himself to the African American community in Detroit as a merchant of silks. As he visited households to sell his goods, he told customers tales from his foreign travels and included lessons learned abroad as to how African Americans could improve their health (Lincoln 1994, 48–50). Apparently Fard was a captivating storyteller—his listeners often asked him to return to their homes.

Fard's lessons quickly turned into religious-based teachings. After introducing religion into his conversations with his customers, Fard began to identify himself as an Arab on a mission from God, sent to the United States to regain the chosen people—black Americans (ibid., 14). To gain the trust of potential converts, Fard relied on Christianity in his initial recruitment activities, reinterpreting familiar Bible stories. As Fard built relationships with his listeners, he taught that the Bible did not espouse an appropriate set of beliefs for African Americans and had been used historically as an instrument of oppression—it was a tool used by whites to justify slavery and oppress black Americans. Instead, African Americans should rely on the Koran for their religious beliefs (Gardell 1996, 51).

Fard was active in Detroit during the Great Depression, which hit African Americans particularly hard. Large numbers of blacks migrated from the South to northern cities such as Chicago and Detroit in search of economic opportunity. However, these opportunities were often quite limited, and newly arriving migrants were often met with violence and discrimination (Clegg 1997, 38). Therefore, Fard's language of economic empowerment among African Americans and his virulent rejection of the violent subjugation of blacks appealed to African Americans (Lee 1996, 20). By 1933, Fard had approximately 8,000 followers, and the Nation of Islam was established with the founding of Temple No. 1 in Detroit (Gardell 1996, 12–14).

Before Fard appeared, a man named Elijah Poole had moved to Detroit from Georgia with his wife, Clara. Soon after he arrived in Detroit, Elijah Poole became involved in Marcus Garvey's United Negro Improvement Association. During this time, Poole began to hear stories of a prophet who taught that Islam was the original religion of blacks in the United States and that African Americans originated in royalty from the holy city of Mecca. In 1931, Poole heard Fard speak at a meeting in Detroit. Poole approached Fard after his speech and informed the latter of a realization he had had during Fard's speech—that Fard was God. From this point, Fard began to teach Poole the lessons he had been sent to communicate to black Americans (Gardell 1996, 58). During this period Elijah Poole rescinded his slave name and took the name Elijah Muhammad.

A Change in Leadership and Organizational Expansion

Because of its perceived antiwhite sentiments, the Nation of Islam was portrayed by the media and the Detroit police as a dangerous and subversive organization. In 1933 Fard was expelled from Detroit after his third arrest—one year before his final disappearance (Lee 1996, 42). Before his expulsion, Fard named Elijah Muhammad his chief minister. Since Fard was God, and since he had appointed Muhammad to bear his message, Elijah Muhammad gained the status of Prophet and First Messenger (Lee 1996, 26). Fard's disappearance, and the persecution of the Detroit police department, led to a period of instability within the Nation.

Because of the organization's perceived vulnerability during this time, other groups attempted to attract membership away from the Nation. Although no particular organization was successful, the overall impact on the Nation was a dwindling membership (Lee 1996, 43).

Because of this new factionalism within the Nation, and because of perceived danger from the police, Muhammad left Detroit and moved to Chicago to establish Temple No. 2. From Chicago, Muhammad revitalized the Black Muslims, and established his leadership as a highly militant and effective one (Lincoln 1994, 16). Elijah Muhammad is responsible for expanding the Nation of Islam, both ideologically and numerically. Under Muhammad, the Nation established businesses, schools, housing, and farms to achieve the goal of self-sufficiency among blacks.

The growth of the Nation continued under Muhammad's leadership, and its teachings reached Malcolm Little, who was serving time in Charleston State Prison. Little converted and changed his name to Malcolm X while he was in prison. In 1952, one year after his release, Malcolm X was named assistant minister of Temple No.1 in Detroit. From Detroit, he was sent by Muhammad to set up temples in Boston and Philadelphia. In June 1954, Malcolm X was appointed head minister of Temple No. 7 in New York City. His thirteen-year tenure as an organizational leader led to the rapid expansion of the Nation's membership (Cone 1995, 91).

Emerging Organizational and Class Divisions within the Nation

After an international journey during which he adopted the beliefs and practices of traditional Islam, Malcolm X left the Nation of Islam in 1963. His departure led to significant changes within the organization. In 1964, Muhammad appointed Louis X, who would later change his name to Louis Farrakhan, minister of Temple No. 7 in Harlem. After Malcolm X's death in 1965, the Harlem temple was the site of many protests by those who blamed the Black Muslims for his assassination. The mosque was internally destroyed by a firebombing, and the organization's future was uncertain. During this challenging period, Louis X proved his skill as a leader and organizer by rebuilding the mosque, and its membership, to become the largest mosque in the history of the Nation. After this success, Elijah Muhammad elevated Louis X to the position of National Representative in 1967 (Gardell 1996, 121).

Elijah Muhammad died in 1975, and the Nation experienced a split in its organization and leadership. Initially Muhammad's son, Warith Deen Muhammad, took over the Nation and changed the organization's theology to a more traditional interpretation of Islam. He began a series of reforms to bring traditional Islamic practice to the Nation and to rid it of its identity as a race-based organization. He changed the name of the organization first to the World Community of al-Islam in the West. Warith Deen Muhammad argued that his father's message was appropriate during a time when African Americans had not been awakened to their history or potential but that the time had come for more advanced Islamic teachings. He lifted the restriction that only African Americans were eligible to be Nation of Islam members in June 1975. This action met substantial opposition from the ranks of ministers and soldiers of the Nation. To prevent an organized backlash against him, Muhammad dissolved the Fruit of Islam, the Nation's unarmed security force. In 1977, Muhammad replaced the symbol of the crescent and star on the Nation of Islam's flag with an image of the Koran. Simultaneously he began to emphasize the importance of American patriotism and integration into white American society (Gardell 1996, 108).

Not all members of the Nation were pleased with Warith Deen Muhammad's changes to the Nation's doctrine. Many followers considered the organization's calls for systemic economic and political change to be critical to its theology. As the opposition to Muhammad grew, Louis X, serving as minister at Temple No. 7, left the United States and traveled throughout Africa and the Caribbean. While he was traveling, Louis X was struck by the racism apparent in every multiracial society he visited, including in Muslim countries. He became convinced that systemic racial oppression was widespread, not only in the United States, and necessitated separatist solutions. Therefore, he actively opposed Muhammad's plans to change the doctrine of the Nation. On November 8, 1977, Louis X officially declared his intention to reestablish the Nation of Islam according to the platform of the Honorable Elijah Muhammad, ushering in the current period of the Nation's history known as the Second Resurrection (Gardell 1996, 154).

The theological and ideological split within the Nation led to an explicit appeal to low-income African Americans by Farrakhan's organization (Mamiya 1982, 145). Unlike Muhammad's group, Farrakhan's reestablished Nation of Islam emphasized separation from white-dominated American society. Because of its focus on integration and economic advancement within the existing political and economic system, Warith Deen Muhammad's organization appealed to middle-class African Americans. Farrakhan, on the other hand, emphasized the unique appeal of his revitalized Nation to low-income African Americans (Marsh 1996, 117).

Warith Deen Muhammad's organization disintegrated by the mid-1980s. In 1986 he was sued by three of Elijah Muhammad's other children for money from their father's estate that had been used to build Warith Deen Muhammad's organization. Muhammad's loss in this case required him to sell the Nation's palace, which Louis Farrakhan bought on July 31, 1988. Upon this purchase, Farrakhan announced that the Nation of Islam had regained its center (Gardell 1996, 137). Even more so than at its founding, the Nation was firmly established as a religious organization committed to low-income African Americans.

At the Intersection of Politics and Faith: African American Political Mobilization

The political relevance of religion to African American politics is well documented. Although scholars debate the usefulness of the black church as a political mobilization tool, there is little disagreement on the relevance of churches to the political history of African American mobilization.[3] The importance of activism and mobilization within black churches during the civil rights movement has been well established—leaders came from the churches, black churches were critical to the political socialization of disenfranchised African Americans, and leaders relied on mobilization within churches for participants in political activities and for fundraising (see Morris 1984; Chong 1991). Scholars have also examined the political activities of churches in the pre– and post–civil rights era. Dating back to the Reconstruction period, churches have been vehicles for organizing African American political resistance (Harris 1999). In the post–civil rights era, scholars have found that black churches provide political mobilization, but they also provide important social services for people who otherwise face difficulty receiving aid from the state or philanthropic organizations (Harris 2005, x).

Unlike the Nation of Islam, black churches have explicitly participated in the political process. Churches organize voter registration drives. Political candidates seek out black churches, clergy encourage church members to talk to everyone they know about candidates, congregants are encouraged to donate to candidates, and collections for candidates may be taken. Church activity politically mobilizes congregants and empowers congregants to believe that political participation is worthwhile. Because of preexisting clerical networks among black clergy and the potential for political mobilization of congregants, politicians pay particular attention to African American churches (Harris 1999).

Although the black church has been politically active, and critical to social movement organizing, it is not a religious institution that is particularly geared to the interests of low-income African Americans. As opposed to the Nation's membership, surveys of African American churches have demonstrated that most black church members are middle class and working class. In their examination of black churches, Lincoln and Mamiya (1990, 269) argue that reaching out to lower-income African Americans is one of the biggest challenges faced by black churches: "as class differentiation has continued, the question is whether Black middle- and working-class churches will continue to devise programs, provide leadership, and reach out effectively to the truly poor. Many poor people do not feel comfortable in middle-income churches."

Additionally, scholars have found that the black church has not been particularly active on policy issues specifically affecting the poor, especially since the 1960s. For example, McLaughlin (2004, 59) finds that African American churches did not have any "measurable involvement in welfare reform policy formation" during the 1996 welfare reform battles. Similarly, Cohen (2004, 104) finds that since the 1960s, churches have primarily worked to implement existing health care policy, rather than to shape policy that might help alleviate the disparities in health care provision for African Americans.

Lincoln and Mamiya (1990) point to the Nation as an alternative to the African American church, particularly for low-income African American men, a segment of the population that black churches have had difficulty recruiting. Lincoln and Mamiya point to several factors that lead to successful recruitment of black men by the Nation: the legacy of Malcolm X as a critic of American society, Islamic acceptance of self-defense, and the conversion of public figures, such as Muhammad Ali.

Additionally, the Nation's outreach in prisons leads to conversions and contributes to the Nation's appeal to low-income African Americans: "many Black men have been attracted to Islamic alternatives because the Muslims have been very active in working in prisons and on the streets where they are, a ministry which is not pronounced in most Black Christian churches" (Lincoln and Mamiya 1990, 391). The appeal of the Nation of Islam to low-income African American women has been less explicit, but the organization has created women's clubs and engaged in neighborhood programming intended to appeal to women.

In some ways, the Nation has filled a void left by some African American churches—directed outreach to low-income African Americans. Interestingly, the Nation's inclusion of Christian doctrine has contributed to its popularity since its founding. During the period of the movement's greatest growth (1955–64), Muslim ministers often spoke to Christian congregations. But once the Black Muslims started to gain substantial negative attention from the black press, congregations became less welcoming. Although the Nation has spoken out against Christianity and the inappropriateness of African Americans following white, Christian doctrine, the Nation has historically been quite willing to work with Black Muslims who are unwilling to give up their Christian faith but are still interested in the Nation's programs of self-improvement and economic uplift (Lincoln 1994, 152). In contrast to the black church, the Nation uniquely appeals to low-income African Americans without requiring that they abandon their existing religious beliefs.

The Nation's critique of economic and political systems in the United States and its call for a radical restructuring of these institutions offer an attractive alternative to black churches, whose political activism has historically focused on changes within existing structures. Although church mobilizations to eradicate Jim Crow segregation and to impose the federal enforcement of voting rights were revolutionary, these goals sought change within the existing system. The Nation's theology and ideology assume that the system is irreparably broken, and therefore call for the establishment of new systems.

The Nation of Islam's Appeal to Low-Income African American

The Nation's outreach to low-income African Americans is also unique among organizations concerned with racial issues. Unlike civil rights organizations such as the NAACP and the National Urban League, the Nation of Islam has historically considered its constituency to be low-income African Americans. In a 1963 photo-essay on the Nation in *Life* magazine, photographer Gordon Parks described the appeal of the Nation to low-income African Americans:

> By their very nature the NAACP and National Urban League cannot match the impact of the Black Muslims. Their leaders do not have the hour-by-hour contact with people who, like the Muslims, suffer the problems each and every day of their lives. While Roy Wilkins of the NAACP is attending an integrated social gathering, or is conferring with constitutional lawyers on vital civil rights issues, Malcolm X of the Muslims is visiting prisoners in jail or a destitute family or addressing a crowd of Negroes on a street corner. (32)

Since its founding, the Nation has aimed its rhetoric and social service programs toward poor blacks, and local leadership has focused on recruiting members from low-income neighborhoods and prisons. Additionally, the Nation's doctrine emphasizes the importance of African Americans gaining economic self-sufficiency. The goal of economic self-sufficiency leads to behavioral regulation by the Nation. According to the organization, achieving middle-class status requires certain behaviors, which are linked to economic success.[4] For example, to attain economic self-sufficiency African Americans must be free from addiction. The doctrine of the Nation prohibits members from consuming drugs, alcohol, or tobacco. Fard taught that the low life-expectancy rate of blacks in the United States as compared to whites was due to poor health habits. Elijah Muhammad also forbade the consumption of traditionally southern African American foods—cornbread, black-eyed peas, and chitlins—which he considered part of a slave diet (Lincoln 1994; Lee 1996).

Muhammad instituted moral codes, based on Fard's instruction, that required absolute adherence on the part of members. These moral codes, while not explicitly based on class, were intended to alter and control the behavior of low-income African Americans (Lincoln 1994; Curtis 2006). As Lincoln explains: "The mass of Muslims are from the Black lower class, with relatively low incomes, and they are encouraged to live respectably and provide for their families" (Lincoln 1994, 18).

According to the Nation's moral code, it is critical that African American families stay together. This goal can be achieved if men and women adhere to their appropriate roles, according to Nation of Islam doctrine. Divorce is permitted by the Nation, but discouraged. Devotion to the family through economic support is demanded of men, and women are instructed to use the family's resources thriftily (Lee 1996, 34). The Nation's doctrine teaches that gambling and credit card use cause blacks to lose money to a system that intends to keep African Americans in economic debt. Additionally, any debt to the white financial system contradicts Elijah Muhammad's call for economic self-sufficiency for African Americans. All of these moral and behavioral codes were viewed as requirements for membership in the Nation—violations of these laws result in suspension from the movement, from thirty days to seven years (Essien-Udom [1962] 1995, 15).

In addition to its moral and dietary codes, many of the Nation's recruiting techniques reflect its focus on low-income African Americans. When seeking to be a member of the Nation, a new recruit is given a letter, which he or she must transcribe perfectly and then present to his or her minister. The letter states the recruit's commitment to the Nation and to Allah. Mamiya (1982, 146) explains how this initiation requirement is indicative of the importance of class within the Nation: "When a poor, uneducated, often illiterate person who can barely write an X for his name, takes the time to copy a letter over and over again until it is perfect, that person is well on his way towards membership in the Nation. The commitment mechanism is a simple test of patience, obedience, and discipline."

While the Nation is unique in its appeal to low-income African Americans, the organization does not shun middle-class support. Beginning as early as 1956, middle-class professionals began to join the movement. In fact, the financial support of middle-class blacks during this period was critical to the Nation's rapid growth (Curtis 2006, 25). Even as the Nation appealed to the middle class, however, it did so with an emphasis on the middle class's historical abandonment of and ongoing obligations to the poor. According to Clegg (1997, 111), "[Muhammad] . . . played upon class tensions among African Americans to make the Nation appear to be the champion of the ignorant, downtrodden lower class and the redeemer of the wily, bourgeois Black who had shirked his responsibility to the race."

The Nation of Islam's Political Engagement

The Nation's religious doctrine has been shaped by founders and leaders to appeal to the African American poor, leading the group to find possible change outside existing political and economic structures. However, the Nation has never completely divorced itself from the existing political system. Does political engagement within the existing system dilute the Nation's calls for extrasystemic change? Or is the Nation able to balance engagement in the political system with its calls for radical change?

According to Muhammad, politics are not an effective means for achieving the goals of the Nation: "politics will not answer your prayers. . . . Politics will not solve the problem of the Negroes."[5] The Nation's rejection of mainstream politics is based on several factors. First, Black Muslims identify with Afro-Asia, not with the United States. W. D. Fard taught that his followers were not Americans and therefore owed no allegiance to the American flag (Lincoln 1994, 16). According to the founding principles of the Nation, only Allah knows justice, righteousness, and righteous government. This knowledge was revealed to the Nation through W. D. Fard and then Elijah Muhammad, and only someone who has this knowledge is able to legitimately rule (Essien-Udom [1962] 1995, 255). Therefore, U.S. politicians are necessarily illegitimate rulers.

The Nation's belief system teaches that the U.S. political system is corrupt, and therefore the Nation's members should refrain from involvement in the system. Muhammad taught that political participation was sinful and that African Americans should withdraw from the political system and devote themselves to economic self-improvement (Essien-Udom [1962] 1995, 258). Even more fundamentally, the Nation's theology states that whites are destined to rule for six thousand years. Muhammad advised blacks to wait for divine intervention, and not to rebel against white rule. This inherently minimizes potential activism, either within or outside the political system (Clegg 1997, 155). According to leadership, a final reason for Nation of Islam members to stay out of politics is that the organization's leadership has sought to keep its numbers a secret. If the Nation one day felt that it was an appropriate time to make demands of the U.S. government, the government would be surprised by the organization's strength (Lincoln 1994, 19).

Despite these rejections of political participation in the Nation's belief system, Elijah Muhammad's verbal admonishments against the political system were often based on the U.S. government's suppression and exclusion of African Americans. Therefore, if the government or political system were to change, it is possible that the Nation's position on political participation might change. In fact, by the 1960s and early 1970s, Elijah Muhammad, while remaining wary of the usefulness of voting for African Americans, did not indicate that it was antithetical to the foundations of the Nation's belief system:

> The Black vote could be cast or not cast. The white citizens of the government are going to win and continue to rule anyway. . . . The Black man should be very serious and careful about his voting because 90% of the Black votes are cast by ones who do not have the knowledge of what they are casting their vote for.[6]

At a speech in Harlem prior to the 1960 presidential election, Muhammad told almost ten thousand African Americans to "go to the voting polls with their eyes and ears open" (quoted in Essien-Udom [1962] 1995, 266). In an endorsement of the political system, Muhammad indicated that African Americans must vote for "good Black politicians" in order to achieve change. Instead of continuing to support the white political structure, African Americans should turn their attention to supporting African American candidates.[7]

Although Muhammad advocated political awareness among NOI members in 1960, the shift to advocacy for active political participation did not happen until the 1980s, when Harold Washington ran for mayor of Chicago. Washington's election in 1983 led Farrakhan to state that electoral politics might be an avenue for change for African Americans (Clegg 1997, 104). Even though he was not registered to vote, Farrakhan maintained a close relationship with Harold Washington, and later described him as a politician who was not afraid or embarrassed to ask for his help mobilizing African Americans in Chicago (Farrakhan 1998). Although Muhammad had indicated that voting might be acceptable for members of the Nation, Farrakhan's endorsement of Washington was a significant shift for the organization. The mobilization of low-income African Americans contributed to Washington's victory and was partially attributable to Farrakhan's participation in the campaign.

Beginning in 1984, Jesse Jackson's presidential campaign gave Farrakhan a candidate to support at the national level. On February 9, 1984, Farrakhan led twelve hundred people to the Chicago Board of Elections to register to vote; Farrakhan also registered for the first time. Upon registering, Farrakhan broke with the Nation's tradition when he stated the importance of voting: "We have no choice between violence and voting. . . . I would rather see us vote" (quoted in Clegg 1997, 104–5). This shift to political participation was not doctrinal; however, it indicated a shift in the Nation's conception of whether change within the political system is worthwhile. Although the system remained corrupt, the Nation's leadership was willing to support actors within that system who might bring change.[8]

In 1990, three members of the Nation ran for political office in Washington, D.C., and Maryland, including a challenger to Representative Steny Hoyer in Maryland's fifth district (Marsh 1996, 131). In addition to political involvement through campaigns, the Nation was politically active through endorsements: Farrakhan endorsed Democratic candidates in a Chicago congressional race and in the Missouri gubernatorial race (Jennings 1992, 67).

In a 1996 interview with John F. Kennedy Jr. for *George* magazine, Farrakhan explained the evolution of political engagement within the Nation. According to Farrakhan, the political system had evolved to a point where members of the Nation might be able to gain benefits from political participation:

> [Elijah Muhammad] took us out of politics and his words were separation. Separation because we needed to heal from 400 years of injustice and alienation from self. And when he had instilled in us a knowledge of self, a love of self and an enlightened self-interest, then, I believe it would be the proper time for us to enter politics, not to be subservient but to go for that which is in our self-interests because it is necessary for us to become politically powerful in order for us to change the reality of our lives. That is in a nutshell where we have moved today. ("Kennedy and Farrakhan One-On-One" 2007)

Because of its political involvement, the Nation was invited to participate in the swearing-in ceremonies of the 103rd Congress. Shortly after, the Congressional Black Caucus entered into an agreement of cooperation with the Nation to work on issues of substance abuse and urban crime among African Americans. The pact also stated that the Nation and the Congressional Black Caucus would work together to achieve these goals, and would not be divided or speak out against each other (Clegg 1997, 116). This cooperative agreement was short-lived and was renounced by the Congressional Black Caucus on February 3, 1994, after Khalid Muhammad, a representative of the Nation, made a particularly anti-Semitic and otherwise inflammatory speech at Kean College (Marsh 1996, 137).

In addition to increased electoral participation by the Nation, the organization became involved with the government by the early 1990s, when it became a major recipient of government contracts, mostly for security at public housing facilities. For the first time, these contracts linked the Nation to state funding and state authority. Perhaps not coincidentally, Farrakhan softened his antigovernment rhetoric as these contracts were being put in place (Clegg 1997, 118).

At the Million Man March in 1995, Farrakhan urged voter registration, although he did not offer a clear political or electoral strategy (Clegg 1997, 125, 128; see also "Kennedy and Farrakhan One-On-One" 2007). On the heels of the march, Farrakhan voted for the first time since the 1984 presidential election in the 1996 election ("Farrakhan Registers to Vote" 1996). Scholars argue that Farrakhan's call to electoral participation at the Million Man March affected voter turnout during the 1996 election. Polls indicated that approximately 1.5 million more African American men participated in the 1996 election than had during the 1992 election. David Bositis, a Senior Research Associate at the Joint Center for the Political and Economic Studies, observed,

> There was only one major relevant event of note in the past year or so that focused primarily on Black men, and that was the Million Man March . . . at which Farrakhan exhorted Black American men to take more responsibility for their lives by registering to vote and voting. In reviewing a variety of possible alternative hypotheses to account for the sharp increase in the Black male vote, I find it highly implausible that there was another factor that rivaled the Million Man March in bringing about this change. (Quoted in Marable 1998, 1)

A Radical Voice or a Mainstream Political Actor?

Is it possible for the Nation to maintain a critique of the U.S. system even as its leadership encourages participation within that system? Unlike earlier Nation of Islam doctrine, which explicitly explained the need to build African American self-sufficiency to combat poverty, Farrakhan's call to political participation has not been accompanied by a defined vision of how African Americans might benefit from the political system. At the Million Man March, and during other speaking engagements and interviews, he has spoken vaguely of a "third force" that might eventually grow into a third party and would serve as an alternative to the Democrat and Republican Parties. This multiracial third force would serve as a voting bloc, ready to leave the two major parties if its interests were not met. However, the third force remains undefined, and Farrakhan has not indicated how this force might form or coalesce to achieve political change within the parties (Farrakhan 1998).

The Nation's future is unknown. Louis Farrakhan's failing health has been noted by the Nation and the national media. His 2008's Saviours' Day speech was considered by many to be Farrakhan's last. Once Farrakhan is no longer the Nation's leader, many wonder what direction the organization will take, and whether it will be able to sustain itself. The Nation puts aside concerns about Farrakhan's replacement, explaining that it is not an organization driven only by its leadership (Paulson 2007). Whether Farrakhan's replacement will be put in place easily or only with some controversy, there is no question that Farrakhan's departure will lead to a period of change for the Nation. Will this change have repercussions on the Nation's political engagement? Would such changes have repercussions for advocacy on behalf of low-income African Americans?

The Nation has not attempted to affect mainstream politics or substantial political change since Jackson's candidacy in 1984. Its own doctrine, coupled with the inherent and ever-present controversy surrounding the organization, limits its ability to translate its appeal to low-income African Americans into mainstream political representation. Additionally, it is important to note that while the Nation issues calls to vote and Farrakhan makes speeches concerning U.S. foreign policy, the organization is not primarily a political one. It does not engage in political advocacy concerning issues that affect low-income African Americans, such as affordable housing or welfare reforms. The organization's advocacy on these fronts is performed through direct-service work.

The Nation's position on the periphery of the political system might serve its constituents better than active engagement, for participation in the political system inherently dilutes the organization's resistance to that system. The Nation's religious, race-, and class-based critiques of the U.S. political and economic system have been unique among both African American religious and advocacy groups. Generally, organizations concerned with racial justice have made issues concerning the poor low priority.[9] Any future decline in the Nation's strength once Farrakhan is no longer the organization's leader might introduce an opportunity for one of these organizations to begin to genuinely represent the needs of the poor, and therefore begin to integrate low-income African Americans into the political system. However, such representation would serve a different purpose than that of the Nation's radical critique of the system. The Nation's position at the intersection of race, religion, class, and gender gives it a unique voice appealing to low-income African Americans without concern about the organization's political acceptability.

Notes

1. As I discuss in detail in this essay, although African American churches have certainly been politically active and relevant, particularly during the civil rights movement, many Christian denominations and organizations have not made a special effort to respond to the needs of the poor.

2. Although the Nation of Islam's political activities draw extensive media and public attention, they go largely unnoticed by scholars of political representation. The Nation's political activities warrant scholarly attention because of the group's unique focus on the interests of low-income African Americans. Scholars (such as Adolph Reed) have examined Farrakhan's leadership but have not discussed the Nation as an organization whose constituency is low-income African Americans. See Reed 1991.

3. On the political importance of the black church, see Harris 1999, Lincoln and Mamiya 1990, Morris 1984, and Smith and Harris 2005.

4. While seeking to attain middle-class status, part of the appeal of the Nation was also a disgust with middle-class leadership and exclusivity within African American churches and political organizations (Essien-Udom [1962] 1995, 83–84).

5. Elijah Muhammad, speech, Washington, DC, May 31, 1959, quoted in Essien-Udom (ibid., 257).

6. Elijah Muhammad, "The National Election," in Muhammed 1973.

7. Elijah Muhammad, "Put Muslim Program to Congress," in Muhammed 1965.

8. In addition to voting, Farrakhan became politically engaged in the Jackson campaign, serving as a campaign adviser. However, the official relationship between Jackson and Farrakhan was short-lived. On July 28, 1984, Jackson publicly ended his relationship with Farrakhan after reports that Farrakhan called the creation of Israel "an outlaw act." This statement fueled the fire of Farrakhan's and Jackson's perceived anti-Semitism and led Jackson to denounce his association with Farrakhan (Marsh 1996, 122). Nonetheless, Farrakhan's involvement with Jackson's campaign led to political engagement by the Nation throughout the 1990s.

9. During the War on Poverty, civil rights organizations were quite active concerning antipoverty policy (see Paden 2008). Otherwise, the interests of the poor have not been a priority of civil rights organizations. Hamilton and Hamilton (1997) find that civil rights groups have made social policy issues a priority, but the authors do not specifically consider social policy that affects the poor.

References

Chong, Dennis. 1991. *Collective Action and the Civil Rights Movement.* Chicago: University of Chicago Press.

Clegg, Andrew Claude III. 1997. *An Original Man: The Life and Times of Elijah Muhammad.* New York: St. Martin's Press.

Cohen, Cathy J. 2004. "Service Provider or Policymaker? Black Churches and the Health of African Americans." In *Long March Ahead: African American churches and Public Policy in Post–Civil Rights America,* ed. R. Drew Smith. Chapel Hill, NC: Duke University Press,

Cone, James H. 1995. *Martin and Malcolm in America: A Dream or a Nightmare?* Maryknoll, NY: Orbis Books.

Curtis, Edward E. IV. 2006. *Black Muslim Religion in the Nation of Islam, 1960–1975.* Chapel Hill: University of North Carolina Press.

Essien-Udom, E. U. (1962) 1995. *Black Nationalism: A Search for an Identity in America.* Chicago: University of Chicago Press.

Farrakhan, Louis. 1998. "Get Out the Vote: A Message to the Grassroots." Speech delivered November 1, Tabernacle Missionary Baptist Church, Chicago.

"Farrakhan Registers to Vote, Kicks Off National Drive." 1996. *Jet,* July 1, 31.

Gardell, Mattais. 1996. *In the Name of Elijah Muhammad: Louis Farrakhan and the Nation of Islam.* Durham, NC: Duke University Press,

Hamilton, Dona Cooper, and Charles V. Hamilton. 1997. *The Dual Agenda: The African-American Struggle for Civil and Economic Equality.* New York: Columbia University Press.

Harris, Fredrick C. 1999. *Something Within: Religion in African-American Political Activism.* Oxford: Oxford University Press.

———. 2005. "Introduction: Black Churches, Activist Traditions, and Urban Political Contexts." In *Black Churches and Local Politics,* ed. R. Drew Smith and Fedrick C. Harris. Lanham, MD: Rowman & Littlefield.

Jennings, James. 1992. *The Politics of Black Empowerment: The Transformation of Black Activism in Urban America.* Detroit: Wayne University Press.

"Kennedy and Farrakhan One-On-One." 2007. Interview with John F. Kennedy Jr., July 31, 1996. FinalCall.com, News, July 17, 2007. www.finalcall.com/artman/publish/Analysis_Statements _and_Briefs_16/Kennedy_and_Farrakhan_-_One_on_One_Interview_3750.shtml.

Lee, Martha F. 1996. *The Nation of Islam: An American Millenarian Movement.* Syracuse, NY: Syracuse University Press.

Lincoln, C. Eric. 1994. *The Black Muslims in America,* 3rd ed. Trenton, NJ: Africa World Press. First published 1961.

Lincoln, C. Eric, and Lawrence H. Mamiya. 1990. *The Black Church in the African American Experience.* Durham, NC: Duke University Press.

Mamiya, Lawrence H. 1982. "From Black Muslim to Bilalian: The Evolution of a Movement." *Journal for the Scientific Study of Religion* 2:138–52.

Marable, Manning. 1998. "Black Fundamentalism: Farrakhan and Conservative Black Nationalism." *Race and Class* 4:1–22.

Marsh, Clifton. 1996. *From Black Muslims to Muslims: the Resurrection, Transformation, and Change of the Lost-Found Nation of Islam in America, 1930–1995.* Lanham, MD: Scarecrow Press.

McLaughlin, Megan E. 2004. "The Role of African American Churches in Crafting the 1996 Welfare Reform Policy." In *Long March Ahead: African American Churches and Public Policy in Post-Civil Rights America,* ed. R. Drew Smith. Durham, NC: Duke University Press.

Morris, Aldon. 1984. *The Origins of the Civil Rights Movement: Black Communities Organizing for Change.* New York: Free Press.

Muhammad, Elijah. 1965. *Message to the Blackman in America.* Chicago: Muhammad's Temple of Islam No. 2.

———. 1973. *The Fall of America.* Chicago: Muhammad's Temple of Islam No. 2.

Paden, Catherine. 2008. "Disentangling Race and Poverty: The Civil Rights Response to Antipoverty Policy." *DuBois Review* 2:339–68.

Parks, Gordon. 1963. "What Their Cry Means to Me: A Negro's Own Evaluation." *Life* 54 (22, May 31): 22–32.

Paulson, Amanda. 2007. "Nation of Islam's Future Uncertain as Farrakhan Prepares to Step Down." *Christian Science Monitor*, February 28, 2.

Reed, Adolph. 1991. "All for One and None for All." *Nation* 252 (3, January 28): 86–92.

Schattschneider, E. E. 1960. *The Semi Sovereign People: A Realist's View of Democracy in America.* New York: Holt, Rinehart & Winston.

Smith, R. Drew, and Fredrick C. Harris. 2005. *Black Churches and Local Politics: Clergy Influence, Organizational Partnerships, and Civic Empowerment.* Lanham, MD: Rowman & Littlefield.

A Demanding Conversation

The Black Manifesto in the Mennonite Church, 1969–1974

Tobin Miller Shearer

In early 1969, Black Power activist James Forman presented the "Black Manifesto To the White Christian Church and the Jewish Synagogues in the United States of America and All Other Racist Institutions" at the National Black Economic Development Conference (NBEDC) in Detroit. With the backing of the conference delegates, Forman demanded $500 million for Christian and Jewish participation in slavery and the ongoing oppression of African Americans. Although Forman was not the first to call for reparations, the former Student Nonviolent Coordinating Committee (SNCC) executive secretary arrested the attention of the white community when he threatened to disrupt worship services. Within a month of releasing his manifesto, Forman marched up the aisle of the Riverside Church in Morningside Heights, New York, and took over the pulpit. As the press followed Forman's ecclesiastical disruptions, opposition grew. A poll by the Gallup Corporation revealed that only 2 percent of the white community and only 21 percent of African Americans supported the Black Manifesto (Newman 2001, 188). Amid this controversy, Forman and his colleagues challenged white Christians throughout the nation and in the rural communities of southeastern Pennsylvania where Mennonites went to church.

The white subjects of this study belonged to the Lancaster Conference, a regional Mennonite governing body responsible for more than three hundred congregations along the eastern seaboard. Mennonites belong to the Anabaptist tradition, which emerged out of the Radical Reformation in the early sixteenth century. Named for church leader Menno Simons, Mennonites believed in separation of church and state. Fleeing persecution for their pacifism, Mennonites emigrated from Europe to Pennsylvania during the colonial period. They emphasized service to the needy, discipleship through mutual correction, community grounded in mutual aid, and nonconformity, a doctrine mandating strict separation from secular influences. By the middle of the twentieth century, Mennonites had, like their Amish religious cousins, become known for pristine farms, distinct dress patterns, and a vigorous work ethic. Centered in a farming community two hours northwest of Philadelphia, the Lancaster Conference supported pastors who led services more likely to be interrupted by roving livestock than reparations requirements.

Those rural Mennonites and their African American interlocutors illuminate the intersection of race and religion because their conversation never should have taken place. Despite their racial homogeneity, Lancaster Conference leaders claimed egalitarian status. They pointed to African American church plants, hosting programs, and service initiatives, as well as a seventeenth-century anti-slavery statement, as proof of their commitments. Furthermore, Lancaster Conference Mennonites held a nonviolence doctrine known as nonresistance. Rural, egalitarian, nonviolent Mennonites should have had little reason to talk about the Black Manifesto. They were removed from urban centers, called to respond nonviolently to intruders, and engaged in service to African Americans. White Mennonites had no reason to discuss Black Nationalism. Nonetheless, five years after the Detroit conference, Mennonites continued a conversation started by Forman.

To understand how white and African American Mennonites sustained that dialogue, a new approach to the Black Manifesto becomes necessary, one that reveals the political space opened up by race and religion. In the past, historians focused on whether denominational leaders rejected or accepted Forman's demands (Lecky and Wright 1969, 18–21; Sousa 1973, 49–54; Frye 1974; Findlay 1993, 212–13; Murray 2004, 212–13). In so doing, they ignored complex, sustained, interracial conversations within religious communities. For example, leaders from the Urban Racial Council (URC), the group responsible for promoting the Black Manifesto among Mennonites, debated, cajoled, and conversed with Lancaster Conference leaders for years after Forman's intervention. In response, Lancaster Conference leaders used the occasion of the Black Manifesto to undergird their commitment to nonviolence—a prime example of Jacobson and Wadsworth's contention that race and religion inextricably intertwine (see the introduction to this volume).

This essay also centers on conversation to evaluate multiple outcomes (Carson 1981, 294–95; Moore 1986, 195; Weisbrot 1990, 284; Wilmore 1998, 240; Lincoln 1999, 115–16; Bedau 2002; Kelley 2002, 12–23; Williams 2005, 40).[1] From 1969 through 1974, members of the URC and the Lancaster Conference talked about racism, violence, and money. Although by 1975 that conversation had fizzled, the dialogue nonetheless prompted unintended consequences. Because the Black Manifesto emboldened African American Mennonites to talk with their co-believers, church administrators funded race-focused programs, African American leaders gained prominence, and race-related dialogue shut down. Demands-focused studies rarely make apparent such mixed outcomes.

The conflicted racial stance of mainline Protestants identified by Antony Alumkal in this volume thus also appeared in a religiously marginal group. Forman, his Black Manifesto emissaries, and Lancaster Conference Mennonites demonstrate the church's ability to resist racism and its immersion in a race-based, white-centered culture. The same people who avoided Forman also sustained interracial conversation prompted by his actions.

Forman's Manifesto

More than any document at the end of the 1960s, Forman's Black Manifesto changed the racial posture of Mennonite and other Christian leaders. Ironically, Forman prompted this shift after disowning the church. Forman came to the NBEDC with a distinguished civil rights record. After he left the SNCC, Forman marched at Selma and garnered the respect of African American clergymen (Carson 1981, 41–42). Despite positive relationships with black church leaders, Forman denounced Christianity for its collusion with slavery and support of economic inequity. His experience in church schools and congregations had led him to become an atheist by his mid-twenties (Williams 2005, 42). Forman thus presented his Black Manifesto on April 26, 1969, with all the passion of a preacher but none of the belief.

Nonetheless, Forman focused on Christian churches for his reparations efforts. The Manifesto called for half a billion dollars in reparations for Christianity's and Judaism's exploitation of African American "resources, . . . minds, . . . bodies, [and] . . . labor" (National Black Economic Development Conference 1969). Although Forman named the Jewish community, he concentrated his subsequent efforts on Christians for postemancipation actions that "degraded, brutalized, killed and persecuted."[2] Payments received would fund media outlets, black-led businesses, welfare collectives, black labor unions, and a southern black-led university. If Christians did not meet Forman's demands, they risked having their offices and worship services interrupted.

Only after Forman carried out his threat did Mennonites pay attention. The day after Forman disrupted services at Riverside Church in Morningside Heights, New York, on May 4, 1969, Mennonites read of Forman's intervention on their local newspaper's front page ("Blacks Defy Church" 1969; Rose 1969, 98). Rather than Manifesto text, they read about Forman "pushing his way past two elderly ushers." More than the monetary demands, the manner of the message received the most attention.

Mennonites continued to read about Forman during the following months. The press followed Forman as he disrupted services, occupied offices, and faced backlash.[3] Reporters emphasized Forman's interruptions and Presbyterian, Southern Baptist, United Church of Christ, and United Methodist leaders' responses. Several officials called the police, and officers removed a woman who disrupted a Catholic service ("Forman Lauds Pastor" 1969; "Protestors Arrested in Churches" 1969; "8 Clergymen Arrested" 1969). Philadelphia activists took even bolder action and removed an electric typewriter from the Presbyterian Church headquarters ("Typewriter Taken as Reparation" 1969). Although the activists later returned the typewriter, they had demonstrated their ability to disrupt both sanctuary and workplace.

The threat of takeovers arrested white Mennonites' billfolds and attention. In response to Forman's demands, Mennonite leaders increased their denominational urban mission programs; Presbyterians and United Methodists also channeled funds internally (General Conference of the Mennonite Church 1969; Poettcker 1969; "Presbyterians Reply to Black Manifesto" 1969; Sousa 1973). White Mennonites subsequently began to talk about the Black Manifesto as they received funding appeals. As was common elsewhere, conversations in the Mennonite church first took place among white people. African Americans had not yet entered the conversation.

Even as Mennonite organizations struggled to respond, Forman intensified his demands. Given that Black Nationalist leaders criticized Forman for having requested insufficient funds, his next move does not surprise (Frye 1974, 68). On June 13, Forman raised the reparations demand to $3 billion (Lecky and Wright 1969, 3). The additional funds would support an independent southern black college (Forman 1970). Financial response to the Manifesto became even more important.

Amid the extensive press coverage, Lancaster Conference Mennonites noted a new threat. Never before had the prospect of worship disruption been so immediate. Even during World Wars I and II, when Mennonites drew public harassment for their pacifism, they experienced little or no disruption when gathered for worship (Juhnke 1989, 208–42; Toews 1996, 107–53; Ruth 2001, 979–83). The unadorned Mennonite meetinghouses offered sanctuary from a hostile world. Worship space sanctity stood ready to be violated by worldly intruders. White Mennonites, like most other white Protestants, noted that the disruption would come covered in dark skin.

Calling for Nonviolence

Bishop Paul Landis was ready to talk. Two months after Forman took over the Riverside service, this young white pastor walked into the Lancaster Conference Peace Committee with a strong interracial record. Demonstrating a dynamic chronicled by Antony Alumkal in this volume, in which leaders embrace antiracism initiatives distrusted by lay members, Landis supported Mennonite pastors who attended Black Power conferences even while facing criticism for his civil rights commitments (New York City Peacemaker Workshop 1968). Nonetheless, Landis eulogized Martin Luther King for his efforts to channel "the flood tide of deep hurt, hate, and revenge into positive, nonviolent efforts," a posthumous assessment also held by other Christian leaders (Landis 1968). Having discussed Mennonite nonresistance with King, Landis felt King's loss keenly and joined other Mennonite leaders in calling for increased involvement with civil rights activities despite substantive backlash.[4]

Landis felt, however, that Mennonites had to deal with violence before talking about reparations. Rather than approach the Black Manifesto as a financial document, on July 10, 1969, Landis and other leaders sent a letter focused on nonresistance to every Lancaster Conference minister. Under the doctrine, many young men opted for alternative service. Nonresistance called its adherents to a greater commitment, however, than the refusal to bear arms. Mennonites also distinguished between Christian nonresistance and secular nonviolence. Lancaster Conference leaders opposed "strikes, boycotts, and organized pressures of any kind" because these methods coerced rather than convinced adversaries (*Christian Nonresistant Way of Life* 1940, 32). By 1969, Lancaster Conference leaders remained committed to pacifism even while debating whether civil rights tactics could be deemed nonresistant (Metzler 1963; Ruth 2001, 1100–1101).

Landis and his colleagues then used the theological language of nonresistance to interpret the Black Manifesto. To be certain, they asked the three hundred Conference pastors to repent of "racial prejudice" and to make "financial resources available" where needed ("Lancaster Conference Peace Committee Responds" 1969; Landis and Shenk 1969; Zook 1970, 65). Landis did so, however, only after focusing on nonviolence. He and his colleagues wrote nearly three times as many sentences about nonviolence as they did about reparations.[5] The Lancaster Conference leaders asked their pastors to "be willing to have our services disrupted" and stressed the "way of love" (Good and Landis 1969). Prior to the Black Manifesto, the Lancaster Conference leaders had not even considered that a Mennonite minister might contact the police to restore worship order. Yet in its aftermath, Landis and his fellow committee members cautioned pastors against "calling the police" or restraining "those who would enter our services" (Good and Landis 1969, 1–2).

This fear of violence from ordained leaders of a nonviolent church can be explained by the church's eroding commitment to nonresistance. In 1942 alone, 30 percent of drafted church members chose a form of military service. Likewise, from 1940 through 1947, more Mennonite men served in the military than in the wartime Civilian Public Service camps. These service records reflected harsh disagreements over how to live a nonresistant life (Toews 1996, 149, 173, 311). Violent members of a nonresistant church had become a new possibility.

In light of these internal debates, Landis and other committee members redirected attention from reparations to nonviolent service. In their penultimate paragraph, Landis and his colleagues quoted an African American who "stated that the Mennonite Church has much more than money to give to the black people" (Good and Landis 1969, 2). They made their point clear. Although African Americans in the secular world asked for money, African Americans in the Mennonite community asked for love, equality, and access to employment. Mennonite ministers knew how to respond to these needs. Tithes from congregations located in one of the "wealthiest farming counties in the nation" supported service, poverty relief, and evangelism rather than the publishing houses, black-led academies, and training centers proposed by Forman (Smith 1941, 784). In stark contrast to a group like the Nation of Islam that, as Paden in this volume points out, brought low-income African Americans into their community, Landis proposed that the ministers serve rather than convert Black Manifesto emissaries.

Three months after Forman's intervention, Lancaster Conference leaders remained unsettled. Landis used the doctrine of nonresistance to discourage Mennonites from paying reparations. Manifesto advocates promoted a financial response based on sacred scripture. All started with theology but arrived at different interpretations. Which perspective would sway the greatest number of church members was unclear. The outcome eventually turned on a common though unexamined aspect of their respective appeals. None of the conference leaders had directed comments to people of color within the church. Although their theologies gave them terms to talk about the Black Manifesto, those doctrines had not encouraged the white Conference leaders to hear African American perspectives. Only after leaders from the African American community initiated discussion did they talk across racial lines.

Landis had responded in ways similar to other denominations. Like many church leaders, he redirected the Black Manifesto demands into familiar territory, in this case service. Some denominations shifted attention to antipoverty programs, others to educational initiatives. Few just paid money. Like the denominational leaders who prescribed solutions for communities of color in Alumkal's study (see Alumkal, this volume), church leaders set their own terms of response. Nonetheless, the religious environment that initially proved so inhospitable to the Manifesto came to host an extended conversation unheard of in the secular community.

Urban Racial Council Responds

John Powell was ready to talk. As this twenty-eight-year-old African American pastor from Detroit strode to the podium before an audience of a thousand Mennonites, Powell prepared to speak frankly. He came to the 1969 biennial assembly of Mennonites in Turner, Oregon, as secretary of the newly formed URC, an advocacy group made up of African American and Latino Mennonites and their white allies (Powell 1970b). Although church officials had invited Powell to speak, those gathered thought he might prove as disruptive as had Forman ("A Response to Racial Tensions" 1969; Smith 1969; Sousa 1973). Powell had previously excoriated white Mennonites for refusing to join demonstrations ("Urban Pastors Meet" 1968). To the surprise of many, by the time Powell finished speaking, he and his audience had begun a conversation that would continue for half a decade.

Powell started the dialogue by plunging into controversy. The church's executive secretary later referred to Powell's speech as "almost traumatic" (Zehr 1970, 5).[6] Another white delegate recalled that Powell "sent shock waves" through the assembly.[7] Such collective distress arose more from the tenor of Powell's comments than from the content of his proposal. Powell stated that Mennonites would have "tarred and feathered" Forman if he had addressed the crowd (Schmucker 1969). Such an accusation irked those who cherished the memory of tarred-and-feathered forebears. Powell's race also added to the controversy. Foreshadowing the mix of Black Power and evangelical terminology that, as Nancy Wadsworth points out in this volume, Tom Skinner would introduce the following year, Powell asserted his racial identity before a racially inexpert audience (Shearer 2008). Rather than praise the church's charity, Powell criticized its integrity. In response, one white delegate pronounced, "If we do what John Powell tells us, they'll have me out of my pulpit and a nigger in there" (Berry et al. 2004).

Such vociferous response masked Powell's careful use of audience-appropriate terms. Knowing that demands did not sit well with congregationally autonomous Mennonites, Powell presented seventeen "recommendations," the first of which called white Mennonites to confess to "sins committed against black people" (Powell 1969b). Powell also proposed that the executive committee of the church's mission board oversee gathered funds. By ceding authority to the denomination's largest program board, Powell sidestepped objections about financial accountability common in other denominations' discussions of the Black Manifesto (Findlay 1993, 212). In this moment of high drama, Powell chose language intended to invite conversation rather than shut it down.

Even though they had modified the proposal's language, URC leaders had not changed the Black Manifesto's focus. Powell asked the delegates to commit themselves to a half million dollars above an already ambitious $4 million budget (Zook 1970, 11–12, 44, 50). He explained that the URC would provide African Americans and Latinos with jobs and education while also solidifying their position in the church (Powell 1969b, 2). Prior to the Turner gathering, the council lacked an official budget, a staff, a clear mandate, and authority over other church bodies. By garnering funds independent of existing church structures, Powell and his colleagues sought to encourage equal, interracial conversation (Powell 1969b, 2).

In the roiling aftermath, white delegates such as Paul Landis lobbied for the proposal. Two days later, the delegates received a six-point motion. Although not the direct apology offered by Southern Baptists three decades later (see Wadsworth, this volume), the motion confessed racial wrongdoing and called for above-budget giving of $6 per member (General Conference of the Mennonite Church 1969). Contrasting his response to Forman's external demands, Bishop Landis supported Powell's internal recommendations. Speaking on behalf of two national committees, Landis moved to accept the money-centered recommendations on Tuesday, August 19 (Urban Racial Concerns 2006). The motion carried.

Initial reaction to the vote seemed promising. Delegates contributed $5,000 that evening to "urban and minority crisis projects," a sum that more than quadrupled the previous evening's offering ("Reporting Guide" 1969; Urban Racial Concerns 2006). Back in Lancaster Conference, editor Mahlon Hess penned a September editorial on reparations and printed an article in which Powell challenged the church to share power (Hess 1969; Powell 1969a). As the executive director of the URC, now funded with the prospect of a half million dollars for each of the next five years, Powell challenged the church to talk frankly about race.

Lancaster Conference delegates returned home from Oregon in late August uncertain of the gathering's outcome. The church had encountered, debated, and supported a Black Manifesto emissary. The very threat that Landis feared would materialize in Lancaster County appeared across the country. Powell's intervention, however, took an unexpected form. Powell disrupted the church by pointing to inconsistencies rather than rushing through sanctuaries. Members of the Lancaster Conference now faced the threat of ongoing disruption. Unlike external Black Manifesto emissaries, internal URC members appeared ready to stay. The prospect of dialoging with them changed the direction of the Lancaster Conference leaders. Rather than prompt ministers to respond nonviolently to pulpit takeovers, Landis and his colleagues prepared themselves for internal conversations about racism.

Religion again showed its complex entanglement with race. The same church leaders who avoided financial response came, at least initially, to support one. The same delegates who dreaded Powell's presentation filled offering baskets. White guilt does not explain the shift entirely. Belief in nonresistance, service across racial lines, support for interpersonal reconciliation, and white racial socialization together shaped the response. As Wadsworth and Jacobson note in the introduction to this volume, race has always been interpolated in religion. The resultant conversations only made the religion-race connection more evident.

A Conversational Roller Coaster

Members of the Lancaster Conference nonetheless gave the URC's conversational initiative a mixed reception. Despite both groups' modified positions, Paul Landis and other members of Lancaster Conference's Peace Committee discussed the URC statement at length in early October but took no common action (Landis 1969b). The Lancaster Conference's Colored Workers Committee addressed Black Manifesto themes more directly during their November meeting. Although white men dominated the leadership structures, small groups of African American and white participants discussed interracial marriage, Christian unity, and financial justice, topics central to then current calls for economic reparations and black separatism (Colored Workers Committee 1964–69). Likewise, on January 4, 1970, Tom Skinner, an African American evangelist from New York City, spoke before a crowd of six hundred people. Local Mennonites listened to Skinner state that the "problem with the Black Manifesto is not James Foreman [sic], but the people and the conditions that make a Foreman necessary" ("Evangelist Urges Gospel for Black Community" 1970). Although he did not endorse Forman, Skinner nonetheless supported the Manifesto. His large Mennonite audience listened with rapt attention. In the five months following Powell's proposal, lay members seemed more interested in conversation about the Manifesto than did ordained leaders.

Landis and other Lancaster Conference leaders initially seemed unresponsive to grassroots members' growing interest in those who promoted the URC agenda. In lieu of direct support, the Conference's leadership employed a familiar strategy. As they had done when faced with worship takeovers, the leaders prepared for conversation with potentially hostile outsiders, in this case Powell and members of the URC, but gave no money. In public, the leaders turned their attention elsewhere. Rather than discuss how the Conference could become involved in the service and fundraising initiatives proposed by the URC, Landis and his colleagues used the pages of the Conference newsletter to interpret church doctrines of nonconformity and submission to authority.[8] Although Landis had backed Powell's recommendations in Oregon, he generated little interest in Black Manifesto conversation.

African American Mennonites grew frustrated with the lack of financial support from Landis and other Lancaster Conference leaders but continued talking with them. In March 1970, Powell reported that the newly named Compassion Fund of the Minority Ministries Council, successor to the URC, had received only $38,075, far below the quarter million dollars necessary to reach the half million mark within a year (Powell 1970c). Perhaps in response to the disappointing giving rate, Powell made some effort to distance the council's appeal from the Black Manifesto, but then wrote glowingly about the Manifesto one week later (Powell 1970d). In the wake of diminished giving, exasperation mounted. African American council associate Hubert Brown, for example, reported on the "bullshit" he encountered among white inner-city Mennonites "all 'decked out' like gods who come to do 'blackie' a favor" (Brown 1970). Yet Brown, Powell, and their associates continued to talk with white church leaders even as funds failed to materialize (Powell 1970a).

In response to the frustration, Landis and his colleagues sought out different conversation partners. Instead of waiting for a Minority Ministries Council preacher to show up unannounced, Lancaster Conference administrators urged local pastors to invite "minority" speakers to preach (Wenger 1970). More than a year after Powell's Oregon speech, Lancaster Conference ministers began to invite African American and Latino leaders into their congregations from a list of pastors unconnected to the increasingly bold Minority Ministries Council.[9] Rather than outsiders over whom the Conference had no authority, the Conference leaders brought in trusted converts accountable to Landis and the other bishops.

Powell and the Minority Ministries Council, however, wanted more from the Lancaster Conference than a list of tame speakers. In early fall 1970, Minority Ministries staff approached Landis about setting up a time to discuss "racist attitudes among" Lancaster Conference constituency (Thomas and Stauffer 1970a). On November 13, Lynford Hershey, a white Minority Ministries staff person hired by Powell to educate white Mennonites, met with nine Lancaster Conference bishops and staff members. Hershey described how he was working in both "indirect and direct" ways to encourage white people to move aside so that African Americans could help themselves (Stauffer 1970). Landis and other bishops in attendance told Hershey about their forthcoming race relations statement, but little else seemed to come of the meeting. Longer-term outcomes of the conversation would not appear for several months.

As he traveled throughout the church, Hershey found lay congregants willing to talk about racial inequities. By November 25, he commented on the "almost unbelievable" gap between white rural Mennonites and Mennonites, both white and from communities of color, who worshipped in the city ("C.P.S.C. At Minneapolis" 1970). Despite that divide, white lay members welcomed Hershey's efforts to "deal with white racism" more readily than did church leaders (Hershey 1970). At least in terms of Hershey's experience, those least threatened by calls to redistribute power were most open to discuss race relations.

Those grassroots conversations came about through a distant and unlikely source. Given that Hershey received funding from Powell based on an appeal prompted by Forman, lay Mennonites had come to talk about race because of the Black Manifesto. The line connecting the NBEDC in Detroit to rural Mennonite congregations in Lancaster ran through a document often thought to have cut off such contact. Although few lay members made the same connection, Powell and his colleagues recognized the antecedent to their efforts and made no attempt to distance themselves from Black Manifesto promoters.

These Black Manifesto roots, when grounded in the religious soil of Mennonite churches, nourished conversations absent in the larger society. The white Mennonites who engaged Hershey and Powell had as difficult a time recognizing structural inequalities as did the white evangelicals studied by Nancy Wadsworth (see Wadsworth, this volume) and others (Patterson 1998). Despite that lack of understanding, the church provided a context for white people in rural locations like Lancaster, Pennsylvania, and Goshen, Indiana, to talk about reparations. The demands of religious identity, ethical conduct, and spiritual integrity prompted white Mennonites who had no other reason to talk about race, to do that very thing. That many had difficulty making systemic connections is less surprising than that they made the attempt at all.

At the leadership level, conversations in the aftermath of the Black Manifesto continued after a slow start. On July 14, 1971, Leon Stauffer, a colleague of Landis, assured Hershey that the Conference's subcommittee on race relations was hard at work (Stauffer 1971). Council members likewise continued to push forward. The day after Stauffer penned his report, Powell and Hubert Brown met with Vincent Harding, a former African American Mennonite minister who had been nominated by Forman to serve on the Black Manifesto's steering committee, in Atlanta to discuss "methods . . . to liberate blacks in the church" (Powell 1971b). Following these meetings, Minority Ministries staff challenged the Lancaster Conference leaders to match public statements about racism with bold action and to refrain from hiring "non-whites that we have taught to act white" (Hershey 1971). Lancaster Conference staff responded by recommending that pastors bring white council staff member Hershey into their congregations (Wenger 1971). As they prepared for Hershey's visit, Landis and other leaders from the Conference kept on talking about a subject that few had anticipated would still be on the church's agenda more than two years after Forman spoke in Detroit.

The Minority Ministries Council built on the ongoing interest by holding an annual meeting in October 1971 that marked the apex of its influence. As council members gathered in the same city where Forman had first presented the Black Manifesto, Powell highlighted a host of new activities. Mirroring the practice of other racial minority caucus groups lodged within majority-white denominations, Powell and other council members disbursed more than $75,000 and laid plans for disbursing $95,000 more. A new alliance between Latino and African American Mennonites had grown. Outspoken council members held influential positions within existing church structures (Minority Ministries Council 1971a). A few white Mennonite executives even expressed support for the council. The secretary of information services for a national Mennonite mission agency supported the Compassion Fund as a means to "recognize our participation as white anglo Mennonites in the overall racist and discriminatory and insensitive patterns in our society" (Powell 1971a). In public, Minority Ministries looked like a healthy conversation partner with church leaders.

During the meeting council members demonstrated their interest in continuing to talk with white Mennonites by rejecting a statement that would have strained relationships within the church. Their decision took on additional significance given the financial constraints facing the council. The Compassion Fund's first-year receipts reached only $100,000 of the $500,000 goal. Receipts in the second year dropped to $60,000. Powell asserted that denominational officials required council staff to submit more detailed financial reports than other departments, a requirement indicative of the church's distrust of council staff, which in turn slowed the pace of giving. As funds failed to materialize, Powell tried to achieve self-sufficiency by proposing that the council develop credit unions and small businesses in racially oppressed communities (Minority Ministries Council 1971b). At the same time, council caucuses reviewed a statement that rejected integration due to Mennonite paternalism (Minority Ministries Council 1971d). In light of the already diminished financial response, numerous Black Caucus members and even more Hispanic Caucus participants objected to the document because "it may hurt the very whites who were friends and were concerned" (Minority Ministries Council 1971c). Despite their reputation as agitators, council members remained invested in relationships with white Mennonites.

Such investment bore fruit in the Lancaster Conference. Although plans for a Minority Ministries' cross-cultural seminar faltered, Landis and his fellow bishops fostered conversations through a variety of actions.[10] In 1972 the Conference published a race relations study guide that, for the first time in the group's history, confessed to racism and lamented a lack of support for "housing, education, employment, and leadership" among racially oppressed communities (Lancaster Conference 1972). Building on other themes prominent in the Black Manifesto, the statement also called Mennonites in the Lancaster Conference to grant "equal power to racially oppressed people" and distribute "economic resources" (Lancaster Conference 1972). One year later, the Conference appointed African Americans such as Harold Davenport to significant leadership positions (Angstadt 1973). The conversation continued through 1974, five full years after the Black Manifesto, when Raymond Jackson, an African American Mennonite minister from Philadelphia, traveled to Kenya to take part in a conference sponsored by the Minority Ministries Council (Powell 1973a). Through Jackson and subsequent reporting, leaders and lay members in the Conference continued to discuss racial inequities in Forman's terms (Bender 1974). Even as late as 1976, a group of Mennonites and their denominational cousins gathered in New Jersey to discuss racism in the church using concepts made popular through the Black Manifesto (Mennonite Board of Congregational Ministries 1976). Although he received little attention by 1976, Forman's controversial document continued to influence Mennonites and other white-majority denominations through groups like the Minority Ministries Council.

Tracing the Manifesto's Legacy

The legacy of the Black Manifesto looks much different when treated as a religious conversation rather than a political demand. Because Forman and his emissaries interrupted work and worship, white Mennonites and other northern Christian groups talked about ecclesiastical racism with African American leaders. Had the Manifesto been a one-sided, unresponsive monologue, such a direct exchange could not have followed. The frank, sustained, interracial discussion also generated new outcomes. Conversation between the Minority Ministries Council and the Lancaster Conference exposed racial inequities, challenged urban missions, and birthed fresh programs. Instead of encouraging churchly strife, a radical document invited careful conversation and measured change.

Those new programs and dialogue emerged amid tensions particular to the practice of religion. In the process of tailoring their comments for Christian— and initially Jewish—audiences, Forman and his emissaries wrote religious documents that invoked countervailing forces. For example, mutual theological commitments among Mennonites grounded conversation about the Black Manifesto even while fostering misinterpretation. Because Powell and Landis held Christian faith and doctrine in common, they had reason to talk. The two men shared confessional commitments to "faith and belief," "the Cross," and "the words of the prophets" as used by Forman in the Manifesto (National Black Economic Development Conference 1969). At the same time, terms like "revolution," "demands," and "colonization" fit Powell's theology but clashed with Landis's. Leaders of the Lancaster Conference preferred to emphasize "the redemptive love of Christ," while Minority Ministries staff focused instead on "paternalism in our churches" (Good and Landis 1969; Landis 1969a; Baer 1970; Minority Ministries Council 1971d; Powell 1971b). Even on the most central of Mennonite doctrines, the two groups differed. Leaders from the Lancaster Conference eschewed any association with the military (Lancaster Conference 1968). Powell and other council staff used military idioms to describe their plans for a "war against prejudice and discrimination" in which they would become "the 'generals' of our troops" and appoint white Mennonites as "foot soldiers" (Minority Ministries Council 1971d; Powell 1969b). Even as Christian commitment brought the groups together, differing interpretations of their theology pulled them apart.

A second religiously initiated tension became evident as the two groups narrated contrasting racial histories. The white Mennonite community in Lancaster thought that it had done race relations well. Community members knew African Americans first received baptism in a Lancaster Conference congregation and felt confident that their approach bested that of civil rights leaders. A Lancaster Conference member claimed, for example, that a predominantly white Mennonite church in Harlem offered "potentially greater gains for the claims of Christ than . . . ten civil-rights marches led by Rev. M. L. King, Jr." (Seventh Avenue Mennonite Church 1965). John Powell and the Minority Ministries Council told another story. In Powell's tale, the Lancaster Conference leaders, pastors, and lay members promoted paternalism. Powell faulted white Mennonites for calling people of color to be more like them than to be like Christ. Rather than participate in a "false kind of integration," Powell and his associates sought to write a history in which they developed "indigenous congregations" and confronted their "white Christian brothers" (Minority Ministries Council 1971d). Their story upended the tale told among the white Lancaster Conference Mennonites. The stories came into such sharp contrast because, as a religious community tasked with spreading their confessional truth to all people regardless of race, it mattered whether they had fulfilled their evangelical task.

Contrasting approaches to systemic injustice also intensified interracial conversation. Like many evangelical communities, white Mennonites had little experience in responding to systemic inequities. From long practice, they knew how to administer service programs based on interpersonal relationships.[11] They knew much less about how to respond to systemwide impersonal forces. Members of the Minority Ministries Council, however, initiated programs that addressed institutional injustice by channeling financial resources to oppressed communities. Both groups stated their intention to right racial wrongs. They disagreed on the means to do so. In particular, Mennonites in the Lancaster Conference found the Council's proposed changes threatening. When they heard Powell's proposals to shift relationally based service to institutionally based advocacy, many felt that their commitment to interracial ministry had been ignored. Although the two groups kept talking, the conversation became strained as interpersonal and institutional visions clashed.

In the end, the conversations collapsed because the money stopped. By the time educational resources on racism reached past the church elite to congregants, Minority Ministries Council staff felt discouraged by administrative restrictions placed on the Compassion Fund, their fiduciary lifeline. When the money dried up, so did much of their influence. Although the council members had once been able to demand that functionaries travel to meet with them, Powell and others soon had to travel to gain a hearing. Already in 1972, church administrators had cut funds for Lynford Hershey's educational program (Historical Committee 2006). By September 1973, John Powell was talking about feeling isolated (Powell 1973b). Soon after, Mennonite Church leaders dismantled the Minority Ministries Council (Historical Committee 2006). In its place, African American and Latino leaders gained a few leadership posts, but the institution that had once advocated on their behalf no longer functioned. The existing theological, narrative, and programmatic tensions identified above proved overwhelming. Less than a year later, Powell resigned (Historical Committee 2006). In short, when the money left the table, the conversation died.

As interracial conversations at the leadership level dwindled, so too did race-focused action. Soon after Powell resigned, white Mennonite leaders across the church turned their attention elsewhere. Even before Powell's resignation, race fell from the agenda of the Lancaster Conference. During the decade following 1972, bishops from the Lancaster Conference discussed race-related agenda twice, once to deny funding for an African American youth ministry team and once to inquire about a local meeting of the Mennonite Church Black Caucus (Lancaster Conference 1977, 1982). Without the Minority Ministries Council to initiate dialogue, white leaders in the Lancaster Conference focused on other pressing matters. Structural reorganization, church discipline, overseas missions, and controversies over charismatic worship garnered their attention (Ruth 2001, 1106–16). In essence, having recognized the disjuncture between their racial self-assessment and that of people of color, leaders in the Lancaster Conference withdrew.

Before its demise, the five-year dialogue initiated by the Black Manifesto nevertheless led to specific, tangible, and at times unexpected outcomes. Within the Lancaster Conference, leaders used the Black Manifesto to strengthen the core doctrine of nonresistance, a move that corresponded with unexpected support for young draft resistors and increased opposition to the Vietnam War (Thomas and Stauffer 1970b, 3). Additionally, administrators from the Conference supported an initiative to hire African American and Latino youth from Philadelphia and other urban centers for summer service programs in their home neighborhoods ("Three Serve Summer Urban Program" 1982). Summer service had formerly been the exclusive province of white rural Mennonite youth. It is doubtful whether this shift would have taken placed as rapidly or at all without Powell and others agitating on the behalf of such initiatives. Rural hosting programs known as "Fresh Air" ventures also received new attention from council members. Lancaster Conference leaders discontinued their Fresh Air program in a slow and attenuated process that can be traced back to 1971. At that time, Powell critiqued paternalism in Fresh Air ventures and called for "stale air" exchanges that would bring white Mennonite children into African American urban homes (Hershey 1971). Changes, even those not sought by promoters of the Manifesto, came about because Minority Ministries staff members and Lancaster Conference leaders talked with each other at length.

The Minority Ministries Council and the Lancaster Conference together demonstrate how the practice of religion both encouraged and quelled a racially demanding conversation. Powell, Landis, and their respective colleagues shared a common religious identity. As Christians they professed belief in core religious tenets regarding salvation, the afterlife, and the importance of evangelism. These beliefs drew them together. At the same time, the two groups applied that doctrine differently. Mennonites in the Lancaster Conference tried to transform individuals through service, whereas the Minority Ministries Council sought to change institutions through advocacy. Furthermore, their shared religious beliefs called them to reconcile broken relationships. Consequently they kept on talking even when their respective theologies clashed. The longer the two groups talked, the more they solidified their positions. As funds for the council diminished and the conversation faltered, the two groups separated with clearer memories of their differences than their shared belief (Berry et al. 2004).[12] In this instance, religious practices and doctrine fostered as much racial division as they did interracial connection.

The mixed legacy of Mennonites' response to the Black Manifesto looks remarkably similar to that of other white-led denominations. Like the Mennonites, groups as widely diverse as Episcopalians, Presbyterians, Seventh-Day Adventists, and Catholics crafted replies focused more on internal concerns than those named in the Black Manifesto (Gingrich 1969). The subsequent conversations roiled with controversy, engaged unexpected interlocutors, and had long-reaching effects. The Methodist Commission on Religion and Race, for example, distributed the Manifesto widely and led leadership-level discussions of the document, while editorials in missions magazines brought the conversation into congregants' homes (Murray 2004, 212–14). As in the case of the Mennonites, those conversations, while sustained far longer than other racial topics in the past, also came to an untimely end.

More notable than the conversation's termination, however, is that it took place at all. A conservative, white religious group discussed a divisive, racial agenda. Leaders examined racial inequities in financial appropriation, resource control, and committee appointment. In addition, the conversation initiated by the Black Manifesto lasted longer within the Mennonite church than in most secular settings and, following the ten-year hiatus noted above, reemerged. In time, Powell returned to the church, and by the early 1990s he held a leadership post at the denominational level (Historical Committee 2006). As part of that appointment, he helped reopen conversation about the Black Manifesto's financial and political themes (Historical Committee 2006).[13] A new generation of leaders in the Lancaster Conference and throughout the church talked about racial inequities in their religious community. Although still one of the whitest and most conservative bodies in the Mennonite church, the Lancaster Conference once again entered a conversation prompted by the Black Manifesto.

The Manifesto was in the end a religious document of remarkable significance. Forman opened conversations among Mennonites and other Christian groups of surprising longevity. A challenge directed at secular groups would most likely not have lasted so long. Lacking Mennonites' concern for reconciled relationship, for example, civic leaders may have summarily dismissed reparations demands. As a result, a shorter, less intense conversation seems almost certain. Yet Forman chose the church. Because he made that decision, Mennonites and other religious groups like them discussed how racial identities fostered financial and institutional inequities. At a time when many white people assumed that the racial revolution died with Martin Luther King, substantive interracial conversation and concrete changes took place.

When treated as a religious document rather than a set of political demands, the Black Manifesto's success or failure appears less important. Although Forman did not raise billions of dollars, he did change how the church talked about and responded to racial injustice. The extended, interracial dialogue that followed the Manifesto unsettled, prodded, and reoriented participants to consider how race shaped their community and their faith. That intense exchange lasted for five years both despite and because of theological, narrative, and programmatic tensions implicit in religious practice. Whether Forman invoked those tensions or was surprised by them is likewise unimportant. As we look back through four decades on the Black Manifesto, the most essential insight to recognize is that Forman's decision to call for reparations from the religious community made possible a demanding conversation in the most unlikely of settings.

Notes

1. The following model an approach to the Black Freedom struggle that evaluates historical actors by their contributions, not their success or failure: Kelley 2002, 120–23; Mariscal 2005.

2. Historical accounts make no mention of Forman or his associates interrupting synagogue services (Lecky and Wright 1969, 17; National Black Economic Development Conference 1969).

3. Events are recounted in several *Intelligencer Journal* articles from that year: Cornell 1969, Owens 1969, and Scott 1969, as well as articles without bylines. A representative selection of these follows: "Blacks Defy Church to Read Demands," May 5, 1; "Reparations Case Presented," May 16, 1; "Forman Lauds Pastor After Rights Sermon," May 12, 1; "Presbyterians Reply to Black Manifesto," May 22, 1; "Typewriter Taken as Reparation," June 5, 1; "Offices of Church Occupied," June 6, 1; "Typewriter Given Back to Church," June 12, 1; "Black Claims Rejected by Baptist Body," June 14, 1; "Protesters Arrested in Churches," June 16, 1; "UCC Denies Reparation to Forman," June 21, 1; "8 Clergymen Arrested for Occupying Church," July 11, 1; "Ex-Local Pastor Target of Sit-in," July 12, 1; "Manifesto Rejected by Church," July 24, 1.

4. Paul G. Landis, telephone interview by author, March 8, 2003.

5. Landis's letter includes three sentences identifying economic reparations as the Black Manifesto's subject, five referring to race relations, and thirteen discussing nonviolent methods.

6. John Powell, telephone interview by author, March 16, 2003.

7. Paul Zehr, telephone interview by author, March 1, 2003.

8. Responses in the *Pastoral Messenger* included Delp 1969, Kniss 1969, Shank 1969, Shenk

1969, and Stauffer 1969, as well as three articles without a byline, all from 1969: "Worth Noting," January, 7–8; "The Lancaster Mennonite Conference, Weaverland Mennonite Church, East Earl, Pennsylvania, March 18, 1969," April, 1–3; and "Report to the Lancaster Mennonite Conference, Mellinger Mennonite Meetinghouse, Lincoln Highway East, Lancaster, Pennsylvania, September 18, 1969," October, 2–4.

9. A number of the ten men listed in Wenger's August 24, 1970, letter to every pastor in the Lancaster Conference—Richard Pannell, Harold Davenport, George Richards, James Harris, Macon Gwinn, Raymond Jackson, Larry Crumbley, Artemio DeJesus, Jose Gonzalez, Jose Santiago—did go on to fulfill a variety of leadership posts in the Conference and throughout the church, but as of Wenger's letter, none of these Lancaster Conference pastors of color had held formal leadership posts with the Minority Ministries Council.

10. Although minutes of the October 30, 1972, Lancaster Conference Peace Committee make reference to plans to explore holding such an event, no follow-up activity appears in the minutes through 1975 (Geigley 1972).

11. Christian Smith and Michael Emerson note that the history of race relations in evangelical communities has often been hampered by a focus on an individualistic "relationalism" in which interpersonal relationships hold primacy over all else, and by an "antistructuralism" in which members of that community refuse to focus on structural realities. Those tendencies were present at both the grassroots and leadership levels among the Lancaster Conference Mennonites (Emerson and Smith 2001, 76).

12. Paul G. Landis, telephone interviews by author, March 8, 2003, April 28, 2005.

13. Starting in 1994, Powell joined the Reference Committee for the Racism Awareness Program of the Mennonite Central Committee.

References

Angstadt, Paul. 1973. "Harold Davenport Talks with Kids." Photograph. File cabinets middle aisle: drawer marked Information Services Picture File, file: Archives—Home Ministries, Children's Visitation Program. Eastern Mennonite Mission, Records Room, Salunga, PA.

Baer, Russel J. 1970. Editorial. *Pastoral Messenger*, January, 4.

Bechler, Le Roy. 1986. *The Black Mennonite Church in North America 1886–1986*. Scottdale, PA: Herald Press.

Bedau, Hugo Adam. 2002. "Compensatory Justice and the Black Manifesto." In *Injustice and Rectification*, ed. R. C. Roberts. New York: Peter Lang.

Bender, Urie A. 1974. "Where Color Doesn't Matter." *Missionary Messenger*, February, 8–9.

Berry, Lee Roy, Hubert Brown, Gerald Hughes, Raymond Jackson Jr., Mattie Cooper Nikiema, and John Powell. 2004. "Urban African American Leaders Interviewed by J. Sharp." Lee Heights Fellowship, Cleveland, OH, July 17.

"Blacks Defy Church to Read Demands." 1969. *Intelligencer Journal*, May 5, 1.

Brown, Hubert. 1970. "Report on the Church and Urban Development Seminar." Washington, DC: Minority Ministries Council. IV-21-4 box 1, MBM Minority Ministries Council, data files 1, A–K, folder: Church and Urban Development 1970, Seminars. Archives of the Mennonite Church, Goshen, IN.

Carson, Clayborne. 1981. *In Struggle: SNCC and the Black Awakening of the 1960s*. Cambridge, MA: Harvard University Press.

The Christian Nonresistant Way of Life. 1940. Lancaster, PA: Peace Problems Committee and Tract Editors of Lancaster Conference District.

Colored Workers Committee. 1964–69. "Colored Workers Committee Notes 1964–1969." File cabinets far wall, first cabinet, top drawer, drawer marked Home Missions Locations and Other General 1956–1964, file: four numbered notebooks. Eastern Mennonite Mission, Records Room, Salunga, PA.

Cornell, George W. 1969. "$500 Million Demand Shocks Church Leaders." *Intelligencer Journal*, May 10, 1.

"C.P.S.C. At Minneapolis." 1970. *Hi-Lights of the Mennonite Publishing House*, November 25, 1.

Delp, Melvin. 1969. "Nonconformity Committee Statement to Conference." *Pastoral Messenger*, April, 5–6.

"8 Clergymen Arrested for Occupying Church." 1969. *Intelligencer Journal*, July 11, 1.

Emerson, Michael O., and Christian Smith. 2001. *Divided by Faith: Evangelical Religion and the Problem of Race in America*. New York: Oxford University Press.

"Evangelist Urges Gospel for Black Community." 1970. *Mennonite Weekly Review*, January 15.

"Ex-Local Pastor Target of Sit-in." 1969. *Intelligencer Journal*, July 12, 1.

Findlay, James F., Jr. 1993. *Church People in the Struggle: The National Council of Churches and the Black Freedom Movement, 1950–1970*. New York: Oxford University Press.

Forman, James. 1970. *Control, Conflict and Change: The Underlying Concepts of the Black Manifesto*. Detroit: National Association of Black Students.

"Forman Lauds Pastor after Rights Sermon." 1969. *Intelligencer Journal*, May 12, 1.

Frye, Jerry K. 1974. "The 'Black Manifesto' and the Tactic of Objectification." *Journal of Black Studies* 5 (1): 65–76.

Geigley, Ray. 1972. "Peace Committee." Salunga, PA: Lancaster Conference, October 30. Peace Committee Minutes, 1962–74. Lancaster Mennonite Historical Society, Lancaster, PA.

General Conference of the Mennonite Church. 1969. "Resolution on Urban-Racial Concerns." Turner, Oregon. I-1-1, Mennonite General Conference, 1898–1971. 1969 Session materials, folder 5/8. Archives of the Mennonite Church, Goshen, IN.

Gingrich, Paul M. 1969. "Black Manifesto: A Study of Reaction by Some Christian Churches." Paper, Church History. Associated Mennonite Biblical Seminaries, Elkhart, IN.

Good, Noah G., and Paul G. Landis. 1969. "Dear Brethren." Salunga, PA, July. Box: Conference Statements. Lancaster Mennonite Historical Society, Lancaster, PA.

Hershey, Lynford. 1970. "Report to: Home Missions Council." Elkhart, IN: Minority Ministries Council. Fourth cabinet of row on far left wall on entering room, second drawer: unmarked, folder: MINORITY MINISTRY COUNCIL 1970–71. Eastern Mennonite Mission, Records Room, Salunga, PA.

———. 1971. "Dear Leon." Elkhart, IN, July 18. IV-21-4 box 1, MBM Minority Ministries, Council, data Files 1, A–K, folder: Education Program 1970–72, Lynford Hershey. Archives of the Mennonite Church, Goshen, IN.

Hess, Mahlon M. 1969. Editorial. *Missionary Messenger*, August, 24, 23.

Historical Committee. 2006. *A Historical Timeline of Minority and Urban Ministry in the United States, 1910–1997*. Mennonite Church USA, September 12. http://www.mcusa-archives.org/Resources/mimorityministriestimeline.html.

Juhnke, James C. 1989. *Vision, Doctrine, War: Mennonite Identity and Organization in America 1890–1930*. Scottdale, PA: Herald Press.

Kelley, Robin D. G. 2002. *Freedom Dreams: The Black Radical Imagination*. Boston: Beacon Press.

Kniss, Lloyd A. 1969. "Worse or Better?" *Pastoral Messenger*, January, 2.

Lancaster Conference. 1968. "Statement of Christian Doctrine and Rules and Discipline of the Lancaster Conference of the Mennonite Church." Lancaster, PA: Lancaster Conference.

———. 1972. "Of All Nations One People: A Study Guide on Race Relations." Salunga, PA: Lancaster Conference of the Mennonite Church, Peace Committee.

———. 1977. "Bishop Board Minutes." Salunga, PA, May 17. Lancaster Mennonite Historical Society, Lancaster, PA.

———. 1982. "Bishop Board Minutes." Salunga, PA, July 15. Lancaster Mennonite Historical Society, Lancaster, PA.

"Lancaster Conference Peace Committee Responds to Black Manifesto." 1969. *Gospel Herald*, August 12, 702.

Landis, Paul G. 1968. "Tribute Lauds King's Life, Work." *Gospel Herald*, April 23, 374.

———. 1969a. "Bishop Board Meeting." Salunga, PA: Lancaster Conference, December 18. Box: Bishop Board Minutes 1964–1969. Lancaster Mennonite Historical Society, Lancaster, PA.

———. 1969b. "Peace and Industrial Relations Committee." Salunga, PA: Lancaster Conference. Peace Committee Minutes, 1962–1974. Lancaster Mennonite Historical Society, Lancaster, PA.

Landis, Paul G., and Norman Shenk. 1969. "Peace and Industrial Relations Committee." Salunga, PA: Lancaster Conference, July 10. Peace Committee Minutes, 1962–1974. Lancaster Mennonite Historical Society, Lancaster, PA.

Lecky, Robert S., and H. Elliott Wright. 1969. "Reparations Now? An Introduction." In *Black Manifesto: Religion, Racism, and Reparations*, ed. R. S. Lecky and H. E. Wright. New York: Sheed and Ward.

Lincoln, C. Eric. 1999. *Race, Religion, and the Continuing American Dilemma*. New York: Hill and Wang.

Mariscal, George. 2005. *Brown-Eyed Children of the Sun: Lessons from the Chicano Movement, 1965–1975*. Albuquerque: University of New Mexico Press.

Mennonite Board of Congregational Ministries. 1976. "Racism Statement by Anabaptists at 'Liberty and Justice' Workshop." Elkhart, IN. Christian E. Charles Collection, Race Relations. Lancaster Mennonite Historical Society, Lancaster, PA.

Metzler, Edgar. 1963. "The Mennonite Churches and the Current Race Crisis." *Gospel Herald*, August 6, 683–4.

Minority Ministries Council. 1971a. "Minority Ministries Council Annual Assembly." Detroit, MI. Fourth cabinet of row on far left wall on entering room, second drawer: unmarked, folder: MINORITY MINISTRY COUNCIL 1970–71. Eastern Mennonite Mission, Records Room, Salunga, PA.

———. 1971b. "Minority Ministries Council Black Caucus." Detroit, MI. Fourth cabinet of row on far left wall on entering room, second drawer: unmarked, folder: MINORITY MINISTRY COUNCIL 1970–71. Eastern Mennonite Mission, Records Room, Salunga, PA.

———. 1971c. "Minority Ministries Council Latin Concilio." Fourth cabinet of row on far left wall on entering room, second drawer: unmarked, folder: MINORITY MINISTRY COUNCIL 1970–71. Eastern Mennonite Mission, Records Room, Salunga, PA.

———. 1971d. "Minority Statement to Mennonite Church." Elkhart, IN. Fourth cabinet of row on far left wall on entering room, second drawer: unmarked, folder: MINORITY MINISTRY COUNCIL 1970–71. Eastern Mennonite Mission, Records Room, Salunga, PA.

Moore, R. Laurence. 1986. *Religious Outsiders and the Making of Americans.* New York: Oxford University Press.

Murray, Peter C. 2004. *Methodists and the Crucible of Race, 1930–1975.* Columbia: University of Missouri Press.

National Black Economic Development Conference. 1969. "Black Manifesto To the White Christian Church and the Jewish Synagogues in the United States of America and All Other Racist Institutions." Detroit, MI: National Black Economic Development Conference.

Newman, Mark. 2001. *Getting Right with God: Southern Baptists and Desegregation, 1945–1995,* ed. D. E. Harrell Jr., W. Flynt, and E. L. Blumhofer, *Religion and American Culture.* Tuscaloosa: University of Alabama Press.

New York City Peacemaker Workshop. 1968. Bronx, NY: Mennonite Peace and Social Concerns Committee; Mennonite Brethren in Christ Churches in New York City Metropolitan Area; Mennonite General Conference, Scottdale, PA (author's collection).

Owens, Joy. 1969. "Rights Panel Asks Justice, Opportunity for Black Man." *Intelligencer Journal,* June 16, 1.

Patterson, Monica Beatriz deMello. 1998. "America's Racial Unconscious: The Invisibility of Whiteness." In *White Reign: Deploying Whiteness in America,* ed. J. L. Kincheloe, S. R. Steinberg, N. M. Rodriguez and R. E. Chennault. New York: St. Martin's Press.

Poettcker, Henry. 1969. "Dear Brother Kaufman." Newton, KS, June 27. VII.R GC Voluntary Service, series 11 Gulfport VS Unit, box 3, folder 71, Black Manifesto. Mennonite Library and Archives, Bethel, KS.

Powell, John. 1969a. "The Urban Racial Council." *Missionary Messenger,* September, 14–15.

———. 1969b. "Urban-Racial Concerns Statement." Turner, OR: Mennonite General Conference.

———. 1970a. "Hesston College Visit." Hesston, KS: Minority Ministries Council. Hist. Mss. 1–784, box 1, Hubert Schwartzentruber Collection, Miscellaneous, folder: Minority Ministries Council, 1970. Archives of the Mennonite Church, Goshen, IN.

———. 1970b. "Minutes Minority Ministries Council Executive Committee." Elkhart, IN: Minority Ministries Council. Fourth cabinet of row on far left wall on entering room, second drawer: unmarked, folder: MINORITY MINISTRY COUNCIL 1970–71. Eastern Mennonite Mission, Records Room, Salunga, PA.

———. 1970c. "The Compassion Fund Is." *Gospel Herald,* March 24, 271.

———. 1970d. "The Minority Ministries Council: A Call to Action." *Gospel Herald,* March 31, 294.

———. 1971a. "Compassion Fund Report." Elkhart, IN: Minority Ministries Council. Fourth cabinet of row on far left wall on entering room, second drawer: unmarked, folder: MINORITY MINISTRY COUNCIL 1970–71, Eastern Mennonite Mission, Record Room.

———. 1971b. "Dear Doctor Harding." Elkhart, IN, July 9. IV-21-4 box 1, MBM Minority Ministries Council, data files 1, A-K, folder: General Correspondence 1969–72. Archives of the Mennonite Church, Goshen, IN.

———. 1973a. "AFRAM to Bring Blacks Together." *Gospel Herald,* July 31, 592.

———. 1973b. "Among Chaos, A Place to Belong." *Mennonite,* September 25, 543–44.

"Presbyterians Reply to Black Manifesto." 1969. *Intelligencer Journal,* May 22, 1.

"Protesters Arrested in Churches." 1969. *Intelligencer Journal,* June 16, 1.

"Reporting Guide for Mennonite General Conference." 1969. *Hi-Lights of the Mennonite Publishing House*, August 19, 3.

"A Response to Racial Tensions." 1969. *Hi-Lights of the Mennonite Publishing House*, August 19, 1.

Rose, Stephen C. 1969. "Putting It to the Churches." In *Black Manifesto: Religion, Racism, and Reparations*, ed. R. S. Lecky and H. E. Wright. New York: Sheed and Ward.

Ruth, John Landis. 2001. *The Earth Is the Lord's: A Narrative History of the Lancaster Mennonite Conference*. Scottdale, PA: Herald Press.

Schmucker, Leonard E. 1969. "Dear Bro. Powell." Inlay City, MI, September 11. IV-21-4 box 1, MBM, Minority Ministries, Council, data files 1, A–K, older: General Correspondence 1969–72. Archives of the Mennonite Church, Goshen, IN.

Scott, Gil. 1969. "'Black Manifesto Is Direct Attack.'" *Intelligencer Journal*, May 26, 1.

Seventh Avenue Mennonite Church. 1965. "Self-Analysis of Congregation in Response to Questionnaire Titled 'Some Questions to Ask When Describing a Church'." Paul G. Landis New York—Seventh Ave. Lancaster Mennonite Historical Society, Lancaster, PA.

Shank, Aaron M. 1969. "Purpose and Objective of the Mennonite Messianic Mission." *Pastoral Messenger*, April, 7.

Shearer, Tobin Miller. 2008. "'A Pure Fellowship': The Danger and Necessity of Purity in White and African-American Mennonite Racial Exchange, 1935–1971." PhD diss., Northwestern University.

Shenk, Norman. 1969. "Pulpit Echoes." *Pastoral Messenger*, October, 8.

Smith, C. Henry. 1941. *The Story of The Mennonites*. Berne, IN: Mennonite Book Concern.

Smith, John Conventry. 1969. "Chronicle of Events at '475,' May 14–July 5, 1969." New York: United Presbyterian Church in the United States of America, Commission on Ecumenical Mission and Relations.

Sousa, William Noel. 1973. "The White Christian Churches' Responses to the Black Manifesto: A Thesis." Master's thesis, University of the Pacific.

Stauffer, Aaron O. 1969. "Liberalism or Conservatism." *Pastoral Messenger*, January, 1–2.

Stauffer, Leon. 1970. "Special Meeting Lancaster Conference Bishop Board Leaders and Peace Committee with Linford Hershey Director Race Education Program, Minority Ministries Council, Elkhart, Indiana." Salunga, PA: Minority Ministries Council. Clarence E. Lutz Peace Committee (Lanc Conf, MCC, VS-IW). Lancaster Mennonite Historical Society, Lancaster, PA.

———. 1971. "Dear Lyn." Lancaster, PA, July 14. IV-21-4 box 1, MBM Minority Ministries Council, data files 1, A–K, folder: Education Program 1970–72, Lynford Hershey. Archives of the Mennonite Church, Goshen, IN.

Thomas, James, and Leon Stauffer. 1970a. "Peace Committee." Salunga, PA: Lancaster Conference, October 15. Peace Committee Minutes, 1962–1974. Lancaster Mennonite Historical Society, Lancaster, PA.

———. 1970b. Peace Committee. Salunga, PA: Lancaster Conference, July 9. Peace Committee Minutes, 1962–1974. Lancaster Mennonite Historical Society, Lancaster, PA.

"Three Serve Summer Urban Program in Philadelphia." 1982. *Gospel Herald*, September 21, 643.

Toews, Paul. 1996. *Mennonites in American Society, 1930–1970: Modernity and the Persistence of Religious Community*. Scottdale, PA: Herald Press.

"Typewriter Taken as Reparation." 1969. *Intelligencer Journal*, June 5, 1.

"Urban Pastors Meet to Air Views." 1968. *Gospel Herald*, June 18, 552.

Urban Racial Concerns. 2006. Mennonite Historical Society 1969 (cited November 15 2006). http://www.mcusa-archives.org/library/resolutions/BlackManifesto1969.html.

Weisbrot, Robert. 1990. *Freedom Bound: A History of America's Civil Rights Movement.* New York: W. W. Norton.

Wenger, Chester L. 1970. "Dear Pastors." Salunga, PA, August 24. Fourth cabinet of row on far left wall on entering room, second drawer: unmarked, folder: MINORITY MINISTERS' APPOINTMENTS 1970, Eastern Mennonite Mission, Records Room, Salunga, PA.

———. 1971. "Lynford Hershey." Salunga, PA, July 27. Fourth cabinet of row on far left wall on entering room, second drawer: unmarked, folder: MINORITY MINISTRY COUNCIL 1970–71. Eastern Mennonite Mission, Records Room, Salunga, PA.

Williams, Lawrence H. 2005. "Christianity and Reparations: Revisiting James Forman's 'Black Manifesto,' 1969." *Currents in Theology and Mission* 32 (1): 39–46.

Wilmore, Gayraud S. 1998. *Black Religion and Black Radicalism: An Interpretation of the Religious History of African Americans.* Maryknoll, NY: Orbis Books.

"Worth Noting." 1969. *Pastoral Messenger,* January, 7–8.

Zehr, Howard J. 1970. "The Mennonite Church, 1970." In *Mennonite Yearbook and Directory,* ed. E. D. Zook. Scottdale, PA: Mennonite Publishing House.

Zook, Ellrose D., ed. 1970. *Mennonite Yearbook and Directory.* Vol. 61. Scottdale, PA: Mennonite Publishing House.

Religion and Race

South Asians in the Post-9/11 United States

Sangay Mishra

South Asians in the United States are a highly diverse group in terms of religious faith. The group includes Hindus, Muslims, Sikhs, Buddhists, Jains, Parsis, and Christians, among others. For South Asians, religion is an important element in a cluster of identities ranging from nation of origin, language, region, and class to caste (the latter especially in the case of Indian immigrants). A panethnic South Asian identity is not an easily acceptable category as the group negotiates multiple identities in a social and political milieu broadly configured by U.S. multiculturalism.

This essay analyzes the racialization of South Asians in the post–September 11, 2001, United States, looking specifically at the interaction of race and religion. In this respect it finds its place in the literature holding that the racialization of South Asians as "others," "outsiders," "foreigners," and "terrorists" is based on their physical appearance, religious affiliation, cultural background, and immigrant status. I make the specific argument that there is a simultaneous homogenizing as well as a differential racialization of Hindu, Muslim, and Sikh South Asians. South Asians experience homogenization through the blurring of religious, cultural, and nation-of-origin distinctions, but they also experience more particularized racialization as Hindu, Muslim, or Sikh. Moreover, religious distinctions, I believe, played an important role in shaping the responses of South Asian communities to the post-9/11 racial targeting, and these distinctions contributed to undermining any possible panethnic South Asian response. Instead, there was a highly fragmented response that also fell along religious lines. I attempt to describe this fragmented response by analyzing the linkages between U.S. multiculturalism's emphasis on particular identities and the increasing tendencies among some immigrant communities to foreground their religious identities in political mobilizations.

The analysis presented here is based on responses from sixty in-depth interviews conducted with leaders and community members of Indian, Pakistani, and Bangladeshi descent in the Los Angeles and New York metropolitan areas between March 2006 and April 2007. Approximately half the interviewees were community activists and leaders associated with different South Asian organizations and half were regular members of the community. Each interview lasted between forty-five and ninety minutes and asked several questions related to the broader processes of political incorporation of South Asians into U.S. politics. A major part of each interview dealt with racial discriminations faced by South Asians in the United States, with specific reference to the post-9/11 period.

The concept of racialization adduced here draws on the framework of racial formation developed by Michael Omi and Howard Winant, who define racial formation "as the sociohistorical process by which racial categories are created, inhabited, transformed, and destroyed" (Omi and Winant 1994, 55). Omi and Winant argue that racial formation is always a contested process and that the meanings and values ascribed to race are inherently unstable. The specific ideological work of attributing meanings and values—they term it the "racial project"—to a particular racial group is never invented out of thin air but is part of a definite historical context, and builds on previous history. The process not only shapes formal policy and defines large-scale meaning but also informs the application of commonsense meanings as far as race is concerned. Racialization is thus the attribution, by formal institutional as well "commonsense" social processes, of meanings and values to different groups based on body types; it works by defining people as racial groups. The racial formation framework offers a way to analyze how certain incidents, such as those surrounding the events of 9/11, highlight and accentuate some of the attributes assigned to a racial group.

South Asians in the United States

The number of South Asians in the United States has increased rapidly in the past twenty years.[1] There are approximately three million South Asians in the United States, of whom more than 80 percent are from India, followed by Pakistan, Bangladesh, Sri Lanka, Nepal, and other countries ("American Community Survey" 2007). The religious composition of South Asians in the United States is very diverse, with a significant majority of Hindus, followed by Muslims and Sikhs, who constitute a sizable portion.[2] Hindu South Asians in the United States are primarily from India or those who migrated from India to the other parts of the world. The majority of Muslim South Asians are from Pakistan and Bangladesh, with a significant number from India as well. Indeed, Muslims of

South Asian descent constitute a significant portion of the American Muslim population. There are different estimates of ancestry of Muslim Americans, but most suggest that South Asian Muslims are the second largest group, after African American Muslims, in the United States.[3] Given their numerical strength, it is not surprising that South Asian Muslims are prominent in American Muslim organizations (Leonard 2005). The Sikh community in the United States is primarily of Indian descent, and according to one estimate, there are 250,000 Sikhs in the United States.[4]

South Asian identity has emerged in the United States over the last twenty-five years as an important panethnic category as a result of both the shared history and cultures of groups in the South Asian subcontinent and the common experience of racialization in the United States. This category, South Asian, is also historically rooted in the Cold War language of the U.S. State Department, which used the term to identify the Indian subcontinent and adjoining areas. It should also be noted here that identities based on the country of origin (Indian, Pakistani, Bangladeshi, etc.) and subnationality or ethnocultural and linguistic identities (Gujarati, Punjabi, Tamil, etc.) are still dominant in the South Asian community. Hence, the panethnic South Asian category as it is developed and deployed is in constant tension and negotiation with other particular identities based on nation of origin, religion, and language.

The early immigrants from the Indian subcontinent were undifferentiated and homogenized in the eyes of the mainstream American population. Even though many of these immigrants were Sikhs and a few were Muslims, all were called "Hindoos" (Jensen 1988). Physical appearance and religion (even though the religious distinctions were often collapsed) were important parts of the racialization of South Asians in this period. South Asian bodies as well as religions were routinely assigned inferior characteristics. The stigmatization and exclusion through whiteness, of course, was faced not only by non-European immigrants. European immigrants—particularly Irish and other Eastern and Southern European immigrants—were also racialized as undesirable and inferior. Their long and tortuous journey to whiteness speaks clearly of the socially contested and changing meanings of racial categories and the power of whiteness to define and attribute meanings and values to groups in relation to itself (Jacobson 1998; Roediger 2005). However, the process of racialization in the late nineteenth and the early twentieth century worked differently for European and Asian immigrants. Alluding to this distinction, Suchen Chan (1991, 61) argues that

Asian immigrants shared many experiences with European immigrants and with oppressed racial minority groups. . . . Like most European immigrants, they started

> at the bottom of the economic ladder. Unlike their European counterparts, however, their upward climb was impeded not only by a poor knowledge of English language, a lack of familiarity with the American way of doing things, limited education and the absence of relevant job skills, but also by laws that severely limited—on racial grounds—the opportunities they could pursue.

The most significant racialized legal barrier to inclusion of Asians and South Asians in the United States was the early twentieth-century naturalization law, which barred them from citizenship.[5]

The current socioeconomic profile of South Asians in the United States is shaped by the three major waves of immigration that occurred after the passage of the Immigration and Nationality Act of 1965. The first wave came under the special skills provision of the 1965 act, which attracted a large number of doctors, engineers, and scientists from India and, to a lesser degree, Pakistan. These immigrants were highly educated, proficient in English, and primarily from an urban background, and they mostly embarked on professional and managerial careers in the United States. The second wave of South Asian immigration, which took place primarily in the 1980s and after, occurred under the family reunification provision of the 1965 act, aimed at bringing to the United States family relatives of the first wave of immigrants (Mazumdar 1989; Prashad 2000). This group did not have the same level of educational or professional training as the first wave and mostly settled on the lower rungs of the professional ladder.

The third wave, which began in the 1990s, has seen a large influx of software professionals and engineers from India to meet the demands of the information technology boom in the United States. These professionals have occupied different levels of the career ladder, depending on their education, training, and the needs of the market. These three waves have largely defined the current demographic profile of South Asians in the United States.

Even though affluent South Asians tend to define the public image of the community, a steady number of Indian, Pakistani, and Bangladeshi immigrants have been joining the ranks of taxi drivers, restaurant and construction workers, and other sectors of the working-class population in the last several years. Thus, a significant and growing sector of working-class South Asian immigrants, alongside the more affluent sector, is now a part of the South Asian community in the United States.

Despite a long history of immigration, South Asians continue to be viewed as racial "others," "outsiders," "foreigners," "inferior," and "threatening," though the notions as to what these terms might reference have evolved over time. The racial targeting of the community in the wake of September 11 attacks has to be situated and analyzed in the context of a changing perception of the group in the post-1965 period, when a significant influx of professionals into the community began. The community, still seen as the "perpetual foreigner," now also acquired the mantle of "model minority."[6] Thus, in the post-1965 period, South Asians found a place in the U.S. racial order with these two different attributes, and the post-9/11 period accentuated the tensions between the attributes of model minority and those of perpetual foreigner.

Post–September 11: South Asians as Outsiders

September 11, 2001, was a critical moment for South Asian and Arab communities in terms of experiencing racialization. There was indiscriminate targeting of people of Arab and South Asian descent of different religious persuasions—Muslims, Sikhs, Hindus, Buddhists, and Christians—along with other brown-skinned people who looked like "foreigners" or "terrorists." They were targeted because they shared or were perceived as sharing the nationality, religion, appearance, and background of those who were involved in the September 11 attacks. The appearance, dress, skin color, and perceived religious background became important markers in the process of racial targeting.

The incidents of racial targeting started even before the U.S. government released any information about those involved in the 9/11 attacks. Within hours of the attack on the Twin Towers, a Sikh was chased down the streets of New York City by a group. The first death in the post-9/11 racial attacks was that of Balbir Singh Sodhi, a Sikh South Asian, who was shot dead in a parking lot in Mesa, Arizona. Local police officials said that Sodhi's killer was heard claiming in a bar that he would kill the "ragheads" responsible for the September 11 attacks (Singh 2002). On October 4, 2001, a forty-nine-year-old Hindu immigrant from India, Vasudev Patel, was shot dead at his convenience store in Mesquite, Texas. His killer, Mark Stroman, said in a television interview that anger over the September 11 attacks led him to target any store owner who appeared to be Muslim. Waqar Hassan, a forty-six-year-old Pakistani Muslim immigrant, was another victim who was killed on September 15, 2001, at his grocery store near Dallas, Texas (Singh 2002). The dynamics of the racialization of South Asian immigrants on the basis of their appearance, dress, skin color, and religion were unmistakable. South Asians, even though familiar with instances of discrimination in public life, were shocked to see the intensity of the suspicion and hostility turned on them in the immediate aftermath of the September 11 attacks.

A report prepared by South Asian American Leaders for Tomorrow (SAALT; 2001) found there were 645 incidents of bias in the time span of just one week, between September 11 and September 17, 2001. These incidents ranged from racial jokes to serious hate crimes such as arson, physical attacks, and shooting. The report noted, "Perceptions played a major role in determining backlash victims, as evidenced by many cases in which victims included Sikhs, Hispanics, a Greek American and others. South Asians were involved in 81 (13 percent) of the reported incidents. Practicing Sikhs, in particular, with their distinct religious traditions were among those who were singled out."

During my research, the media accounts of blanket targeting, racial profiling, and hate crimes were echoed by leaders and members of Indian, Pakistani, and Bangladeshi communities in the broader Los Angeles and New York metropolitan areas. One of the most common themes that emerged from these interviews was the image of outsider or foreigner being ascribed to South Asians. After the events of 9/11, this image of foreigner or outsider was often conflated with the image of a terrorist.

The trope of foreigner is, of course, an old one in U.S. history. It has been applied to both European and non-European immigrants. European immigrants—particularly Irish, Italian, and Jewish—also faced this stereotype, but they were able to shed their "foreigner" stereotype over time. However, the racialization of Asian immigrants of the nineteenth century as outsiders and inassimilable evolved and persisted as what many scholars term "perpetual foreigner" (Tuan 1998; Kim 1999).

Many South Asian immigrants realized the depth of the perpetual foreigner perception only in the post-9/11 period. A sixty-five-year-old South Asian woman in New York City referred to her family's experiences in the following words:

> I must say that the community felt frightened in the beginning. . . . My son did have an unpleasant experience. I mean unpleasant verbal abuse, let me put it that way. He was at Princeton. . . . He is dark, he looks like a Palestinian actually. Every body thinks he looks like a Palestinian. . . . My son is sort of dark-skinned. He and his wife were coming out of a restaurant . . . and some white kids, who were obviously very drunk, started abusing him and saying, go back to your country, what are you doing here. I think what it did to my son, who came here [to the United States] when he was not even three and who has never seen himself as black. . . . But he said for the first time, I looked at myself and realized that I was not white. They were seeing me as something different.[7]

Appearance and skin color were used to mark him as an outsider. The racialization of South Asians as foreigners or outsiders, irrespective of length of stay, place of birth, and self-identification, is unmistakable here.

A forty-one-year-old Pakistani immigrant based in New York City aptly expressed the deep sense of exclusion that South Asians were confronted with after 9/11 attacks. He noted:

> When I came in [to the United States] I was like, yes! I belong here. I felt like I am in the right spot and right society. This is the society where I should be. But the 9/11 incident has changed it a little bit. For a couple of years (after 9/11) I really thought I should move back to Pakistan, although I am an American citizen. . . . Yeah, there was public anger and bashing, but more by the government agencies, the FBI and INS. I live in Brooklyn, in the middle of the community, and people were being picked up right and left of me. If you go home and you see a couple of blocks where FBI agents are all looking around, basically for those guys who ran out of their (immigration) status . . . they have done no criminal activity whatsoever. All they were guilty of was that their status ran out, which is true for millions and millions of immigrants of different ethnicities. So only one ethnicity was being targeted, which totally made me feel not being welcomed. Not so much by the public but by the government actions. . . . I totally felt like I don't belong here any more.[8]

One of the repercussions of September 11 was thus a particular construction of South Asians that combined the outsider perception with threatening images circulating in the media. South Asians felt compelled to make loud gestures showing their patriotism and commitment to the United States. Talking about the reaction of the South Asian community in the New York metropolitan area immediately after 9/11, a thirty-year-old South Asian woman of Indian descent from Northern New Jersey said:

> One of the things I could see was a lot of South Asians putting the American flag on their cars. A lot of shops and businesses, they hung the American flag. One of the people I know who did it was my brother. He still has a five-foot American flag stuck outside his house. He is the only South Asian in his community, everyone else there is white, and he does experience the unease of being out of place. That was his first move. I think a couple of days after September 11, he went out and got the flag and hung it. I think that was an obvious marker of how South Asians in specific and nonwhite Americans in general might feel the need to articulate their belonging and support.[9]

But even the public display of patriotism was not enough to stop the spate of racial targeting in the period.

Being Muslim and an Immigrant Is a "Double Whammy"

Despite all South Asians being the potential targets of attack in the days following the September 11 attacks, religious differences played an important role in the ways in which different South Asian communities were treated. A fifty-two-year-old Muslim of Indian descent from the New York metropolitan area pointed to the challenges of being a Muslim immigrant in the post-9/11 United States. He said:

> Especially the Muslims are affected very much. I think in the immediate aftermath everybody was painted with a broad brush, whether you were Muslim or not, as long as you were brown. As long as you looked different, you were looked at with suspicion. . . . However, [there was] less tolerance towards Muslim immigrants. So if you are an immigrant and a Muslim, it is a double whammy. You have to work through two hurdles.[10]

As noted earlier, one of the features of racialization is the lumping together of groups, thereby obliterating internal differences. In the immediate aftermath of 9/11, all South Asians and Arabs were lumped together and racialized as threatening, outsiders, and unpatriotic, but as time passed, certain groups, particularly Muslims and Sikhs, felt more targeted and under attack.

In light of the prominent presence of Muslims among South Asian immigrants, the profiling and targeting of Muslims in the United States affected a large number of South Asian immigrants. A New York–based Muslim South Asian from Pakistan explained the specific targeting of Muslims by law enforcement agencies in the post-9/11 period:

> Early on I think it was true for everyone [South Asians], but it looks like the law enforcement agencies have gone through their training and they have been told: this is a Sikh turban and this is a Muslim turban, so be aware. If you get this turban, let them go, but this turban, stop them. So they went through that change of their manual of training and it is now mostly the South Asian Muslim community.[11]

The specific targeting of Muslims of both Arab and South Asian descent sent shock waves through these communities all over the United States. The American Civil Liberties Union (ACLU) documented the harrowing details of indiscriminate arrest, police abuse, lack of legal support, and family separations resulting from a large number of deportations (ACLU 2004a, 2004b). Even the governmental agencies acknowledged the indiscriminate nature of arrest and deportations when the ACLU and other civil rights organizations pressed them to disclose the number of people who were arrested in the aftermath of September 11. The Office of Inspector General's report in 2003 accepted that the arrests were "indiscriminate" and "haphazard," and also that Immigration and Naturalization Services (INS) regularly arrested people who had no connection to criminal activity, let alone terrorism (U.S. Department of Justice 2003).

The government went a step further in targeting Muslim immigrants when it announced the infamous Special Registration drive in August 2002—the National Security Entry-Exit Registration System (NSEERS). As a part of this mandatory drive, the Justice Department required all nonimmigrant aliens entering from certain designated countries (all of them Muslim-majority countries except North Korea) to register with local INS INS offices for interrogation and fingerprinting by a given date. The rule stated that nonimmigrant males sixteen years and older from identified countries would need to report to INS upon arrival; then every thirty days after arrival and upon events such as change of address, employment, or school; and, finally, on departure from the United States.[12] The Special Registration, presented as neutral and benign, unfolded in a way that led to painful consequences and created an environment of unprecedented fear among Muslim communities across the United States. It became a tool for selectively enforcing immigration laws in the Muslim community (Aizenmann and Walsh 2003). When the process of special registration was completed, 13,000 men of the total 83,000 who complied with the special registration were set to be deported. The targeting and profiling of the entire Muslim community were unmistakable in this period. Commenting on the treatment of Muslims in the United States after September 11, Vijay Prashad (2005, 585) writes:

> The government began to play the game of six degrees of separation, picking up anyone who knew one of the hijackers or worshipped at the mosque they attended, or whose name appeared in their address book, or whose name came up in interrogation of anyone picked up for these reasons, or again anyone who had been under the government's dragnet as radical Islamists in one form or the other.

Sikhs were another religious group specifically targeted in the aftermath of the September 11 attacks. Even though Sikhs had encountered negative reactions to their turban long before September 11, the attacks on the Twin Towers changed the meaning of the turban in a more fundamental way. The popular imagination conflated the Sikh turban with the terrorists who had perpetrated the attacks. Turbaned Sikhs became easily accessible proxies for terrorism in the popular mind, and the religious, cultural, and racial differences became easy fodder for racialization of the Sikh community.

The attacks on Sikhs, however, should not be seen merely as a case of mistaken identity. They are a continuation of the long history of racialization of immigrants as strangers and outsiders. In American popular culture, we find numerous racial slurs such as "towelhead," "raghead," "camel jockey," and "sand nigger" directed against Arab, Sikh, and other South Asian immigrants. Thus, it was the long history of racialization of immigrant groups that easily fed into the emotions that led to both homogenizing and differential targeting of Sikhs, Muslims, and other South Asians in the post-9/11 context.

South Asian Mobilization against Racialization: U.S. Multiculturalism and Religion

The long history of racialization of South Asian immigrants in the United States—based on skin color, appearance, language, immigration history, culture, and religion—was sharpened in the post-9/11 period, leading to a sense among South Asians that they fell under the gaze of suspicion. Even though the suspicion was translated into the systematic targeting of Muslims and random attacks on Sikhs, Hindus, and others, all South Asians were made to realize that they still remained outsiders. This blanket racialization of South Asians could have been a potential mobilizing moment based on panethnic solidarity against racism. However, the actual response of South Asians in the post-9/11 period suggested there was little mobilization based on panethnic solidarity against racial targeting. Rather, the political responses of South Asian communities were shaped primarily by religious, national, and class-based distinctions, with religious differences being one of the most important factors.

While responding to the post-9/11 racialization in a fragmented manner may seem a natural response because of religious differences among South Asians, there is another possible reason for this phenomenon. I propose that the lack of panethnic solidarity among South Asians in fighting racialization during this period was directly linked to how U.S. multiculturalism shapes the political orientation and responses of immigrant and minority communities. It is important, therefore, to contextualize the post-9/11 responses of South Asian communities not just in terms of their religious differences but within the broader context of multicultural ideological and institutional practices in the United States as well.

The official political discourse in the United States took a multiculturalist turn in the post–civil rights era. This turn was the product of a series of movements led by religious and racial minorities that included struggles by Catholic and Jewish religious minorities from the early to the mid-twentieth century, and the civil rights movement led by the African Americans in the 1960s. The multiculturalist turn represents a very different approach to racial, religious, and cultural minorities when compared with the assimilationist era, when the Americanizing campaign was the credo of the day and those of different religious, ethnic, and racial persuasion were supposed to be assimilated into the "mainstream culture" (Handlin 1951). Multiculturalism, in contrast, is based on the idea of positive acceptance and equal treatment of religious, cultural, and racial differences (Taylor 1992; Kymlicka 1995).

While initially some scholars welcomed it as tolerating differences, multiculturalism has also been critiqued for becoming an instrument to manage and control differences. These critics point to multiculturalism's emphasis on horizontal (nonhierarchical) differences and its tendency to treat all differences as equivalent, which ends up obscuring the issue of the power of whites over nonwhites (Mohanty 1993; Davis 1996; Kim 2004). In other words, multiculturalism essentializes racial differences and denies they have been constructed also through dominance. Hazel Carby (1992) argues that issues of power, domination, and racial discrimination rooted in racial hierarchy are framed as misunderstandings arising out of cultural differences. Multiculturalism's complete disregard for racial hierarchy and its inability to locate the process of continued and changing racialization in that hierarchy sets the stage for a framework in which racial, cultural, and religious differences are seen as immutable and groups are expected to live up to their discrete religious and cultural differences. This framework also encourages the view that issues of racial discrimination and targeting are to be approached primarily through the lens of discrete, singular identities, which renders it difficult to conceive of and develop a broader antiracial coalition. Thus, the lack of broader antiracial South Asian panethnic mobilization in response to the post-91/11 incidents of racial targeting in favor of preserving a Hindu, Sikh, or Muslim identity could be explained in part by the existence of multicultural ideological framework that essentializes identities and obfuscates hierarchies.

A closer look at specific Hindu, Muslim, and Sikh responses to racialization shows how religious groups have negotiated the multicultural framework that tends to produce a fragmented response to racialization. Religion is one of the most important identity frameworks through which immigrant communities view their social and political experiences (Warner 1998; Kurien 2007). Since the U.S. social and political institutions encourage the use of religious identity as a valid mode of public identity and expression, there is a trend toward the explicit foregrounding of religious identities among immigrant communities, even though religion is only one of the identities that immigrants inhabit. Thus, very often, the cultural recognition of an ethnic group has taken the form of religious recognition. The example of Hindu Indians is a case in point. One of the important instances of recognition of the Hindu immigrant community by U.S. political institutions was the celebration of a Hindu religious festival, Diwali, by President Obama at the White House in 2009, the first by a sitting president of the United States.

Another such act that got wide publicity in the Indian American community was the opening of a U.S. Senate session in 2007 with a Hindu prayer. A priest was invited to perform the Hindu prayer before the Senate opened its proceedings on July 12, 2007. It was a gesture on the part of the U.S. Senate to recognize the importance of Hinduism in the United States. Both these examples point to the increasing importance of religious recognition and acceptance in multicultural practices of the U.S. political institutions. They also suggest both the importance of religious framing within the immigrant communities and the potential of this framing to be used for political interventions.

Analyzing the case of Hindu immigrants from India, Prema Kurien emphasizes the role of multicultural institutions in foregrounding the role of religion. She argues (2007, 3–4),

> The relationship between U.S. Hinduism's institutionalization, politicization, and transnationalism is mediated through multiculturalism. Multiculturalism leads to the institutionalization of ethnicity and to ethnic formation among groups as individuals face pressure (both from the wider society and from within the ethnic community) to organize into groups on the basis of cultural similarity and to have ethnic representatives "speak for the community" and its concerns.

Hinduism thus enters the broader American society through the institutions of multiculturalism. Kurien observes that Hinduism to a certain extent seems also to be acting as a substitute for an ambiguous racial identity for Indian immigrants of Hindu descent. Hindu American organizations, building on the general emphasis on religious identity, have started occupying multicultural spaces as the community's representatives, and these spaces provide opportunities for framing the issues and concerns of the community in primarily religious terms. It is important to point out that besides multiculturalism's encouragement of religious identity and representation through religion, there is also a transnational dimension of this mode of political representation. For instance, the resurgence of mobilization around Hindu identity and the consolidation of political Hinduism in India have contributed immensely to the politics of representation through religious mobilization among Hindus in the United States.[13]

The salience of religious identity among South Asian communities in general clearly shaped the ways in which they responded to the post-9/11 environment. Research interviews and the analysis of organizational responses to the post-9/11 events suggest that the dominant interventions from different sectors of the South Asian community could be broken down primarily on the lines of religious identity, with some slippage between religious and national identity. The Indian immigrant community, being a Hindu-majority community, foregrounded its Hindu identity to distinguish itself from Muslims, and mostly remained silent on the issue of racial targeting in this period. Asked about the possibility of a united campaign against racial targeting of the type that followed September 11, a seasoned New York–based first-generation activist from Indian community said:

> Hindus must be supporting Sikhs on that sort of campaign but I don't see any way that Pakistanis, Indians, and Bangladeshi can meet. The religion is a big divide—it really is. It is not only a feeling, but it is there in practical life also even in India, I think. Hindus don't trust Muslims, whether they [Muslims] would go for India or for Pakistan. This is really a problem, though it should not be, but it is, and that can be reflected here also. Religion is a big factor.[14]

This statement points to possible fault lines occurring along the divides of religion and national origin within South Asian communities in the United States, and also to the transnational dimensions of the divide. The politics of religious conflict pursued by Hindu political formations in India and the ongoing conflicts between India and Pakistan have further led to deep distrust between Hindus and Muslims, which also shaped the ways in which groups responded to the post-9/11 environment in the United States.

Referring to the responses of South Asians amid the atmosphere of fear and intimidation in the days and months following 9/11, Vijay Prashad writes, "rumors flew about that the Indian embassy in Washington asked its nationals to wear bindi, to distinguish 'Indians' from Arabs and Afghans. . . . Talk of the bindi went about as a way for some to suggest it as an adequate sign of being a Hindu, or at least not a Muslim" (Prashad 2005, 585). The sentiments of distinguishing Hindus from Muslims or "Indians" from other nationals were heard in that period. Journalist Sarah Wildman quoted Rajiv Malhotra, president of the Infinity Foundation, on this issue: "a lot of Hindus suddenly have started realizing they better stand up and differentiate themselves from Muslims or Arabs" (Wildman 2001). Hindu organizations, as well as most other Indian community organizations, chose not to speak out on the issue of racial targeting in the post-9/11 period.

The framework of mobilizing on the basis of discrete religious identities rather than mounting a panethnic response in the post-9/11 period was not limited to any one group. This trend could be seen in the case of Muslim and Sikh interventions as well. A major part of the campaign against racial targeting in the post-9/11 period was undertaken by Muslim organizations, consisting of South Asian and non-South Asian Muslims, as well as by Sikh organizations.[15] These groups came out very strongly against racial targeting and hate crimes, but they also mobilized mostly along religious lines rather than on the basis of a panethnic South Asian identity or by building a broader racial coalition. Sikhs mobilized through Sikh organizations, and the post-9/11 period saw the formation of important Sikh civil rights organizations, such as the Sikh American Legal Defense Fund (SALDEF), which came into existence in 2004, and the Sikh Coalition, which was formed in the New York area in the immediate aftermath of September 11. These organizations worked for Sikh Americans through advocacy, legal, and media campaigns and played an important role in highlighting hate crime attacks on Sikhs all across the United States. However, it is important to note that the Sikh response to the post-9/11 racial targeting was primarily focused on attacks on Sikhs who were "mistaken" for Muslims. A mobilization based on Sikh religious and cultural identity could not evolve into a broader panethnic or antiracial coalition, even though the racialization processes lumped all these groups together. Once again, the multicultural institutional and ideological logic can be seen at work here that encourages groups to view and frame racialization in terms of a discrete and singular religious or cultural identity.

Muslims were the hardest hit among South Asians in the post-9/11 period. There were a number of initiatives among Muslim South Asians against racial targeting and hate crimes during that period. Since they were targeted as Muslims in the immediate aftermath of the September 11 attacks, the mobilization along religious lines was understandably the most immediate response. The Council of American-Islamic Relations (CAIR) was one of the most important organizations to campaign against violations of Muslims' civil rights by the law enforcement agencies, and also campaigned to highlight the targeting of Muslims in the post-9/11 period. CAIR spoke on behalf of Muslims of different ethnic and national backgrounds and became one of the most important organizations working to defend the civil rights of Muslims in the United States. The organization came out with a number of reports after 2001 that drew attention to attacks on and instances of discrimination against Muslim Americans. Besides CAIR, a number of nation-of-origin-based organizations also took on the issue of racial and religious targeting of South Asian Muslims. Pakistani American organizations in New York and Los Angeles such as the Coney Island Avenue Project, the Council of Pakistani Professionals, the Council of People's organizations, and the Council of Pakistani American Affairs were actively engaged with the issue of racial discrimination and hate crimes directed against South Asian Muslims. The response of Muslim South Asians, along with other Muslims in the United States, suggested that mobilization on the lines of Muslim religious identity was perhaps the most effective strategy in the aftermath of 9/11. It is important to note that the possibility of a broader panethnic mobilization also existed, since South Asians from different regions, culture, ethnic, and religious background were being homogenized and targeted because of their physical appearance and were collectively being racialized as "outsiders" and "threatening." However, different groups chose to foreground their particular religious identities while responding to the post-9/11 environment. The pattern of responses emerging from descrete Hindu, Muslim, and Sikh organizations suggests that the multicultural ideological and institutional framing contributes to the promotion of existing religious, ethnic, and cultural identities, leading to a mode of political response that eschews panethnic solidarity.

The religion-based mobilization of most mainstream South Asian groups was particularly surprising when contrasted to the existence of a parallel trend of organizing, albeit small, based on broader panethnic South Asian solidarity. A number of organizations both in Los Angeles and in New York did organize on the basis of panethnic South Asian identity in the post-9/11 period, although they had limited influence in South Asian communities. The South Asian Network (SAN) in the Los Angeles area worked with a few Muslim and Sikh organizations, and together they played an important role in responding to post-9/11 hate crimes and in countering the atmosphere of fear among South Asian immigrants in the area. Similarly, South Asian organizations such as Desis Rising and Moving, the Coney Island Avenue Project, the New York Taxi Workers Alliance, the Council of People's Organization, the South Asian Youth Association, and many small advocacy and service organizations in New York City actively mobilized against racial targeting, special registration, and deportations. Similarly, organizations such as SAALT actively intervened on this issue in Washington, D.C., and coordinated with other civil rights and ethnic organizations at the national level to develop a broader antiracial coalition to work against racial targeting of

South Asians and Arabs. However, they remained smaller and marginal attempts at mobilizing South Asians against post-9/11 racial targeting.

The foregrounding of religious identity by different South Asian groups in the post-9/11 period was consistent with a multicultural institutional and ideological paradigm that encourages discrete, singular, and immutable identities. The literature on race and minority politics has often presented religion as a unifying force promoting the cause of social justice and racial equality (Harris 1994; Wood 1999). However, analysis of the racial targeting of South Asians and their responses in the post-9/11 period suggests that religious identity can also work against a broader panethnic and antiracial mobilization. The analysis points to the role of multicultural institutional and ideological practices in facilitating the politics of exclusive religious identity at the cost of a broader panethnic mobilization against racism.

Notes

1. The term "South Asian" in the United States is traditionally understood to refer to seven countries, namely, Bangladesh, Bhutan, India, Maldives, Nepal, Pakistan, and Sri Lanka.

2. There are varied estimates of the number of Hindus in the United States. According to Harvard's Pluralism Project, there are 1.3 million Hindus in the United States. This figure is based on the 2004 *World Almanac*. The American Religious Identification Survey in 2008 estimated the number closer to 1.2 million. See the website for the Harvard Pluralism Project, http://pluralism. org/resources/statistics/tradition.php#Hinduism, and that for the American Religious Identification Survey, www.americanreligionsurvey-aris.org.

3. According to one estimate, African Americans account for 42 percent of the American Muslim population, followed by South Asians (24.4 percent), Arabs (12.4 percent), Africans (6.2 percent), and Iranians (3.6 percent). This estimate is based on "The Muslim Population in the United States: A Brief Statement," by Fareed H. Nu'man (1992). Another, 1999 estimate by Ilyas BaYunus and Moin Siddique (cited in Leonard 2005) gives different groupings and percentages: African American (30 percent), Arab (33 percent), and South Asian (29 percent). These numbers suggest that South Asian Muslims constitute a large part of the immigrant Muslim population in the United States (all figures from Leonard 2005).

4. See the website http://pluralism.org/resources/statistics/tradition.php#Sikhism.

5. The racial naturalization laws were applied to all nonwhite immigrants, and the issue ultimately reached the Supreme Court in 1923 in *Bhagat Singh Thind v. U.S.* The Court ruled that immigrants from India are not eligible for citizenship because they are not white. Ian Haney López (1996) has discussed the racial prerequisite naturalization cases carefully and linked them to the construction of "whiteness" in legal and social discourse.

6. The discourse of model minority came in the context of placing certain Asian American groups vis-à-vis African Americans. The discourse claims that Asian Americans are culturally inclined to strive hard and achieve better economic and social standing compared to blacks. Hence, certain minorities are models to be followed, whereas others are culturally dysfunctional. This dis-

course tries to take racism off the table by doing an ahistorical analysis and pitting one minority's performance against another's. The educational and economic profile of a section of South Asian immigrants in the post-1965 period was ideally suited for the model minority discourse.

7. Interview, New York City, February 10, 2007.

8. Interview, New York City, March 7, 2007.

9. Interview, Madison, NJ, November 11, 2006.

10. The expression was used by one of the interviewees to describe the status of Muslims in the post-9/11 United States. Interview, New York City, February 7, 2007.

11. Interview, New York City, March 3, 2007.

12. All twenty-five countries included in the special registration were predominantly Muslim countries from Africa, the Middle East, South Asia, and Southeast Asia, with the exception of North Korea. This program was scrapped subsequently.

13. The emergence of Rashtriya Swayamsewak Sangh (RSS), Vishwa Hindu Parishad (VHP), and the Bhartiya Janata Party (BJP) in Indian politics since the 1980s has brought political Hinduism to the front and center of Indian politics. The anti-Muslim and anti-Christian campaigns of these groups have defined their political project of striving for a Hindu state. The ascendance of this political trend in India has contributed to a particular kind of political mobilization based on religious identity among Hindus of Indian descent in the United States (Mishra 2009).

14. Interview, Long Island, NY, November 13, 2006.

15. The Council on American-Islamic Relations (CAIR) is one of the leading civil rights organizations active among American Muslims on issues of racial profiling and hate crimes against Muslims. The Sikh Coalition and SALDEF are some of the leading Sikh civil rights organizations.

References

Aizenmann, Nurith, and Edward Walsh. 2003. "Immigrants Fear Deportation after Registration." *Washington Post,* July 28.

American Civil Liberties Union. 2004a. *America's Disappeared.* New York: American Civil Liberties Union.

———. 2004b. *How Deporting Immigrants after 9/11 Tore Families Apart and Shattered Communities* New York: American Civil Liberties Union.

"American Community Survey, 2007." 2007. http://www.census.gov/prod/2007pubs/acs-05.pdf.

Carby, Hazel. 1992. "The Multicultural Wars." *Radical History Review* 54:7–18.

Chan, Sucheng. 1991. *Asian Americans: An Interpretive History.* Boston: Twayne.

Davis, Angela. 1996. "Gender, Class, and Multiculturalism: Rethinking 'Race' Politics." In *Mapping Multiculturalism,* ed. Avery Gordon and Christopher New Field. Minneapolis: University of Minnesota Press.

Handlin, Oscar. 1951. *The Uprooted: The Epic Story of Great Migration That Made the American People.* Boston: Little, Brown.

Haney López, Ian F. 1996. *White by Law: The Legal Construction of Race.* New York: New York University Press.

Harris, Fredrick C. 1994. "Something Within: Religion as a Mobilizer of African-American Political Activism." *Journal of Politics* 56 (1): 42–68.

Jacobson, Matthew Frye. 1998. *Whiteness of a Different Color: European Immigrants and Alchemy of Race.* Cambridge, MA: Harvard University Press.

Jensen, Joan M. 1988. *Passage from India: Asian Immigrants in North America*. New Haven, CT: Yale University Press.

Kim, Claire J. 1999. "The Racial Triangulation of Asian Americans." *Politics and Society* 27 (1): 105–38.

———. 2004. "Imagining Race and Nation in Multicultural America." *Ethnic and Racial Studies* 27 (6): 987–1005.

Kurien, Prema. 2007. *A Place at the Multicultural Table: The Development of American Hinduism*. New Brunswick, NJ: Rutgers University Press.

Kymlicka, Will. 1995. *Multicultural Citizenship*. Oxford: Oxford University Press.

Leonard, Karen. 2005. "American Muslims and Authority: Competing Discourses in a Non-Muslim State." *Journal of American Ethnic History* 25 (1): 5–30.

Mazumdar, Sucheta. 1989. "Race and Racism: South Asians in the United States." In *Frontiers of Asian American Studies*, ed. Gail M. Nomura, Russel C. Leong, Stephen H. Sumida, and Russel Endo. Seattle: Washington State University Press.

Mishra, Sangay. 2009. Political Incorporation and Transnationalism:South Asian Immigrants in the United States. PhD diss., University of Southern California.

Mohanty, Chandra Talpade. 1993. "On Race and Voice: Challenges for Liberal Education in the 1990s." In *Beyond a Dream Defferred: Multicultural Education and the Politics of Excellence*, ed. Becky Thompson and Sangeeta Tyagi, 41–65. Minneapolis: University of Minnesota Press.

Nu'man. Fareed H. 1992. "The Muslim Population in the United States: A Brief Statement." American Muslim Council, December. www.uga.edu/islam/muslimpop_usa.html.

Omi, Michael, and Howard Winant. 1994. *Racial Formation in the United States: From the 1960s to the 1990s*. New York: Routledge.

Prashad, Vijay. 2000. *Karma of Brown Folk*. Minneapolis: University of Minnesota Press.

———. 2005. "How Hindus Became Jews: American Racism after 9/11." *South Asian Quarterly* 104 (3): 583–606.

Roediger, David. 2005. *Working towards Whiteness: How America's Immigrants Become White*. New York: Basic Books.

Singh, Amardeep (for Human Rights Watch). 2002. *We Are Not the Enemy: Hate Crimes against Arabs, Muslims, and Those Perceived to Be Arab or Muslim after September 11*. New York: Human Rights Watch Publications.

South Asian American Leaders for Tomorrow (SAALT). 2001. *American Backlash: Terrorists Bring War Home in More Ways Than One*. Washington, DC: South Asian American Leaders for Tomorrow.

Taylor, Charles. 1992. "The Politics of Recognition." In *Multiculturalism and Politics of Recognition*, ed. Amy Gutmann, 25–74. Princeton, NJ: Princeton University Press.

Tuan, Mia. 1998. *Forever Foreigners or Honorary Whites? The Asian Ethnic Experience Today*. New Brunswick, NJ: Rutgers University Press.

U.S. Department of Justice, Office of the Inspector General. 2003. *The September 11th Detainees: A Review of the Treatment of Aliens Held on immigration Charges in Connection with September 11th Attacks*. Washington, DC: U.S. Government Printing Office.

Warner, Stephen. 1998. "Immigration and Religious Communities in the United States." In *Gatherings in Diaspora: Religious Communities and the New Immigration*, ed. S. Warner and J. Wittner, 3–34. Philadelphia, PA: Temple University Press.

Wildman, Sarah. 2001. "All for One." *New Republic*, December 24.

Wood, Richard L. 1999. "Religious Culture and Political Action." *Sociological Theory* 17 (3): 307–32.

Ambivalent Miracles

The Possibilities and Limits of Evangelical
Racial Reconciliation Politics

Nancy D. Wadsworth

One of the great wonders of religion is its profound pliability. Not only can different collectivities wield the same religion for opposite purposes but a group that once drew on a faith-based meaning system to found a particular mission can also, in a changed historical context, adjust that system to fuel a reformed set of objectives.

Such is the case with racial change advocates inside conservative evangelical Protestant communities in the United States.[1] These believers draw on religious resources to break from a racially fractured past and build a more integrated and "reconciled" American evangelicalism.[2] Among their objectives are "racial reconciliation" and the proliferation of intentionally multiethnic churches. Casting a vision of racially integrated Christian communities, participants struggle with how to bring together cultural groups—black, white, Latino, Asian, and others— that have long been sociologically and to some degree theologically divided on matters of race (Emerson and Smith 2000). In that effort, they carry with them the unique cultural resources and faith-based framings they have inherited from their religious and racial subcultures.[3] But as they engage across racial lines, they also develop new collective resources, new methods and concepts that facilitate but also delimit their movement for racial change. On the whole, evangelical racial change advocates passionately pursue social change on race matters, but often resist using the political realm to do so. That complex dynamic presents an interesting puzzle for scholars of race, religion, and politics.

The few secular researchers who have tracked new evangelical racial change efforts so far have tended to discount the social and political value of such efforts, evaluating the likes of faith-based "racial reconciliation" as manifestations of neoconservatism and white racial retrenchment (Diamond 2000; Stricker 2001; Newton 2005).[4] Such judgments, I believe, are not simply a product of political bias against conservative evangelicals (though they are often that). They also result from a secular orientation largely blind to the cultural contexts that so profoundly inform how ordinary people apply religious resources to navigate larger societal issues. Political scientists are especially predisposed to secular bias when studying measurably political acts (e.g., voting, donating political funds, running for office). Because we give less attention to cultural phenomena until they appear on a political stage, the discipline has frequently been surprised when religious movements like the Christian Right "suddenly" explode into the political limelight.

Scholars of race in American political life need more than an analytical orientation that critiques religion-based phenomena such as evangelical racial change efforts through a secular lens. Frameworks for interpreting racial politics would do better to illuminate the complex ways in which the particular cultural characteristics of evangelical communities—or of any religious or other subcultures—inform such efforts, and with what results.

Given that conservative evangelical Christians (whites, at least) have been one of the *last* groups in American political life to attempt to substantively address what Gunnar Myrdal in 1944 called "an American dilemma" of racial inequality, an obvious question for scholars is what these recent racial change efforts might signal politically and sociologically in the larger culture. Are they just another manifestation of what Howard Winant (1997, 2004a) calls a "neoconservative race project" that individualizes racial inequality and remains apathetic toward the nation's abiding systemic racial injustices? Do evangelical racial change initiatives represent recycled incarnations of classic evangelical purification rituals that fantasize liberating a (white evangelical) community from its particular sins while leaving larger power configurations essentially untouched?[5] Advocates of progressive racial policies might ask whether the boundaries of evangelical racial change efforts reflect a rejection of the great American social tradition of fighting political injustice in an era when material racial inequalities have only grown wider in the United States. In short, do racial change initiatives among evangelical conservatives do more political harm than good?

To begin to answer such inquiries, evangelical racial change efforts should be understood not as a variation of some secular racial project but as a distinct kind of racial project, what I call *religious race bridging*.[6] A racial project is a conceptual framework that influences people's reactions to or promotion of race-related policy, or a set of ideas that frames the way people think about race and judge proposals for addressing race issues. Religious race bridging is a means of employing faith-based resources to bring members of different racial groups together for the purpose of cross-racial engagement designed to inspire individual and corporate change within the spiritual body.[7] This racial project reveals distinctive collective navigations at the intersections of race and religion in American political life worth understanding. The evangelical racial change movement reveals how not only secular discourses about race and power but also specific elements of the religious setting, such as theology, identity, and spiritual discourse, inform and complicate different communities' responses to U.S. racial problems. The political claims—and critiques—expressed by this racial project emerge organically from the cultural context and thus have culturally specific implications. I submit that for now, in the context of an American political culture that finds few ways of substantively engaging the difficult topic of race, the collective forums created by this racial project do more good than harm.

Depoliticized Racial Change?

I focus here on the two primary types of racial bridging initiatives exhibited in theologically conservative evangelical communities: the "racial reconciliation" efforts of the 1990s and the more recent multiethnic church movement.[8] The term "racial reconciliation" in particularized usage refers to a discourse (a set of beliefs, narratives, and practices) that articulates a theology of racial "sins" and offers individual and collective methods for overcoming them in order to create a more racially reconciled Christian community. Such a discourse emerged in the late 1960s, peaked in the mid-1990s, and still circulates in many evangelical circles. The multiethnic church movement, which has been gaining ground in the 2000s, is informed by and extends the racial reconciliation discourse. It aims to build evangelical churches with intentionally multiethnic congregations in which multiracialism is seen as evidence of a Christian community fulfilling its divine mission.

Both initiatives were originally informed by explicitly political, faith-based critiques of racial inequality in Christian communities by evangelicals of color. Both seek to transform race relations in evangelical communities in substantial, not superficial, ways. And both have indeed influenced some identifiable shifts in American evangelicalism. Yet each has been marked, from the mid-1990s forward, by a politically circumscribed and at times explicitly apolitical character. Evangelical racial change advocates—whites as well as people of color—consistently express nervousness and resistance to seeing their movement assume politicized dimensions or pursue political goals. While they see their efforts as producing real "miracles" in the immediate worlds of their lives and their spiritual communities, most participants remain ambivalent about contributing to or constructing an earthly politics of evangelical racial change.[9]

That religious race bridging by conservative evangelicals defies easy categorization according to Winant's (2004a, 2004b) influential "racial projects" framework makes it amenable to a number of potential political manifestations. Religious race bridging is undeniably influenced by conservative and individualist approaches to race that constrain its potential trajectory. But it also draws from competing, more radical and critical influences. Religious race bridging offers an indispensable path to meaningful cross-racial engagement that resonates for evangelical Christians and without which most cannot imagine applying their hopes for racial change to any kind of cohesive near- or long-term, direct or indirect political objectives. In other words, if evangelical racial change efforts are ever to link up with matters of political justice, of more concrete matters of racial equity, substantive cross-racial forums like these have to be created, and must in themselves reflect social change.

Additionally, evangelical racial change efforts reflect a phenomenon that has not been identified by scholars: a critique by people of color of politicized or overly programmed racial change initiatives in the post–civil rights movement era that, they feel, fail to address deeper spiritual and interpersonal obstacles that hamper "real" communion among people across race boundaries. These participants worry that politics, or any secularization of their model, might corrupt important spiritually based processes for achieving "true" or "deep" racial change. Through such perspectives, religious race bridging articulates an alternative, not simply a conservative, race project in American political life. Despite the limitations for which we outsiders might justifiably critique it, it is an alternative to mainstream secular race projects worth understanding in a multidimensional way.

In this essay, I first set evangelical racial change efforts within the larger context of evangelical race relations. I then consider some of the scholarly frames available for interpreting these efforts and assert the analytical value of a religious race-bridging model. Finally, I draw on perspectives from participants I've interviewed to identify the key expressed motivations behind the distinctive racial project of religious race bridging and to analyze the rationale many participants use to circumscribe the political limits of their activities.

Evangelicals' Racial Epiphany

The detailed history of evangelical race relations has been chronicled elsewhere (Emerson and Smith 2000, chaps. 2–3; Gilbreath 2006, chaps. 4, 7). To contextualize the racial change initiatives discussed here, though, we must grasp a few key elements of this history.

Before the twentieth-century civil rights movement, the story of race in

American evangelicalism is a story of inequality, turmoil, and prolonged seg-regation, albeit interrupted with moments of what Harvey (2005) calls racial interchange—intercrossings and sharing of cultural practices such as worship and revivals, which could only temporarily (if at all) override the race-based structural divisions that characterized Christian churches. In the country's first century, most African Americans and indigenous people were either forcibly converted under slavery, or relegated to third-class status inside white churches, or prevented from autonomously practicing their own religions, Christian or otherwise.[10] The Civil War and its aftermath divided evangelicals into separate denominations according to racial makeup or positions on slavery. The Southern Baptist Convention, for instance, was born through its defense of slavery, while the National Baptist Coalition, the African Methodist Episcopalian church, the Church of God in Christ, and other denominations were created by blacks ex-ercising their hard-won freedom. With few exceptions (the early Pentecostal movement being one), this de facto racial segregation of American Christianity did not change and was rarely challenged at the institutional (denominational) level until the civil rights movement. The extent of racial separation in U.S. evan-gelicalism is reflected by the fact that today, more than 90 percent of churches are still populated almost exclusively by members of one racial group (DeYoung et al. 2003).

If there was an early catalytic moment for what later became racial reconcili-ation and the multiethnic church movement, it was delivered by a charismatic young black preacher named Tom Skinner.[11] A converted ex-gang leader, through-out the 1960s Skinner led his Harlem Evangelistic Association to a distinctively black evangelical mission inspired by civil rights and black power, a mission he delineated in several books.[12] In 1970 he delivered the keynote address at a large annual youth gathering called Urbana 70. In a thundering oration, "The U.S. Racial Crisis and World Evangelism," Skinner critiqued the American Christian community's failure to address the "sad state of race relations" in and beyond the church (67). Articulating a radically Christian praxis, he lambasted misguided orientations within white evangelicalism that justified status quo domestic and foreign policies, ignored the plight of the inner city, or perpetuated prejudice. He also critiqued the separatism of Black Power, which he saw as theologically empty. "You will never be a radical," he urged the assembled, "until you become a part of [Christ's] new order, and then go into a world that is enslaved; a world that is filled with hunger and poverty and racism and all those things that are the work of the devil. Proclaim liberation to the captives . . . go into the world and tell men who are bound mentally, spiritually, and physically, 'The Liberator has come!'" (68).

Skinner's liberation theology challenged both white evangelicals and established black clergy to employ their religious resources to challenge racial inequality. Although his larger body of engaged theological race critique was too radical for some, over the next decades it inspired a generation of leaders, many of color and a few whites, to build urban, race- and poverty-related ministries and to challenge racial divisions among evangelicals.[13] Leaders like John Perkins, the African American prophet of Christian community development, and Jamaican American reconciliation preacher Samuel Hines became champions of racial reconciliation in the evangelical world (Emerson and Smith 2000, 54–55).[14]

The heart of early racial reconciliation theology (developed and extended by subsequent advocates) was the belief that racial division, hostility, and inequality are sins in the eyes of God. Therefore, God directs a divine imperative for Christians to recognize these sins and become reconciled to each other across racial and ethnic lines (following the Christian model of substitutionary atonement, whereby humanity is reconciled to God through his sacrifice).[15] The framework asserts that Christians must acknowledge their personal and collective racial sins, commit to changing through a spiritually grounded, relationship-based process, and work to end racial divisions, resentments, and inequalities.

According to Yancey (2003), the early black advocates of racial reconciliation articulated a four-step model:

- *Developing primary cross-racial relationships,* such as close friendships and support groups. Some evangelical racial change advocates maintain that "this [interpersonal, relational] aspect of King's vision was largely abandoned [after the civil rights movement] in pursuit of political rights and economic opportunities" (Emerson and Smith 2000, 54).

- *Recognizing and remedying social structures of inequality,* such as unequal access to quality housing and education. Early reconciliation leaders identified indifference and inaction in the face of injustice as sins equal to racism, robbing all parties of unity.

- *Acknowledgment and repentance, by whites,* of their personal, historical, and social "sins" as the main benefactors of an unequal, racialized society.

- *Forgiveness, by African Americans* (later, all Christians of color), of whites individually and corporately when they ask, and repentance and release of lingering anger and resentment.

As the racial reconciliation movement emerged in the 1970s and 1980s, these messages had some influence on white evangelicals such as Billy Graham and Jerry Falwell, who came to reconsider their segregationist practices or previous silence on racial justice issues (Snowball 1991; Gilbreath 1998). They also generated discussions about race and racism within evangelical forums such as Graham's popular *Christianity Today* (*CT*) magazine (Emerson and Smith 2000, chap. 3). For the most part, though, racial reconciliation and multiethnic church ministry initiatives didn't seem to penetrate the mainstream of white evangelical discourse until the 1990s.

In a decade steeped in race-related scandals and crises, including the O. J. Simpson trial, Louis Farrakhan's Million Man March, the establishment of the Advisory Board to the President's (Clinton's) Initiative on Race, and the Abner Louima–New York police brutality scandal, racial reconciliation articles in *CT* began to proliferate. After about 1992, an emergent racial reconciliation literature reproduced what seemed to be a growing interest within evangelical communities in self-critically grappling with racial issues.

Broadly, three themes marked the proliferation of race-related topics in evangelical literature. First was the phenomenon of white Christians identifying and publicly apologizing for racism, either as individuals or, more typically, as representatives of their religious organization. The highest-profile moments in the evangelical racial reconciliation discourse of the 1990s were public apologies by leaders of denominational organizations (sometimes accompanied by rituals such as ceremonial foot washing). Five prominent meetings related to racial issues occurred in evangelical denominational organizations between 1994 and 1998 (Lee 1994; Morgan 1995a; Tapía 1997). A now famous example was the Southern Baptist Convention's 1995 issuance of a formal apology for slavery and racism. The apology included this astonishing statement: "We apologize to all African Americans for condoning and/or perpetuating individual and systemic racism in our lifetime, and we genuinely repent of racism of which we have been guilty, whether consciously or unconsciously" (Maxwell 1995, 28). Internal critiques of white evangelical racism continued to emerge in books by pastors and in the evangelical press through the end of the decade (Findlay 1997; Davies, Hennessee, and Teresa 1998). This literature continues to expand, although tempered by the acknowledgment that racial transformation is a slow and sometimes disappointing process.[16]

A second theme in the rise of racial reconciliation discourse was the importance of identifying and understanding the quotidian racial divisions that separate Christians. This topic was addressed by a wave of reconciliation articles and "partnership" books published in the Christian press, often co-authored by pastors. Through accounts of the authors' personal journeys toward reconciliation, partnership models offered guidance for cross-racial relationship building. Such personal experience testified to the power of and challenges to committed cross-racial relationships. For instance, *He's My Brother: Former Racial Foes Offer Strategy for Reconciliation*, co-written by a prominent southern urban Baptist preacher and a former Ku Klux Klan member, presented scriptural justifications and a point-by-point plan for doing racial reconciliation. Others chronicled the experience of engaging in multiethnic efforts to rebuild and revitalize urban churches (Perkins 1995; Washington, Kehrein, and King 1997). Evangelical magazines provided a steady backdrop of coverage of race-related issues.[17]

Also within this theme, evangelical magazines ran some fairly critical articles and editorials about white Christian racism (Stanton 1994a; Myra 1995). A pivotal intervention was a 1993 article by Andrés Tapía in *CT*, "The Myth of Racial Progress," in which forty-one African American leaders critiqued racial attitudes in the evangelical community, directly challenging white evangelicals to face the music. Following that, *CT* pursued a beat on race-related events in different denominations, tracking issues such as Christian interracial marriage, inner-city challenges, and local church reconciliation efforts and publishing profiles of evangelical leaders of color.

Some of these topics arose in evangelical literature in the context of a third theme: the growing Promise Keepers men's movement, which, early on, placed a core emphasis on racial reconciliation (Stanton 1994b). As one of the largest, most successful, and most visible evangelical movements ever, Promise Keepers was an influential vanguard racial reconciliation organization. Former University of Colorado coach Bill McCartney pursued a vision (from God, he attested) of building a multiracial men's movement. Committed to building a racially diverse organization from leadership on down, Promise Keepers set an example by hiring people of color in key leadership positions, including a multiracial board of directors (McCartney 1997). By the late 1990s, racial reconciliation was a major focus at Promise Keepers' stadium events. Eventually the organization took the radical step of eliminating entrance fees to its rallies in order to attract a more diverse audience (Green 1997). Nine Promise Keepers staff members I interviewed at the movement's height expressed pride in being part of that, and more than one had held prestigious positions on other race-related councils, such as President Clinton's advisory board on race.

In sum, racial reconciliation efforts proliferated at several levels in the 1990s: at the grassroots level of local congregations, in Christian denominational institutions, and in organizations like Promise Keepers. But when white evangelicals became involved in reconciliation discourses, the political element espoused by the early generation of evangelical race activists (step 2 of the four-step model) largely disappeared. A full analysis of why this happened is beyond the scope of this essay, but I concur with Emerson and Smith that white evangelicals lacked the ideological repertoire through which they could effectively recognize and respond politically to the structural and systemic factors influencing racial inequality in the United States.

For a time under the leadership of Ralph Reed, the political and conservative Christian Coalition also took up the language of racial diversity and reconciliation, but it tended to embrace the neoconservative approach of addressing racial inequality through civic faith-based organizations rather than through systemic reforms. In 1996, Reed announced the Christian Coalition's "Racial Reconciliation Sunday" campaign to raise $1.5 million to help repair black southern churches besieged by arson (Sack 1996). A short-lived effort called the Samaritan Project also sought to attract black and Latino Christians of color to the Christian Coalition's mission by addressing issues of inner-city problems, education, family values, and poverty (Seelye 1997). Despite Reed's interest in white evangelicals' acknowledging their racist past and in attracting a more diverse constituency, these efforts apparently were not embraced by the Christian Coalition's leadership, and disappeared after Reed left the organization in 1997 (see Jacobson, this volume.)

As the evangelical racial reconciliation discourse developed in the 1990s, with white evangelicals increasingly invested and more voices of color engaged in the discussions, racial reconcilers added new elements to the four steps delineated by the movement's early pioneers. After identifying these, I'll discuss evangelical racial change efforts as a religious race-bridging project.

Bridge building. After the steps of repentance and forgiveness of racial sins, participants were encouraged to reach beyond their racially homogeneous church communities and get to know members of other groups. This took the form of committed cross-racial relationships, church partnerships, collaborative volunteer work, and organizational collaboration.

Promoting diversity. Racial reconcilers encouraged creating racially diverse, rather than institutionally segregated, congregations, parachurch organizations, and denominational structures. A major manifestation of this principle was the expansion of the multiethnic church movement. Organizational bodies such as Promise Keepers also sought to produce more racially representative organizations through culturally sensitive recruiting practices, leadership structures, and marketing.

Avoiding politics. As evangelical racial change efforts became more widespread and scrutinized by the secular media, advocates stressed relationship building and distanced their movement(s) from politics. Without necessarily prohibiting political responses, they consistently interpreted them as spiritually fraught and therefore less likely to create long-term change than spiritually based interpersonal and intercommunity efforts.

Religious Race Bridging as a Racial Project

As Antony Alumkal discusses in this volume, sociologist Howard Winant's "white racial projects" schema has influenced scholars' understanding of race and privilege in the post–civil rights era in the United States.[18] Evangelical racial reconciliation and the multiethnic church movement are not exclusively white racial projects, since they were developed by and include people of color. But religious race bridging by evangelicals *is* a race project, and understanding it enables observers to better comprehend the complex distinctiveness of these faith-based racial change efforts as an alternative to mainstream secular race discourses.

The following list summarizes the key categorical elements of Winant's (2004a) white racial projects framework. In the remainder of this essay I use statements from the racial reconciliation and multiracial church movements to delineate how these efforts, as a religious race-bridging project, relate to and depart from Winant's categories, and why it matters.

Far Right
- Sees "unalterable" racialized difference between white and nonwhites (Winant 2004a, 6)
- Rejects the possibility of integration, reconciliation
- Explicitly racist
- *Examples:* Ku Klux Klan, Christian Identity

New Right
- White backlash via covert and coded racism
- Capitalizes on political mobilization of white fears
- Codes policies that benefit racial minorities as "unfair"
- Admits token minorities, but refuses to challenge white privilege
- *Examples:* George Wallace's campaign, Southern Strategy, Reagan Democrats

Neoconservative
- Seeks to preserve white advantages through denial of racial difference (Winant 2004a, 7)

- Appeals to supposedly race-blind universalist, individualist norms to defend free-market social policies
- Refuses to engage in "race thinking," ignoring ongoing discrimination and institutionalized racial inequality
- Seeks change through the private arena
- *Examples:* Anti-affirmative action policies; critiques of "mul-ticulturalism"; faith-based initiatives as an alternative to government intervention

Neoliberal
- Seeks to reduce white advantage by constructing a "transracial political agenda"
- Combines white and minority interests into strategic coalition politics
- Deemphasizes ongoing racial hostility and inequality in search of common interests
- *Examples:* William Julius Wilson, Barack Obama

New abolitionist
- Critiques and seeks to disrupt the partnership between U.S. capitalism and the invention of whiteness
- Sees race and racism as central to U.S. political culture and history
- Acts from a "race traitor" positionality
- *Examples:* Noel Ignatiev, David Roediger

Winant's white racial projects schema categorizes people, groups, and policy perspectives along a spectrum of racial frames circulating in contemporary U.S. political culture. At the racist extreme are explicitly hostile, segregationist populists—racist "old-schoolers," so to speak—from the Ku Klux Klan to the racist Christian Identity movement (Barkun 1994). At the progressive end are radical "race traitors" who name, deconstruct, and reject white privilege to develop a principled antiracist politics (Ignatiev and Garvey 1996). In between are proponents of New Right, neoconservative, and neoliberal race projects, all of which, in Winant's critique, fail, though in different ways, to fully acknowledge the abiding "racial dualism" and "deep-seated structural racial conflicts endemic to U.S. society" (Winant 2004a, 8–9). New Right racial projects channel white backlash through covert and coded racism pioneered by the likes of George Wallace and extended in the so-called Reagan revolution. Neoconservatives deny racial difference and refuse to engage in "race thinking" by appealing to universalist, individualist, and private-sphere frames that discount structural racial inequities. Neoliberals acknowledge racial inequities but try to build political coalitions through "transracial" political agendas that assume commonality, at the expense of fully recognizing ongoing racial hostilities.

Mary Stricker (e.g., 2001), a student of Winant's, found that white Promise Keepers engaged in racial reconciliation processes had more trouble recognizing structural inequalities than did their counterparts of color, and thus leaned toward "color-blind" understandings of race that minimized racial difference. Emerson and Smith (2000), who studied racial attitudes among a spectrum of evangelicals (few of whom were actively involved in reconciliation or multiethnic church efforts), reached similar conclusions. Whites, they found, quickly minimized or dropped matters of social justice or equality between races in favor of a "spiritually and individually based" view of social justice. "Some of the white elite evangelicals attempted reconciliation," they summarize, "but incompletely. The problem with whites' conception of reconciliation, many [blacks] claimed, was that they did not seek true justice—that is, justice both individually and collectively" (58). Because of the different ideological "toolkits" Christians employ to identify and interpret racial inequality, white evangelicals (especially those functioning in racially homogeneous environments) tend to see through lenses of "accountable freewill individualism, relationalism, and antistructuralism" (76–78). Blacks, in contrast, identify structures of inequality and draw from a theological tradition that enables them to critique and challenge that inequality through system-changing efforts (67).

Such scholars are correct that white evangelicals have trouble recognizing both the benefits of white privilege and the social and political structures that perpetuate it. But in this respect, white evangelicals differ very little from what scholarship reveals about most whites.[19] The only relevant difference is that evangelicals often are affiliated with religious traditions that have sculpted theology in particular ways to anchor their worldview. However, in my interviews with and ethnographic research among people directly involved with racial reconciliation or multiethnic church efforts I've witnessed processes occurring that are considerably more nuanced than a reiteration of white privilege or neoconservatism. While evangelical racial change efforts undeniably reflect neoconservative elements such as structure-blind individualism, they also express neoliberal and neo-abolitionist commitments with broader social change orientations. More important, these racial change advocates summon their own distinctively faith-based resources to channel racial change processes through the religious race-bridging project.

Religious race bridging, as distinct from other race projects, holds out faith that the spiritual and cultural resources of evangelicalism, be they theological frames or rituals such as public apology and forgiveness, can enable Christians to overcome divisive obstacles. Faithful use of these resources, advocates believe, will foster significant change inside Christian communities and create new *collective* relationships. Done correctly, they maintain, such faith-based approaches to race can uniquely bridge the following divides:

- Between self and other

- Between attitudes or misunderstandings and awakening or epiphany

- Between negative feelings (resentment, fear, anger, mistrust) and healing through engagement and relationship

- Between the sins of the past and the reconciling contemporary present

- Between one community and another of a different race or culture

- Between the collective awakening of the church and the will to engage with real racial problems in and beyond the church

To fairly evaluate such efforts, scholars must recognize that this religious racial-bridging project, though influenced by other racial projects in Winant's schema, is its own animal. Although some evangelicals of color have understandably critiqued racial reconciliation as disingenuous or short-sighted, many participants claim that it (and multiethnic church communities) met a distinctive set of needs not effectively addressed by other secular or politicized race discourses. They attest that evangelical racial change efforts in part achieved this because they avoided politics and resisted the temptation to turn racial change efforts into "programs and projects." Through such delimiting of their distinctive racial change discourse, religious race bridging arguably provides a stage for cross-racial engagement without which evangelical communities, long fractured by race, cannot possibly conceive of more politically engaged critiques of structural and systemic racism. To support this claim, I focus on first, the bridging between past and present, and second, emphasizing relationship over "programmatic responses" to race.

Bridging Past and Present

In ways critics have overlooked, evangelical religious race bridging attempts to meaningfully address white evangelicals' failure to sufficiently challenge, and contributions to (in Winant's terms), the Far Right racial project. Whether or not outsiders see them as superficial, gestures like public apologies and statements of wrongdoing ("sin") by evangelical denominational leadership were, in a sense, the only logical starting point for whites to begin responding to the critiques evangelicals of color had been advancing for decades. After all, pioneers like Tom Skinner and John Perkins had practically begged white evangelical organizations to come clean about the racism in their past. As evangelical reconcilers such as Tom Tarrants, former Klan leader-turned-reconciler, pointed out, tracing almost any southern (but also northern) evangelical roots historically reveals the racist damage done by whites who identified as Christian. Racial reconciliation discourse offered a framework to start identifying the legacies of racism in white evangelicalism.

For this reason, developments such as the Southern Baptist Convention's apology for slavery felt pertinent even to many skeptical evangelicals of color. Drawing on the Christian ritual of confession, the organization wrote into its "Resolution on Racial Reconciliation" ("SBC Renounces Racist Past" 1995) explicit statements such as the following:

> WHEREAS, Our relationship to African-Americans has been hindered from the beginning by the role that slavery played in the formation of the Southern Baptist Convention; and
>
> WHEREAS, Many of our Southern Baptist forbears defended the right to own slaves, and either participated in, supported, or acquiesced in the particularly inhumane nature of slavery; and
>
> WHEREAS, In later years Southern Baptists failed, in many cases, to support, and in some cases opposed, legitimate initiatives to secure the civil rights of African-Americans. . . .[20]

Racial reconciliation discourse also urged recognition not only of acts but also of "theological racism" (Harvey 2005), or the use of biblical interpretations to justify the oppression and mistreatment of people of color: "Racism profoundly distorts our understanding of Christian morality, leading some Southern Baptists to believe that racial prejudice and discrimination are compatible with the Gospel." Where theological racism fueled extreme expressions of white supremacy (Far Right racial projects) in the past, religious race bridging seeks ways to weed out elements of that racism from contemporary evangelical thought and replace them with a theology of divinely ordained racial equality and reconciliation.

Reconciliation discourse also provided evangelicals a framework for tracing links between theological racism at the fringes of a white supremacist system and at its very center. Certainly not all evangelicals ran in lynch mobs. But reconcilers framed racial segregation "eleven o'clock Sunday morning" as a phenomenon that developed along the same spectrum. This narrative provided a surprising mechanism through which even some former extremely racist Christians were able to apologize for their or their family's racist past. While reconcilers of color I've met read such apologies as a beginning, not an end, they also often described them as a significant first step. Raleigh Washington, the African American head of Promise Keepers' Racial Reconciliation division in the late 1990s, illustrated how evangelical reconcilers saw reconciliation as a process capable of creating "miraculous" reversals:

> I got a letter from a man who heard me speak [at a Promise Keepers rally] and he said that my message so touched his heart, he turned around and hugged the first black guy. He went back to Alabama and he burned his Klan robe. He took my challenge and he went out and he made friends with a black man and he brought that man to Washington, D.C. to "Stand in the Gap" [a 1997 Promise Keepers gathering].[21]

Most people actively involved in racial reconciliation did not have direct connections to the Far Right, but the facts of a longer, uglier past were, for many, precisely what had to be reconciled. Spiritual rituals such as offering testimony, undertaking acts of repentance, and seeking forgiveness were mechanisms for facilitating that process.

This use of a faith-based framework to build a bridge from a dark past to a brighter present through recognition of the historical "sin" of racism also carries through the multiethnic church movement. In books by movement architects, in seminars about how to build multiethnic churches, and in testimonies from participants, an acknowledgment of historical racism often (though not always) frames discussions of what is happening in the present (DeYoung et al. 2003; Yancey 2003). For example, at multiethnic church conferences black evangelical sociologist George Yancey often delivers a PowerPoint primer called "Divided by Faith" that draws on secular scholarship to explain the "historical and cultural context of the racial divide in the U.S."[22] Beyond fostering credibility with participants of color, recognitions of race history in the church seem to provide a platform for articulating both the need for and the newness of multiethnic church efforts.

From Resistance to Relationship

The mandate to cultivate meaningful, long-term cross-racial relationships before, or instead of, channeling racial reconciliation into programs and projects permeates the evangelical religious race-bridging model. But rather than reading it as an expression of a narrowly neoconservative, "color-blind" race project, I suggest we consider the relationship-building mandate as a framework that affords the creation of a faith-based bridge from disempowering or alienating feelings about race to meaningful engagement across difference. Participants inside evangelical racial change efforts see relationship building as the most tangible and immediate means of transforming individual consciousness and thereby engendering meaningful crossing of racial barriers in churches, organizations, and society more broadly. What surprised me was that not only guilt-ridden whites claimed to experience "miraculous" epiphanies about race through cross-racial relationships; people of color, too, described these relationships as rewarding, healing, and even emotionally liberating, if also challenging. They also reported that the rewards of such relationships derived precisely from being nurtured outside the secular realm of programs and projects, policy initiatives, or race politics. Distinct from their white counterparts, who may have leaned toward a neoconservative-style rejection of structural policy remedies, evangelicals of color often criticized such initiatives as "white" solutions.

Reconcilers and participants in the multiethnic church movement tended to be wary or explicitly critical of more politicized approaches to racial change, on three main grounds. First (the relational argument), they saw the spiritually anchored, relationship-building model as deeper and more rewarding, and therefore better for creating long-term social change, than political models. Many read the secular realm, the world outside their spiritual communities, as fraught, ineffective, or potentially contaminating (the contamination argument). Third, some argued that secular political approaches to racial change, which had been implemented since the civil rights movement without creating "true" racial transformation in the social world, were inadequate because they lacked a spiritual component.[23] (This is the antiprogrammatic argument.)

Relationships over Programs

As the reconcilers interviewed put it, institutionalized efforts, necessary though they might be as short-term solutions, were incapable of producing the "heart change" that could lead to long-term social change because they had no spiritual core and did not attend to building committed relationships. One Latino reconciler expressed the relational argument in combination with the antiprogrammatic argument:

> [U]nderstand that institutional racism became institutionalized because of individual racism. So if you want to change institutional racism, you don't start from the institution, you start from people. Because the very people that created the problem are the people that can change it. In some sense, you have to hit it from both ends to turn this humongous ship around. But the greatest influence and effect that you can have in terms of a change agent is at the one-by-one, man-to-man, woman-to-woman relationship.[24]

Coming from white reconcilers, it would be easy to interpret this common refrain (through Winant's framework) as a kind of veiled racism that rejects truly reparative political solutions to race problems. But the critique by reconcilers of color of church-based or secular programs and projects designed to create racial change as typically white and therefore inadequate approaches provides another perspective.

Three examples from different interviewees illustrate the issue:

> Anglos, for the most part, are programmatic, whereas people of color are relational. . . . [I]f you really want to understand them, you've got to be in relationship with them. (African American Promise Keepers leader)

> I think a lot of times, the government viewpoint with our Native Americans is to somehow pay them off with programs or projects, and both those issues aren't going to work. . . . The government basically tried to I think somehow cover their guilt and shame and turn us into programs, economical things, school programs, clothing programs and so on . . . they realized it didn't work, so they gave us over to the churches to deal with. . . .most part, are programmatic, whereas people . . .
>
> Instead of turning us into programs, [the churches] turned us into projects. . . . In the early or mid-1800s, they divided Native America, so that major denominational groups would take over different parts of the Indian nations. . . . [T]hat's how they tried to somehow give us restitution or restoration—turning us into programs and projects; programs from the government viewpoint, projects from the church viewpoint. (Native American Promise Keepers leader)

> The Body of Christ has become very programmatic, so we want to program reconciliation, and that's very similar to legislating reconciliation. When in reality it's got to be founded on the establishment of relationships. (Latino Promise Keepers leader)

The above statements come from staffers of Promise Keepers, which firmly maintained a nonpolitical, nonpartisan identity and thus depoliticized the racial reconciliation model in favor of the relational one. Yet minimizing the role of participants of color in the evangelical racial reconciliation movement hobbles our understanding of how the religious race-bridging project works.

In interviews with more than forty racial reconcilers and participants in the multiracial church-building movement, I've met only a few who advocated for a *more* politicized faith-based racial change project. Many interviewees of color are self-described as Democrats, supporters of the civil rights movement, "economic liberals," or simply "not conservative on race issues," yet they expressed a common wariness about allowing their movement to be "co-opted" into a political mode. These reconcilers seemed willing to trust their faith in a spiritually based reconciliation model to challenge divisive beliefs and attitudes, partly because of their disillusionment with approaches they felt had been tried all too often. "There's never been true ownership [with government-sponsored programs]," said a Native American Promise Keepers leader. "There's a lot of compassion, but if you put compassion with programs and projects you get paternalism. . . . But if you put compassion with, say, a working together, an interdependence where [people] feel it's theirs, then you begin to get a lot of confident people in power."[25] Or, in the words of one Latino, with programmatic responses to racial problems, "what we do is generate a cycle of dependency, and we demoralize people—that's what the welfare system has done. I've seen it firsthand."[26]

Through the antiprogrammatic critique, most evangelical reconcilers maintained that politicized racial change models, though necessary at certain historical periods (e.g., Reconstruction or the civil rights movement), could not cut through the attitudes, beliefs, and behaviors that anchor racism. They believed the spiritual arena offered a more penetrating approach. "Affirmative action was the right thing to do because you had to force people to do the right thing," said a Latino reconciler. "But the reason it didn't work was that relationships were not a part of it." The same person maintained, as did others, that the Christian community had abdicated its social responsibility, and this was why Christians had to get involved with social change efforts on the ground: "So now we expect the government to take care of the poor and needy," he complained. "But God didn't assign that role and responsibility to the government; he gave that role to us as Christians."[27]

"Contaminated" Politics

Many reconcilers also saw the political realm as potentially destructive to Christians, and to the racial reconciliation process itself. The contamination argument regards the political realm as characterized by conflict and dominated by non-Christian interests. A Promise Keepers staffer commented that although "we can always be challenged with the seductiveness, power of politics as different political factions may try to challenge us as an organization to take a certain stance," Promise Keepers needs to resolutely refuse to etch out a political position on racial reconciliation. In one way or another, reconcilers of color often expressed the desire to preserve a line between the formal realm of politics and the cultural realm of racial reconciliation.

Many evangelical reconcilers also doubted that the secular world, or any other religious perspective, is capable of engaging in racial reconciliation; they perceived Christianity specifically as uniquely providing them the necessary tools that they believed other perspectives could not provide. Raleigh Washington articulated this in the context of having spoken to President Clinton's advisory panel on race in 1997. His view was that the religiously inspired "incentive to love one another" could not be replaced with "political logic":

> Inside the church we teach love your neighbor as yourself. The president says he wants a One America campaign, we ought to have relationships—but nothing drives it. . . . So this is how we do it from a secular viewpoint: we gear up for the fight. When the church is saying that the answer is we must love one another. . . . But how do you love? I think you need a power within yourself that's greater than yourself to do something that you would not naturally do yourself.[28]

Another way of framing this perspective is that evangelical religious race bridging is a "public-minded" discourse (the term Washington used with me) that focuses on and, by its own admission, can only effectively speak to one public: (Christian) believers. There is a cynicism to the evangelical perspective, a belief that only Christians are compelled by an authority beyond themselves to create "true" reconciliation.[29] When I asked one white Promise Keepers reconciler if racial reconciliation was possible outside Christian settings, he replied frankly, "Not effectively. No matter what my opinion is, I still have to hear what God has to say and if I consider God to be my Father, I have no options, obedience is required. Do you obey apart from love? No, you can't. . . . It's not that racial reconciliation can't happen at all [outside Christianity]. It just won't happen in a widespread fashion because people aren't willing to go there. . . . There's no compelling reason for them to stretch themselves."

A More Complex Racial Project

I wish to underscore the following: Although there are clearly elements of the evangelical race-bridging project that can be read as neoconservative (turning away from government solutions, seeking change through the private arena), evangelical racial change advocates for the most part view their objectives not through a neoconservative lens per se but through the distinct racial reconciliation lens, through their religious race-bridging toolkit. Their ambivalence about politics is specific to their vision of the processes needed to create racial change inside *their* communities, communities that are frequently their primary sources of identity. Time and again, they return to a few core ideas central to evangelicalism: that "God" must be at the center of the process, that it has to involve real relationships, that healing and epiphany happen through direct engagement with real people guided by a spiritual process.

Even with these distinguishing, nonsecular characteristics, evangelical racial change efforts also constitute a neoliberal race project in some obvious ways. They seek to name white privilege and the history of white racism and to decenter those through rituals of apology, witness, and repentance, the development of cross-racial relationships, and multiethnic community building. Relationships, according to reconcilers of color, are critical precisely because they don't allow whites to remain oblivious to their privilege, or their counterparts of color to stew in distrust. Whether outsiders are comfortable with such faith-based processes is beside the point; participants in them see them as meaningful vehicles of social change. These efforts, especially multiethnic church building, also seek, through the guiding narrative and resource of shared faith, to, in Winant's terms, "combine their interests," to literally bring a diverse community together under the same roof. It may be a church rather than a political party or an interest group. Still, these religious race-bridgers express the very neoliberal sentiments that cross-racial community should never mean uniformity and that people should be not only free but also encouraged to express the styles and values of their racial or ethnic culture next to others of different cultures. While few are inclined to articulate the anticapitalist critiques Winant attributes to the neoabolitionist race project, participants in evangelical racial change efforts do, as far as I've seen, recognize that race and racism have been at the center not only of American political culture but also of the culture of American evangelicalism, the legacy they most hope to change.

Conclusion

At the largest evangelical church-building conference in the nation, in April 2008 leaders in the multiracial church movement had earned, for the first time, their own section at the conference. Their seminars over the four-day event drew 75–150 people, most pastors of multiethnic churches. Participants saw themselves as rebels inside the conference and critiqued its still dominant model of church building, the "homogeneous unit principle," which advocated growing churches in demographically homogeneous communities. Mark DeYmaz, a movement leader who helped set up Mosaix Global Network, a social network and clearing-house for emergent multiethnic church efforts, cast a vision for the future. He called it the "20/20/20 Plan": 20 percent of U.S. churches by 2020 would meet the minimum threshold of 20 percent diversity (members of nonmajority groups in the church) (see also DeYmaz 2007). Participants couldn't wait to go home and take up the challenge. At the closing session, this deeply ethnically diverse circle of men (and a few women) linked hands and fervently prayed for change.

Circumscribing racial change efforts inside evangelicalism serves several pur-poses. It means that participants do not have to replace religious authority with state authority; they are allowed to explore their differences without necessarily revealing or having to defend their partisan attachments (at least initially); and they can draw on the resources they find meaningful for engaging race issues in their own communities. Perhaps these forms of racial change will never trans-late into organized responses to structural and systemic racial inequalities that perpetuate the racial wounds evangelical racial change advocates seek to heal. But perhaps this depoliticized form of religious race bridging creates organic, culture-based conversations that put participants on a gradual path to such in-sights. In my interviews with multiracial church pastors in 2008–9, a majority said they could imagine their church beginning discussions about, or challeng-ing political policy related to, the racially charged issue of immigration. They said they wanted to protect their immigrant members and that it seemed like the right thing to do in the eyes of God. Maybe they will.

To understand the intertwined dynamics of race and religion in American political life, scholars must attend to religious racial change efforts. As more multiethnic church communities emerge, more participants come into contact with people whose racial and socioeconomic realities are different, and through that process they may become educated to the policy matters that affect them. Ongoing racial progress may come of that, especially in the realm of education reform, which concerns so many ordinary parents. Alternatively, an increasingly multiracial American evangelicalism might generate more fear-based cross-racial coalitions geared to limit the rights of certain Americans, as has happened in battles against same-sex marriage (Wadsworth 2008). My hope is that we will continue to build analytical frameworks and critiques that do not simply dismiss religious racial change efforts—even those we secular scholars might not relate to—but rather seek to understand the resources they navigate and the communities they reflect.

Notes

1. Conservative evangelicals generally ascribe to a literalist reading of the Bible, traditionalist positions on a number of social issues, the importance of a "born-again" conversion experience, a belief in Christ's second coming, and a commitment to evangelism (Green 2004). Conservative evangelicalism is not just a white phenomenon; according to the 2000 National Election Survey (Version 2, http://sda.berkeley.edu:7502/cgi-bin/hsda3), fully 59 percent of blacks, 30 percent of Latinos, and 36 percent of whites identified as evangelical Christian.

2. Though I am sympathetic to the genuineness of the evangelical racial change efforts I study, it bears mentioning that I am neither evangelical nor a participant in the phenomena discussed.

3. Swidler (1986) and Emerson and Smith (2000, 76) refer to such frameworks as "tool kits."

4. Christian sociologists studying evangelical racial change efforts, such as Emerson (e.g., Emerson and Smith 2000), Yancey (2003), and others, are considerably less dismissive. Indeed, some of these scholars actively promote such efforts. While recognizing that white and nonwhite Christians tend to interpret racial issues in drastically different ways, these writers have focused primarily on the sociology of evangelical racial change, not on the movement's political orientation.

5. James Morone helped me by publicly posing this irritating question (as well as "Does this represent some kind of 'opiate of the sincere'?") in an earlier incarnation of this essay, as a paper delivered at the 2007 meeting of the American Political Science Association in Chicago. See his *Hellfire Nation* (2003) for a savvy exploration of other forms of "come-outerism" in U.S. history.

6. I borrow the term "bridging" from social capital literature. "Bridging social capital" happens when some groups engage or cooperate with others, and in the process "generate broader identities and reciprocity" (Putnam 2000, 23). Evangelical racial change advocates are bridging across racial or ethnic communities, and sometimes across what I call religious racial traditions (e.g., the black church). Paul Lichterman (2005, 2008) first helpfully used the term "race-bridging" in his sociological study of evangelical racial change efforts. I wish to broaden the concept to "religious race bridging," a term that can potentially be employed beyond the evangelical context. Lichterman largely does not explore the political dimension of these efforts.

7. My focus is restricted to communities that predominantly identify as theologically conservative. The tradition of *progressive* faith-based racial change among progressive evangelicals like Jim Wallis is not analyzed here. See also my "Bridging Racial Change: Political Orientations in the Multiracial Church Building Movement" (2010).

8. "Multiethnic" and "multiracial" are almost interchangeable terms in this movement, but "multiethnic" could, for example, describe a congregation of Asians or Latinos from different national origins—which might require boundary crossing as significant to participants as crossing racial divides.

9. Reflecting this paradox, my larger book project, which explores the dimensions of this move-

ment in much greater depth, is provisionally titled "Ambivalent Miracles: Conservative Evangelical Racial Change Efforts in American Political Culture."

10. See Harvey 1997, Loescher 1948, Manis 1987, Marsden 1980, Nelson 1981, Ammerman 1990, and Luker 1991.

11. Most of the description below is drawn from Gilbreath 2006. Smith and Emerson (2002) also discuss the influence of Skinner on evangelical racial change efforts.

12. These include *Black and Free* (1968), *How Black is the Gospel?* (1970), and *Words of Revolution* (1970).

13. Of Skinner's radicalism, John Perkins noted in 1994: "After he confronted an audience, people would be glad when someone like me came along, because I seemed moderate in comparison" (quoted in Gilbreath 2006, 64).

14. In 1993 Skinner and Patrick Morley, a white Christian business executive, launched Mission Mississippi, a Jackson-based racial reconciliation ministry, but Skinner's leadership was cut short when he died unexpectedly in 1994. The likes of Jesse Jackson, Maya Angelou, Betty Shabazz, and Louis Farrakhan attended his funeral.

15. For a full-blown articulation of an evangelical theology of racial unity, see DeYmaz 2007, chaps. 1–3.

16. Gilbreath (2006) captures the disappointments many supporters of the movement feel. A lot of the multiracial church-building books analyze what does and doesn't work, based on trial-and-error experiences.

17. To give a sense of the titles from the racial reconciliation flood: George Grant and D. James Kennedy, *The Changing of the Guard: The Vital Role Christians Must Play in America's Unfolding Political and Cultural Drama* (Nashville, TN: Broadman & Holdman, 1995); Danny Duncan Collun, *Black and White Together* (MaryKnoll, NY: Orbis Books, 1996); Fumitaka Matsouka, *Out of Silence: Emerging Themes in Asian American Churches* (Cleveland, OH: Pilgrim Press, 1995); Glen Loury, *One by One from the Inside Out* (New York: Free Press, 1995); Marcus Mabry, *White Bucks and Black-Eyed Peas* (New York: Scribner, 1995); and Curtiss Paul DeYoung, *Coming Together: The Bible's Message in an Age of Diversity* (Valley Forge, PA: Judson Press, 1995).

18. Winant's "white racial projects" argument appears in Winant 2004a and Winant 2004b, chap. 4. My references come from the former.

19. For more on the dynamics of white privilege, see Bush 2004, Steyn 2001, and McIntosh 1989.

20. For the text of the resolution, see http://www.sbc.net/resolutions/amResolution.asp?ID =899. See also "SBC Renounces Racist Past," 1995.

21. Raleigh Washington, Promise Keepers, interview, Promise Keepers Headquarters, Denver, CO, July 16, 1998.

22. I listened to this lecture and interviewed Yancey while attending the Multi-ethnic Churches track at the Exponential 08 church planting conference, Orlando, Fl, April 21–24, 2008.

23. Some 70 percent of the thirty reconcilers I interviewed made direct comments to this effect.

24. Elizár Pagán, Promise Keepers, interview, Denver, CO, April 23, 1998.

25. John Lansa, Promise Keepers, interview, Denver, CO, June 1, 1998.

26. Pagán interview, April 23, 1998.

27. Ibid.

28. Washington, interview, July 16, 1998.

29. In the 1990s, I saw a deep lack of awareness among evangelical reconcilers of other reconciliation movements in the world—such as between indigenous groups and governments, in South Africa, across ethnic divides, and so forth.

References

Ammerman, Nancy Tatom. 1990. *Baptist Battles*. New Brunswick, NJ: Rutgers University Press.

Barkun, Michael. 1994. *Religion and the Racist Right*. Chapel Hill: University of North Carolina Press.

Bush, Melanie E. L. 2004. *Breaking the Code of Good Intentions*. Lanham, MD: Rowman & Littlefield.

Davies, Susan, E. Hennessee, and Paul Teresa. 1998. *Ending Racism in the Church*. Cleveland, OH: United Church Press.

DeYmaz, Mark. 2007. *Building a Healthy Multiethnic Church*. San Francisco: John Wiley & Sons.

DeYoung, C. P., M. O. Emerson, G. Yancey, and K. C. Kim. 2003. *United by Faith: Multiracial Congregations as a Response to the Racial Divide*. New York: Oxford University Press.

Diamond, Sara. 2000. *Not by Politics Alone*. New York: Guilford Press.

Emerson, Michael O., and Christian Smith. 2000. *Divided by Faith: Evangelical Religion and the Problem of Race in America*. New York: Oxford University Press.

Findlay, James F. 1997. *Church People in the Struggle: The National Council of Churches and the Black Freedom Movement, 1950–1970*. New York: Oxford University Press.

Gilbreath, Edward. 1998. "The Jackie Robinson of Evangelicalism." *Christianity Today*, February 9, 52–57.

———. 2006. *Reconciliation Blues*. Downers Grove, IL: InterVarsity Press.

Green, John C. 2004. "The Religious Landscape in American Politics." Pew Forum on Religion & Public Life. https://www.uakron.edu/pages/bliss/docs/Religious_Landscape_2004.pdf .

Green, Marcia Slacum. 1997. "At Assembly, a Call to Bring the Races Together." *Washington Post*, October 5, A16.

Harvey, Paul. 1997. *Redeeming the South: Religious Cultures and Racial Identities among Southern Baptists, 1865–1925*. Chapel Hill: University of North Carolina Press.

———. 2005. *Freedom's Coming: Religious Culture and the Shaping of the South from the Civil War through the Civil Rights Era*. Chapel Hill: University of North Carolina Press.

Ignatiev, Noel, and John Garvey. 1996. *Race Traitor*. New York: Routledge.

Lee, Grady. 1994."Pentecostals Renounce Racism." *Christianity Today*, December 12, 58.

Lichterman, Paul. 2005. *Elusive Togetherness: Church Groups trying to Bridge America's Divisions*. Princeton, NJ: Princeton University Press.

Lichterman, Paul, Prudence Carter, and Michele Lamont. 2008. *Race-Bridging for Christ?* New York: Russell Sage Foundation.

Loescher, Frank Samuel. 1948. *The Protestant Church and the Negro: A Pattern of Segregation*. New York: Association Press.

Luker, Ralph. 1991. *The Social Gospel in Black and White: American Racial Reform, 1885–1912*. Chapel Hill: University of North Carolina Press.

Manis, Andrew Michael. 1987. *Southern Civil Religions in Conflict: Black and White Baptists and Civil Rights, 1947–1957*. Athens: University of Georgia Press.

Marsden, George M. 1980. *Fundamentalism and American Culture: The Shaping of Twentieth Century Evangelicalism, 1870–1925*. New York: Oxford University Press.

Maxwell, Joe. 1995. "Black Southern Baptists: The SBC's Valiant Efforts to Overcome Its Racist Past." *Christianity Today,* August 14, 27–31.

McCartney, Bill (with David Halbroo). 1997. *Sold Out: Becoming Man Enough to Make a Difference.* Waco, TX: Word Publishing.

McIntosh, Peggy. 1989. "White privilege: Unpacking the Invisible Knapsack." *Peace and Freedom,* July/August, 10–12.

Morgan, Timothy C. 1995a. "First Stride in a Long Walk." *Christianity Today,* February 6, 48.

———. 1995b. "Racist No More? Black Leaders Ask." *Christianity Today,* August 14, 53.

Myra, Harold. 1995. "Racial Reconciliation Begins with You." *Christianity Today,* March 9, 18–19.

Myrdal, Gunnar. 1944. *An American Dilemma: The Negro Problem and American Democracy.* New York: Harper Brothers.

Nelson, Douglas J. 1981. "For Such a Time As This: The Story of Bishop William J. Seymour and the Azusa Street Revival." PhD diss., University of Birmingham.

Newton, Judith Lowder. 2005. *From Panthers to Promise Keepers.* New York: Rowman & Littlefield.

Perkins, John. 1995. *Restoring At-risk Communities.* Grand Rapids, MI: Baker Books.

Putnam, Robert D. 2000. *Bowling Alone: The collapse and Revival of American Community.* New York: Simon & Schuster.

Sack, Kevin. 1996. "A Penitent Christian Coalition Offers Aid to Burned Churches." *New York Times,* June 19, U.S. Politics.

"SBC Renounces Racist Past." 1995. *Christian Century,* July 5, 671–72.

Seelye, Katherine Q. 1997. "Christian Coalition Plans Inner-City Program." *New York Times,* January 31. http://www.nytimes.com/1997/01/31/us/christian-coalition-plans-inner-city-program .html (accessed March 15. 2009).

Skinner, Tom. 1970. "The U.S. Racial Crisis and World Evangelism." www.urbana.org/articles/ the-us-racial-crisis-and-world-evangelism-1970.

Snowball, David. 1991. *Continuity and Change in the Rhetoric of the Moral Majority.* New York: Praeger.

Stanton, Glenn T. 1994a. "Will the Promise Keepers Keep Their Promises?" *Christianity Today,* March 7, 30–33.

———. 1994b. "Will the Promise Keepers Keep Their Promise?" *Christianity Today,* November 14, 35.

Steyn, Melissa E. 2001. *Whiteness Just Isn't What It Used to Be: White Identity in a Changing South Africa.* Albany: State University of New York Press.

Stricker, Mary. 2001. "A New Racial Ideology for the Christian Right? The Meaning(s) of Racial Reconciliation within the Promise Keepers Movement. PhD diss., Temple University.

Swidler, Ann. 1986. "Culture in Action: Symbols and Strategies". *American Sociological Review* 51:273–86.

Tapía, Andrés. 1993. "The Myth of Racial Progress" *Christianity Today,* October 4, 16.

———. 1997. "After the Hugs, What?" *Christianity Today Online,* February 3, 54.

Wadsworth, Nancy D. 2008. "Race-ing Faith and Fate: The Jeremiad in Multiracial 'Traditional Marriage' Alliances. *Race/Ethnicity: Multidisciplinary Global Contexts* 1 (2): 313–41.

———. 2010. "Bridging Racial Change: Political Orientations in the Multiracial Church Building Movement." *Religion & Politics* 3 (3): 439–68.

Washington, Raleigh, Glen Kehrein, and Claude V. King. 1997. *Break Down the Walls.* Chicago: Moody Press.

Winant, Howard. 1997. *Behind Blue Eyes: Whiteness in Contemporary U.S. Politics.* New York: Routledge.

———. 2004a. "Behind Blue Eyes: Whiteness and Contemporary U.S. Racial Projects." In *Off White: Readings on Power, Privilege, and Resistance*, 2nd ed., ed. Michelle Fine et al. New York: Routledge.

———. 2004b. *The New Politics of Race*. Minneapolis: University of Minnesota Press.

Yancey, George A. 2003. *One Body, One Spirit: Principles of Successful Multiracial Churches*. Downers Grove, II: InterVarsity Press.

Racial Justice in the Protestant Mainline

Liberalism and Its Limits

Antony W. Alumkal

While the Christian Right has been the focus of considerable scholarly and media attention for the past two and a half decades, it is hardly the only politically significant sector of American religion. The so-called mainline Protestant denominations experienced declines in both political power and membership during the last half century, yet they continue to maintain a significant public presence in many areas of American life (Wuthnow and Evans 2002).

This essay discusses the racial justice–related discourses and practices of the five largest mainline Protestant denominations: the United Methodist Church, the Evangelical Lutheran Church in America, the Presbyterian Church (U.S.A.), the Episcopal Church, and the United Church of Christ.[1] I argue that mainline denominations mirror the diversity and conflict of racial ideologies in the larger American society, particularly the majority white population, in the post–civil rights era. While mainline denominational leaders continue to call for substantive measures to bring about greater racial equality, mainline laypeople mostly prefer to maintain the racial status quo. Racial minority leaders in mainline denominations give their white colleagues a mixed scorecard, sometimes criticizing the latter group's "paternalism" and sometimes commending its efforts to bring about great "empowerment" of racial minorities. And while mainline Protestantism's historical commitment to intellectual respectability has translated into attempts to draw from social scientific perspectives on race, this has not prevented mainline church leaders from frequently approaching racial issues in simplistic ways. Despite all of this, mainline denominations play important roles in furthering racial justice through numerous types of public advocacy.

The data for this study came primarily from documents related to racial issues produced by mainline denominations, including official social statements on race, mission statements, strategy blueprints, reports of actions, internal assessments, and antiracism training literature. Additionally, I drew on interviews with five individuals, one from each denomination in this study, who was or had been employed by a mainline church's racial justice unit.[2]

Additional data for this study came from an unusual and unexpected, but ultimately quite valuable, experience of participant observation. During the academic year 2004–5, the Iliff School of Theology, where I teach, was formally charged by the United Methodist Church with being a racist institution. Consequently, I and other faculty members interacted with members of the United Methodist Church's official racial justice unit, the General Commission on Religion and Race. My participation in these events provided me with data normally unavailable to social scientists. After presenting a broad picture of mainline denominations' racial dynamics based on the above-mentioned documents and interviews, I discuss how the Iliff case study further refines our understanding.

Mainline Denominations and Their Social Location

The term "mainline" refers to a set of Protestant denominations that for much of the twentieth century could be regarded as a type of unofficial religious establishment in the United States. The mainline denominations included Episcopalians, Congregationalists (a predecessor body to the United Church of Christ), Disciples of Christ, and major denominations associated with the Lutheran, Methodist (excluding African American denominations), and Presbyterian traditions. Religious groups not considered to be part of the mainline churches included evangelical and fundamentalist denominations, Pentecostals, the Roman Catholic Church, African American denominations, Eastern Orthodox bodies, sectarian Christian groups such as the Jehovah's Witnesses, and non-Christian religions. Mainline denominations formed the bulk of the Federal Council of Churches in the first half of the twentieth century and the National Council of Churches after its founding in 1950. As Wuthnow and Evans (2002) note, the term "mainline" has become problematic, insofar as these denominations account for less than a tenth of the American population and this proportion continues to shrink. Yet these denominations continue to exercise considerable social influence, even if their "quiet" style, noted by Wuthnow and Evans, contrasts with the more aggressive style of the Christian Right. The influence comes in no small part from the fact that mainline denominations have a disproportionate number of members with above-average income and educational levels.

Racially, the mainline denominations are characterized by overwhelmingly white lay memberships. While precise data do not exist for the Episcopal Church or the United Church of Christ, the Evangelical Lutheran Church in America (2007a) reports that 97 percent of its members are white, the Presbyterian Church (U.S.A.) (2006) reports 92 percent, and the United Methodist Church (2007) reports 91 percent for members living in the United States.[3]

Past Studies of Race and the Mainline

What little literature exists on racial dynamics in the contemporary Protestant mainline denominations consists primarily of studies of congregations. Ammerman (1997) and Foster and Brelsford (1996) describe mainline congregations grappling with issues of racial diversity. Jeung (2005) describes Asian American "panethnic" (i.e., composed of multiple Asian ethnic groups) congregations in the San Francisco Bay Area and how their theology, ritual, and activism reflect mainline denominations' racial projects.

The only recent study of contemporary mainline churches' racial dynamics focusing on denominational structures and policies is Bradford Verter's (2002) essay, "Furthering the Freedom Struggle: Racial Justice Activism in the Mainline Churches since the Civil Rights Era." Verter is a diligent historian who gathered an impressive array of primary and secondary sources. He offers many insightful observations concerning mainline churches' efforts to advance racial justice, including the limitations of these efforts. However, his analysis is seriously undermined by an inadequate framework. As Verter states regarding his study:

> I here focus exclusively on relations between blacks and whites. A number of scholars and activists (including officers within mainline denominations) have argued for a conception of racial justice that looks beyond a biracial model to examine conflict between and among multiple racial and ethnic groups. My decision to pursue a narrower course was determined by the centrality of black/white relations to both the historical and the current efforts of the churches. Previous research into the dynamics of racism concentrating on the African American experience has provided valid models for understanding the experience of other people of color. Thus neither the validity of the insights gained from the present study nor the possibility of their broader application should be compromised by my focus on black/white relations as a starting point for analysis. (207n4)

There are several problems with Verter's arguments. While the historical racial justice efforts of the churches (i.e., those occurring before and during the civil rights movement) may have focused on black/white relations, current efforts are clearly multiracial in focus, with considerable attention devoted to immigrants and refugees from Asia and Latin America. In fact, some of Verter's own findings contradict this biracial framework. For example, he notes that in the 1970s, the programmatic concerns of the mainline hierarchies began to include the liberation struggles of Chicanos and Native Americans. Verter refers to this shift in focus as part of "the mainline's retreat from racial justice" (189), avoiding the more obvious conclusion that it reflected a broadening of racial justice concerns. Essentially, Verter employs a type of circular logic in which only issues related to African Americans are legitimately classified as "racial," and therefore mainline churches' racial justice advocacy remains focused on African Americans.

As for the argument that the experiences of African Americans can be extrapolated to other racial minorities, it is doubtful that this is informed by any consultation of the literatures on Asian Americans, Latinos, or Native Americans. The literature on Asian Americans analyzes their simultaneous status as the "model minority" and as "perpetual foreigners" (Takaki 1989; Tuan 1999), a situation with no correspondence in the African American experience. And the Native American experience has often been marked by forced acculturation and assimilation (often involving the work of Christian churches), again in sharp contrast to the African American experiences of segregation (Takaki 1979; Tinker 1993). In sum, Verter provides no convincing rationale for ignoring racial minorities other than African Americans in a study of mainline denominations' racial justice advocacy. Consequently, in this essay I analyze the racial dynamics of mainline denominations as a multiracial phenomenon.

Finally, Verter's account of mainline churches' racial justice efforts in the post–civil rights era often ignores evidence of positive progress. This is particularly apparent in his extensive discussions of racial minority complaints of "paternalism" on the part of white mainline church officials. While these complaints do exist, they represent only one side of a dialectic between what racial minority leaders call paternalism or tokenism, on the one hand, and what these leaders call the empowerment of racial minorities on the other. I discuss this dialectic in greater detail below.

Racial Formation Theory and the Mainline Denominations

My analysis in this essay is strongly informed by racial formation theory, which Nancy Wadsworth references in her essay in this volume. Michael Omi and Howard Winant (1986, 1994) present racial formation theory in their book, *Racial Formation in the United States,* and Winant expands the theory further in his books, *Racial Conditions* (1994), *The World Is a Ghetto* (2001), and *The New*

Politics of Race (2004). Omi and Winant describe the racial order in the United States in the post–civil rights era as one of a "racial hegemony" that replaced an earlier period of "racial dictatorship." Winant (1994, 29) defines hegemony succinctly as "a system in which politics operates largely through the *incorporation* of oppositional currents in the prevailing system of rule, and culture operates largely through the *reinterpretation* of oppositional discourse in the prevailing framework of social expression, representation, and debate" (italics in the original).[4] Racial hegemony in the contemporary United States, according to Omi and Winant, operates through the adoption by the state and key societal institutions of political initiatives and cultural narratives drawn from competing "racial projects." Proponents of each racial project seek to advance their own conception of the significance of race.

In *Racial Conditions,* Winant (1994, 31) presents the first version of his conceptual map of major racial projects shaping racial hegemony in the United States.[5] On the conservative extreme is the "Far Right," which represents race in terms of inherent, natural characteristics and which presses for open racial conflict in defense of "white rights." Next is the "New Right," which understands racial mobilization as a threat to "traditional values" and which engages in racial coding (e.g., complaints about busing or quotas) to advance its cause. In the center, Winant places "neoconservatism." This project denies the salience of racial difference and pushes for a "color-blind" state. Finally, Winant argues that the remains of the civil rights movement had by the 1990s evolved into two loosely knit racial projects on the left, "pragmatic liberalism" and "radical democracy." As Winant further elaborates, "In the former group I include the surviving civil rights organizations, the liberal religious establishment, and the Democratic party. In the latter group I include 'grass-roots' organizations that continue to function at the local level, cultural radicals and nationalist groups that have avoided mystical and demagogic pitfalls, and survivors of the debacle of the socialist left who have retained their antiracist commitments" (28).

Given that Winant places the "liberal religious establishment" (which would presumably include mainline denominations) in the pragmatic liberal category, it is worth examining this project in further detail. As Winant describes the racial discourse associated with pragmatic liberalism, "Racial identities serve to organize interests and channel political and cultural activities; as long as principles of pluralism and tolerance are upheld, a certain degree of group identity and racial mobilization can be accepted as the price of social peace" (31). He then describes the corresponding political/programmatic agenda as "Cultural and political pluralism; affirmative action as 'goals, not quotas.' State racial policy as moderating and eroding the legacy of discrimination" (31). Pragmatic liberalism stands in contrast to radical democracy, which involves the celebration of racial difference while advocating "state racial policy as redistribution" and the "extension of democratic rights and of societal control over the state" (31).

The pragmatic liberalism described above is a common orientation among mainline church officials. However, an accurate description of mainline denominations would present them as sites of competing racial projects ranging from conservative to radical. And while we can identify some general tendencies (e.g., laity holding more conservative views than clergy and whites holding more conservative views than people of color), diverse racial projects can be found within all subgroups in these denominations. The story of racial justice efforts in the mainline churches is to a large extent a story of clashing racial projects, as I discuss below.

Finally, racial formation theory describes race operating not only as competing ideologies but as a structural reality. Race continues to structure social life in the United States despite widespread denial of the significance of race, particularly among whites. As Winant (2004, 34) argues,

> [My white students] know they are supposed to reject racism, and indeed they consider themselves nonracists. But they also need racism: it protects their jobs, their property, their neighborhood schools, their "standard of living." Their psychic demand for "security" is still served by it; their feelings of vulnerability are still figured racially. Their racial privileges—and the contradictions inherent within them—are the lineaments of their social identities.

Race as a structural phenomenon in the broader society manifests itself in mainline denominations in the form of racially segregated congregations, with most racial minorities worshipping in a small number of congregations in which they predominate, while the bulk of mainline congregations feature overwhelmingly white memberships. In these latter congregations, common Euro-American values and styles are taken-for-granted parts of congregational cultures. As I discuss below, this racial structure seriously undermines denominational efforts at recruiting racial minorities.

The Racial Discourse of Mainline Denominations' Leaders

In line with racial formation theory, my first task in this analysis is to determine the basic features of mainline denominations' racial discourse with regard to the churches' understandings of identity, difference, and the meaning of race, as well as the political programs that follow from these understandings. The document that has shaped racial discourse among mainline religious leaders more than any other in the last three decades is "Policy Statement: On Racial Justice," which was produced by the National Council of Churches of Christ in the U.S.A. (1984). The document begins by affirming that all humanity is created in the image of God. Racism is therefore an expression of idolatry, replacing faith in God with "belief in the superiority of one race over another or in the universality of a particular culture" (1). The document also argues that Christians have a special responsibility to oppose racism, given that "[i]n Christ God challenges racism and promises its defeat" (2). However, the task of challenging racism is not only for Christians but is shared by Christians with "all people of goodwill" (17). Citing New Testament verses (1 Corinthians 12:13 and Galatians 3:28) that speak of diverse people in the early church (Jews and Greeks, slaves and free, males and females) being united together in Christ, the document argues that modern Christians should have the same appreciation for diversity "without confusing unity with sameness" (2). Here the document's authors seem to be rejecting a melting-pot model of assimilation.

The document begins to draw heavily from the social sciences as it turns from discussion of the church to the larger society. While not explicitly citing the work of sociologist Mark Chesler (1976), the document embraces his definition of racism as "racial prejudice plus power" (4). Furthermore, it stresses that racism operates not simply on the personal level but also at the institutional and systemic levels. In one of its more controversial passages, the document argues that whites in the United States have controlled the overwhelming majority of sources of power. It continues by arguing "Racism in the United States can therefore be defined as white racism: racism promulgated and sustained by the white majority. . . . The complete dominance and institutionalization of white racism in the United States makes 'reverse racism' nearly impossible because the victims of racism lack power" (5).

Turning to recommendations for future action, the document calls on predominantly white denominations to address their legacies of institutional racism by giving racial minority members greater authority within all types of church structures. The document also details an ambitious agenda for how denominations should combat racism at both the national and the global level. The national-level agenda includes advocating "aggressive social, economic, and employment policies" to further the economic well-being of all, especially racial minorities who bear disproportionate economic challenges (21). The document further states the authors' support for affirmative action policies. "We support goals, quotas, and other remedies of affirmative action when used as *minimum*, but not *maximum*, measures of participation. We call for a restructured economic system based on a cooperative model in place of current competitive and comparative models that promote profit at the expense of others" (21, italics in original). Finally, the document calls for reform of immigrant and refugee policies, arguing that nonwhites are not treated as favorably as European whites.

Several features of "Policy Statement: On Racial Justice" are worth commenting on. First, the political agenda advocated in the document most closely resembles not pragmatic liberalism but radical democracy, given the document's emphasis on the redistribution of resources through government intervention. Second, the document's descriptions of racism as involving institutional and structural phenomena draw heavily on concepts from the social sciences. Third, by arguing that in the United States only whites can be racist, the document not only precludes the possibility of racial minorities acting in racist ways against whites but also precludes the possibility of racial minorities acting in racist ways against each other. Finally, and related to the previous point, the document treats power nearly as an all-or-nothing phenomenon. Racial minorities are depicted as virtually powerless rather than as simply having lesser degrees of power than whites.[6] Thus, we can see a type of dualism in the document's conceptualization of race.

Turning to statements on racism and other racial justice material produced by individual mainline denominations, we find in nearly all of them heavy reliance on the discourse from "Policy Statement: On Racial Justice," sometimes in the form of verbatim quotations. The "racial prejudice plus power" definition of racism remains the standard in mainline denominations. All of the mainline denominations included in this study have statements supporting affirmative action, though not necessarily in terms as strong as those found in "Policy Statement: On Racial Justice." Regarding the insistence that only whites can be racist in the United States (since only they possess power), most official mainline documents agree. An example is this argument in the United Methodist Church's antiracism study and action guide, *Confronting the Sin*, which upholds this understanding of racism in rather dogmatic terms: "Remember our earlier definition of racism as the power of one racial group in a society to enforce its racial prejudices against other groups in the society through the major institutions of society. Many white persons object to this definition of racism. They resist the clear implication of this definition that only whites can be racists, that racial and ethnic minority persons cannot be racists. However, the definition is correct" (Jenkins 1997, 16).

By the mid-1990s, however, some mainline church leaders were beginning to depart from the earlier National Council of Churches' statement by insisting that it was possible for racial minorities in the United States to be guilty of racism. For example, in 1994 the bishops of the Episcopal Church produced a statement entitled "The Sin of Racism." While arguing that racism in the United States primarily flows from white privilege, the statement did not spare other racial groups from criticism:

> If racism is to be overcome, and our culture attain true inclusivity based on pluralism and diversity, there is a great deal of confessing that must go on all sides: confession that relates to our complicity in the genocide of native peoples, confession by whites of their continued advantage based on unearned privilege, confession by blacks of our co-dependence and participation in that corrupt value system, confession by both blacks and whites of our collusion in the racist dynamic which excludes Asian, Native Americans, and Hispanics, confession by all of us of our dependency upon violence as a means of controlling others and settling disputes. (Episcopal Church 1994)

Significantly, this view rests on a different understanding of power than that found in "Policy Statement: On Racial Justice," one that does not define racial minorities so starkly as powerless people. A viewpoint similar to the one above can be found in the 1998 statement "Erasing Racism," produced by the Consultation on Church Union. This organization was formed to increase interdenominational unity and included five mainline denominations—the Episcopal Church, the United Methodist Church, the Presbyterian Church (U.S.A.), the United Church of Christ, and the Christian Church (Disciples of Christ)—and three African American denominations—the African Methodist Episcopal Church, the African Methodist Episcopal Church Zion, and the Christian Methodist Episcopal Church. "Though white racism is clearly dominant in the United States and many other places, particularly as a consequence of colonialism, it is a naïve denial of the universality of sin and its injustices to assume that racism is exclusively a white offense. No ethnic group is immune from the infection of ethnocentrism" (Consultation on Church Union 1998, 359).

Three of the five mainline officials interviewed for this study shared that they had seen a slow shift toward a more complex discussion of race in their respective denominations. The Episcopal official noted that there has been more discussion of interminority conflict since 9/11 and that there is now "a handful of people in leadership positions discussing this." She also noted that the Episcopal Church's Hispanic membership is undergoing a "browning" as light-skinned Cuban Americans are being joined by an increasing number of darker-skinned Dominican Americans. This has led to some discussion of racial prejudice taking place within the Hispanic community. The United Methodist Church official noted that there are similar discussions in his denomination about racial prejudice among Hispanic Americans. He also noted that there are emerging discussions about how the church should minister to multiracial persons without asking them to choose one category of identity. Finally, the United Church of Christ official noted that at the denominational headquarters, "we are trying to generate curriculum about multiracial and multicultural conversation that is not just black and white conversation but a brown and white or a yellow and brown."

Finally, it is worth briefly comparing the racial discourse of mainline leaders with that produced by American evangelical leaders, as discussed in my previous work (Alumkal 2004) and in Nancy Wadsworth's essay in this volume.[7] Evangelical leaders tend to focus on individual transformation as the solution to racism, and they are indifferent or even hostile to efforts to transform social structures. Mainline leaders take a more holistic approach that involves transforming both individuals and social structures. Anecdotal evidence suggests that some evangelical leaders are turning to social scientific studies of race for guidance, but at this point they remain a minority. In contrast, it is the norm for mainline leaders to draw heavily (if simplistically at times) from the social sciences. Finally, evangelical leaders' proposed solutions to racism often exclude those who are not Christian (and even Christians who are not theologically conservative),[8] while mainline leaders seek interfaith cooperation in overcoming racism.

Advocacy

From the discourse found in mainline statements on race and other race-related texts, we turn to mainline denominations' actions in the political and social sphere. As noted earlier, at least some mainline racial discourse reflects the radical democracy project. This tendency is less evident in mainline denominational social action, which is constrained by issues of feasibility and consequently hews more closely to the pragmatic liberal project.

Central to mainline churches' advocacy on behalf of racial and other political concerns are the denominations' Washington, D.C., offices. Olson (2002, 55) describes these offices as pursuing a "peace and justice" agenda by "advocating human rights at home and abroad, working to preserve the environment, questioning U.S. use of military force, and above all else fighting for the disadvantaged." These offices lobby members of Congress and officials in the executive branch (including the president) concerning legislation and government policy about which the offices have concern. The mainline denominations' offices in Washington have lobbied for legislation regarding hate crimes, affirmative action, Native American policy, refugee and immigration policy, and "environmental racism." These offices also offer amicus curiae briefs in important federal cases.

In addition to lobbying the federal government, mainline denominations engage in race-related advocacy at the local or community level. Some of this work is authorized directly by the denominations' central offices, often in cooperation with local congregations. For example, in 1989 the Presbyterian Church (U.S.A.) established the Native American Ministry Project in the Los Angeles area. According to a report by the denomination, the minister running the project "not only responds to the spiritual needs of Native families, but also social needs and justice issues" (Presbyterian Church [U.S.A.] 2000a).

The Evangelical Lutheran Church in America's Lutheran Immigration and Refugee Service (LIRS) combines lobbying efforts with direct assistance to immigrants and refugees. According to the denomination's "Message on Immigration," the LIRS "resettles refugees, advocating on behalf of detained asylum seekers, assists unaccompanied children, offers pastoral and legal counsel to persons without legal status, aids persons with the citizenship process, and helps newcomers learn to live in a new country" (Evangelical Lutheran Church in America 1998). Most of the work by the LIRS has been on behalf of persons from Asia and Latin America, though people of Arab and Middle Eastern descent received increasing assistance following 9/11. The LIRS has recently been working with other faith-based organizations and immigrant advocacy groups to lobby members of Congress regarding the issue of immigration reform, advocating for legislation "promoting family unity, safeguarding human rights and workers' rights, ending marginalization, and providing a path to permanence" (Evangelical Lutheran Church in America 2007b).

The United Church of Christ combined racial justice and environmental concerns in 1987 by publishing a study on environmental racism. Verter (2002, 196) notes that while other activists and agencies had noted a correlation between race, income, and zoning of hazardous waste, the United Church of Christ "made resistance to environmental discrimination feasible by sponsoring leadership summits, training workshops, development grants, and protests, helping to transform what had started as a local complaint into a nationwide issue." Twenty years later, the United Church of Christ continued to shine a spotlight on environmental racism with its report "Toxic Wastes and Race at Twenty: 1987–2007" (United Church of Christ 2007).

Further examples of mainline advocacy at the local level come from individual congregations acting on their own initiative. Some of this activity has been documented in sociological studies of congregational life (e.g., Ammerman

1997; Jeung 2005). However, it is important to note that congregations actively engaging in racial justice efforts make up a small minority of congregations affiliated with mainline denominations; the reason for this is detailed below.

The Ideological Divide between Leaders and Laity

While the mainline denominations are able to do significant work in support of a liberal agenda on race and other social issues, there are constraints on this work. Perhaps the most important factor limiting the success of the mainline denominations' racial agenda is the ideological gap that separates leaders (including denominational officials and clergy) from the lay members. This division between leaders and laity in the mainline was first noted in the 1960s. A "new breed" of mainline clergy emerged who freely mixed religion with an antiwar, antipoverty, pro–civil rights political agenda. But as Hadden (1969) observed, the majority of lay members were not persuaded to support this agenda. In the decades that followed, the increasingly voluntaristic nature of religious commitments, which meant that churches could not depend on the loyalty of their flocks but had to compete for religious "consumers" in an open market, further eroded the ability of mainline leaders to influence laity on political matters (Roof and McKinney 1987). In fact, mainline laity simply mirrored the political opinions of the white middle class from which they were predominantly drawn.

One of the denominations in this study, the Presbyterian Church (U.S.A.), has extensively studied the opinions of its lay and clergy members through its Presbyterian Panel surveys. Recent surveys have revealed the continuation of the ideological gap between lay and clergy. For example, in the 1999 Presbyterian Panel survey, 63 percent of specialized clergy (denominational officials, campus chaplains, etc.) and 49 percent of parish pastors favored affirmative action ("preferences") for African Americans in hiring and promotion, in contrast to only 16 percent of lay members (Presbyterian Church [U.S.A.] 1999b, A-16).

A second denomination in this study, the Evangelical Lutheran Church in America, conducted a survey of clergy and lay members in 1988 in an attempt to understand opinions on the connection between faith and social action. The survey found that the majority of clergy approved of churches being involved in racial justice, foreign policy, and other social issues. However, laypeople exhibited a different pattern. "[T]hose activities which endeavor to affect the community by 'spiritual' means or by transforming or serving individuals tend to be seen favorably, and those which in any way seem to involve the congregation in politics—even where it plays an essentially neutral role, as in hosting candidates' nights open to all contenders or promoting discussion of local government policy within the congregation—tend to be seen less favorably" (Hart 1990, 10). Furthermore, there was little relationship between the views of individual clergy and the members of his or her congregation. The research report speculated on the reason for this disconnect:

> One possible explanation is that congregations are simply not very "ideological" places. That is, the bonds among members within a congregation, and between members and pastor, may not be based primarily on shared beliefs and values (even religious ones, let alone political and social ones), but rather on factors such as sharing a life and history. Furthermore, it is likely that not many discussions go on about social issues, especially in light of responses showing that a sizeable minority of members do not want to have such discussions take place. (Ibid., 22)

The report went on to say that, given that pastors generally hold more liberal political views than members of their congregations, this lack of discussion of political issues made pastors' jobs easier by helping to avoid conflicts.

Further evidence of the divide between mainline leaders and laity can be seen in the sparse interest among congregations in the antiracism training curricula developed by mainline racial justice units. All of the denominations in this study have antiracism curricula available to congregations and other denominational units. Some denominations (or geographic sections of denominations) require leaders working in their offices to undertake antiracism training. However, most of the officials interviewed for this study indicated that only a small minority of congregations were taking advantage of this training.[9]

The gap between leaders and laity is especially problematic with respect to the generally liberal-leaning social statements issued by denominations, statements that are each supposed to represent the collective view of their respective denomination. I found denominational leaders responding to this situation in at least two ways. First, they generally reject the idea that denominational social statements should be decided simply by majority lay opinion. As the Evangelical Lutheran Church in America report mentioned earlier argues,

> [T]hese data should not be taken to define what stance the ELCA *should* take. As the church, we try to be faithful to God's call as best we can discern it, rather than passively following the views of a majority as discovered in surveys like this one. On the one hand, the voices of lay members of the church are one important witness to God's call, and deserve to be listened to with care and respect. . . . Such knowledge, however, is no substitute for theological and ethical discernment. (Hart 1990, 2–3; italics in the original)

The report, which was written by the Evangelical Lutheran Church in America's director for research, attempts to strike a balance between lay and leader authority. We can see a stronger position taken in the Presbyterian Church (U.S.A.)'s "Facing Racism" statement, which bluntly criticizes mainline laypeople for not following the antiracism agenda of denominational leaders:

> While the social policies and pronouncements of denominations continue to emphasize inclusiveness and justice, these do not translate in the hearts and minds of Christians who participate in the electoral and political process. Christians are passive in the face of attacks on affirmative action and the adoption of regressive social policies at the local, state, and national levels. (Presbyterian Church [U.S.A.] 1999a, 6)

A second response to the ideological gap between denominational officials and laity is to describe social statements as "teaching documents." This perspective is expressed in the Evangelical Lutheran Church in America's *Guiding Perspectives for Social Statements* booklet. "Church members are called upon to give social statements serious consideration as they form their own judgments. In their use as teaching documents, their authority is persuasive, not coercive" (Evangelical Lutheran Church in America 2000, 1). Such a stance is consistent with the respect for pluralism that mainline denominations traditionally have held. However, the evidence strongly suggests that few mainline laypeople are finding the social statements of their denominations to be persuasive. Returning to the racial formation theory perspective, we can say that the majority of mainline laypeople, like members of the white middle class more broadly, continue to be influenced by conservative racial projects (particularly the neoconservative and New Right projects), which deny that racial minorities in the United States experience significant oppression.

My reading of the divide between mainline leaders and laity regarding racial justice issues differs from that offered by Robert Wuthnow in *The Quiet Hand of God*. Wuthnow cites survey data showing that a large majority of the American public is interested in "achieving greater equality for racial and ethnic minorities in our society," along with a number of other social issues. He then argues:

> These data suggest that church leaders need not apologize for the stands they have taken, nor should they worry that nobody else cares about these issues. What may be contested are specific programs and strategies for advancing some of these issues, not the fact that the issues themselves are important. (Wuthnow 2002, 384)

This argument misses how in the post–civil rights era the language of racial equality has been rearticulated by conservatives in ways fully compatible with the maintenance of the racial status quo, which is to say continued racial inequality. It is on behalf of a "color-blind" agenda that proponents of the neoconservative and New Right projects dismantle state policies designed to reduce racial inequality (Omi and Winant 1994; Winant 2004). In other words, it is precisely the "specific programs and strategies" that differentiate between racial projects that challenge white privilege and those that preserve it. Furthermore, Bonilla-Silva and Forman's (2000) study of white U.S. college students found that these individuals frequently express racially egalitarian views on surveys, only to contradict these views during interviews by giving derogatory statements about racial minorities. In sum, I believe Wuthnow underestimates the difficulties that mainline leaders face in promoting racial justice.

The Uphill Pursuit of Diversity

All of the mainline denominations in this study have official goals to increase racial and ethnic diversity. Such goals are consistent with the pragmatic liberal project's embrace of cultural pluralism (Winant 1994). It should be noted, however, that not all racial minorities support such goals, as they represent the possibility of draining members from African American denominations and other racial minority religious communities.

Two mainline denominations, the Presbyterian Church (U.S.A.) and the Evangelical Lutheran Church in America, have set specific, and perhaps unrealistically high, diversity targets. In the case of the Evangelical Lutheran Church in America, the denomination resolved at its 1987 Constituting Convention[10] to have 10 percent racial minorities (up from 2 percent) by 1997. Yet by 1999, racial minority membership was only 2.6 percent. A 2000 document evaluating the Evangelical Lutheran Church in America's progress noted that "at this current rate, it will take the ELCA over 100 years to achieve the 10 percent goal" (Inskeep 2000). The Presbyterian Church (U.S.A.) set a similarly ambitious goal in 1998 of having 20 percent racial minorities (up from 4.7 percent) by 2010 (Presbyterian Church [U.S.A.] 1998). However, the 2000 Presbyterian Panel survey revealed that two-thirds of pastors in the denomination believed this goal will not be realized. Furthermore, only 8 percent of lay members were even aware that the goal existed (Presbyterian Church [U.S.A.] 2000b).

Why do mainline denominations have such difficulty implementing their goals of attracting racial minorities? One of the main reasons is that denominational outreach goals, while set by the central offices, largely depend on the local congregations for implementation. (The exception to this is when mainline offices plant new congregations designed to serve racial minority communities.) Given the competitive nature of the religious marketplace, mainline congregations cannot afford to alienate their core constituencies, which for most of them consist of white members. Consequently, most mainline congregations attract only those racial minorities that are comfortable assimilating into an existing congregational culture shaped by white (and often middle-class) norms. Predominantly white congregations that are genuinely interested in racially diversifying—to the point that they are willing to change worship styles, music, and general congregational cultures—remain the exception rather than the rule (Emerson and Kim 2003). Denominational offices can set goals and monitor progress, but they can do little to enforce these goals.

Evidence of congregations' lack of compliance with diversity goals can be found in the 2000 Presbyterian Panel survey. Only 29 percent of pastors and 18 percent of lay members agreed that their congregations had made it a priority to become more racially and ethnically diverse (Presbyterian Church [U.S.A.] 2000b, A-10). In the United Methodist Church, a 2000 report by the General Commission on Race and Religion complained that denominational mandates for developing strategies for increasing diversity were not being carried out at the local level (United Methodist Church 2000). Again, we see that mainline laypeople are following different racial projects than those of mainline leaders, with the result that most mainline congregations do little to attract or accommodate racial minorities, and white privilege remains an embedded feature of congregational cultures.

"Paternalism" versus "Empowerment"

The mainline denominations' difficulties with racial minorities go beyond the quantitative issue of failing to attract large numbers of people. They also include the qualitative issue of often failing to include racial minorities as full equals who have the ability to influence policy, rather than simply trying to incorporate minorities into white-controlled structures. Materials produced by minority-member caucus groups and materials produced by denominational committees studying racial matters, which are predominantly staffed by racial minorities, both frequently complain of "tokenism" and "paternalism," describing these as situations in which white leaders refuse to yield adequate power to racial minorities. At the same time, it must be recognized that mainline denominations have made real progress toward empowering their racial minority constituencies.

Mainline racial minorities make several specific complaints, which can be found in denominational reports. One of the most frequent complaints is that they are being asked to assimilate into a Euro-American church culture, rather than the church changing to meet their needs. For example, a 2000 report by the United Methodist Church's General Commission on Religion and Race argued that "The Black constituency is constantly being asked to 'give up' something to be part of the 'inclusive' church" (United Methodist Church 2000, 13). The Evangelical Lutheran Church in America official interviewed for this study expressed similar concerns about her denomination. She affirmed that the Evangelical Lutheran Church in America had done a good job of increasing representation by racial minorities. However, the sharing of power lagged behind. "We bring people in but we don't give them the voice to make the institution a truly multicultural church."

A second frequent complaint is that white leaders often assume they know what is best for racial minorities rather than being willing to listen to them. An example of this second complaint can be found in the Presbyterian Church (U.S.A.)'s (2000a) "Comprehensive Strategy for Ministry with Native Americans." The document discusses white Americans' long history of mistreatment of Native Americans, a history that includes actions by the Presbyterians. The document then argues that this history affects current ministries to Native Americans. "Part of the legacy is remnants of paternalism in the type of connections PC(USA) entities have with Native American congregations. By far, most of the relationships with Native American churches are not true partnerships, but paternalistic relationships in which another church or church entity only does things for the Native church on its own terms" (ibid.).

Despite concerns about tokenism and paternalism, mainline racial minorities also describe the opposite situation, which they describe as successful "empowerment." The 1992 report by the United Methodist Church's General Commission on Religion and Race defined empowerment this way:

> Empowerment is to facilitate people making decisions about their own destiny; identifying their own visions and needs and determining how best to meet those needs. Empowerment is the way of ensuring that barriers are removed and doors opened to persons traditionally denied access to power—to information, to resources, to opportunities.

Racial minority leaders in mainline denominations point to a number of examples of moves toward greater empowerment. The United Methodist Church official with whom I spoke told me that the area in which his denomination has been most successful in instituting racial justice was "getting racial minority people in positions of leadership." Additional examples of empowerment can be found in denominationally funded programs run by and for racial minority members. Both the Episcopal Church and the Evangelical Lutheran Church in America operate programs for African American youth that are staffed by African American adults and designed to produce future church leaders.

Another example of progress toward empowering racial minority constituencies can be seen in the Presbyterian Church (U.S.A.)'s decision to alter its normal governance structures to serve the needs of Korean Americans in the denomination. The Presbyterian Church (U.S.A.) has attracted by far the largest number of Korean Americans of any mainline denomination, primarily because of historical ties between American Presbyterian missionaries and the Christian churches in South Korea. In 2005 the denomination had 50,000 Korean Americans out of a total membership of 2.4 million (Presbyterian Church [U.S.A.] 2005). To accommodate the needs of Korean American pastors and lay leaders, many of whom have limited English ability, the Presbyterian Church (U.S.A.) allows Korean American congregations to bypass the normal governance structure, which divides the denomination into presbyteries based on region of the country, and instead affiliate with special Korean American presbyteries. A sign of Korean Americans' clout within the denomination was the election of Syngman Rhee, a Korean American, to the highest leadership post in the denomination in 2000. This is not to say that tensions between Korean Americans and the denominational hierarchy do not remain, but clearly, Korean Americans have taken major steps toward self-determination.

From a racial formation theory perspective, that racial minorities simultaneously experience mainline denominations as paternalistic and as empowering reflects the fact that these denominations are sites with competing racial projects. To a large degree, racial minorities make complaints of paternalism against white leaders (and probably some racial minority leaders) who reflect the pragmatic liberal project. These complaints focus particularly on the significant concessions that this project makes to white privilege. Conversely, racial minority descriptions of empowerment suggest radical democratic projects struggling to find fuller expression within the confines of mainline denominations.

Lessons from the Iliff Investigation

Having presented a broad picture of mainline denominations' racial dynamics, in this final section I turn to the specific case of the Iliff School of Theology and its interaction with the United Methodist Church's racial justice unit. The relevant question now is how this case study furthers our understanding of mainline racial justice.

A summary of the 2004–5 events is as follows. Iliff had hired David Maldonado in 2000, thereby becoming the first mainline seminary in the United States with a Hispanic president. However, it was not long before tensions appeared between Maldonado and an ever-increasing number of faculty members over a wide range of issues. In May 2004 the chair of the board of trustees announced the early retirement of President Maldonado, with specifics regarding the circumstances of the retirement left undisclosed. At the request of a former and a current trustee, the United Methodist Church decided to investigate the events at Iliff leading to Maldonado's retirement. The Review Team included members from the United Methodist Church's University Senate, the body that oversees the church's institutions of higher education, and the General Commission on Religion and Race, the church's official racial justice group. The Review Team included both whites and people of color. In the fall of 2004 the Review Team interviewed ninety individuals, among them faculty, staff, students, trustees, and retired President Maldonado.

The Review Team's report, which was made public on November 2, 2004, was harshly critical of the school, charging that institutional racism was responsible for Maldonado's retirement. It also recommended that the University Senate place Iliff on immediate "listing with public warning," threatening the school with the loss of denominational funding if reforms were not instituted (University Senate and General Commission on Religion and Review Team 2004). The University Senate quickly accepted this recommendation. On November 15, 2004, five Iliff faculty members of color (myself included) released a public letter responding to the Review Team's report. The letter expressed concern that the Review Team had ignored the faculty of color and their leadership roles in the school. The letter also criticized the failure of the report to "speak any word regarding the accountability shared by President Maldonado" in addition to the accountability shared by faculty and trustees.[11]

In April 2005 a second Review Team, with some members from the previous team plus some new members (including a new chair), came to Iliff. Meeting with the faculty members of color as a group, they apologized for the fact that the first Review Team's report did not adequately note their contributions to the school. After their site visit, the second Review Team concluded that Iliff had fulfilled the recommendations outlined in the report. Iliff was removed from "listing with public warning" without fanfare.

What can we learn from this case study? First and foremost, we see the consequences of the mainline denominations' insufficiently nuanced (that is, dualistic) conceptualization of race I discussed earlier. The tendency toward simplistic dualism was the single most striking characteristic of the work of the Review Team sent to investigate Iliff. In their interviews with Review Team members during the investigation, most racial minorities on the faculty insisted that the situation at Iliff was a complex one. Their argument was that institutional racism was a factor in the unraveling of Maldonado's presidency, but it was also true that he had made some serious errors in leadership that ultimately made his relationship with the faculty unworkable. The Review Team report not only ignored racial minority faculty members' criticisms of Maldonado, it also ignored their very presence in the school in order to portray the conflict as one between a white faculty and a president of color—in other words, to paint a dualistic picture of racial dynamics at Iliff. Many members of the Iliff community complained that the report contained prefabricated (or "boilerplate") descriptions of institutional racism that had little relationship to the specifics of the Iliff case. This suggests that the Review Team lacked the conceptual tools to conduct a competent investigation.

The case study also cautions us against understating the influence of mainline churches' racial justice units within their respective denominations. As I discussed earlier, these units have limited impact on the attitudes of mainline laypeople or on the behavior of congregations. However, the events at Iliff suggest that in the United Methodist Church, the racial justice unit exercises considerable power among the denomination's central offices. The United Methodist Church's General Commission on Religion and Race was able to persuade the University Senate to exert financial pressure on one of its seminaries, in the form of threatening to cut off Iliff's nearly $1 million annually in funding if it did not comply with the Review Team's recommendations. This is clearly more than a token level of power. Which other mainline racial justice units, if any, wield similar institutional power in their respective denominations is a question that merits further investigation.

Conclusion

Mainline denominations reflect the complexity of race in the post–civil rights era. The racial attitudes of mainline denominations' laypeople closely match those common in the broader white middle-class population from which they are mostly drawn—there is widespread denial of the significance of race even as race continues to structure social life. While some mainline church racial justice units may wield significant power among denomination central offices, as was illustrated by Iliff's experience of being disciplined by the United Methodist

Church, most mainline laypeople exhibit little enthusiasm for their leaders' efforts at promoting racial justice in the wider society or racial diversity in their congregations. Yet conflicting racial ideologies between leaders and laypeople are only part of the story. Leaders themselves are divided between those advocating more moderate (i.e., less challenging to structures of white privilege) forms of liberalism and those advocating radical democratic policies. In all of this, we can see the limits that efforts at promoting racial justice encounter under conditions of racial hegemony.

Yet despite these limits, the mainline denominations still serve an important function in contemporary American society regarding race. With racial justice concerns having long ago been relegated to the margins of the political process, mainline denominations, along with historically black denominations, are among the few institutions voicing concern about continued racial inequality. If they are to play this prophetic role more effectively, mainline church leaders need finally to move past the simplistic dualism that has undermined much of their past thinking related to race. Moving forward will require drawing on one of the main strengths of the mainline Protestant tradition—the willingness to allow new knowledge from scholarship and an ever-widening circle of human experience to transform theology and practice.

Notes

1. While some scholars would include the American Baptist churches among large mainline denominations, I did not include them in this study for two reasons: first, they have a larger evangelical constituency than the other denominations in this study, and second, a significant number of American Baptist congregations are dually affiliated with an African American denomination. Both factors would make the American Baptist churches an outlier in this study.

2. The interviews ran roughly thirty minutes each. Four were conducted over the phone and one was conducted in person in the official's office.

3. The United Methodist Church has a global membership, with 30 percent of its members living outside the United States, most of these in Africa.

4. "Oppositional currents" refers to attempts to challenge those in society exercising dominance. In the context of racial hegemony, this refers to attempts to challenge the system of white dominance.

5. Nancy Wadsworth's essay in this volume references the second version of Winant's map. I find the original version more useful for my analysis of mainline denominations.

6. Omi and Winant appropriately criticize this conception of power and its resulting understanding of racism. "In the modern world, 'power' cannot by reified as a thing which some possess and other's don't, but instead constitutes a relational field. The minority student who boldly asserts in class that minorities cannot be racist is surely not entirely powerless. In all but the most absolutist regimes, resistance to rule itself implies power" (1994, 188n65).

7. I am aware that mainline denominations include many members and congregations that self-identify as evangelical. In other words, mainline and evangelical represent overlapping rather than mutually exclusive religious categories. However, the overlap becomes less pronounced in moving from mainline congregations to denominational central offices.

8. Many American evangelicals use the word "Christian" when they mean "evangelical Christian," with the implication that only those who subscribe to typical evangelical beliefs can be counted as authentic Christians.

9. Three of the officials emphasized that the antiracism efforts were at least partially successful. The Evangelical Lutheran Church in America official shared that interest in antiracism training appeared to be growing in her denomination. The Episcopal Church official shared her belief that some denominational leaders were underestimating the interest in antiracism training among congregations. The United Church of Christ official was the most optimistic. "[Antiracism training] is widespread, but I couldn't give numbers. Having traveled around nationally, I can say that people are very passionate."

10. The Evangelical Lutheran Church in America was formed in 1987 from a merger of three smaller Lutheran bodies, all of which had overwhelmingly northern European memberships.

11. Other signatories were Edward P. Antonio, Vincent Harding, Alberto Hernández, and George E. Tinker.

References

Alumkal, Antony W. 2004. "American Evangelicalism in the Post–Civil Rights Era: A Racial Formation Theory Analysis." *Sociology of Religion* 65:195–213.

Ammerman, Nancy. 1997. *Congregation and Community.* New Brunswick, NJ: Rutgers University Press.

Bonilla-Silva, Eduardo, and Tyrone A. Forman. 2000. "'I'm Not a Racist, but . . .': Mapping White College Students' Racial Ideology in the USA." *Discourse and Society* 11:50–85.

Chesler, Mark. 1976. "Contemporary Sociological Theories of Racism." In *Towards the Elimination of Racism,* ed. Phyllis A. Katz. New York: Pergamon Press.

Consultation on Church Union. 1998. "Erasing Racism: A Strategy Paper for COCU's Quest for a Racially Just Unity." *Midstream* 37:357–85.

Emerson, Michael O., and Karen Chai Kim. 2003. "Multiracial Congregations: An Analysis of Their Development and a Typology." *Journal for the Scientific Study of Religion* 42:217–27.

Episcopal Church. 1994. "The Sin of Racism." http://www.episcopalchurch.org/peace-justice/article_63.asp.

Evangelical Lutheran Church in America. 1998. "A Message on Immigration." http://www.elca.org/socialstatements/immigration.

———. 2000. "Guiding Perspectives for Social Statements." Chicago: Evangelical Lutheran Church in America, Division for Church and Society.

———. 2007a. "Fascinating Facts Brought to You by the ELCA Department for Research and Evaluation." Evangelical Lutheran Church in America, Department for Research and Evaluation. http://www.elca.org/research/fyifacts/html.

———. 2007b. "LIRS Continues Comprehensive Immigration Reform Advocacy." Evangelical Church in America, Lutheran Immigration and Refugee Service. http://www.lirs.org/News/AdvoUpdate/Advo200707.html.

Foster, Charles R., and Theodore Brelsford. 1996. *We Are the Church Together: Cultural Diversity in Congregational Life.* Harrisburg, PA: Trinity Press International.

Hadden, Jeffrey K. 1969. *The Gathering Storm in the Churches.* Garden City, NY: Doubleday.

Hart, Stephen. 1990. "Faith, the Church, and the World: How ELCA Members See the Connections." Chicago: Evangelical Lutheran Church in America, Office for Research, Planning and Evaluation.

Inskeep, Kenneth W. 2000. "An Evaluation of the 1991 Evangelism Strategy." Chicago: Evangelical Lutheran Church in America, Department for Research and Evaluation.

Jenkins, Elaine. 1997. "Confronting the Sin." Washington, DC: United Methodist Church, General Board of Church and Society and General Commission on Religion and Race.

Jeung, Russell. 2005. *Faithful Generations: Race and New Asian American Churches.* New Brunswick, NJ: Rutgers University Press.

National Council of the Churches of Christ in the U.S.A. 1984. "Policy Statement: On Racial Justice." Racial Justice Working Group of the Division of Church and Society. New York.

Olson, Laura R. 2002. "Mainline Protestant Washington Offices and the Political Lives of Clergy." In *The Quiet Hand of God: Faith-Based Activism and the Public Role of Mainline Protestantism,* ed. Robert Wuthnow and John H. Evans. Berkeley: University of California Press.

Omi, Michael, and Howard Winant. 1986. *Racial Formation in the United States: From the 1960s to the 1980s.* New York: Routledge.

———. 1994. *Racial Formation in the United States: From the 1960s to the 1990s,* 2nd ed. New York: Routledge.

Presbyterian Church (U.S.A.). 1998. "Racial Ethnic/Immigrant Church Growth Strategy." Office of the General Assembly. Louisville, KY.

———. 1999a. "Facing Racism: A Vision of the Beloved Community." Office of the General Assembly. Louisville, KY.

———. 1999b. "Presbyterian Panel: Public Role of Presbyterians—August 1999." Research Services. Louisville, KY.

———. 2000a. "Comprehensive Strategy for Ministry with Native Americans." http://www.pcusa .org/nativeamerican/strategy.htm.

———. 2000b. "Presbyterian Panel: Racism and Racial Justice." Research Services. Louisville, KY.

———. 2005. "Korean Congregational Enhancement." http://www.pcusa.org/korean/index.htm.

———. 2006. "FAQ/Interesting Facts." Research Services. http://www.pcusa.org/research/ statistics_faq.htm.

Roof, Wade Clark, and William McKinney. 1987. *American Mainline Religion: Its Changing Shape and Future.* New Brunswick, NJ: Rutgers University Press.

Takaki, Ronald. 1979. *Iron Cages: Race and Culture in 19th-Century America.* New York: Oxford University Press

———. 1989. *Strangers from a Different Shore: A History of Asian Americans.* Boston: Little, Brown.

Tinker, George E. 1993. *Missionary Conquest: The Gospel and Native American Cultural Genocide.* Minneapolis: Augsburg Fortress Press.

Tuan, Mia. 1999. *Forever Foreigners or Honorary Whites? The Asian Ethnic Experience Today.* New Brunswick, NJ: Rutgers University Press.

United Church of Christ, Justice and Witness Ministries. 2007. "Toxic Wastes and Race at Twenty: 1987–2007." http://www.ucc.org/assets/pdfs/toxic20.pdf.

United Methodist Church, General Commission on Religion and Race. 1992. "Report to the 1992 General Conference." Nashville: United Methodist Church.

———. 2000. "Report to the 2000 General Conference." Nashville: United Methodist Church.

———. 2007. "GCFA Report." Nashville: United Methodist Church.

University Senate and General Commission on Religion and Race Review Team. 2004. "Report of the Special Review of Iliff School of Theology."

Verter, Bradford. 2002. "Furthering the Freedom Struggle: Racial Justice Activism in the Mainline Churches since the Civil Rights Era." In *The Quiet Hand of God: Faith-Based Activism and the Public Role of Mainline Protestantism*, ed. Robert Wuthnow and John H. Evans. Berkeley: University of California Press.

Winant, Howard. 1994. *Racial Conditions: Politics, Theory, and Comparisons*. Minneapolis: University of Minnesota Press.

———. 2001. *The World Is a Ghetto: Race and Democracy Since World War II*. New York: Basic Books.

———. 2004. *The New Politics of Race: Globalism, Difference, Justice*. Minneapolis: University of Minnesota Press.

Wuthnow, Robert. 2002. "Beyond Quiet Influence? Possibilities for the Protestant Mainline." In *The Quiet Hand of God: Faith-Based Activism and the Public Role of Mainline Protestantism*, ed. Robert Wuthnow and John H. Evans. Berkeley: University of California Press.

Wuthnow, Robert, and John H. Evans. 2002. Introduction. In *The Quiet Hand of God: Faith-Based Activism and the Public Role of Mainline Protestantism*, ed. Robert Wuthnow and John H. Evans. Berkeley: University of California Press.

Contributors

ANTONY W. ALUMKAL is Associate Professor of Sociology of Religion at the Iliff School of Theology and serves on the editorial board of the journal *Religions*. He is the author of *Asian American Evangelical Churches: Race, Ethnicity, and Assimilation in the Second Generation* (2003).

CARLOS FIGUEROA received his doctorate in Political Science and Historical Studies from the New School for Social Research, specializing in American political development, U.S. religion and race politics, American and African American politics and political thought, Latino politics in the United States, and interpretive approaches to policy development. His current research explores the intersection of Quakerism and racialism in the context of U.S. insular territorial politics in early-twentieth-century U.S. imperialism. He was born in Rio Piedras, Puerto Rico, and grew up in New York City and central New Jersey.

ROBERT D. FRANCIS is Director of Advocacy and Policy for Lutheran Services in America (LSA), an alliance of the Evangelical Lutheran Church in America (ELCA), the Lutheran Church–Missouri Synod, and their more than three hundred health and human service organizations. Prior to joining LSA, he worked in public policy for Sojourners and then the ELCA. Francis came to public policy work from a background of direct service, including time as an inner-city high school teacher and social worker in Chicago. His articles have been published in the *Journal of Lutheran Ethics*, *The Christian Century*, and *Sojourners*. He holds a master's degree in Social Science from the University of Chicago.

SUSAN M. GORDON holds a doctorate in Political Science from the University of Chicago. She is the author of the article "Integrating Immigrants: Morality and Loyalty in U.S. Naturalization Practice," which appeared in *Citizenship Studies*.

EDWIN I. HERNÁNDEZ, a Research Fellow with the Center for the Study of Latino Religion, is Senior Program Officer for Research, Education, and Congregational Initiatives at the DeVos Family Foundations. A sociologist of religion with a doctoral degree from the University of Notre Dame and a master's of divinity from Andrews University, he investigates Latino religious experience, theological education, congregational studies, and the role of religious leaders in sustaining the life and commitment of socially engaged congregations. His most recent publications are "Gathering of Hope: How Religious Congregations Contribute to the Quality of Life in Kent County" (2008) and the edited book *Emerging Voices, Urgent Choices: Essays on Latino/a Religious Leadership* (2006).

ROBIN DALE JACOBSON is in the Political Science Department at the University of Puget Sound. Her work focuses on immigration politics and the politics of race in the United States. She is author of *The New Nativism* (2008). Her current project looks at issues surrounding the detention of immigrants.

ROBERT P. JONES is the founding CEO of Public Religion Research Institute (PRRI), a nonprofit, nonpartisan research and education organization specializing in work at the intersection of religion, values, and public life. He is a member of the national steering committee for the Religion and Politics Section at the American Academy of Religion and is an active member of the Society of Christian Ethics and the American Association of Public Opinion Research. He holds a doctorate in religion from Emory University and a master's of divinity from Southwestern Baptist Theological Seminary. Before founding PRRI, Jones worked as a research fellow at several think tanks in Washington, D.C., and served as Assistant Professor of Religious Studies at Missouri State University. He is the author of two academic books—*Progressive & Religious* (2008) and *Liberalism's Troubled Search for Equality* (2007)—and numerous peer-reviewed articles on religion and public policy.

JONATHAN I. LEIB is Associate Professor in the Department of Political Science and Geography at Old Dominion University. His research in political geography, cultural geography, and geographies of race and ethnicity has appeared in numerous journals, including *Political Geography*, *Cultural Geographies*, *The Professional Geographer*, *Journal of Geography*, and *Journal of Race and Policy*.

Jessica Hamar Martínez is a doctoral candidate in the Department of Sociology at the University of Arizona. She is also the Project Manager of the Chicago Latino Congregations Study through the Center for the Study of Religion and Society and the Center for the Study of Latino Religion at the University of Notre Dame. Her current research focuses on Latino religious affiliation and the roles of Latino congregations in the lives of their members.

Eric Michael Mazur is the Gloria and David Furman Professor of Judaic Studies at Virginia Wesleyan College, Norfolk. He is the author of *The Americanization of Religious Minorities: Confronting the Constitutional Order* (1999), co-author of *Religion on Trial: How Supreme Court Trends Threaten Freedom of Conscience in America* (with Phillip E. Hammond and David W. Machacek, 2004), co-editor of *God in the Details: American Religion in Popular Culture* (with Kate McCarthy, 2001; 2nd edition, 2010), and editor of *Art and the Religious Impulse* (2002) and *The Encyclopedia of Religion and Film* (2011). He is currently working on a book-length manuscript, "Church and State in America."

Sangay Mishra holds a doctoral degree in Political Science from the University of Southern California, Los Angeles. His research focuses on the political incorporation of South Asians in the United States. He is currently a Postdoctoral Fellow at the University of Southern California. His areas of expertise are racial and ethnic politics, with a special focus on immigrant political incorporation, citizenship, transnationalism, religious identity, multiculturalism, and immigration policy. His essay, "The Limits of Transnational Mobilization: Indian American Lobby Groups and the India-U.S. Nuclear Deal," appeared in an edited collection, *The Transnational Politics of Asian Americans*.

Catherine Paden is Assistant Professor of Political Science at Simmons College. Her research and teaching interests focus on social movements, racial politics, interest groups, and how underrepresented groups gain political representation. Her current research examines the impact of local civil rights and economic justice organizing on national policy and interest group priorities. She is the author of *Civil Rights Advocacy on Behalf of the Poor* (2011), which assesses whether and how low-income African Americans gain representation in antipoverty legislative battles. She holds a doctorate from Northwestern University.

Milagros Peña is Associate Dean of the College of Arts and Sciences and Professor of Sociology and Women's Studies at the University of Florida. She received her doctorate in Sociology from the State University of New York at Stony Brook.

She is the author of *Latina Activists across Borders: Grassroots Women's Organizing in Mexico and Texas* (2007), which was awarded the 2008 Distinguished Book Award by the Latino/a section of the American Sociological Association. Peña co-edited with Edwin I. Hernández the book *Emerging Voices, Urgent Choices: Essays on Latino/a Religious Leadership* (2006). She is also the recipient of a 1995 Fulbright-Hays/Garcia Robles Research Award and author or co-author of multiple books, journal articles, and reports.

Tobin Miller Shearer is Assistant Professor of History at the University of Montana and the coordinator of the African-American Studies Program there. He is the author of *Daily Demonstrators: The Civil Rights Movement in Mennonite Homes and Sanctuaries* (2010) and co-author of *Set Free: A Journey Toward Solidarity against Racism* (2001) Shearer is a frequent lecturer on twentieth-century U.S. religion, the civil rights era, and the Anabaptist community.

Nancy D. Wadsworth is Assistant Professor of Political Science at the University of Denver. Currently she studies cultural and historical aspects of American politics, particularly racial and religious social change movements. She is preparing for publication a book-length manuscript, "Ambivalent Miracles: Evangelical Racial Reconciliation Efforts in American Political Culture."

Gerald R. Webster is Professor and Chair of the Department of Geography, the University of Wyoming. He is the author of more than seventy refereed articles and book chapters, including work appearing in *Political Geography, The Professional Geographer, Geographical Review,* the *Journal of Geography,* and *The Southeastern Geographer.*

Italicized page numbers refer to tables or graphs.

Abbott, Lyman, 68–73; *America in the Making,*
69–70, 73; Christian evolutionary racialist theory of, 18, 68–69, 70–71, 72–73, 74;
on confrontation between races, 69–70;
on dependent peoples, 68–69, 71–72, 74;
on Lake Mohonk Conference attendees as
guests of Smiley, 65, 67; in Lake Mohonk
Conference leadership, 68, 69, 72–73,
76n29, 77n31; as *Outlook* magazine editor,
68, 74, 76n26
Abington School District v. Schempp (1963), 45
"Addressed to White Liberals" (Smith), 109
Advisory Board to the President's Initiative on
Race, 255, 256, 267
affirmative action, 47, 259, 281
African Americans: as category on naturalization form after 1940, 93; and Christian
Coalition's redefinition of religious identity,
177, 179–82, 257; civic and political involvement by race/ethnicity, *158*; Confederate
battle flag as viewed by, 104, 108, 110,
118, 120; in evangelical racial reconciliation politics, 249–70; federal government
in incorporation of, 38; Forman's "Black
Manifesto" and Mennonite church,
207–30; and geographic origin as criterion
for citizenship, 83; immigrants attempt to
distinguish themselves from, 90; increasing public participation of, 41; in mainline
Protestantism, 277–78, 292; Mennonites,
208, 212, 213, 216, 218, 219, 220, 221; migration north during Great Depression,
192; Million Man March of 1995, 202, 255;
and "model minority" discourse, 246n6;
multiple fields affect voting behavior of,
140; Muslims, 233, 246n3; political mobilization among, 195–97; race and Southern
identity, 107–8; race as predictor of voting
behavior, 139–40, *141*; religion in enduring
and overcoming racism, 2, 18; support for
Kerry by race, 133, *134*; variable definitions
of blackness, 14. *See also* black church; civil
rights movement; Nation of Islam; slavery
African Methodist Episcopal Church, 118, 253,
283
African Methodist Zion Episcopal Church,
118, 283
Ali, Muhammad, 196
Alumkal, Antony W., 21–22, 209, 213, 258
America in the Making (Abbott), 69–70, 73
American Civil Liberties Union (ACLU),
238–39
American Enterprise Institute, 171
American Family Association, 119, 170
American Friends Service Committee, 76n10
American Indian Religious Freedom Act
(1978), 42
Americanism, 87, 88, 89, 90, 91, 94

American Jewish Committee, 85, 93

American Values Survey, 145n2

Amish, 45, 50, 52n12, 208

Anabaptists, 207

anthropological view of race, 82, 90

anti-Semitism, 92, 93

Armenians, 83, 85, 89, 98n8

Asians: in evangelical racial reconciliation politics, 249; immigration acts stop all immigration from Asia, 98n5; Jews as Asiatics, 86; in mainline Protestantism, 277, 278; as "model minority," 278. *See also* Chinese; Indians (Asian)

assimilation, 87–91; Jews' either/or approach to, 83, 91, 96; mainline Protestantism demands of minorities, 291; multiculturalism contrasted with, 241; reconciling difference and, 91–97; segmented, 92. *See also* melting pot

Ayers, Edward, 108

Baptists: increasing power over time, 15; and mainline Protestantism, 295n1; in the South, 111; Southern Baptist Convention, 119, 170, 214, 253, 255, 262; split over slavery before Civil War, 112

Barnes, Roy, 107, 120

Barrett, James, 90

Beasley, David, 116, 118

Beecher, Henry Ward, 65

Benedict, Ruth, 92

Benjamin, Philip S., 66

Berea College v. Commonwealth of Kentucky (1908), 42–43, 45

Berkson, Isaac, 87, 91

Bessinger, Maurice, 114

Bhartiya Janata Party (BJP), 247n13

Bible: King James, 44; literalism, 165, 270n1; Nation of Islam's Fard on, 192; reading in schools, 45; traditionalists versus modernists on, 145n4

Biblical View of Slavery, The (Bessinger), 114

Birth of a Nation, The (film), 106

black Americans. *See* African Americans

black church: and Christian Right, 173; in civil rights movement, 8, 23n9, 118, 120, 195; class orientation of, 195–96; conservatism of black Protestants, 127–28, 172–73; geographic location of, 130; and mainline Protestant diversity goals, 289; moral values as political issue in, 135, *136*; Nation of Islam's political involvement compared with that of, 191, 195–97; origins of, 112, 253; political activity of, 8, 195; on political party friendliness toward religion, 137, *137*; religious orientations of, *131*; seen as voting Democratic, 128–29, 131–32, 139; as target of violence, 103, 119, 179–80; traditionalists in, 130; white evangelicals and black Protestants compared, 129–32, 145n3

"Black Manifesto To the White Christian Church and the Jewish Synagogues in the United States of America and All Other Racist Institutions" (Forman), 207–30; conversations nourished by, 217; legacy of, 219–24; Methodists' response to, 223; public opinion on, 207; reparations demanded by, 207, 209, 210, 211, 212, 214, 215, 217, 224; Urban Racial Council promotes, 208, 213–16

Black Muslims. *See* Nation of Islam

black women: intersectional approach to, 10; Nation of Islam's appeal to low-income, 196; in Nation of Islam's moral code, 198

Board of Education of Kiryas Joel v. Grumet (1994), 46

Board of Indian Commissioners, 61

Boas, Franz, 82, 92

Bob Jones University v. United States (1983), 45, 52n13

Bonilla-Silva, Eduardo, 289

Bonner, R. E., 105

Bositis, David, 202

Bourdieu, Pierre, 128, 129, 138

Bowen v. Roy (1986), 42

Brelsford, Theodore, 277

bridging social capital, 270n6

Brown, Hubert, 216, 217–18

Brown v. Board of Education (1954), 46–47, 106

Bryce, James, 77n30

Buchanan, Pat, 175
Buddhism: as expression of overall American religion, 94; South Asians, 231; targeting of Buddhists after September 11, 235
Burgess, Larry E., 66
Burwell, Rebecca, 159
Bush, George H. W., 131, 145n6
Bush, George W.: black Americans' support for, 140, 173; church attendance and support for, 132–33, 141; on immigration, 171; Latino support for war in Iraq, 152, 153, 154, 158, 164; Muslim Americans defended by, 1; values voters' support for, 133, 134; white Americans who were not Protestants vote for, 145n6; white evangelicals' support for, 130
Butler, Judith, 14

Calhoun-Brown, Allison, 173
California: Christian Coalition expands in, 176–77; Proposition 187 of, 175, 176, 181; recall election of 2003 in, 182
Campaign for Immigration Reform, 165
Carby, Hazel, 241
Catholicism. See Roman Catholicism
Cato Institute, 171
Census Bureau, 50
centrists, 130, 145n4
Chamberlain, Houston Stewart, 85
Chan, Suchen, 233–34
Charlton, Paul, 63
Cherokee Nation v. Georgia (1831), 41
Chesler, Mark, 281
Chicago: Latino Congregations Study, 159–63, 166–67; Nation of Islam moves headquarters to, 193; Harold Washington's mayoral campaign, 200
Chinese: debate over immigration of, 7, 23n7; feelings of vulnerability after 9/11, 97
Chinese Exclusion Act: of 1864, 99n23; of 1882, 81, 83
Christian American (Christian Coalition), 175, 176, 177, 178, 179, 181
Christian Coalition: in California, 176–77; expanded agenda rejected by, 184; on immigration, 175–85; "Minority Myths Exploded: Poll Shows Minorities Hold Traditional Values" survey, 180; multicultural movement compared with, 178; "Muslims and the Judeo-Christian World—Where to From Here?," 182–83; organizational decline since late 1990s, 172, 182, 183–84; privileges religion over race, 177–79; and race, 177–82; "Racial Reconciliation Sunday" campaign, 257; redefines religious identity, 177, 179–82; on religion in American identity, 20, 178; rewrites its racial-political identity, 174, 257; "Road to Victory" conference of 1991, 176; Samaritan Project, 180–81, 257; victim stance assumed by, 178; voter education brochure in Spanish, 181
Christian Identity movement, 258, 259
Christianity: Abbott's Christian evolutionary racialism, 18, 68–69, 70–71, 72–73, 74; America characterized as Christian nation, 22n3, 88, 178–79; Americanism equated with, 89; civilization associated with, 6, 85; in Confederate flag debate, 19, 113–20; de-Christianization of U.S. during and after World War II, 94; home-schooling by conservatives, 50; as racialized, 5; segregation supported by, 23n8; in slavery debate, 6, 112, 114–15, 120, 209; whiteness associated with, 2. See also Bible; Protestantism; Roman Catholicism
Christianity Today (magazine), 255, 256
Christian Methodist Episcopal Church, 283
Christian Right: aggressive style compared with mainline Protestantism, 276; black evangelicals not mobilized by, 173; decline of organizations in, 183–84; and immigration, 170–86; political scientists taken by surprise by, 250; as predominantly white, 172–74, 184; and race, 170, 171–74; Republican Party support in, 173; scholarly attention paid to, 128; on values voters, 134; in Winant's racial project framework, 258. See also Christian Coalition
Christian Science, 36
Christians for Comprehensive Immigration Reform, 184

Christian Union (weekly), 68

Christmas, 89

Church of God in Christ, 253

citizenship: for Chinese, 7, 23n7; geographic origin as criterion for, 83–86; nonwhites excluded from, 81–82, 86–87; public education for, 44, 49–50; race and religion in co-creation of, 74; religious tests for, 6

Citizenship Day, 94

Civil Rights Act (1866), 39, 41, 46–47, 52n6

civil rights movement: black church in, 8, 23n9, 118, 120, 195; Confederate battle flag and, 103, 106, 116; Lost Cause civil religion as backlash to, 115; multiculturalist turn after civil rights era, 241; and poverty, 204n9; racial projects of remains of, 279; Southern Christian Leadership Conference, 8, 9, 118; in Southern history, 103

Civil War, 103, 111, 112, 113, 114, 117, 120

Civil War (Reconstruction) Amendments: and Chinese citizenship, 7, 23n7; Fifteenth Amendment, 7, 41, 23n7; Fourteenth Amendment, 7, 43; and Native American rights, 41

class: civil rights movement and poverty, 204n9; distinctions among South Asians, 234; intersection with other categories, 11, 15; low-income African Americans as primary constituency of Nation of Islam, 189, 191, 194, 195, 196, 197–99, 212; of mainline Protestantism, 276, 286; as not static, 14; orientation of black church, 195–96; religion's constitutional protection contrasted with, 16

Clegg, Andrew Claude, III, 199

Clinton, Bill, 131, 145n6, 255, 256, 267

Cohen, Cathy J., 196

Cohen, Jon, 135

Collins, Lee, 108, 109–10

color-blind understandings of race, 174, 176, 260, 264, 279, 289

Combs, Roberta, 182, 183

Compassion Fund (Minorities Ministries Council), 216, 218, 221

Coney Island Avenue Project, 245

Confederate battle flag: African American view of, 104, 108, 110, 118, 120; Christianity in debate over, 19; and civil rights movement, 103, 106, 116; in "culture wars" context, 116; history of, 104–7; race and religion in opposition to, 118–20; race and religion in support of, 113–17; religious dimension of, 105–6, 114; at state capitols, 104, 107, 116–17, 118, 119–20; on state flags, 107, 108, 115, 117, 118–19, 120–21; as white symbol, 108, 109–11

Confronting the Sin (United Methodist Church), 282

Congregationalists, 276

Congressional Black Caucus, 201–2

Conservative Jews, 95, 99n20

Constitution of the United States, 33–55; First Amendment, 38; religion protected under, 16–17. *See also* Civil War (Reconstruction) Amendments

Consultation on Church Union, 283

"coolie" labor, 7

Corbett, Henry W., 7

Cortez, Luis, 167n4

Council of American-Islamic Relations (CAIR), 244–45, 247n15

Council of Conservative Citizens, 119–20

Council of Pakistani American Affairs, 245

Council of Pakistani Professionals, 245

Council of People's Organizations, 245

Cox, Daniel, 145n2

Cripps, John Thomas, 114, 115, 117

Crist, Raymond, 85

critical race theory, 108–11

Crossfire (film), 92

Crumbley, Larry, 225n9

"culture wars," 116

Darwinism, 82, 84

Davenport, Harold, 219, 225n9

Davidson, Charles, 114–15

Davis, Jefferson, 106, 113

Declaration of Independence, 33, 51

DeJesus, Artemio, 225n9

Democratic Party: black Americans who are

not Protestant vote for, 131; black Protestants seen as voting for, 128–29, 131–32, 139; church attendance and support for, 132–33, 139; "God gap" attributed to, 127, 128, 132–33; "God problem" for, 127, 128, 136–37; Latino religion and political identification, 150, 152, 158, 164; pragmatic liberalism of, 279; race as predictor of voting for, 139–40; Reagan Democrats, 258, 259

Desis Rising and Moving, 245

Dewey, John, 44

DeYmaz, Mark, 269

Dillingham Commission, 82

Disciples of Christ, 276, 283

discrimination: against Jews, 90; reverse, 47. *See also* segregation

diversity: Jewish intellectuals promote, 93; mainline Protestantism's goals for, 289–90; political aspect of religious, 94–95; positive images begin to appear, 92

"Divided by Faith" (Yancey), 263

Diwali, 242

Dixiecrat Party, 106

Dole, Bob, 131, 145n6

Drachsler, Julius, 87

Dred Scott v. Sanford (1857), 35, 81

Du Bois, W. E. B., 4, 108–9

Eagle Forum, 170

Eastern European immigrants, 82, 83, 84, 90, 98n5, 233, 236

education. *See* public education

education reform, 269

Emerson, Michael O., 129, 131, 225n13, 257, 270n4

Employment Division, Department of Human Resources of the State of Oregon v. Smith: 1988 case, 42; 1990 case, 42

empowerment, 291–92

Engel v. Vitale (1962), 45

environmental racism, 285

Episcopal Church: in Consultation on Church Union, 283; empowerment for minorities in, 292; in mainline Protestantism, 275, 276; white membership of, 276–77

Epperson v. Arkansas (1968), 45

"Erasing Racism" (Consultation on Church Union), 283

Esperanza, 165

essentialism, 241

establishment, 5

Ethics and Religious Liberty Commission, 170

ethnicity: cultural recognition through religious recognition, 242; Jewish intellectuals promote term, 87, 91; panethnic Asian mainline Protestant congregations, 277; race and, 39–40, 91; South Asians as panethnic, 231, 233, 240, 245. *See also* multiethnic church movement; race

Eubanks, Bobby, 117

eugenics, 82, 90

Evangelical Lutheran Church. *See* Lutherans

evangelical Protestantism: black evangelicals not mobilized by Christian Right, 173; black Protestants and white evangelicals compared, 129–32, 145n3; characteristics of, 270n1; division over slavery, 253; geographic location of, 130; on immigration, 171; increasing public participation of, 36; Latino, 150, 154, 159–63, 165, 167n3; mainline denominations versus, 23n8, 296n7; marginalized by forces of modernism, 15; moral values as political issue in, 135, *136*; on political party friendliness toward religion, 137, *137*; racial reconciliation movement, 249–74; religious orientations of, *131*; on solution to racism, 284; in the South, 111, 130; traditionalists in, 130, 270n1; vote favors Republicans, 128, 129–32, 139, 145n3

Evans, Hiram Wesley, 83

Evans, John H., 276

Everson v. Board of Education (1947), 45

Executive Order 9981, 41

"Facing Racism" (Presbyterian Church [U.S.A.]), 288

faith-based initiatives, 8, 259

faith-versus-works doctrine, 35

Falwell, Jerry, 255

Families First on Immigration, 170, 185n1

Family Research Council, 134, 171

family reunification provision of nationality Act of 1965, 234

"family values" policies, 8

Fard, W. D., 191–92, 198, 199

Farrakhan, Louis: becomes National Representative, 193; failing health of, 203; increasing involvement with political mainstream, 190; Jesse Jackson endorsed by, 201, 204n8; Million Man March of 1995, 202, 255; Nation of Islam reestablished by, 194; on third force in politics, 202–3; on voices of the poor, 190; on voting, 189, 190, 201, 202; Harold Washington endorsed by, 200

Far Right, 258, 262, 263, 279

Feder, Don, 181

Federal Council of Churches, 276

federal government: as guarantor of freedom of conscience, 36, 38; incorporates those beyond Euro-American Protestant culture, 38; legislation on Native American religion, 42; liberated from nongovernmental systems, 37; mainline Protestants lobby, 284–85; radical individualism and the state, 48–50; stages of development of, 35, 51n1. See also Supreme Court

federalism, 35–36

Fessenden, Tracy, 48

field (Bourdieu), 138

Fifteenth Amendment, 7, 41, 23n7

Figueroa, Carlos, 18–19

First Amendment, 38

Flint, Colin, 110

Fordice, Kirk, 178

foreigners, trope of, 236. See also immigration

Forman, James, 207, 209–10, 218, 219, 220, 224

Forman, Tyrone A., 289

Foster, Charles R., 277

Fourteenth Amendment, 7, 43

Fox, George, 57–58, 63, 64, 66

Francis, Robert D., 20

Frank, Jerome N., 91

Frank, Leo, 98n9

Frankfurter, Felix, 45

Franklin, Bobby, 121

free exercise of religion: free speech claims associated with, 38; in redefinition of religion in 1940s, 94; in Virginia Declaration of Rights, 35. See also religious liberty

free speech, 38

Fruit of Islam, 194

Furman, Richard, 112

Garcia, F. Chris, 149

García Bedolla, Lisa, 15

Gates, Merrill E., 76n24

gender: intersection with other categories, 11, 15, 34; religion's constitutional protection contrasted with, 16

General Allotment Act (1887), 41

Genesis, 39

Gentleman's Agreement (1906), 99n23

Gentleman's Agreement (film), 92, 98n13

geographic origin, 83–86

Georgia Committee to Save the State Flag, 108, 109

German Americans, 88

Ghost Dance movement, 42

Gilbreath, Edward, 271n11

Gitlow v. New York (1925), 35

golden rule, 94–95, 99n19

Goldsboro Christian Schools, 52n13

Gone With the Wind (film), 106

Gonzalez, Jose, 225n9

Gordon, Susan M., 19

Gore, Al, 131, 145n6

Graham, Billy, 255

Grant, Madison, 84

Grant, Ulysses S., 42

Greeley, Andrew M., 129, 173

Green, John, 130

Guiding Perspectives for Social Statements (Evangelical Lutheran Church), 288

Gwinn, Macon, 225n9

habitus, 138

Hadden, Jeffrey K., 286

Ham, curse of, 6, 22n6, 39

Hamilton, Dona Cooper and Charles V., 204n9

Hancock, Anne Marie, 10, 24n14
Harding, Vincent, 218
Harlan, John Marshall, 42–43, 45
Harlem Evangelistic Association, 253
Harris, James, 225n9
Harrison, Earl G., 93
Harvey, Paul, 113, 253, 262
Hassan, Waqar, 235
Hattam, Victoria, 87
Hawkins, Russell, 129, 131
Hazard, Henry, 93
Hebrew Free Loan Society, 95
Hebrew Immigrant Aid Society, 95
Hennington v. Georgia (1896), 51n4
Herberg, Will, 92, 96–97
Heritage Foundation, 171
Hernández, Edwin I., 20
Hershey, Lynford, 216–17, 218, 221
He's My Brother: Former Racial Foes Offer Strategy for Reconciliation (Perkins and Tarrants), 256
Hess, Mahlon, 214
Higby, William, 7
Hill, Michael, 113–14
Hill, Samuel S., Jr., 150, 162
Hinduism: as expression of overall American religion, 94; "Hindu" as racial category, 8, 233; Hindus distinguish themselves from Muslims, 243; mobilization against racial targeting, 243–44; multiculturalism and cultural recognition of, 242–43; political, 243, 247n13; South Asians, 231, 232, 246n2; targeting of Hindus after September 11, 235
Hines, Samuel, 254
Hinshaw, David, 60
Hispanics. *See* Latinos (Hispanics)
Hollingshead, August, 96, 97
home-schooling, 50
Hoover, Herbert, 88
Hout, Michael, 129, 173
Hoyer, Steny, 201
Hunter, Joel C., 184

Ignatiev, Noel, 259
Iliff School of Theology, 276, 292–94

immigration: assimilation urged on immigrants, 87–91; bureaucracies use geography and religion in defining race, 19; California Proposition 187 and, 175, 176; Christian Coalition and, 175–85; Christian Right and, 170–86; Jewish immigrants, 80–102; Latino response to debate, 165–66; Lutheran Immigration and Refugee Service, 285; "Policy Statement: On Racial Justice" on, 282; as racialized, 80, 170, 171, 181; religion foregrounded in political mobilizations, 231, 241–44; Republican Party on, 171, 175; South Asians, 231–48
imperialism: Abbott on, 69, 70, 71–72; beginning of modern U.S., 56; Lake Mohonk Conference debates on, 18, 57, 62, 63, 66
Indian Citizenship Act (1924), 41
Indian Civil Rights Act (1968), 41
Indian Reorganization (Wheeler-Howard) Act (1934), 41
Indians (American). *See* Native Americans
Indians (Asian): "Hindu" as racial category, 8, 233; South Asians, 231–48; *United States v. Bhagat Singh Thind*, 40, 42, 246n5; as white, 83. *See also* Hinduism; Sikhs
individualism, radical, 48–50
Inner Light, 58, 60, 61, 64, 74
integration: *Brown v. Board of Education*, 46–47, 106; Confederate battle flag as symbol of opposition to, 106; desegregation of military, 41; Warith Deen Muhammad emphasizes, 194; racially integrated Christian communities, 249
intersectional scholarship, 9–17, 34, 24n15, 24n17
Irish, 13, 86, 233
Islam: African American Muslims, 233, 246n3; Christian Coalition's "Muslims and the Judeo-Christian World—Where to From Here?," 182–83; Christianity forced upon African Muslims, 6, 253; Congress opened with Muslim prayer, 179; as expression of overall American religion, 94; Farrakhan on racism in, 194; Hindus distinguish themselves from Muslims, 243; mobilization by

Islam (*continued*)
Muslims against racial targeting, 244–45; Muslim feelings of vulnerability after 9/11, 97, 238–40; Obama believed to be Muslim, 1, 2, 3, 50; planned Islamic center in downtown New York, 1; as racialized in U.S., 13; religion makes Muslims' Americanism suspect, 88; South Asians, 231, 232–33. *See also* Nation of Islam

Jackson, Jesse, 180, 201, 203, 204n8
Jackson, Raymond, 219, 225n9
Jackson, Robert H., 45
Jackson, Stonewall, 105, 113
Jacobson, Matthew, 39, 98n13
Jacobson, Robin Dale, 20, 85, 208, 215
Jefferson, Thomas, 35–36
Jehovah's Witnesses, 36, 38, 50, 276
Jeung, Russell, 277
Jewish Committee of New York City, 85
Jewish Community Center, 95
Jewish Theological Seminary, 93, 98n16
Jews: assimilation urged for, 88–91; deracializing of, 19, 91–94, 96, 97; desire to maintain their cultural uniqueness, 89, 90, 96; discrimination against, 90; either/or approach to assimilation in, 83, 91, 96; Forman's "Black Manifesto" names, 207, 209, 220; and geographic origin as criterion for citizenship, 83–86; as Hebrew race, 86, 87, 93–94; increasing public participation of, 36, 40–41; "Jewish or American" dichotomy, 81; Judaism as expression of overall American religion, 92, 94, 96–97; marrying outside their faith, 99n20; in multiculturalist turn, 241; Nation of Islam's anti-Semitism, 202, 204n8; race, national identity, and changing circumstances of immigrants to U.S., 80–102; religion becomes more civic, 95; religious difference of, 88, 89; trope of the foreigner applied to, 236; Western versus Eastern, 83–84, 86; as white, 80, 87, 88, 89, 96, 97
Jim Crow. *See* segregation
job advertisements, 90

Johnson, James A., 23n7
Jones, Bob, III, 119–20
Jones, Robert P., 20, 145n2
Jones, Rufus M., 65
Jones-Correa, Michael A., 150, 162
Judaism. *See* Jews
Judeo-Christian tradition: Islam and, 179, 182–83; Jewish intellectuals promote concept of, 93; Reed on, 179; whiteness associated with, 3

Kallen, Horace, 87, 91
Kazin, Alfred, 91
Kennedy, John F., 40, 51
Kennedy, John F., Jr., 201
Kennedy, Robert F., 106
Kennedy, Ruby Jo Reeves, 92
Kerry, John: black Protestants' support for, 130; church attendance and support for, 132–33; positions contradict Catholic Church, 53n17; support by race, 133, 134; values voters' support for, 133, 134
King, Desmond, 174, 177, 181, 185
King, Martin Luther, Jr., 211, 220, 224, 254
Korean Americans, 292
Kroeber, Alfred, 91
Ku Klux Klan, 83, 85, 106, 256, 258, 259
Kurien, Prema, 242

Lake Mohonk Conference: Abbott in leadership of, 68, 69, 72–73, 76n29, 77n31; attendees of, 75n4; as battleground for imperialism, 18, 57, 62, 63, 66; context of emergence of, 60; influence of, 75n4; name changes of, 75n4; pragmatic Quakerism at, 61–62, 64; Quaker business meetings compared with, 65–66; racialism of, 18–19, 61; Smiley in creation of, 60–61; Smiley screens guests and speakers, 65, 66, 67; unanimity sought by Smiley at, 64–68; on worth of other races, 56
Land, Richard, 170
Landis, Paul, 211–12, 214, 215, 216, 217, 218, 219, 220, 222
Langer, Gary, 135

Latinos (Hispanics): and Christian Coalition's redefinition of religious identity, 180, 257; Christian Right and social views of Catholics, 173; congregational context and political lives of, 150–51, 159–63, 164; ethnic identity related to religious worship in, 150; in evangelical racial reconciliation politics, 249, 264–65, 266; issues of importance to, 8, 153–54, 155, 164; as largest and fastest-growing ethnic group, 149; look to religious leaders for political guidance, 151; in mainline Protestantism, 278; majority identify as Catholic, 150; Mennonites, 213, 218, 219, 221; on "moral values" issues, 153–54; political participation by, 149, 154–57, 156, 157, 158; political party alignment, 153; problematic nature of "Latino," 149; racism among, 283–84; religion and political behavior of, 20, 149–69; religious intensity and political alignment among, 152; religious leaders and politics, 161, 162, 163; support for George W. Bush's management of war in Iraq, 152, 153, 154, 158, 164; support for Kerry by race, 133, 134; "two-pronged" approach of religious leaders, 159

Layman, Geoffrey, 132

League of the South, 110–11, 113–14, 115

Leal, David L., 150, 162

Lee, Daniel, 39

Lee, Robert E., 113, 121

Lee, Wen Ho, 97

Lee v. Weisman (1992), 45–46

Leib, Jonathan I., 19

liberalism, pragmatic, 279–80, 282, 284, 289, 295

liberation theology, 254

Lichterman, Paul, 270n6

Lincoln, C. Eric, 196, 198

Lippmann, Walter, 91

Lochner v. New York (1905), 35

Lost Cause civil religion, 113, 114, 115–16

Louima, Abner, 255

Lutheran Immigration and Refugee Service, 285

Lutherans: diversity goals of, 289; formation of Evangelical Lutheran Church, 296n10; ideological divide between leaders and laity in, 286–88, 296n9; Lutheran Immigration and Refugee Service, 285; in mainline Protestantism, 275, 276; as other, 39; power sharing with minorities, 291, 292; white membership of, 277

Lyng v. Northwest Indian Cemetery Protective Association (1988), 42

MacCulloch, Diarmaid, 59

Maddox, Lucy, 69

Madison, James, 48–49

Mahler, Sarah J., 150

mainline Protestantism, 275–98; advocacy by, 284–86; antiracism training curricula of, 287; commitment to intellectual respectability, 275; conflicted racial stance of, 209; decline in power and membership of, 275, 276; denominations of, 275; diversity goals difficult to achieve, 289–90; versus evangelicals, 23n8, 296n7; ideological divide between leaders and laity, 21–22, 286–89, 295; Iliff School of Theology investigation, 292–94; Latino, 150, 159–63, 165; lobbying federal government by, 284–85; monopoly over American culture declines, 36–37, 44, 45; "new breed" of clergy in, 286; past studies on race and, 277–78; paternalism attributed to, 290–91; pragmatic liberalism of, 280; racial discourse of leadership of, 280–84, 295; racial formation theory and, 278–80; segregation in, 280; social location of, 276–77; term as problematic, 276; white memberships in, 276–77, 289

Malcolm X, 193, 196, 197

Maldonado, David, 293, 294

Malhotra, Rajiv, 244

Mamiya, Lawrence H., 194, 196, 198

Manis, Andrew, 116, 118, 120

Marshall, Louis, 85

Martínez, Jessica Hamar, 20

Martínez, Lisa M., 149

Mazur, Eric Michael, 18, 81, 95

McCartney, Bill, 256

McCloskey, Robert, 35

McCollum v. Board of Education (1948), 45

McLaughlin, Megan E., 196

melting pot: Christian Coalition on, 182; Fordice on, 178; "Policy Statement: On Racial Justice" on, 281; triple, 92

Mennonites, 207–8; Forman's "Black Manifesto" and, 207–30; Fresh Air rural hosting program, 222; gap between urban and rural, 217; Lancaster Conference of, 207, 208; in military service, 212; nonresistance doctrine of nonviolence of, 208, 211–12, 222; peace churches, 52n12; Powell's recommendations to, 213–15; public harassment for their pacifism, 210; on reconciled relationships, 21, 223–24; urban mission programs of, 210, 220, 222

Methodists: *Confronting the Sin*, 282; in Consultation on Church Union, 283; diversity goals of, 290; Forman's "Black Manifesto" distributed by, 223; global membership of, 295n3; Iliff School of Theology investigation, 292–94; in mainline Protestantism, 275, 276; more complex discourse of race in, 283–84; power sharing with minorities, 291–92; split over slavery before Civil War, 112

Miles, William Porcher, 105

military: depicted as integrated in World War II films, 92–93; desegregation of, 41

Miller, Watson B., 98n14

Miller, Zell, 109–10

Million Man March (1995), 202, 255

Mills, James, 117

Minersville School District v. Gobitis (1940), 50

minorities: fear of growing power of, 3; in mainline Protestantism, 280, 289–92; "model minority" discourse, 235, 246n6, 278; multiculturalist turn results from movements of, 241; racism in, 282–84, 295n6. *See also* ethnicity; race; *and specific groups by name*

Minorities Ministries Council, 216–17, 218–19, 220–23

"Minority Myths Exploded: Poll Shows Minorities Hold Traditional Values" (Christian Coalition), 180

Miranda, Jesse, 167n4

Mishra, Sangay, 21

Mission Mississippi, 271n13

Mississippi College, 119

Mississippi Religious Leadership Conference, 119

"model minority" discourse, 235, 246n6, 278

modernists, 15, 130, 145n4

Montagu, Ashley, 92

"Moral Defense of the Confederate Flag, A," 116

moral values: "family values" policies, 8; Latino concern about, 153–54; Nation of Islam's moral code, 198; as political issue, 127, 134, 135; values voters, 127, 132, 133–36; variation in meaning of, 135–36

Morley, Patrick, 271n14

Mormons: increasing public participation of, 36; polygamy, 15, 39–40; Supreme Court reduces territorial authority of, 51n5

Morone, James A., 6, 270n5

Mosaix Global Network, 269

Muhammad, Elijah, 192–93, 194, 198, 199, 200

Muhammad, Khalid, 202

Muhammad, Warith Deen, 193–95

multiculturalism: Christian Coalition compared with, 178; Christian Coalition opposes, 181; criticisms of, 241; emphasis on particular identities, 231, 240–46; neoconservative critiques of, 259; in official political discourse, 240–41

multiethnic church movement: combining their efforts, 268; as extending racial reconciliation discourse, 251; Mosaix Global Network for, 269; politics avoided by, 261, 264; positive and negative potential of, 269–70; proliferation of intentionally multiethnic churches, 249, 251; on racial division as sin, 263; as racial project, 258; relationship building in, 264; Skinner as catalyst for, 253. *See also* racial reconciliation movement

multiracial persons, 284

Musgrove, Ronnie, 115

Muslims. *See* Islam

"Muslims and the Judeo-Christian World—

Where to From Here?" (Christian Coalition), 182–83
Myrdal, Gunnar, 250
"Myth of Racial Progress, The" (Tapía), 256

National Association for the Advancement of Colored People (NAACP), 197
National Baptist Coalition, 253
National Black Economic Development Conference (NBEDC), 207
National Council of Churches of Christ in the U.S.A., 281–82
Nationality Act (1965), 234
National Origins Act (1924), 83–86, 234
National Security Entry-Exit Registration System (NSEERS), 239
National Survey of Latinos (Pew Hispanic Center), 151–52
National Urban League, 197
Nation of Islam, 189–206; agreement with Congressional Black Caucus, 201–2; anti-Semitism of, 202, 204n8; behavioral regulation by, 197–98; black church compared with, 191, 195–97; cooperation with Christians, 196–97; economic self-sufficiency as goal of, 193, 197–98, 202; Farrakhan reestablishes, 194; Farrakhan's future replacement, 203; founding of, 191–92; founding doctrines of, 189; future political course as unknown, 202–4; government contracts for, 202; identifies with Afro-Asia, 199; low-income African Americans as primary constituency of, 189, 191, 194, 195, 196, 197–99, 212; middle-class support for, 198–99; moral code of, 198; Elijah Muhammad becomes head of, 192–93; Warith Deen Muhammad as leader of, 193–95; organizational and class divisions within, 193–95; prison outreach of, 196; shift away from consciously apolitical body, 20–21, 189–90, 199–202; on whites, 199
Native American Graves Protection and Repatriation Act (1990), 42
Native American Ministry Project, 285
Native Americans: Christianity forced upon, 6; continued marginalization of, 41–42; image changes in World War II films, 93; mainline Protestant advocacy for, 285; in mainline Protestantism, 278; Presbyterian ministries to, 291; seen as needing religious conversion, 42; Smiley on Board of Indian Commissioners, 61
nativism, 13, 171, 172, 175, 176, 181
neo-Confederate groups, 110, 113–14, 116, 119
neoconservatism: of Christian Coalition, 257; on dismantling state policies that reduce inequality, 289; racial reconciliation movement seen as manifestation of, 249, 250, 260, 264, 268; in Winant's racial projects schema, 250, 258–59, 279
neoliberalism, 259–60, 268
new abolitionism, 259, 260, 268
New Right, 258, 259, 279, 289
New York Taxi Workers Alliance, 245
9/11. See September 11, 2001
Noll, Mark, 33–34, 35, 45, 51n1
Northwest Ordinance (1787), 52n11

Obama, Barack: believed to be Muslim, 1, 2, 3, 50; Diwali celebrated by, 242; election as transformation, 51; as neoliberal, 259; as "postracial," 50; racial otherness equated with religious otherness, 2, 3; Wright denounced by, 1
Olson, Laura R., 284
Omi, Michael, 171–72, 177, 232, 278, 279, 289, 295n6
Open Secret (film), 92
Orren, Karen, 35
Orthodox Christians, 88, 94, 276
Orthodox Jews, 95, 99n20
Ottoman Empire, citizenship refused to immigrants from, 85, 89, 98n8
Outlook (magazine), 68, 74, 76n26
Owen, Dennis E., 150, 162

Paden, Catherine, 20–21, 212
Pannell, Richard, 225n9
Parents Involved in Community Schools v. Seattle School District #1 (2007), 18, 47
Parks, Gordon, 197
"partnership" books, 256

Pascoe, Peggy, 82
Passing of the Great Race, The (Grant), 84
Patel, Vasudev, 235
paternalism, 290–91
Paul III, Pope, 42
peace churches, 52n12
Peace Policy (Grant), 42
Peña, Milagros, 20
Penn, William, 59, 76n22
Perkins, John, 254, 262, 271n13
Pew Forum, 139, 146n10
Pew Hispanic Center, 150, 151, 153, 154
Philippines: Abbott on, 68, 69, 71–72; Filipino as category on naturalization form after 1940, 93; Smiley on, 62, 63; U.S. acquires, 56–57
Pierce v. Society of Sisters (1925), 45
Plessy v. Ferguson (1896), 43, 46–47
pluralism: Christian Coalition focuses on, 178–79; gradual integration of European nonwhites, 40–41; Jewish intellectuals promote, 87, 91, 93; of pragmatic liberalism, 279–80, 289
"Policy Statement: On Racial Justice" (National Council of Churches of Christ in the U.S.A.), 281–82, 283
political behavior: African American political mobilization, 195–97; conservative backlash, 8; Dixiecrat Party, 106; Nation of Islam in, 189–206; political Hinduism, 243, 247n13; Quakerism and racialism in early twentieth-century U.S., 56–79; race and religion as competing forces affecting voting behavior, 138–40; race and religion in discourse of, 3, 127–48; religion and Latino political behavior, 20, 149–69; religion foregrounded immigrant in political mobilizations, 231, 241–44; religious tests for participation, 36, 81. *See also* Christian Right; Democratic Party; Republican Party
polygamy, 15, 39–40
polygenesis, 6
Ponce v. Roman Catholic Apostolic Church (1908), 51n4
Powell, John, 213–15, 216, 217–19, 220–22, 223

pragmatic liberalism, 279–80, 282, 284, 289, 295
Prashad, Vijay, 239, 243
Prejudice (film), 92
Prentiss, Craig, 39
Presbyterians: "Comprehensive Strategy for Ministry with Native Americans," 291; in Consultation on Church Union, 283; diversity goals of, 289, 290; empowerment of Korean Americans in, 292; ideological divide between mainline Protestant leaders and laity in, 286, 288; in mainline Protestantism, 275, 276; Native American Ministry Project, 285; paternalism attributed to, 291; Presbyterian Panel surveys, 286, 290; white membership of, 277
Princeton Religion and Politics Survey, 157
Progressive National Baptist Convention, 118
Promise Keepers, 256, 257, 260, 263, 265–66, 267
Proposition 187 (California), 175, 176, 181
Protestant-Catholic-Jew (Herberg), 92, 96–97
Protestantism: assimilating immigrants into, 88; disestablishment of, 49; as engine of racial dynamism, 39–44; as expression of overall American religion, 92, 94, 96–97; in first phase of federal institutional development, 35–36; freedom of conscience in, 48; Latino religion and political identification, 150–67; loses its monopoly over construction of meaning, 49, 95; mainline versus evangelical denominations, 23n8, 296n7; in public education, 44–45, 48; race associated with non-Protestantism, 39; radical individualism replaces group-based constructions of identity, 33–34; social gospel, 69; Supreme Court decisions make nearly complete break with, 38; transition from Protestant nationalism to Republican Protestantism, 36–38; whiteness associated with, 2–3. *See also* black church; Christian Right; evangelical Protestantism; mainline Protestantism; *and specific denominations by name*
public education: *Brown v. Board of Education,*

46–47, 106; education reform, 269; versus home-schooling, 50; questions of race religion and, 34, 44–47

public opinion: Abbott on reshaping, 68–69; intersection of race and religion in, 20; in shaping U.S. policy, 77n30

Puerto Rico, 56–57, 68, 69, 71–72, 73

Quakers: American Friends Service Committee, 76n10; evolution of, 57–60, 59; Hicksite versus anti-Hicksite, 58; Inner Light in, 58, 60, 61, 64, 74; pragmatic Quakerism, 61–64, 66, 67, 71; and racialism in early twentieth-century U.S. politics, 56–79; and slavery, 58, 75n9; splits within, 58; unity and consensus in, 64–68

race: and American constitutional order, 33–55; as "American dilemma," 250; broad interpretations of, 80; Census Bureau expands self-definition option, 50; Christian Coalition and, 177–82; Christianity as racialized, 5; Christian Right and, 170, 171–74; color-blind understandings of, 174, 176, 260, 264, 279, 289; commonsense ideas of, 82, 90; in Confederate battle flag debate, 113–20; conservative backlash against civil rights era, 8; and ethnicity, 39–40, 91; evangelical racial reconciliation movement, 249–74; ideologies in flux in early twentieth century, 81–83; immigration as racialized, 80, 170, 171, 181; as intimately integrated with other categories, 34; Jews deracialized, 19, 91–94, 96, 97; loosened from group definition, 50; and national identity of Jewish immigrants to U.S., 80–102; non-Protestantism associated with, 39; Obama as "postracial," 50; Old Testament in construction of, 39; in political discourse, 3, 127–48; Protestantism as engine of racial dynamism, 39–44; and public education, 34, 44–47; Quakerism and racialism in early twentieth-century U.S. politics, 56–79; "race traitor" positionality, 259; racial justice in mainline Protestantism, 275–

98; racial projects, 250–51, 252, 258–59, 279; radical individualism replaces group-based constructions of identity, 33–34; and religion as co-constituted, 3–4, 18; religion as racialized, 2–3, 4–9, 19, 39–40, 96, 231, 235, 238–40, 244–46; religion deracialized, 94; religious race bridging, 250–51, 270n6; scholarly approaches to religion and, 9–11; scientific conceptions of, 82, 90; social construction of, 174; South Asians racialized, 231–48; and Southern identity, 107–8; as structural phenomenon, 280, 282, 294; terrorists racialized, 183; theological racism, 113, 262–63; variable definitions of, 14; Winant and Omi's racial formation theory, 171–72, 232, 278–80. *See also* African Americans; Asians; integration; Latinos (Hispanics); Native Americans; racism; segregation; whites

Race: Man's Most Dangerous Myth (Montagu), 92

Race and Democratic Society (Boas), 92

Races of Mankind, The (Benedict), 92

racial formation theory, 1–29, 34, 208

racial reconciliation movement, 249–74; ambivalence about, 251; as antiprogrammatic, 264–66; as depoliticized, 251–61, 264–68; emergence of, 251; at evangelical church-building conference, 269; four-step model of, 254; history of, 252–58; meaning of term, 251; as neoconservative, 268; as neoliberal, 268; new elements added to model, 257–58; on politics as contaminated, 267–68; potential of, 261–63; as public-minded discourse, 267–68; on racial division as sin, 254, 262; as racial project, 258–61; relationship building in, 264; scholarly attitude toward, 249–50; topics in literature of, 255–56, 271n17

"Racial Reconciliation Sunday" campaign (Christian Coalition), 257

racism: environmental, 285; evangelical Protestant response to, 284; Farrakhan on Islamic, 194; Forman's "Black Manifesto" on, 207–30; ideological divide between main-

racism (*continued*)
  line Protestant leaders and laity on, 287, 288, 296n9; institutional, 259, 265, 281, 293, 294; in minorities, 282–84; "Policy Statement: On Racial Justice" on, 281–82; "racial prejudice plus power" definition of, 281, 282, 295n6; racial reconciliation movement on sinfulness of, 254, 262; religion in African Americans enduring and overcoming, 2, 18; reverse, 281; scientific, 82, 84, 90; theological, 113, 262–63; of Winant's Far and New Rights, 258. *See also* segregation
radical democracy, 279, 282, 284, 295
Rahall, Nick Joe, 179
Rashtriya Swayamsewak Sangh, 247n13
Reagan, Ronald, 258, 259
Reconstruction Amendments. *See* Civil War (Reconstruction) Amendments
Reed, Adolph, 23n9
Reed, James A., 84
Reed, Ralph, 175, 178–79, 180, 185n3, 257
Reform Jews, 95, 99n20
religion: and American constitutional order, 33–55; becomes civic, 95; change in role since Civil War, 33; as chosen, 12–14; in civic republicanism, 5; Confederate battle flag associated with, 105–6, 114; in Confederate battle flag debate, 113–20; crosscuts every other identity category, 17; as cultural backbone of U.S., 4–5; deracialization of, 94; as engine of Supreme Court dynamism, 35–38; equal protection under the law, 16–17; exclusion from intersectional research, 12–17; foregrounded immigrant in political mobilizations, 231, 241–44; freedom of, 6, 36, 39–40, 42; institutions lose their monopoly over construction of meaning, 49, 95; and Latino political behavior, 20, 149–69; as not easily situated in respect of power, 14–17; pliability of, 249; in political discourse, 3, 127–48; as privatized, 13; and public education, 34, 44–47; and race as co-constituted, 3–4, 18; racialization of, 2–3, 4–9, 19, 39–40, 96, 231, 235, 238–40, 244–46; redefinition during and after World War II, 91–95, 96; scholarly approaches to race and, 9–11; segregation at eleven o'clock Sunday morning, 2, 263; segregation of religious communities, 8–9; in Southern identity, 111–13, 120; theological racism, 113, 262–63. *See also* Buddhism; Christianity; Hinduism; Islam; Jews; Sikhs
Religious Land Use and Institutionalized Persons Act (2000), 42
religious liberty: American Indian Religious Freedom Act of 1978, 42; as founding precept, 6; in Story's jurisprudence, 36; Supreme Court affirms congressional authority to prohibit Mormon polygamy, 39–40
religious race bridging, 250–51, 270n6
religious tests for political participation, 36, 81
reparations, 207, 209, 210, 211, 212, 214, 215, 217, 224
Republican Party: Christian Coalition's ideas mainstreamed into, 184; Christian Right support for, 173; church attendance and support for, 132–33, 139; friendliness toward religion attributed to, 136–37; on immigration, 171, 175; Latino religion and political identification, 150, 152, 158, 164, 166; outreach to black evangelicals by, 140; Southern Strategy, 258; values voters seen as voting for, 127, 132, 133–36; white Americans who were not Protestants vote for, 145n6; white evangelical vote favors, 128, 129–32, 139, 145n3
"Resolution on Racial Reconciliation" (Southern Baptist Convention), 262
reverse discrimination, 47
reverse racism, 281
Rey, Terry, 150
Reynolds v. U.S. (1878), 40
Rhee, Syngman, 292
Rhoads, James, 66
Richards, George, 225n9
Riverside Church (New York City), 207, 209–10
"Road to Victory" conference (Christian Coalition), 176

Roberts, John, 47

Robinson, Carin, 173

Rockford Institute, 171

Rodriguez, Samuel, 167n4

Roediger, David, 90, 259

Roman Catholicism: anti-Catholic sentiment in 1928 election, 88; as expression of overall American religion, 92, 94, 96–97; increasing public participation of, 36, 40–41; John F. Kennedy's election, 40, 51; Latino religion and political identification, 150–67; marginalized in nineteenth century, 15; in multiculturalist turn, 241; nativist opposition to Irish Catholics, 13; religion makes their Americanism suspect, 88; social teachings of, 165

Rosenfeld, Isaac, 91

St. Andrew's Cross, 105, 111, 114

Saint Francis College v. Al-Khazraji (1987), 40, 52n7

Samaritan Project (Christian Coalition), 180–81, 257

same-sex marriage, 140, 146n12, 270

Samuel, Maurice, 84

Santa Fe Independent Schools District v. Doe (2000), 46

Santiago, Jose, 225n9

Sapir, Edward, 87

Schlafly, Phyllis, 170, 175

school prayer, 45–46

school vouchers, 47

scientific racism, 82, 84, 90

secularism, Protestant freedom of conscience and, 48

Secure Borders, 170

segregation: Abbott on Anglo-Saxon role in, 71; in *Berea College v. Commonwealth of Kentucky,* 42–43; black church in movement against, 118, 120, 197; Christianity supports, 23n8; Confederate battle flag as emblematic of, 104; at eleven o'clock Sunday morning, 2, 263; expulsion of blacks from white Southern churches, 112; in mainline Protestantism, 280; of religious communities,

8–9, 253; in Southern churches, 103; states' rights justification for, 50; white evangelicals reconsider, 255

"separate but equal" doctrine, 46–47, 106

separation of church and state, 94, 207

September 11, 2001: George W. Bush defends American Muslims after, 2; concern about Muslim immigration after, 182–83; South Asian immigrants after, 235–46

Seventh-Day Adventists, 36

Shaare Tefila Congregation v. Cobb (1987), 40, 52n7

Shearer, Tobin Miller, 21

Sheldon, Lou, 170

Sherbert v. Verner (1963), 38

Siemen, Evelyn, 34

Sikh American Legal Defense Fund (SALDEF), 244, 247n15

Sikh Coalition, 244, 247n15

Sikhs: mobilization against racial targeting, 244; number in U.S., 233; among South Asian immigrants, 231, 232; targeting after 9/11, 236, 238, 239–40, 243

Silberman, Charles, 93

Simons, Menno, 207

"Sin of Racism, The" (Episcopal Church), 283

Skinner, Tom, 213, 215, 253–54, 262, 271nn13–14

Skowronek, Stephen, 35

slavery: Christianity in debate over, 6, 112, 114–15, 120, 209; Confederate battle flag as emblematic of, 104, 120; "coolie" labor compared with, 7; *Dred Scott v. Sanford,* 35, 81; forcible conversions of slaves, 6, 253; Forman demands reparations for, 207, 209, 210, 211, 212, 214, 215, 217, 224; Mennonite opposition to, 208; Quakers and, 58, 75n9; Southern Baptist Convention apologizes for, 214, 255, 262

Smiley, Albert K., 60–68; and Abbott's Christian evolutionary racialism, 18, 69, 74; on Board of Indian Commissioners, 61; creation of Lake Mohonk Conference, 60–61; on Inner Light, 61, 64, 74; on nonpartisanship, 56, 62; pragmatic Quakerism of,

Smiley, Albert K. (*continued*)
61–64; screens Lake Mohonk Conference
guests and speakers, 65, 66, 67; as spiritual
in his liberal theology, 64; traditional Quak-
erism invoked by, 63–64; unanimity sought
by, 64–68
Smiley, Daniel, 67
Smith, Al, 88
Smith, Christian, 129, 225n13, 257
Smith, Lillian, 109
Smith, Rogers M., 57, 174, 177, 181, 185
social gospel, 69
Sodhi, Balbir Singh, 235
Sons of Confederate Veterans, 114
Souls of Black Folks, The (Du Bois), 108–9
South, the, 103–24; evangelical Protestants in,
111, 130; race and Southern identity, 107–8;
religion in Southern identity, 111–13, 120.
See also Confederate battle flag
South Asian American Leaders for Tomorrow
(SAALT), 235–36, 245
South Asian Network (SAN), 245
South Asians, 231–48; category rooted in Cold
War language, 233; legal bar to citizenship,
234; mobilization against racialization,
240–46; as model minority, 235, 246n6;
number in U.S., 232; otherness and foreignness attributed to, 234–35, 236–37, 245;
as panethnic, 231, 233, 240, 245; religious
identities as basis for political mobilization
among, 243–44; after September 11, 235–
46; socioeconomic profile of, 234; targeting
after September 11, 235–40; tension and
negotiation with particular identities, 233;
waves of immigration of, 234; working-
class, 234. *See also* Indians (Asian)
South Asian Youth Associations, 245
Southeast Asians, 21
Southern Baptist Convention, 119, 170, 214,
253, 255, 262
Southern Christian Leadership Conference, 8,
9, 118
southern European immigrants, 82, 83, 84, 90,
98n5, 233, 236
Southern Party, 115

Southern Strategy, 258
Special Registration drive, 239
special skills provision of Immigration and
Nationality Act of 1965, 234
Spiritualism, 36
Stainless Banner (flag), 104–5
Stars and Bars (flag), 104, 121
Stauffer, Leon, 217
Stepick, Alex, 150
Stone Mountain (Georgia), 113
Stone v. Graham (1980), 45
Story, Joseph, 35, 36
Stricker, Mary, 260
Stroman, Mark, 235
Student Nonviolent Coordinating Committee
(SNCC), 207, 209
Sun Dance, 42
Supreme Court: in distancing of government
from Protestant foundation, 37–38; negoti-
ates intersection of race and religion, 34;
on public education, 44–47; on race not
limited to binary categories, 40, 52n7;
religion as engine of dynamism of, 35–38;
understanding of religion in approach to
race of, 18
Sutherland, J. H., 56
Syrians, 83, 87, 89

Tapía, Andrés, 256
Tarrants, Tom, 262
Tate, Randy, 185n4
teaching documents, 288
Ten Commandments, 45
terrorists: racialization of, 183; targeting of
brown-skinned after September 11, 235–40.
See also September 11, 2001
Thind, Bhagat Singh, 40, 42, 246n5
Thurmond, Strom, 106
Tocqueville, Alexis de, 4, 49
tokenism, 290, 291
Torcaso v. Watkins (1961), 38, 51n2
traditionalists, 130, 145n4, 165, 270n1
Traditional Values Coalition, 170
Travieso, Martin, 77n33
Trilling, Lionel, 91

Trueblood, Benjamin F., 66, 67
Truman, Harry, 41
Truth about the Confederate Flag, The (Weaver), 114
"20/20/20 Plan," 269

Union of American Hebrew Congregations, 85
United Church of Christ: in Consultation on Church Union, 283; environmental racism studies by, 285; ideological divide between leaders and laity in, 296n9; in mainline Protestantism, 275, 276; on multiracial individuals, 284; "Policy Statement: On Racial Justice," 281–82, 283; white membership of, 277
United Methodist Church. *See* Methodists
United States v. Bhagat Singh Thind (1923), 40, 42, 246n5
United States v. Macintosh (1931), 37
United States v. Seeger (1965), 38
University of California Regents v. Bakke (1978), 47
Urbana 70, 253
Urban Racial Council (URC), 208, 213–16
"U.S. Racial Crisis and World Evangelism, The" (Skinner), 253
USS *Dorchester*, 92–93

values, moral. *See* moral values
Verter, Bradford, 277–78, 285
Vidal v. Girard's Executors (1844), 36
Virginia Declaration of Rights (1776), 35
Virginia Statute for Religious Freedom (1786), 35–36
Vishwa Hindu Parishad, 247n13
voting rights, 197

Wacquant, Loic, 138
Wadsworth, Nancy D., 21, 85, 146n12, 213, 208, 215, 217, 278, 284
Wald, Kenneth D., 150, 162
Walker, Charles, 110
Wallace, George, 106, 258, 259
Walvin, James, 57
Warren, Earl, 47

Washington, Harold, 200
Washington, Raleigh, 263, 267
Washington Weekly Review (Christian Coalition), 183
Watson, Justin, 178
Weaver, John, 114
Webster, Gerald R., 19, 111
Weiss, Rick, 53n16
welfare reform, 196, 203
Wenger, Chester L., 216, 225n9
West, Cornell, 139
"What Would Jesus Do?," 120, 121
whites: Americanness conflated with whiteness, 108, 109; black Protestants and white evangelicals compared, 129–32, 145n3; as category on naturalization form after 1940, 93; Christianity associated with whiteness, 2; Christian Right as predominantly white, 172–74, 184; civic and political involvement by race/ethnicity, *158*; Confederate battle flag as symbol for, 108, 109–11; conservative backlash by, 8; critical race theory and whiteness, 108–11; evangelical racial reconciliation movement, 249–70; evangelical vote favors Republicans, 128, 129–32, 139, 145n3; extreme right and whiteness, 110–11; freedom of religion as white privilege, 6; Jews as white, 80, 87, 88, 89, 96, 97; looking white, 82, 90; in mainline Protestant denominations, 276–77, 289; moral values as political issue for evangelicals, 135, *136*; Nation of Islam on, 199; nonwhites excluded from citizenship, 81–82, 86–87; on political party friendliness toward religion, 137, *137*; Protestantism associated with, 2–3; provisional whiteness, 90; race and Southern identity, 107–8; racism seen as phenomenon of, 281, 282, 283; religion in construction of whiteness, 39; religious orientations of evangelicals, *131*; South Asian immigrants' journey to, 233; support for Kerry by race, 133, *134*; "white man's burden," 83; whiteness as unmarked, 5, 108, 260
Wildman, Sarah, 244

Wildmon, Don, 119

Wilkins, Roy, 197

Will, George, 135

Wilson, Catherine E., 151, 159

Wilson, Charles Reagan, 111–12, 113

Wilson, Pete, 176

Wilson, William Julius, 259

Wilson, Woodrow, 87

Winant, Howard: on racial formation, 171–72, 232, 278–80; on "racial prejudice plus power" definition of racism, 295n6; on racial projects, 250, 252, 258–59, 261, 268, 279, 289; on racial terrain, 177

Wisconsin v. Yoder (1972), 45

World Community of al-Islam in the West, 194

Wright, Jeremiah, 1, 2

Wuthnow, Robert, 157, 276, 288–89

Yancey, George A., 254, 263, 270n4

Zelman v. Simmons-Harris (2002), 47, 50

Zorach v. Clauson (1952), 46